Being and Caring

———————————————

Victor Daniels and
Laurence J. Horowitz

Being and Caring

SAN FRANCISCO BOOK COMPANY, INC.

San Francisco 1976

Printed in the United States of America

Library of Congress Cataloging in Publication Data

Daniels, Victor, 1941–
    Being and caring.

    Bibliography: p.
    Includes index.
    1. Humanistic psychology.   2. Self-actualization (Psychology)   I. Horowitz, Laurence J.,
        1925–   joint author.   II. Title.
BF204.D36   158'.1   75-43975
ISBN 0-913374-29-6

Simon and Schuster Order Number 22284

Trade distribution by Simon and Schuster
A Gulf + Western Company

10 9 8 7 6 5 4 3 2 1

Contents

Preface

In our first few years, we all live with the faces we were born with. Beyond that, we start wearing the faces and living the lives we've created for ourselves.

We all write, direct, and act the parts we play in the theatre of our lives. These roles grow out of how we feel about ourselves and how we want our world to see us. We are all sometimes terribly tragic, sometimes hilariously funny, and sometimes exquisitely absurd. As we live and act, we can find ways to please ourselves, rather than just pleasing other people.

In recent years, many psychological understandings and techniques have come into popular use. Each has the advantage of originality; each has the disadvantage of being partial, of overemphasizing one part of the personality. We have synthesized these understandings—the wisdom of such writers as Perls, Rogers, Jung, Skinner, Freud, Berne, Reich, and many others—and created an approach that involves the systematic development of each important part of your personality. And since there is, in our view, a direct and immediate relationship between good psychology and good philosophy, we have drawn into our book the wisdom of great philosophers and prophets of the East and West. For them too, the goal was the life that *feels good* to a person.

We have tried to make the mysteries less hidden—to "de-mystify" what all these people have said, saying simply and directly what others have often stated in complicated ways. You can find ways of using these insights that fit your own life.

Several central themes run through these pages. To move toward being a whole person and toward feeling good on a moment-by-moment and day-to-day basis, each of us needs *self-acceptance*. Each of us needs *self-direction*, the ability to know who we are independent of the expectations and pressures of other people. We also need a firm sense of *responsibility*, not leaving to others what we must do for ourselves. We can all increase our *awareness* of what's going on both inside us and outside us. And we can find ways to be more *caring*, generous toward others and toward ourselves.

In these chapters, you can join us in a journey of growth in which these five principles are interwoven in such a way that they become a single fabric. We illustrate key ideas with personal stories, and we suggest exercises that can lead to useful changes in behavior and awareness. There is a logic to the order of the chapters, and the insights of the latter chapters can be absorbed more quickly after the earlier chapters are read. A comprehensive index is included to guide you to information that can help you with particular problems and dilemmas.

What we have written here is in part a synthesis of what we have studied and taught. It is in part a gift left to us as witnesses to the lives of the many people we have counseled, taught, and known as friends. And it is partly a record of our own struggles and joys.

Our emphasis is on the person-to-person of author to individual reader, of us to you, so that you can use the book by yourself as your own program of personal growth. We have also included exercises for more than one person, so you can use it in a group, a class, or with a partner. We suggest that as you read, you relate what you're reading at any given moment to your own life and experiences. Don't worry about what you've read before or about what's coming next.

As we wrote, we came to realize that we needed to pull together our experiences and points of view so that the "I" statement could be made and be true of both of us. Some of the tales in these pages are from Larry's life, some from Victor's. We speak of them all as "I," and it doesn't matter which is which. We call this the "generic I." We intend no "more conscious than thou" statement in these pages—as an older brother said on reading some of the chapters: "You know all this stuff—how come you're still such a schmuck?" We hope you'll join us in our appreciation of our mutual humanity.

If you use this book by yourself, you may want to keep a journal of your experiences to help you reflect more fully on the events in your life. If you read the book with another person, both of you might read a given chapter or section, and then spend some time sharing the thoughts and feelings you've had in response to it and doing the exercises you can do together.

Many people find meeting with a class or group of others who are also reading the book to be a rich experience. The key to making such a class or group successful is to share the feelings, events, and experiences from your own lives that are called out by the exercises and by what you've read. (The surest way to deaden such a group is to exchange opinions rather than share experiences, to analyze and theorize rather than listen to and appreciate one another.) We recommend starting each session with an exercise, then taking a little time to tell what happened in the exercise when that seems appropriate. If you're not reading the book in connection with a class, you might arrange to have a group sponsored by your community center, church or temple, or other neighborhood institution. Or you could put up a notice on the bulletin board at work or at your laundromat that you'd like to meet with a group of other people who are also reading the book. This is called the "laundromat wash-and-dry group counseling process."

If you want your friends to read the book so you can talk about it with them, you can make them, us, and the publisher happy by telling them about it, or even buying them a copy. It's a great present for birthdays, weddings, confirmations, and bar mitzvahs. For funerals, it's too late.

This book is dedicated to our families, friends, colleagues, and students, with whom we continue to live and learn.

Students, lovers, and colleagues gave us continual riches in material, ideas, and support. Virginia Horowitz provided us with valuable contributions in areas of nonverbal communication and body movement—and lunch and dinner. Sally Jean Nelson's sharing of ideas and anecdotal material added important substance to these pages. Gordon Tappan's comments on Jung, dreams, and symbols have been exciting and useful. So too the suggestions of the gentle Zen monk Jakusho Kwong Sensei, and the perspectives on awareness provided by healer and Gestalt Therapist Robert K. Hall. Gene Alexander contributed important ideas to our treatment of emotion. We are also grateful to our many colleagues at California State College, Sonoma, who have influenced our ways of living and thinking and who have created a unique working and learning environment. We are indebted to Harold H. Kelley and Bertram H. Raven of UCLA, and Albert Bandura, John Krumboltz, and Arthur Coladarci of Stanford University, who guided us through the scientific training that was so important to our professional growth. We appreciate Marge Bader's careful editing of our first draft, and the generous efforts of Kay Smith, LaVerne Thomas, and Jeannie Hofstetter, who contributed extensively of their time during the preparation of the manuscript. And we are grateful for the valuable suggestions of the many students who read our early drafts. We appreciate the consideration Paul Horowitz and Neena Horowitz showed in accommodating their living environment to the needs of our working environment. And we thank John Stevens at Real People Press for allowing us to quote extensively from *Gestalt Therapy Verbatim*.

I

Basic Understandings

1 *Judging and Letting Be*

"Pass no judgment, and you will not be judged; do not condemn, and you will not be condemned; acquit, and you will be acquitted; give, and gifts will be given you . . . . for whatever measure you deal out to others will be dealt to you in return" (Luke 6: 37-38, quoting Jesus).

We all know the feeling that many American Indian tribes call "bitterness in our hearts."

When I feel this bitterness in my heart, I tend to pass harsh judgment on whoever or whatever comes my way. As I pass judgment, I strengthen this bitterness inside me.

A person who is habitually harshly critical makes a hard life for himself or herself. Few things steal more vitality, or cast a darker shadow on one's life, than the habit of judging, condemning, and criticizing.

To see this for yourself, as you go through a day be attentive to the judgments and put-downs you hear people make. How do they affect the atmosphere and mood of a situation? How does the judging and condemning seem to affect the people who are doing it?

Sometimes my judgments are obvious, loud and clear enough for everyone to hear. Other times they're subtle—just an instant of tightness, a momentary narrowing of my eyes, a flash of thought that's gone almost before I notice it.

The Judger's key message is that the person or thing judged is *not okay*. To judge myself is to say to myself, "I am not okay as I am right now. I should be different" (Harris).

Evaluating, liking, and judging

Often I must make decisions; I must choose among alternatives. "Yes, this one is better for my purposes than that one." "If I do this, we will be better off than if I do that." I call this *evaluation*. Evaluation is considering the *effects* of a process. Is the process helpful or harmful? To whom? In what ways? Under what circumstances? What are the *consequences* of doing this? Some people use the word "criticism" or "judgment" for this appraisal. Here we use those words differently.

Liking or disliking is basically a feeling process. I *prefer* this or that, from some deep place inside me.

My likes and dislikes are partly the wisdom of my organism, partly the result of helpful learning that protects me and keeps me out of trouble, and partly the result of harmful learning. Harmful learning includes certain kinds of accidental learning brought about by chance circumstances, as well as conditioned responses that were once appropriate but are no longer so. These obsolete ways of thinking and feeling make it hard for me to act in healthy and satisfying ways now.

When I pay attention to my liking and disliking, I naturally become more fully aware of my likes and dislikes, of what I want to do and don't want to do; and I discover that these sometimes contradict what I've learned I "should" like and dislike.

Judging, as we use it here, is negative. When I judge, I condemn, I criticize, I put down. Out loud or in my mind, I call you bad, not okay. What I say often boils down to "My way is right, and you're not only wrong, but are also some kind of fool."

Many of my judgments I've borrowed from my parents and friends and other sources. I've taken over their opinions and attitudes and made them my own. I've also borrowed their judgmental emotional habits and filled them out with my own content, for my own purposes.

Judgments are mostly projections. Not realizing that *I feel hostile* toward you, I label *your action* as stupid or ridiculous. Thus I define *you* in terms of *what's happening in me.*

My inner meaning when I call something good, or tasty, or beautiful, etc., is that *I like it,* or please myself about it. My meaning when I call it bad or crummy is that I dislike it, or displease myself about it.

My judgment is often a disguised preference, especially when I'm afraid I'll have to defend or justify my preference. When I judge, I can pretend I'm operating from "the way things are," instead of from my feelings, and thereby avoid how I feel.

When I'm straight with myself, my words and attitudes show that I call things *as I see them.* I don't pretend to call them "as they are." So instead of saying, "It's good," I say, "I like it." Instead of "It's bad," I say, "I don't like it." This isn't easy, for old habits can be strong.

If, for instance, I'm really angry at what another man does, I'm often tempted to yell, "You idiot!" or something more colorful. If I do, I have him as wrong, and odds are he gets pissed off at me in return. He wants to have himself as right, and the only way he can do that is to have me as wrong.

But suppose I follow the advice of Carl Rogers, one of the noted psychologists of our time. I can tell the man how angry I feel without calling him names. I might say something like "I'm really mad at you for doing that!" I can even sound as loud and angry as I would if I were calling him names.

But since I'm not calling him names or saying he's no good, he's less likely to feel so pushed against the wall that he can defend himself only by lashing out at me.

At first you may have a hard time telling the difference between judgments and evaluations. The best way to develop a clear sense of which is which is through experience, by paying attention to both kinds of events.

If you don't know how to be evaluative in a nonjudgmental way, what you say to me may seem like a put-down even if you don't mean it to be.

If I'm insecure, I might not be able to tell the difference even when you speak in a clearly evaluative way, and I might take it as a judgment or a put-down regardless of your manner.

Still, I'm more likely to hear you when you *tell me you are angry or upset*, or when you *point out the effects of what I do*, than when your words or voice imply that somehow you're superior and I'm inferior.

Putting yourself down

The commonest form of self-judgment is the put-down: "That's so stupid of me!"

All these pangs of annoyance and uptightness about myself add up to many dark hours. Other people reflect back the dark feelings I cast toward them, making my world grayer still.

I get angriest with other people when they do the things I dislike in myself.

Most people who put others down a lot put themselves down a lot too. A few, by contrast, blind themselves to their dissatisfaction with themselves and project their own "faults" onto everyone else.

How many times a day, in how many ways, do you judge yourself? Take your job: "I'm only a housewife"—or a dimestore clerk—or a janitor —or whatever.

Why "only"?

Perhaps, like most of us, you sometimes feel inferior.

Inferior compared to what? Compared to what you might realistically expect to be and do, given the background and the breaks you've had?

Of course not. That way you'd come out right where you are.

Every person has an easy time with some things and a hard time with others, even though it may *seem* as if some people are "good at everything."

Instead of judging yourself as good or bad, you can relax by appreciating that you're different from anybody else. You're not just this or that—you're a whole collection of abilities and potential ways of being.

You can improve your skill at doing almost anything, once you get rid of your image of yourself as "no good at it."

If you're weak in one thing, you're potentially strong in a complementary thing. A person not so good at book learning can be loaded with common sense.

Some people think that being down on themselves helps them change. It does just the opposite. If I don't like something in myself, my mind plays all kinds of tricks to keep me from noticing when I act the way I don't admire. I have to work twice as hard to be aware of what I'm doing than I do when I feel all right about my actions. Accepting what I'm doing makes awareness of it easier.

Here is one of the most important statements in this book: At this point in your life, at this moment in time, *however you are, it's all right for you to be that way.* To feel what you feel, to think what you think, to do what you do. What is, is. What you are, you are, even though you can begin today to move in directions that will help you feel better with your life tomorrow.

The story of John Mendoza

John Mendoza is twenty-two years old. He dropped out of school, has no trade, and has never had a regular job. He lives in a subdivided basement room with his mother, younger brother, and two sisters.

John knows that most of society does not think well of someone like him. Over and over, his life experience and environment keep telling him, "You're a failure, you're not making it. You've never had it and you're not going to get it and your kids probably won't either."

By now, he's begun to buy that. He's started to say to himself, "It doesn't matter *what* I do. There's no way for me to come out a winner."

John is smart enough to see what's in it for the Man to put him down, to keep him in his place. What he doesn't see is that by putting himself down, he's doing the Man's job for him.

If I'm John Mendoza, I don't have to cooperate with the Man's attempt to make me feel incompetent. In fact, I'm pretty damn capable in lots of ways. That's real.

It's not easy for me to accept all that. When I do, I'm going to feel scared. As I realize that I'm keeping myself down by feeling incompetent, I face my built-in demand to do something to make my life better. I don't have to buy the "failure script" society has written for me anymore.

Some people like John never make it. Some do. I *guarantee* you this: If you keep sitting around full of self-pity, buying the failure package, you're going *nowhere*.

You may be angry about your situation. You can use that anger to hurt yourself, tightening your muscles against each other, making your guts churn, and turning your anger into a brooding resentment that dominates your day and stops you from doing anything. Or you can use it as a source of energy to do something for yourself.

We've all got what it takes to *start* developing the abilities we need to make it. Once you start down the road toward making it, you *are* making it, right then.

It may take a while to get where you want to go—but what else have you got to do that's better than learning how to be good to yourself?

WORKING WITH JUDGMENTS

A judgment can be a starting point for getting in touch with things that are going on in me or in my relationship with you.

What I do with my judgment is the main thing. Do I let it out, or do I keep it to myself? If I reveal to you my judgment of myself or of you in such a way that we can use it as a starting point for dialogue, we just might learn to understand each other.

Here's a way to explore your judgments of yourself:

✳ *"The trouble with you"*

Sit back and take a couple of minutes to relax.

Now say to yourself, "The trouble with you is . . . ," "What's wrong with you is . . . ," "You should . . . ," "You shouldn't . . . ," and so on. Go through all the criticisms you can think of to lay on yourself.

Stay aware of your physical feelings as you do this. Pause occasionally to listen to your own words. How does your condemning voice sound? Do you recognize anyone besides yourself in that voice?

Now change places in your mind, and become the you who has just been criticized. How do you respond to these criticisms and "shoulds"? Do your replies follow any consistent pattern?

Now, if you're in a group, get together with the other members and share your experiences. Talk in the first person present tense: "As my critic, I say . . . ," etc. (Adapted from J. Stevens, 60–61)

Working with the wrist counter

Counting judgments with a wrist counter* is usually an effective way to become aware of when and what and how you judge, and to decrease your judging.

Counting judgments is the starting point for using the wrist counter to increase your awareness of *any* way of acting.

Be sure to begin by counting only your judgments. Otherwise you might become aware of some unwanted way of acting and gradually become more and more self-critical and depressed: "I'm so awful! I really want to quit yelling at my kids, and I do it *so* much. I guess I'm just a lousy parent. I didn't even realize how much I yelled at them before I started counting."

If you work on your habit of judging before you work on anything else, the whole process is different. Suppose you're counting how many times a day you yell at your kids. You yell once and punch the counter. Then you immediately start to condemn yourself for yelling. But since you're already in touch with your judgmental process—you've punched that counter—you notice, "Hey, I'm running that one again," and you cancel a whole sequence of feeling crummy about yourself that might have lasted for several minutes.

After you've used the counter to aid your awareness of judgments for as long as you need to, you can use it to work on many other ways of behaving.

Then later, when you're working on something else and you find that you've slipped into putting yourself down again, you can lay aside that other project and focus on judging again.

---

*Wrist counters are available in sporting goods stores and departments. (Golfers use them for scorekeeping.) They count up to ninety-nine, and are worn on the wrist like a watch. Those we've seen run from about $1.50 to $4.00. Adequate ones could probably be made of plastic and sold for fifty cents or less.

✳ Counting judgments

As soon as you get up in the morning, pay attention to your judgments of yourself or of anyone or anything else. Notice every instance of judging and criticizing, whether aloud or silently.

If you say to yourself, "What an awful dress she has on!"—notice as you do it. Each time you condemn anything, punch your wrist counter once.

At first maybe you'll even be self-critical when you notice yourself being critical. Forget that; more of the same you don't need.

Pay attention with the attitude of "noticing" yourself, not "catching" yourself. It's the difference between "Oho! There I go again!" and "Damn! I'm doing it again. Will I never learn?" In the latter case, you would punch your counter twice—the second time for putting yourself down for judging.

After a while, you and your fault-finding will start to be old friends. You'll find it easier to hear yourself when you judge. You'll be aware of the tightness in your jaws and stomach, the shallow breathing, and the narrowness in your voice that goes along with judging. After a few days or weeks, when you start to get down on yourself for something, you'll be alert to what you're about to do and you won't do it. You won't even have to try to stop. It happens automatically.

As you become more aware of your criticisms, they'll come less and less often.

"SHOULDS"

Every judgment or criticism has a "should" at its center. Things "should" be a certain way, and if they're not, they're bad: "I should do this, you should do that, she ought to do the other thing . . ."

How many times a day do you get mad at yourself, or at least a little irritated or upset, because you didn't do what you think you "should" have done? How many times a day do you hand out advice about what somebody else "should" do? How often does someone else get angry with you because you didn't do what that person thinks you "should" have done?

"Should" carries a quality of absoluteness. The things I "should" do are RIGHT, and the things I "shouldn't" do are WRONG. And that's that.

In my life, I do what I do. My action brings certain consequences. If I don't confuse myself by thinking, "I should have done something else," I can see those consequences and learn from them. When my mind is busy with what I "should" have done, I don't find out as much about what happened as a result of what I *did*.

Every time I say "you should" to someone else, I deny that person a chance to learn from his or her own experience.

All this does not mean that you shouldn't have "shoulds." We all have "shoulds." If you try to not have any, you'll blind yourself to the ones you do have.

Just *pay attention* to your "shoulds" and "should-nots." Notice especially the *impossible* "shoulds," like "what I should have done." You'll soon find out which "shoulds" have real value for you and which ones don't.

SAYING "YES" TO YOURSELF

✳ *Appreciating yourself*

Do this in your imagination.

Take five minutes to *brag about yourself.* Mention every good thing you know about yourself. Overdo it. Describe all the things about you that make you wonderful.

The key is not to generalize, but to stay very specific. *How* am I such a superb person? In what particular ways?

As you do this, listen to how you hedge and qualify your appreciation of yourself. Where do you have a hard time giving yourself credit? Which is easier for you: appreciating yourself or putting yourself down?

Indian sage Meher Baba speaks of two kinds of perfection. One kind is the gradual change from being "imperfect" to being "perfect." The other is the perfectness of each thing that exists, just as it is right now.

One day as I sat by a creek listening to its voices, I reached into the water and scooped up a handful of stones. I looked at them glistening wetly for a minute or two, and suddenly realized that every stone was perfect. Some had intricate designs. Others were hard and good for cutting things. One was a nice shape for throwing. A couple were poetic in their ordinary grayness. There weren't any "good stones" or "bad stones." Every stone was absolutely perfect.

It's the same with people. Here and now, I'm an absolutely perfect me, and you're an absolutely perfect you. No one in the world can be as perfect a You as You are.

Listen to one of Bugental's clients:

"Mom and Dad were trying so hard but they were so scared. And I was scared too. . . . And what were we frightened of? Just of being ourselves! . . . (She is weeping hot, quiet tears as she talks.) And that's what I've been running from: by being so bright or pretty or popular or successful or all the other things I've tried to be. I've been trying to be those things instead of just being me" (Bugental, 274).

Consider this Zen story:

When Banzan was walking through a market he overheard a conversation between a butcher and his customer.

"Give me the best piece of meat you have," said the customer.

"Everything in my shop is the best," replied the butcher. "You cannot find here any piece of meat that is not the best."

At these words Banzan became enlightened. (Reps, 32)

There are at least two equally valid ways to understand this story.

Suppose I walk into the butcher shop and look at one piece of fine lean meat, one piece with a lot of fat and bone, and one piece that's three weeks old and smells a little strange.

If I have to eat, every piece is not the best. You can keep the three-week-old meat, thank you, and if I can afford it, I'd rather have the prime-quality lean. You can tell me that the old piece is the best lousy meat available, but it's still a lousy piece of meat for eating. The meat *is a functioning part of my life,* and I evaluate it in terms of how well it fulfills my functions.

However, there's also a lot of the world that I'm basically a spectator to. Suppose I walk into the butcher shop to buy cheese. I can see that three-week-old meat hanging there, and I know it's part of the butcher shop just like everything else. From where I stand then, every piece of meat is the best. But I'm glad I'm buying cheese instead of meat.

Having things okay *does not mean* making yourself "feel okay" about troublesome conditions in your own life that you might be able to change. There the task is to get in touch with exactly how things are not okay, and set out to find some remedies. Saint Theresa of Avila said it beautifully: "Lord, grant me the serenity to accept the things I cannot change, the courage to change the things I can, and the wisdom to know the difference."

I have some choice about how I feel. I can feed my uptightness or I can relax. As I work to change harmful conditions, I can feel hostile and angry and bitter or I can feel full and alive and in harmony with myself and my life. My experience is that I'm usually more effective when I'm relaxed than when I'm uptight.

When no harm is being done, I can let the people and things and events in my world be and appreciate them as they are, or I can feel upset about this or that. In either case, the situation is as it is. My choice is whether I feel good or bad about it.

As an old Chinese poem points out,

> In the landscape of spring
>   there is neither better nor worse;
> The flowering branches grow naturally,
>   some long, some short.

People around you are just trying to live as best they can. If you feel a tendency to get down on them for something, look at yourself: *Are you willing to give the time to show them a better way,* and do it nonjudgmentally so they'll be able to hear?

(I've found that when I want to advise another person, the way that works best for me is *sharing.* Not "You should do this . . .," but "Something that often works well for me is . . .")

Here is the last point of this chapter. Read it carefully: *Don't demand that you be nonjudgmental about things you really do judge.*

Perhaps you are a Jew whose family was murdered by the Nazis, and you do not find it in your heart to forgive an ex-SS trooper when you meet him.

Perhaps you are a mother whose only son came home from Vietnam in a casket, and you cannot bring yourself to forgive those who sent him there.

Perhaps you are a Black or Chicano or Poor White who spent months or years in prison for an offense for which an influential businessman or politician would have got off on probation, and have had a hard time getting work since your release because you're an ex-con.

As you feel the bitterness that lingers in you still, be gentle with yourself. If you forgive no one else, at least forgive yourself.

Nietzsche had a word for us: "I know of the hatred and envy of your hearts. You are not great enough not to know hatred and envy. Be great enough, then, not to be ashamed of them" (158–59).

2 Your Own Way

Others can hold your hand for only so long. Then they can do no more. There comes a point where you must find your own direction.

Zen monk Bill Kwong tells his students, "I can't make you high. You must find your own tools. My presence here is like a dream. Soon the dream will be over."

Many American Indian cultures have a deep respect for each person's individual way.

A Navajo, for example, seldom speaks for another person. If a Navajo man is asked what his wife thinks about something, he is likely to reply, "I don't know. I haven't asked her." A father who is offered a good price for his child's bow and arrow will let the boy decide whether or not to sell, and respect the boy's decision not to sell even though the child may badly need the clothing the money would buy.

A Navajo mother allows her child space to make his or her own mistakes, to suffer pain or grief or joy and learn from experience. She teaches not by giving orders—"Don't touch that!"—but by pointing out cause-and-effect relationships: "If you touch that, you'll burn your finger." She knows that the freedom to explore and learn from what happens is an important step in developing self-reliance (Lee, 8, 12, 13).

Letting others move me

Few of us have learned to fully trust our own sense of what means most to us, and accept it as our guide.

At several points in my own life, I abandoned paths that were important in my journey in order to get the safety and love I knew no other way to get.

A kid who hears, "You don't like chocolate, you like vanilla!" enough times is likely to start believing it.

Actually the child is hearing the grownup say not only "You like vanilla," but also *"I want you to like vanilla."*

If I'm the grownup, I'm giving the child a double message: "You have no choice—you're going to get vanilla" and "I want you to *feel that you have a choice*, even though I'm choosing for you."

My straight message is "I want you to like vanilla, and I'll approve of you if you do." When I say that, you have room to reply, "I know you want me to like vanilla, but I prefer chocolate, thank you."

Whenever I want your approval so much that I'll do anything you want me to, in order to please you, I make you my judge.

In order for me to do what *I* want to, instead of what *you* want me to, I've got to be willing to approve of myself even when you don't approve of me.

Just as you can want me to want something, *I* can want me to want something. I take other people's messages about what I should want into me, and then one place in me tells the rest of me what to want.

When I don't feel quite right about something I seem to want, I pay attention to see whether I really want it, or have just learned to think I do. Freud called this *introjection.*

As children, and sometimes as adults, we are often asked to *introject,* to swallow whole, the ways that others prescribe for us.

When I swallow my food whole, barely chewing it, I don't digest it well. It may come back into my mouth so that I have to chew it again before it stays down. When I bite off a piece I can manage, and chew it thoroughly, I digest it and it becomes a part of my body.

In the same way, I may need to bring out and chew through ways of being that I've swallowed whole at one time or another in my life. Then I can reject what has no value for me, and assimilate what has.

Erich Fromm gives an example of the introjection process:

> [The child] is taught to suppress the awareness of hostility and insincerity in others; . . . children [are not] so easily deceived by words as adults usually are. They still dislike somebody "for no good reason"—except the very good one that they feel the hostility, or insincerity, radiating from that person. . . .
>
> . . . The child is taught to have feelings that are not at all "his" . . . to be uncritically friendly. . . . Friendliness, cheerfulness, and everything that a smile is supposed to express, become automatic responses which one turns on and off like an electric switch. (EFF, 242–43)

A child doesn't, of course, have to go along with the parents' demand to become someone other than he or she is. Time and time again, I've been amazed at the different personalities the various children in a family are choosing for themselves, and at how different these are from what

I'd have predicted just by knowing the parents. Within any family, each child has real choices as to his or her own direction, and takes them, just as you and I have.

✳ Steppingstones

At the top of a sheet of paper write, "I was born." Take five minutes to reflect on the most significant turning points or periods in your life that brought you to where you are today. Jot down a single word or phrase to describe each of these important steppingstones.

When you're done, take at least fifteen minutes to think about, or discuss with another person, your thoughts and feelings as you recall these stepping-stones. Then talk with the other person about the steppingstones he or she wrote down.

If you're in a group, when all the pairs have finished their conversations, have the members take turns in sharing with the rest of the group their feelings about the events they wrote down. (This exercise is suggested by Jungian analyst Ira Progoff.)

The script

Each of us, says psychiatrist Eric Berne, has a script that tells us what to do in our lives. It was written for us in part by parents, friends, teachers, and any other authorities we came in contact with: "There's your script—don't forget to follow it!"

Our scripts are also our own doing. As I grew up, I rewrote the script that others gave me so that it fit who I was and what I wanted for me. Then I conveniently "forgot" that I did the rewrite job, so I could blame others when I didn't like what I was doing.

Many of my problems as an adult come from trying to fit my old script. Until I realize I'm acting out a 10- or 20- or 30-year-old script, I may be stuck with some pretty ineffective, unproductive, and sometimes even self-destructive behavior.

For instance, many adults have a hard time saying no. Long ago they got scripts that said, "Good boys and girls never say no." Most children in that situation rewrite their scripts. "I don't dare *say* no, but I can *behave* no." I may still do that, saying yes, and then behaving no.

✳ Looking at your script

Think about each of the major stages in your childhood and youth. At each stage—at ages five through eight, for instance—imagine that one of your parents (or some other relative or whoever was the important adult in your life at that point) hands you a script. You look at it and see a one-sentence title. Your parent's prescription for you is in that title, and underneath it may be more specific instructions.

For each prescription, jot down that one-line title. Below it, in a few words or a line, write your response to your parent's statement. Do this for each prescription at each stage of your life, before you read on.
. . .

Now look at what you've written. Do you say yes to your parent's statement? Do you say no and choose some other way? Do you say yes but resolve to act some other way?

Now, with each prescription you accepted, imagine a way you can rebel against or sabotage it. Then go one step further and consider how you can find your own way, a way that suits you but may not exactly either agree with or rebel against the prescription. If you like, you can do this last part in conversation with another person or a group.

Those who raised us meant well. As I raised me, I meant well. We were all doing the best that we knew how.

Yet, yesterday's world was a simpler world. Different groups of people tended to live more by themselves. To do exactly as my father and his father before him did was more fitting then than it is now.

Some of my father's ways are useful to me. So are some of my grandfather's ways that my father has forgotten or discarded. For instance, my grandfather knew how to live with fewer goods and less fuel and power than my father is accustomed to. As our resources and energy supplies grow scarcer, I can learn from the style of life my grandparents knew. I can draw from my roots at the same time that I find my own directions.

When I order or persuade you, I try to get you to do what I want you to do instead of what you want to do. I implicitly ask you to accept me as your authority—to take a step backward from being in touch with yourself, from making your own decisions, and from learning to be your own person. I want you to be "my person" instead. Ordering and persuading are *attempts by one person to rob another person of his or her self-determination.*

I want to stop persuading others in part because I don't like others to persuade me. I'm more likely to listen when you *inform* me than when you try to persuade me.

When I talk to you, I'd best remember that you can tune me out completely.

One of my relatives was deaf from birth. As a youngster he had a hearing aid that could be turned up and down. Imagine his mother's frustration when she would start yelling at him and see him reach up and turn the hearing aid down. "What am I supposed to do—tell him to turn it up so he can listen to me scream?" How absurd can you get?

We all have the option this deaf child had. He had to tune out observably. We can do it on the sly. *We only have to listen when we want to.*

When I inform you rather than persuade you, I leave you free to choose your own direction. Unfortunately, our culture is persuasion-oriented; we need to make a basic shift from persuading to informing.

AUTHORITY

I rely on authority every day, from the weatherman to my mechanic to my attorney, etc. These authorities have knowledge or skill in certain areas. This is *informational authority.* I try to avoid being influenced by the opinion of someone who's famous but who knows no more than I about the matter at hand, like a movie star's opinion about politics or soap.

In *power-based authority*, someone else has the upper hand, and I must do that person's bidding either to get rewards he or she controls or to avoid punishment. The authority may range from an obvious one like a parent or boss or jailer to a disguised one like "public opinion"—my friends will think badly of me if I don't accept their way.

Power-based authority has many ways of trying to appear legitimate. There's the *defensive authority*: it always has a way to justify itself. There's the *attacking authority*: challenge it and too bad for you. There's the *benevolent despot*: "I'll help—all you have to do is . . ." There's the *"good" fascist*: "I know what's good for you—I'll give you what you want and even more besides."

There is also *anonymous authority*, the atmosphere of subtle suggestion that pervades our social life, disguised as common sense, science, psychic health, normality, or public opinion (Fromm, EFF, 167–68).

So often, comments Krishnamurti,

We do not ask. We want to be told . . . whereas to ask a question is to ask it of yourself. . . .

Leaders destroy the followers and followers destroy the leaders. . . .

I will first reject what the church, what society, what my parents and friends, what every person and every book has said . . . , because I want to find out for myself (FK, 21, 83, 121).

Kabir adds: "You don't grasp the fact that what is most alive of all is inside your own house, and so you walk from one holy city to the next . . ." (8).

In Talmudic studies a good Jew has first to find arguments in disagreement with every one of God's commandments. Only then is he allowed to discover how he agrees with them. He works through and defines each of his principles of conduct for himself, rather than accepting them on prior authority.

I get along best when I make "how it works when I try it" my ultimate authority, knowing that at any one moment, I don't have the final answers and may well be wrong (May, MSFH).

When I check what others say against my own experience, I'm less likely to make errors like this one:

A certain man . . . believed to have died regained consciousness, lifted the coffin lid, and cried out for help.

"It is not possible," . . . said the mourners, "because he has been certified dead by competent experts."

"But I am alive!" shouted the man. . . .

[A judge who was present said], "Now, we have heard what the alleged deceased has had to say. You fifty witnesses tell me what you regard as the truth."

"He is dead," said the witnesses.

"Bury him!" said the expert.

And so he was buried.

(Story from the Chishti Dervish Order, in Shah, WS, 120)

Authority and society

Authority [too often] . . . would maintain itself at any cost, even the fearful cost of destroying the man himself and those who accept his authority, and those who oppose it as well . . .

Seek no authority over the lives of men. . . . But seek a way into the hearts of men through Love and Understanding (Naimy, 129–30).

When I hold a rigid "the-rules-are-the-rules" attitude, instead of considering this particular person in this particular situation, I'm indicating that I don't trust my own judgment.

In government, schools, and industry, countless regulations govern minute details of an employee's or student's behavior that have no relation to his or her activities there.

We can learn from other cultures. In Japan, an employee at any level can make a suggestion that does not just pass into a superior's hands for acceptance or rejection, but must be circulated throughout the company, so that workers at all levels can consider it. In China, often the workers choose their supervisors and then the supervisors choose *their* supervisor, instead of all the decisions being made from the top down.

Even within an institution as it is, we can do a lot. My colleague Red Thomas comments that "half the time 'the authorities' don't know what's going on. If you can do a job and you can take a few risks, you often discover that you have much more freedom than you think" (quoted in Bugental, 230–31). You don't have to accept the limits you're told you have.

SELF-DETERMINATION

You must do it for yourself

"What is done for you—allow it to be done," said the Sufi Khawwas. "What you must do yourself—make sure you do it" (quoted in Shah, WS, 247).

If you take my advice or anybody else's as to what you "should" or "shouldn't" do, you'll be living borrowed pieces of other people's lives instead of your own life. And that includes this advice!

You can come to know yourself far better than anyone else will ever know you. No one is more suited to be you for you than you are.

In the long run, finding your own way is often easier than trying to do what someone else tells you to. A hard task I choose for myself is often easier than a simple one that another person gives me.

Nietzsche's Zarathustra says, "This is my way; where is yours?—thus I answered those who asked me 'the way.' For *the* way—that does not exist" (307).

Any moment in your life, you're determining your direction. Through what you focus on and what you choose to do, you're implicitly saying, "This is where I want to go."

Thinking for someone else tends to keep that person from growing. Everyone needs some frustration in order to learn to stand on his or her own two feet. We can stunt someone's growth by giving him or her too much.

Consider this Zen story:

The student Tokusan used to come to the master Ryutan in the evenings to talk and to listen. One night it was very late before he was finished asking questions.

"Why don't you go to bed?" asked Ryutan. Tokusan bowed, and lifted the screen to go out. "The hall is very dark," he said.

"Here, take this candle," said Ryutan, lighting one for the student.

Tokusan reached out his hand, and took the candle.

Ryutan leaned forward, and blew it out.(P. Pauper Press)

Light your own way.

Finding your direction

Self-determination is more than rebellion. It means taking explicit responsibility for your own growth process.

How do I know if the direction I choose is a growing one? If it leads me to make better use of my potential, I'm willing to call it growth.

There are many paths to follow, but not all are easy for all of us. An easy way for one person is a hard way for another. You don't have to waste your energy trying to make a hard way easy. If you choose your own path, you'll change in ways that fit who you are, and not in ways that are alien to you.

✳ What you need for yourself now

Relax, close your eyes, and imagine the following:

You are walking on a path through a forest. You come upon some kind of barrier. Notice everything you can about the barrier; then find a way to deal with it.

On the other side of the barrier, you'll find yourself in a place that provides you with something you need, and tells you something important about your life now. Don't try to "make yourself imagine" certain things, but allow whatever comes spontaneously to come.

After you've finished, if you're with another person, share your fantasies and what they meant to each of you. Then, if you're in a group, each of you tells the rest of the group what you learned about the other person and about yourself, and others in the group do the same.

When you act in new ways, you may feel strange, or stiff and stilted, as you try something out. The new way may be very natural, but still feel unusual, just as a new method of throwing a ball or holding a baseball bat may seem odd at first. That same feeling can come as you learn new ways of being with other people. As you learn the new way better, it will come to seem more usual.

But while the feeling of unusualness lasts, you get something extra. It's easier to be aware of what's happening with you when you're first learning some new way, before it comes to be a habit. That intense awareness can be a rich event.

Something new that you try might seem only a small part of your life. If you feel discouraged remember the words of the ancient Chinese sage Lao-tzu:

> Difficult things of the world
> can only be tackled when they are easy.
> Big things of the world
> can only be achieved by attending to
> their small beginnings. . . .
> A tree as big as a man's embrace springs
> from a tiny sprout.
> A tower nine stories high begins with a
> heap of earth.(91, 93)

We typically notice and applaud only the tower nine stories high, and forget that there was *ever* only a heap of earth. We learn to distrust our ability to accomplish anything when we let our eyes rest only on the finished product.

NOURISHMENT AND POISON

I can nurture and nourish myself in ways that help me grow, or poison myself in ways that stop my growth.

I can nurture and nourish you in ways that help you grow, or poison you in ways that stop your growth. As Greenwald points out, when someone or some circumstance is nourishing for you, you feel good, full, and alive. When a person or circumstance is toxic for you, you feel bored, irritated, drained, and exhausted.

In some ways I poison myself. In some ways my father poisoned me and my mother poisoned me, just as in some ways I poison my children.

Sometimes my mother got poisonous toward me by being unwilling to accept the good things I had done and putting me down for not having done enough. When I did something good on Tuesday, it was: "How come you didn't do it on Sunday too?"

I introjected that attitude—took it into me. Sometimes I still do that.

But more often now, when I start doing that, I'm aware enough of what I'm doing that I can stop myself short, and be with myself in more nourishing ways.

Every time a person's stinger flashes out to poison someone else, a little valve opens and the poison also shoots through the person who does the stinging.

A while back I knew a woman who mirrored this process very well. I could always tell when she was ready to sting with her poison: her whole face grew tight and ugly and ominous.

The more I give you my aliveness, the more I nourish you. The more I give you my exhaustion and my ennui and demand that you work hard to stay with me, the more I poison you.

Ignoring someone is also a potent form of poison. I can make you invisible by poisoning you with my ink eradicator. A sexist male can make the individual woman disappear by treating her as an object. A white racist can make the black person disappear by treating him or her as a nonperson.

Help can be poison too. Sometimes my help can sabotage your attempt to learn to take care of yourself.

When one person throws a poison dart, it can trigger a poison place that already exists in the other person. When your dart fails to activate my own poison place, your poison doesn't faze me. I can feel compassion for you when you're in your poison place without having to poison myself too.

One time Fritz Perls, who developed Gestalt Therapy, was finishing a difficult film. When we got together afterward, he was bushed. I said, "Wow, nice day, blah-blah-blah," and he said, "Listen, I really don't have the energy for bullshit. Let's go somewhere and you can tell me what you want."

We found a place, sat down, and talked for a long time. As we parted, Fritz said, "I was so tired that I wanted to talk for fifteen minutes and go to sleep. We've talked for an hour and a half and I'm completely refreshed." He was able to use what was going on with us to nourish and revitalize himself.

The torturer, saboteur, and assassin

There dwells a fearsome trio of poisoners inside almost every one of us: the torturer, the saboteur, and the assassin.

My *torturer* is the place inside me that won't let me be as I am or let the world be as it is, even though I'm not willing to make any changes.

My torturer keeps hammering away, telling me that I and my world should be different. I find nothing good for me in what's happening, but don't do anything to change my situation.

When I'm out to torture myself, I convince myself that whatever I do and experience is wrong. If I feel hurt, I think I shouldn't feel hurt. If I feel good, I think I shouldn't feel good. When I mess things up, instead of thinking, "Well, where do we go from here?" I condemn myself and make self-defeating statements. I find a way to lose no matter what I do.

My *saboteur* is my tendency to re-create the Wreck of the Old '97 in my day-to-day existence. I tell myself, "I can't," and find some way to fail. I may have a good program, but I don't let myself follow it. If I know how to get a good payoff in a situation, I do exactly the opposite of what's required. If I *do* get where I'm going, I make things hard for myself along the way.

But after I've screwed up today, I'll probably find some energy to come back and screw up again tomorrow. My saboteur doesn't put me completely out of business.

My *assassin* is the way I deaden and kill myself: "Why even try? I know I'll fail." I immobilize myself. My assassin stops me cold and makes it very hard for me to go on. I feel there's no way I can do anything good for me or for you. If I do get up enough energy to start moving again, my assassin may creep up when I'm not looking and blast me again from another angle.

Nourishing me and you

Each time I feel and act in a nourishing way toward me or toward you, my sac of poison shrinks a little. I feel better with me and with you.

I don't always have to want to nourish you. Sometimes I hear you needing and I don't want to give. Nevertheless, when I hear you say again, "I know you don't want to give, but I still need," I may be willing to give even though it's not so easy for me then; and I'll feel good about it if I do. At other times, I need to take some time just to nourish myself.

When I'm being nourishing, I experience a clarity about what I want for me and from you. My aliveness flows from me to you, picks up your aliveness, and comes back to me.

I find my aliveness as I discover and follow my own directions. In the old Judaic tradition, a person pleases God most not by acting like God's chosen prophet Moses, but by being most fully himself or herself.

3 *Responsibility*

When a leaf blows across the street in the wind and I pick it up, I *choose* to pick it up. When a fierce gust knocks me into a tree, that's something *done to me*, not something I do. I'm responsible only for being there where the wind is blowing.

Even when strong external forces are present, I have some power to check out those forces and to choose whether I want to let them act on me. On a windy day I can choose to stay inside the house. There are few situations in our lives in which we have no effect at *all* on what happens to us.

I can easily trick myself into *thinking* I have no effect. "I had to do it—there was no choice," I tell myself. Actually, even when I'm following orders, *I decide* whether I'll do as ordered or else risk doing what seems right to me, even though that may be against my orders.

Response-ability, says Perls, is a misused word. It "means the ability to respond: the ability to be alive, to feel, to be sensitive" (GTV, 100).

It doesn't mean "obligation." It doesn't mean "duty."

Duty—what is that, anyway?

One way or another, it's something I've been directed to do without asking *why*. I do it automatically, without accepting responsibility for my actions—like a robot, not a human being.

Perls sees growth as a move from letting others be responsible for you to taking responsibility for yourself. He often refused to give a person the support he or she was used to getting from others, in order to help that person learn to stand on his or her own two feet.

As I begin to see how I still hang on to some of my helpless childhood ways, so that the people around me will do things for me, I move from manipulating others for support toward developing self-support.

Keeping a person dependent can cause hostility, especially when double messages are involved.

I may say, "I want you to go out and do something on your own," while my actions tell you loudly that I want you to depend on me, and, what's more, I'll give you lots of goodies if you do.

A teacher may tell his or her pupils, "Just listen to what I tell you to do and do it," and at the same time demand that they be responsible for their own behavior.

Few people like to be put in those kinds of situations.

As long as I assign the cause of my behavior to my "unconscious" or my parents or my past, I can't change. If Mama did it to me, she's the one who must undo it if it is to be undone. If she has gone out of my life, presumably I'm stuck with what she did.

I may still be angry with her for what she did to me when I was a child: "See what you've done!" is my message to her. "Now that I give you all this power, I want you to *undo* what you've done." The trouble is, she can't. I'm the only one who can.

I don't have to give up being bitchy or angry or jealous or doing anything else I do. But I do need to stop thinking that I act in these ways only because of my ancient history.

I can scrap some of the scripts I wrote as a child for roles I played as a child that I'm still trying to live, and write new scripts to fit my life as it is now.

When I make an *excuse*, I defend or justify or explain what I do by assigning responsibility for my action—or inaction—to some agent beyond my control. "I have no choice but to do that . . . ," I may say, or "I can't do that . . . because of the weather" or ". . . because of my wife." An excuse almost always follows the word "because" or its equivalent.

I can use something inside me as well as something outside me as an excuse. "The difficulty was due to my 'obstinacy,' " or "My 'unconscious' made me do it." If I can write off my actions to some "thing" inside me that I can't control, *I* have no responsibility for what I do.

BLAME

When I have a grudge against someone, I tend to make that someone responsible for everything I find wrong.

"I bet she left that there!"

"I bet she took my favorite mug with her when she moved out." (Naturally, two days later the mug shows up.)

When I blame you, my desire to judge and punish is often what's at work. I blame you when I'm angry because your action made things turn out differently than I wished. If not through my words then through my manner and tone of voice, I can put all the responsibility for what happened on you, in a way that implies what you did was "wrong" or "bad."

What you did may not seem wrong to you at all. But if you're not aware of what's happening inside me and inside you, one of your old fear places might get hooked in—one where Mom or Dad or Teacher stood there shaking a finger and said "bad boy" or "bad girl," and you felt guilty at having done "wrong." Out of that past conditioning, you feel "wrong" now.

Blame breeds resentment. "It's your fault!" is a red-flag phrase. It is to a person what a matador's cape is to a bull.

The hooker in blame is that smidgen of truth in what you said or implied. I can seldom say, "That's just what *you* feel—it has nothing to do with me." When a person's blamer goes to work, it's very canny. It knows exactly where to go *zap*, where to pick out that nasty kernel of truth. A put-down artist is an expert at zeroing in on where you feel bad about yourself and making you feel even smaller there.

Two messages get mixed up in blame: my statement of how I feel ("I'm angry and disappointed") and my evaluation of you ("Scum like you shouldn't be allowed on the street"). My feelings about the situation are often hidden in my "you-are-bad" message, instead of being said straight out.

If I want to keep you on the defensive, I'll keep blaming you. As long as you defend where I attack, I have the upper hand. I control the action. To get out of that cycle, you respond by telling me your feelings: "When you talk to me that way, I want to walk away," or you comment on my process: "I hear you sounding upset about what happened."

Even when I tell you how I feel in response to what you did in a clean and nonblaming way, you might still sometimes *feel* blamed, because of events in your personal history. Also, if I'm *really* upset, I can be doing my best not to blame you and still sound as if I am.

I'll do no one any good by blaming myself for blaming you. The most useful thing I can do is to stay as aware as I can of what I'm doing, and to stay as open as I can to how you feel in response.

There's a difference between the blaming we all do and the blaming a chronic blamer does.

As a chronic blamer, I blame others for everything that doesn't go as I want it to go. I'm likely to have relatively few friends, and the friends

I do have will be cautious around me, to avoid doing things that might provoke my blaming.

If I'm stuck in this kind of blaming, admitting it to myself is a real step forward in my growth.

I'm especially suspicious of my own "Why did you do . . . ?" questions, which are often a way of attacking and blaming.

One way I can start to get out of my own blaming process, and help open up communication between us, is by taking responsibility for my part in what happened: "I see this part of it as mine," I say, and leave it to you to assume whatever responsibility you want to accept for yourself.

I can protect myself against other people's blaming. *I am not obliged to accept anyone else's evaluation of me.* When I depend on what others think of me, as Brice points out, I'm "vulnerable to being made to feel bad by every ill-dispositioned person I happen to meet.

"There are few of us," says Brice, "who have the presence of mind to say, 'Oh, no! That's *your* truth. That's not *the* truth!' . . . Trust your feelings; when you wince, someone has blamed you" (and usually they've also hit a sore spot).

Self-blame

I may blame myself in those areas where I feel the least adequate: "I'm so blemished that there's nothing I can do. I'm helpless."

Using self-blame in this way is a device to avoid responsibility. I'm not really blaming myself—I'm blaming the circumstances or people in my past that made me as I am.

If I accept the responsibility for my own troubles, I can no longer use my "helplessness" or "inadequacy" as an excuse to avoid doing anything to change. I can say to myself, "I got into this; now I can get myself out of it and into a situation I'll feel better about."

Theresa finds herself in such a situation. She is depressed. She describes herself as a total failure socially. People don't like her, and when they see her coming they walk away.

She's willing to admit that she does nothing to involve herself with others, but she uses that to say, "You see how inadequate I am?" This self-fulfilling statement of her helplessness is a way of saying to herself and her world, "See? I have no capacity to do other than that which I blame myself for." Theresa takes her blaming statement of "Look at all these things I'm doing wrong!" to define her whole existence.

I don't have to let my self-blame stop me from changing in ways I need to change.

Recently my daughter saved her money to buy a minibike.

I said, "I don't like them. They're noisy, you probably won't take care of it, etc., etc., but if that's what you want I'm not going to stop you."

Then I heard myself throwing roadblock after roadblock in her way. I thought, "That's really a dirty trick. I don't want you to have the bike but I don't want you to think I'm stopping you. So I present myself as fair, reasonable, and a nice guy, while I try to manipulate you into thinking it's too much bother and you didn't really want it anyway."

I went through the process of blaming myself. I had a choice there. I could say, "Boy, am I defective! Oh well—too bad. I'm so defective I can't do anything about it."

Instead I said, "That's a lousy thing to do. I don't want to leave it there—I want to undo that." I talked with her again and changed things, clearly having to take responsibility for what I'd done.

Taking responsibility for all my urges, impulses, feelings, and actions means I can no longer use "I did it unconsciously" as an excuse. Instead, I can view my unconscious as a resource I want to stay in touch with, not as a vague "force" that takes away my power and my responsibility for what I do.

WHAT'S YOURS AND WHAT'S MINE

In most cases, what happens between you and me results from what we both do. You *anger yourself, feel hurt, feel good,* etc., in response to what I do. I can't, all by myself, make you angry, hurt your feelings, or make you feel good. You've got to be willing to use my input to go to one of those places.

Usually the most I can do is *create the situation* in which you feel hurt or afraid or angry or pleased or joyful. If I didn't do or say what I did, you probably wouldn't have felt or thought or done what you did in response.

Try this: for the next thirty seconds *don't think about watermelons.*

See what's happening? Anything I say or do has the potentiality to set up a train of associations in your mind. Before I say something to you, I can ask myself, "Do I want to set those thoughts going in you?" If I know you well enough to be pretty sure where you'll go in response to what I say, and I go ahead and say it, I'm sending you there.

Usually, though, I don't know where you'll go with what I say or do. In that case, I can take responsibility only for my action. I have no responsibility for your response.

A few years ago I arranged to buy a hundred and forty-five acres of forest land. I bought a plot for myself, and friends of mine bought the rest in parcels of ten or fifteen acres each.

Had I not set up the deal, none of us would be living there now. Responsibility for arranging the purchase was mine. But since then we've each done our own thing with our parcel of land. Some of us have built fancy houses, some have built simple shacks, some are deeply in debt, some have left the land in its natural state. I am not responsible for what anyone except me has done.

Taking responsibility only for my own actions and letting other people take responsibility for theirs takes a big load off my shoulders.

When you and I are involved in any kind of a growing relationship, it's necessary for both of us to share. If I'm working on our mutual growth while your energy is somewhere else, we get nowhere. If you sit there playing dead while I'm working hard, I get tired of trying to carry you. I start setting goals for you. Then I no longer accept you as you are.

In any relationship, the kind of energy that comes out is the responsibility of everyone involved. No one person can singlehandedly make the process happen as it does.

I can respond to the messages you send out in whatever way I want to. I don't have to respond the way you want me to. But as long as I believe "*You* make me mad!" "*You* put me uptight!" "*You* make me happy!" and so on, I'm helpless. When I realize that *I* make myself feel bad, I can learn to stop doing that and to make myself feel good instead.

People who are having trouble in their relationships often make statements that boil down to "If only *you* would be different, *I* could be okay" or "I was all right till you came along."

If I insist, "This isn't fair" and "You're doing it to me," I put it all on the other person. I give away my power. I make myself the victim. How strange that, when I feel dissatisfied about something that involves both of us, I claim that *you* aren't doing it right!

Ben and Maureen had problems in their sexual relationship that each laid at the other's doorstep.

"You don't take the time for long, gentle lovemaking anymore—you're not as caring as you were when we were first together," complained Maureen. "I want you to be soft and tender and really in touch with me."

"You expect me to do everything," countered Ben. "I like some lusty sensuality every now and then, but you always say, 'Don't do this, don't do that, don't do the other thing.' You get upset at everything I do, but never take the initiative to make love the way you want to."

Ben and Maureen never did straighten out that problem. Later, in another relationship, Maureen began to discover how passive and sexually unadventurous she was, and learned to stop turning off her sexuality and to take a more active role in lovemaking. Ben began more fully appreciating the sexual act as a process of deep communication and sharing, and less often lost touch with his partner. Without each other to blame for their problems, Ben and Maureen both recognized what they were doing to create those problems, and changed their behavior.

ONLY YOU CAN DO IT

A monk asked: "How does one get emancipated?"
The master said:"Who has ever put you in bondage?"(D.T.Suzuki,106)

Do you promise yourself that someday you'll work on the things you need to work on in your life?

Do you believe yourself when you say "someday" as a child believes an adult when he or she says, "Just a minute"?

What do you need to do to be good to yourself? How do you evade asking yourself that question? Once you've asked it, how do you answer it? By evasion, or by doing something for yourself?

How do you let the expectations of people in your past define what you can and can't do for yourself today?

Do you expect someone else—like a psychologist or social worker—to solve your problems for you?

So many people I meet describe how things are *done to* them that change their lives. They describe themselves as though they were objects—totally manipulated and totally powerless, and close themselves to understanding how they let their lives be determined by outside events and other people's expectations. Their justifications of why they can't change close every door that might be open to them, and they keep on losing, and feeling bad.

✳ *Subject and object*

Sit comfortably and close your eyes. Imagine yourself as an *object*. Things are being done to you.

After a few minutes, have a new fantasy. In this one you're the *subject,* the doer, the controller, the creator.

Stop reading now and have your fantasies, and then continue on below.
. . .

Now, looking back at your fantasies, ask yourself, "How do I allow myself to get "done-to"? What kinds of things do I allow myself to fantasize? What kinds of power do I allow myself when I'm the doer?"

If you're doing this in a group, get together with three other people and share your experiences.

Whatever I'm doing, I'm creating a whole mood, whether it be a vigorous thing or a shoulder-slumping droopy nothingness or whatever.

I may stay out of touch with what's happening inside me by "keeping everything under control," for instance. If so, I can start paying attention to *how* I control myself, to my ways of *holding back* from expressing myself freely and living fully. I can discover how I stop myself from moving and flowing with my feelings and surroundings. Then, if I've been constricting my throat and tightening my voice, I can relax my neck and open my vocal cords. If I've been pulling in my chest and hunching my shoulders, I can drop my shoulders, breathe deeply, and let energy flow into my body. Just as I've learned to control myself, I can learn to release that control when appropriate.

We often say, "I can't," when the truth is "I won't." "I can't quit injuring myself . . . can't stop abusing other people . . . can't cut down my spending," etc. It's a handy dodge.

Usually when I say, "I can't," I haven't worked at whatever is facing me, or I've done so half-heartedly. This "can't" seems to make life easy, fixing things so I don't need to put out any effort. I'm not responsible—"It's not possible, that's all."

Here's something you can do:

✳ I can't, I won't, and I try

Be on the alert for those moments when you are about to say, "I can't." Each time you hear your "I can't" coming up, substitute "I won't." If that's too hard a statement for you, say "I can't right now." Instead of "I'm not able to," say "I'm not willing to." Instead of "I'm unable to," "I'm unwilling to." As you practice this, you'll start to detect when others use "I can't" to cover up what's really happening with them or to disown responsibility.

"I try" is another copout. Usually if I want to do something badly enough, I can do it. "I tried" implies "I can't." Usually it means I didn't want to badly enough, but I don't want to admit it. "I tried" often brings pity and the "poor baby" routine from others. Often you can simply say, "I did it," or "I didn't do it," and leave out the "trying" entirely.

The source of all security is inside me. I get nowhere if I put it on the world around me: "If only this were so, then I would be secure."

When my environment is oppressive, as it is for many people at various times in their lives, or even throughout their lives, I must find the kind of security that comes from getting in touch with my own sense of who I am, with my own self-worth. Then I can use my knowledge of myself to counter the oppressive environment: to change it so that my right to safety and self-determination begins to exist in the world around me as well as in my consciousness.

"All this is so hard!" you may say. "I have so many handicaps! So many strikes against me!"

I can't fix you up. Neither can your counselor. The door of opportunity doesn't open with an electric eye. Some people have more handicaps than others, but everyone has his or her share. We all have our sack of rocks to bear.

I think here of my friend and colleague Anne. Anne was born with severe cerebral palsy. Her distorted words came slowly and with difficulty. She moved her limbs in spasmodic jerks. During her early years she was considered severely mentally retarded.

Her parents put her in an institution, but she refused to stay. Brought home, she insisted on going to school. So Anne—who was not a pretty girl—went to school and suffered many jibes and jokes, but also got support and appreciation for her strength. She went through high school and college.

I met her when she asked to be an intern at the school for handicapped children I directed. Her internship included psychometrics, psychological testing, curriculum design, and parent consultation. She was one of the best interns I had, and she knew how to be good to herself.

Your quest is not to get the messiah to come but rather to move yourself toward him, assert the Hasidim of Pshiskhe.

4 *Awareness*

My awareness is my life. It is the source of my survival. My lack of awareness is my limit, and could mean my end.

So long as I'm not aware of what I'm doing now, I can't do anything different. When I notice what I'm doing, I can choose either to continue doing that or to do something else.

The world I know exists for me through my awareness, and the world you know exists for you through yours.

Many people use their eyes to look only at clothes and appearances, and their ears to hear only words and phrases. They don't see the forgotten language of body talk, and don't hear the music and rhythm that underlie our words. The environments they grew up in blunted their natural sensitivities, and did not teach them those sensitivities that can be learned.

We can develop greater sensitivity by developing our awareness. Awareness is not the same as knowledge. Awareness occurs in the present, whereas knowledge is a file cabinet of information we learned in the past. In the following exercises, you can explore your own awareness.

✳ *The awareness continuum*

Out loud to another person, or silently to yourself, describe what you are aware of from moment to moment.

Begin each sentence with "Now I am aware . . ." and describe what you are aware of. For example, "Now I am aware that the sun is making golden patterns on the floor. Now I am aware that my mind keeps going back to something that happened to me yesterday. Now I am aware of feeling a pain just below my left shoulder blade," and so on.

As you describe what you are aware of, pay special attention to *specific details* of what's going on. Avoid generalities. Instead of "I'm aware of the way I'm sitting," you might say, "Now I'm aware that I'm sitting with my left foot up on the couch and my body slumped sideways."

You may find yourself thinking, "The things I'm aware of in the now are so simple and trite and obvious." That's okay. We are often so blind to the obvious that there's real value in learning to be aware of it.

If you're talking to another person, he or she can help you stay in the present. When you say something that isn't an awareness of a present event, the listener says, in a nonjudgmental way, "you've wandered."

If you're doing this with another person, after five or ten minutes, switch so that the other person talks and you listen. (Adapted from Perls, Hefferline, and Goodman, 31–32, 82–83)

When you first try the awareness continuum, you may often drift off into daydreaming or thinking about the past or future. That's normal. As soon as you notice that you're no longer talking about your present experience, say so—"Now I am wondering who will win the election," etc. Then bring your attention back to "Now I am aware . . ." and continue.

If too much happens for you to describe, skip over what has become the immediate past and tell only what's happening right now. Stay with what's clear and obvious in your awareness. You can use the awareness continuum with what "happens" in you as well as with what you do "on purpose"—with your spontaneous as well as your deliberate experience.

In the next exercise, you can be aware of the spontaneous movement and flow of your waking consciousness, without restricting your attention to the present.

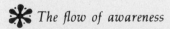 *The flow of awareness*

If it's handy, put on some relaxing but unobtrusive music.

Lie down on your back or sit comfortably, opening or closing your eyes whenever you wish. Let your mind drift freely wherever it wants to.

As you do this, you'll probably soon notice that some of the time you're aware of events in your body and in your immediate surroundings, and some of the time your consciousness is filled with fantasies and daydreams, thoughts and images, memories and anticipations. You spend part of your time in your awareness process and part of it in your fantasy process.

Get a sense of the natural ebb and flow of what happens in your own mind—with what you do with your awareness from one moment to the next.

When you've finished this "flow of awareness," go right on to the next exercise:

❊ The editor's exercise

Take a pen and a sheet of paper. Continue the "flow of awareness" exercise, with one change: Each time something new comes into your awareness, jot down one or two words to describe it.

Do this for at least ten minutes, right now. Then continue reading below. . . .

Now, keeping before you your list of what has just passed through your mind, take another sheet of paper. Imagine that you are a newspaper editor doing a front-page layout. Lay out a front page that reflects the content of your own awareness.

What's your headline? What are the major issues? What are the brief news flashes that come into your awareness just for a moment? What do you put down in the corners?

Now look at your front page. Where does the biggest share of your awareness go? What news sources do you favor to the exclusion of what others? Are you most attuned to sensations in your body, sights and sounds around you, or thoughts and fantasies?

If others are doing the exercise along with you, compare your "front pages" to get a sense of the different kinds of events you report.

BE RICH AND BEAUTIFUL

We blind ourselves to so much in our lives that could be rich and beautiful! Part of this narrowing of our awareness is the result of the taboos learned from a parent's constant "Don't do this, don't do that, stop that!" even when the child is doing nothing harmful. This prevents the child from finding out what is harmful and what isn't. It can create an anxious, resentful personality, as the child learns to fear that everything he or she does might be wrong.

Many children who have reading problems have grown up with such taboos. Their parents endlessly warn them, "Don't look here, don't look there, don't open the drawers, don't open the closets, don't be curious, don't stare . . ." The children learn how to not look, and then generalize and apply this habit of not looking to the written word. Much of their natural curiosity has been turned off.

Feeling upset can be a barrier to awareness too. When we're upset, we can completely lose our sense of what's important.

Joseph Wood Krutch tells of a duck who was frantic in protecting her young. She flew in a flurry even at well-meaning human friends who had cared for her for years. If they kept coming close, she'd forget what she was disturbed about and even attack her own little ducklings.

Awareness, judging, and acceptance

Awareness and acceptance go hand in hand. Full awareness is seeing what is. Judging people and things "bad" or "wrong"—or even as "right" or "good"—usually gets in the way of awareness. What my judge sees and what is may not be the same.

Tom complained to me about his delayed reaction time. Time and time again he would think of something he "should have said" a couple of hours before.

At work one day, for instance, his foreman said, "Tom, that window frame on the left side of the building should have been set in." Tom felt confused and embarrassed, mumbled something in reply, and went on with his work. Two hours later he was eating his heart out because he just remembered that he couldn't set the frame in because the other workers didn't have the joists up.

Tom carried around a lot of anger that he didn't let himself feel. For him, anger was somehow "wrong" and "bad." The foreman's criticism triggered some of that anger, but Tom was so afraid of his anger that he hid it beneath confusion and embarrassment.

When Tom began to stop judging his feelings, he began to be more aware of them and to speak out when it was appropriate, instead of bottling himself up and feeling bad later. Eventually he was able to talk to the foreman—not in ways that would get him fired, but in ways that clearly stated his position, like "I would have set it in, but the joists weren't up."

When I accept what I do, think, or feel as being how I am now, without judging my behavior as "right" or "wrong," I can see what I'm doing clearly. Only when I'm aware of what I'm doing do I have the option of doing something else. That accounts for the seeming paradox that *being willing to have yourself okay as you are right now makes change easier.*

You can begin moving into a *growth circle.* Judging less allows you to be more aware. Increased awareness helps you be alert to when you judge.

There is no good or bad awareness—no "my awareness is better than yours." The important thing is knowing what you're doing, whatever that is.

WORKING WITH AWARENESS

Buddha used the term "mindfulness" for awareness. He advised people to be aware of every area of themselves and their lives.

Shunryu Suzuki says of Buddha, "He watched himself, and he watched others with the same eyes that he watched stones or plants, or anything else. He had a very scientific understanding" (102).

✳ *People-watching*

This is something you can do almost anywhere. Kids have a lot of fun with it.

Suppose you're sitting in a restaurant, waiting for the waitress to come. Look at the people around you, one at a time, and give a label to each posture, each movement. Such labels can carry great force. They can sum up much about a person.

A lot of what goes into the label you assign is your own projection. Even so, this exercise teaches you to look at people more carefully, to see them and yourself more clearly and in a more focused way.

A useful way to start expanding my awareness is to assume that I'm not so aware of what I do. For if I assume I know myself, I close myself to discovering anything except what I already think I know.

The great thing to understand, as Perls notes, is that awareness—by and of itself—can be curative, bringing constructive change. We can rely on the wisdom of our organism. But there's a wild card: Though awareness almost always leads to change, it doesn't always lead where you think you want to go. For example, Gestalt Therapist Robert K. Hall notes that when a couple with problems undergoes therapy and becomes more aware, they may get together or they may split up. What happens with awareness is unpredictable. That's both the delight and the frustration of it.

Have you ever noticed how some people look straight ahead as they walk along, as if they had blinders on? They can pass people they know and seem not to see them—or even in fact not see them—unless they're in the direct line of sight.

I used to do that. I was afraid that others would be offended if I broke into their privacy. In my world each person lived inside a glass box, and I couldn't reach or look into another's box without permission.

At last I realized that most people preferred a "hello" or a friendly nod to my "respect for their privacy." It wasn't respect at all. It was fear: fear of what might happen if I "intruded."

Here's something you can do. For half a day, smile and nod at everyone you pass or meet, even strangers. For the other half, scowl and look away from everyone.

What do you discover?

With awareness you don't need to "figure out" why something is happening. (In other contexts, "figuring out" sometimes has value. When it intrudes on your ability to be aware, then your tendency to "figure out" is part of what you need to be aware of.) Awareness itself can lead to understanding. As you get in touch with what's going on, you will start to sort your puzzle out.

Staying with immediate awareness short-circuits your reasoning, computing mind that uses your fixed beliefs to blind you.

If I insist on using my computing mind to analyze what's happening, I can ask questions like "What's in it for me to act as I do? What triggers my action? What leads to what, and when do I do these things that I'm concerned about?"

The important thing is not to think about what you *usually* do and feel, but to pay attention to what you're doing and feeling *now*.

When awareness is painful

Mark took his son on a camping trip in the wilderness with a group of other fathers and sons. Mark's son died on the trip. No one really knew what happened—one morning he just didn't wake up.

The well-meaning minister at the funeral told the family not to grieve, because the boy was with the angels. For six months, the family members pretended they had no grief, and the tensions almost destroyed the family. Finally they became aware that they were all sitting on their grief, and gave themselves permission to grieve. After that things got better.

In India there is a tradition that the person who was closest to the one who died tells the story of the beloved one's death over and over again to each new visitor. Then the visitor often relates a similar story from his or her own experience. As the bereaved person keeps retelling the story, he or she begins to live with the fact of the death. The stories others tell in reply can provide some sharing and consolation. In this manner, the awareness of death becomes a part of the reality of life.

When you are in sorrow, *be* sorrowful. When you feel bored, *be* bored. These states, which you so often try to escape, are keys to transformation. When you escape them, you remain the slave of your worries and fears, and learn nothing. When you stay aware of what you experience, you begin to know who you are.

✳ Exaggeration

If you feel bored, be *terribly* bored.

If you're sorrowful, go into the very center of your sorrow. Exaggerate it. Wail, moan, and roll on the floor if that's what you feel like doing.

If I can push myself until I am completely filled with sorrow, beyond the limits I would ordinarily go to, then my sorrow comes into perspective. I begin to know the limits within which it is real for me. I know it in its proper proportion to the rest of life.

Then, since I've been to the very bottom of my deep black pit, as far as this kind of experience is concerned, I need no longer run away and hide from these thoughts and feelings.

You can do this with any way of thinking or feeling you want to know more fully.

You can also do it with joyful and happy thoughts and feelings. Do you allow yourself the fullness of your joy and laughter, or do you stop short there too?

Awareness and exaggeration work even when you're confused. Be aware of how you confuse yourself, and you'll have an easier time sorting your confusion out. When I try to figure out how to be not confused, I usually get more confused than ever. Bill Kwong comments, "When the fog is there, don't pretend it isn't. Just see the fog."

II

Responsibility

5 *Creating Your World*

My environment may open many doors to me, or it may restrict me. As an extreme example of restriction, consider a prison: the kinds of stimulation available are very limited, and there's a limited number of people to be with.

Anywhere a person lives, be it a ghetto, a suburb, or a high-rise apartment, can be a jail if it builds in important limitations. Any family can be a prison for the children who grow up in it.

Some of our environmental "jails" are, in basic ways, more restrictive than others. A person who lives in a ghetto has to hustle to find any kind of job at all, and *really* work to find a job that fits his or her own directions and potentialities. A middle-class person has more opportunities available.

Within the limits set by my environment, I can choose how I let the forces around me influence me. Deliberately or by default, I can select the way I am wherever I am.

This is true even for a man in prison. The institution has said to him, "We'll tell you who and how to be by regimenting every moment of your life."

The guy in the joint can choose to buy that. He can focus completely on that day ten years from now when he's due to get out; he can get suckered into putting most of his daily life into pleasing that parole board that will meet in several years. Or he can choose to live each day as it comes, and stay in touch with what he's experiencing, what he's responding to, and how he's responding. That way he can maintain his aliveness, instead of letting ten years of his life be a void. Those who stay in touch this way have a lot less "Hard Time" than those whose lives depend completely on "The Day I Get Out." People have, among other

43

accomplishments, written books, studied law, developed programs for prison reform, and initiated political movements while doing time.

When I'm in New York City, I begin to talk and move a little faster than when I'm in the country. The very vibrations of the city affect me. Still, I stay true to myself. When I was growing up in New York, I chose never to rush for a subway train; after all, another train would pull in soon. As I walked down the station steps, people invariably pushed by me to get to *that* train. Often they glanced back with anger because I walked slowly instead of rushing. I knew, as many of them didn't, that none of us had to let the rhythm of the subway become the rhythm of our lives.

If, like Hermann Hesse's Siddhartha, I live by an ageless, ever-flowing river, and choose to live *with* that river, its voices slowly seep into my being. In a sense I become that river. The river can be the flow of the lives of the people around me, and *their* voices can seep into my being. If I'm in touch with my existence, I become the rich and vital parts of the river. If not, I may become its ill-tempered, shallow, and uncaring parts.

Today I live in a forest, but I could go back to living in the city tomorrow and be happy there. I've learned to allow myself to be wherever I am. Environment is important, but what I do with my environment is even more important.

As a teen-ager living in Bellevue, Nebraska, I was miserable. I hadn't learned how to find many good things for myself in that environment, and was overjoyed when we moved away. Today I could find ways to get what I need and to feel good even in Bellevue.

Some parts of my world open doors to fuller ways of living and experiencing, while others close them.

Take a look at the things you watch and read. How does each one affect the way you feel and what you think about? Next time you watch TV, turn off the picture and just listen to the sound awhile. Now turn off the sound and just watch the picture. In each case, be sensitive to how the program or commercial manipulates your thoughts and feelings. You're making all those things you watch and read and listen to part of your life.

With everything you make part of your life—your friends, your job, your residence, the other places where you spend your time—you can ask yourself, "Do I *want* to make that part of me?"

This question has both a personal and a political aspect. The personal aspect is "How am I affected by my environment?" The political aspect is "What's in it for my environment to have me accept the messages it's giving me?"

Many of our social institutions seem to want me to be available for ready manipulation. If I feel inadequate about making my own decisions, I give up my power, my responsibility, and my right to define who I am to big business, the media, government agencies, and other influential groups.

Once I understand how my social environment wants me to be, and why, I can more wisely choose which people and events in my environment I want to make part of me, and which ones I don't.

✳ *This is my existence*

In the course of an ordinary day, take five or ten minutes for this exercise in each of the places that is part of your day, including where you are right now.

During that time, get fully in touch with the place. Pay attention to people and things and events that you're usually not aware of, as well as those you usually notice.

As you slowly and carefully touch and look and listen, ask yourself, "Who here is like me? Who here is not? What in this place is like me, and what is not? *How* are these people and things like me? How are they alien to who I am?"

Does this evaluation suggest any changes you want to make in how you arrange your environment, or in where you spend your time?

I CREATE MY OWN EXISTENCE

Stephen writes, "I used to drink and drive a lot, and I used to therefore get in a lot of wrecks. . . . I began to figure out that it wasn't like an accident at all, you know, it was something that I bought, asking for it."

If I trace my problems back to their source, it almost always turns out that, in some way, *I chose them*. If I apologize for being alive, for instance, people will treat me as though I have no right to be here.

If I ask for something as though I don't expect to get it, the chances are I won't.

"You wouldn't possibly be willing to . . . ?" "I don't suppose I might . . . ?"

The way I ask a question tells the other person what kind of answer I expect. I can ask a question in a way that makes it easy to reply "No" or "I don't know," or in a way that leads to "Yes" or "Sure I will."

I might say: "It's all right if I . . . , isn't it?" or "What can you tell me about . . . ?" Or alternatively: "Do you have any . . . ?" or "Do you know . . . ?"

Whether I get a yes or a no often depends on which I ask for.

When I was asked to move to another office, I said to myself, "I better check the place I'm supposed to move into."

Then I thought, "No, the man who's asking me to move knows what I need, and he told me that the new office is almost exactly like the one I have." I made one feeble attempt to get a key to the place, didn't get it, and gave up trying.

After the movers had moved in my things, I finally saw the office. It was terrible—so noisy I couldn't carry on a conversation. I'd been done-to, and I was angry. I was just as angry at allowing myself to get done-to as at getting done-to.

In my daily life, I can give myself at least as much consideration as I give others. I don't have to set myself up to be a victim.

My world is not something that exists separate and apart from me. "If I want to describe a man," says my colleague Bernd Jager,

> I must also describe his surroundings. I must look at where he acts and lives, and where he fails to act and fails to live. I stand here in the classroom and look at you. The way each of us is here comes from who we are. In your faces, I see opportunities—roads along which to go.
>
> Suppose there is a depressed woman standing here beside me. To her, your faces might look like closed doors. The room seems narrow and repressive, and she's not aware of much outside her. She sees fewer differences among people. They're more like a blur—gray and uninviting. She's there in the room in a way different from the way I'm there. If we assume that she and I are in the same room, we make a mistake.

George A. Kelly and his colleagues studied "laziness" in schoolchildren. Kelly writes:

> [It] became apparent . . . that the teacher's complaint was not neces-sarily something to be verified or disproved, but was, rather, a

construction of events in a way that made the most sense to her at the moment.

One technique we came to use was to ask the teacher what the child would do if she did not try to motivate him. Often the teacher would insist that the child would do nothing—absolutely nothing—just sit! Then . . . we would ask her to observe how he went about "just sitting." Invariably the teacher would be able to report some extremely interesting goings on . . . some teachers found that their laziest pupils were those who could produce the most novel ideas, others that the term "laziness" had been applied to activities that they had simply been unable to understand or appreciate.

In another context Kelly says, ". . . our clients were making their choices, not in terms of the alternatives *we* saw open to them, but in terms of the alternatives *they* saw open to them. It was their . . . daily mazes that they ran, not the 'pure realities' that appeared to us to surround them. . . . The child's temper tantrum is, for him, one of the few remaining choices left."

In Kelly's view, a person is "not a victim of his past, only the victim of his construction of it" (345–54).

I AM WHAT I DO

At the height of a battle, a soldier runs out into the line of fire to help his wounded buddy. The next day, he sits in his foxhole all day long. From moment to moment and day to day, he can choose whether to act in a way you or I would call "brave."

That same soldier is six feet tall. He was six feet tall yesterday and he'll be six feet tall tomorrow. He can't choose to be five-feet-seven instead. In the same way, a table is a table, and can't choose to become something else instead.

This is what Jean-Paul Sartre means when he distinguishes between an *action* and an *attribute*. "Six-feet-tallness" and "tableness" are *attributes*. They can't be changed. "Bravery" is different. It's based on *actions*. There's no such thing as "a brave man," declares Sartre. If a man *usually acts bravely*, that's all we can say. His acts define him.

Suppose I feel sad. When I feel sad in my usual way, I can predict what my sadness will be like. I know how I'll probably get out of it, because I know how I got out of it before. Yet even as I act sad, Sartre suggests, I know I can't hang on to my sadness. Let a stranger suddenly appear and I lift up my head. I assume a lively cheerfulness. I no longer act sad, though I may promise myself more of the same torture when the stranger has gone.

What happened? I *made myself sad*. Then I made myself cheerful.

When I live with the idea that I'm "sad" or "a coward" or whatever, I blind myself to the fact that *I create* these ways of thinking and feeling in myself. As I begin to recognize that I could act otherwise, and feel otherwise too, I gain a new measure of choice in my life.

The kind of learned pattern of showing my sadness that Sartre describes differs from a real feeling of sadness *as I uniquely experience it now*.

If I'm really with the sadness I feel today, when Sartre's stranger appears, I will stay with my sadness. I will relate to the stranger from where I am.

I have seen this in times of tragedy. When there is a severe illness, a death, a great disaster, people don't just suddenly snap out of it.

Here's a way to explore how you create and maintain your ways of feeling and behaving:

✳ *Echoes of the way I feel*

As you go through a day, you describe yourself to others and to yourself. Pay attention to how you do this. What favorite stories do you reel off again and again, and what do they tell you about yourself? Who talks to you about their feelings, and which of those feelings sound like your own? What about the music you listen to? How is it like you? If you read newspaper stories and magazine articles, which ones fit who you are and which ones don't? Do any of them say anything about how you act or feel?

What do you learn from this about *how you gather data to use in creating your own world?*

On the other side of the ledger, who do you allow to tell you the ways in which they've changed? Which among the songs and stories of renewal and change do you read and listen to? How much of the information you select helps keep you where you are, and how much of it helps you move into other places?

There's an illusion many people hide behind: "I'm not what I seem to be—I'm better than my deeds suggest."

People who say this use their images of what they "are" to keep from facing what their actions paint them as: "That's not who I *really* am." Sometimes they have a hard time telling the two apart. If I'm trying to be my illusion of who I am, I may not want to be aware of who I am in fact.

I may abuse and bully and tyrannize other people. I think, "People misunderstand me. I'm not a bully. It's the evil in other people that makes me do the things I do."

If I'm unwilling to work at behaving as the "kind person at heart" I think I am, I'm likely to rationalize: "My deeds don't represent me. I'm 'good at heart,' and that's what counts."

When I deny my acts as statements of myself, I blind myself to things that everyone else can see. Though we may claim that our deeds don't represent us, in fact they do. Though we may claim that we can't act otherwise, in fact we can.

ACTION AND ITS RESULTS

> He is wise
> Who acts without lust or scheming
> For the fruit of the act:
> His act falls from him,
> Its chain is broken . . .
> He acts, and is beyond action.
>
> *The Bhagavad-Gita*

I *am* the risks I run to be me. The risks I'm willing and unwilling to take are statements of who I am and who I am not.

We can almost never know enough to be sure what's going to happen as a result of what we do. We can only guess, assume, and expect, with varying degrees of certainty.

At this moment, under these circumstances, with the knowledge I have now, I make my choice. I live with its results. The conditions of my life today are the result of choices I made yesterday.

Everyone "blows it" now and then. If I think as clearly and act as honestly and wisely as I know how, that's all I can do.

We can't help some of our suffering, but we ourselves create the rest. We don't have to do that. We can learn to take our failures and our half-successes as a normal part of life. My "errors" and "defeats" sometimes teach me more than my successes. In an important sense they aren't failures at all.

When I try to avoid feeling responsible for what I did yesterday, I blind myself to doors that are open now. When I blame others for what happened to me, I keep myself from seeing how I shape my own destiny. As I learn how I create my life, I find more ways to feel good, because I know the choice of doing that is mine.

Learning to take responsibility is as important for a child as for an adult.

When I hurt somebody, it's important for me to perceive the harm in such a way that I can't deny it. Only if you experience the consequences of your actions will you develop a true sense of responsibility.

The other day I was sitting in a laundromat when a small boy came over and closed the window next to me.

It was a hot day. I said, "I'd like that open." He opened it again, looked at me, and went off to do something else. His mother glanced over from across the room, then went on putting her laundry in the machine.

The child was learning that he can act independently and that what he does has certain consequences for other people and for him. He was learning to be responsible for his actions.

Many mothers in this situation would immediately say, "Now don't you bother that man!" and then come over, open the window again, and say to me, "I'm very sorry," scolding the child and leading him away. Their children learn to be directed from outside and to carry out orders. They don't learn to do things for themselves.

How often and how automatically many of us deny responsibility when something goes wrong!

"It wasn't my fault!"

"I couldn't help it!"

Watching a child, it's easy to see how it all gets started: "But Billy did it first," Johnny protests, or "It was Suzie's idea."

Mother replies, "Well, then run along and play, and do behave yourself next time."

See what's happening?

By accepting his excuse, Johnny's mother is teaching him *to believe that he is not responsible for what he does.*

The way this works with reward-oriented learning is that when Johnny doesn't do what he's been told he has to do to earn a certain reward, but comes up with some excuse, he gets the reward anyway.

As an adult, I find ways to reward myself for excuses and statements of helplessness that once got me what I wanted, but now sabotage my ability to do things for myself.

Self-righteousness

When Jesus was teaching, he associated with prostitutes, tax-gatherers, and many others who were looked down on by the "respectable" people of his time. He felt no ill will toward people who had done many hurtful things if they were willing to be open with themselves and change. He was less warm toward "virtuous" people who were blatantly self-righteous.

If I'm self-righteous about what I do, I admit no possibility that my act might not be altogether wise. The more sure I am of my righteousness, the more likely I am to blind myself to anything that doesn't fit what I want to believe.

When I'm willing to look carefully at the effects of what I do, I become aware of the ways I affect myself or others.

The Latin root of the word "repentance" means to *change one's behavior*. Saying "I'm sorry" won't do it.

Saying "Oh, Father, forgive me, I've been so bad! I repent, I repent, I repent!" won't do it.

Acting differently will.

The wider context

In small ways we may not even recognize, most of us contribute to larger events that happen in this world. I uphold the law as I pay my taxes. I maintain our society by the clothes that I wear. I act to keep things as they are by often neglecting to work for issues and candidates that offer real change.

When I face important issues in this world, I sometimes feel hopeless. Anything I could do seems so insignificant as to be hardly worth the bother. Yet, if I think the issue is important, I do what I can anyway.

As you and I act, others may take heart and be stirred to action too. But if you wait for me and I wait for you—welcome to Zombieland.

6 *Guessing and Projecting*

When I started out as a psychologist, I worked in a school in a community where an Aleutian family had recently arrived. The whole family looked as if it had just walked off the wrapper of an Eskimo Pie bar.

The principal suggested that the boy's hair, which was cut in the traditional Eskimo style, be cut shorter. The father immediately cut off *all* the boy's hair. The next day, the child came into the classroom, put his head on his desk and his jacket over his head, and would not come out. This behavior was referred to me as a problem, with the child attached to it.

I made several assumptions about the boy's behavior. I thought of castration fears associated with having his hair cut off. I thought of anthropologists' findings that some tribes cut off the hair of a person they are excommunicating. But no matter what I thought of, I got nothing back from the boy that fit my interpretations.

Finally I asked directly, "Eddie, why do you have your jacket over your head?"

He peeked out from under his jacket and replied, "It's cold."

When we gave him a knit cap to wear until his hair grew back, he was just fine.

I can't see into your mind. I can watch what you do, hear what you say, think about these things, and weave them all into a guess about what's happening with you. Then, like a projector in a movie theatre, I project my guess back onto you, and assume that it corresponds to what's happening in you.

Often, of course, I don't realize that it's a guess at all. I think I "know" what's happening with you. Guesses about what's happening inside other people are sometimes called "inferences" or "interpretations." But a guess is a guess, whatever it's called. It may be fairly accurate or it may not.

I can use my guesses about others to find out about myself. I'm most likely to see in you the kinds of things I'm most tuned in to picking up. Often, what I imagine that you're thinking and feeling is what I would think and feel if I were in your place.

Here's something to try:

 Projection onto objects

Pick out any object around you, and imagine you're that object.

Tell another person what you're like as that object. Think of as many aspects of being it as you can.

Another way to do this is for you both to imagine being the same object, and then share your experiences.

In your daily life, you can imagine being different objects at different times and see what common themes stand out.

The image I project onto you may be pretty accurate, or it may not. I may distort my view of what's happening so that things seem the way I want them to be, or the way I'm afraid they'll be.

When his teen-age daughter starts dating, a father may remember his own teen-age exploits with girls. He may assume that the boy with whom his daughter is going out will do exactly what he did during his own adolescence, or what he didn't do but wanted to, and imagined that everyone else was doing.

People whose projections are often accurate tend to keep their imaginings about others firmly rooted in what they see and hear.

People who are most often mistaken in their projections are usually the ones who are most certain they "know how other people really are." By being so sure, they close themselves to changing their ideas when new information comes along. Even when the stuff they take from inside themselves and project onto the other person isn't really in that person, they insist that it is.

Someone who wants to believe that a certain trait exists in another person can always find some "proof" that what he or she sees in the other person is really there. The smallest detail can take on great significance. The projector is amazingly talented at elaborating, at exaggerating, and at dismissing contradictory evidence, and needs just one confirming instance to feel total certainty—"Aha! I knew it all the time!"

What we're unwilling to recognize in ourselves

"How can you say to your brother, 'My dear brother, let me take the speck out of your eye,' when you are blind to the plank in your own?" asked Jesus (Luke 6:41–42).

Freud usually used the word "projection" in a more limited sense than we're using it here. He used it for the process of looking for traits in other people that we're not willing to see in ourselves, or accept as ours if we do see them.

You've probably seen this process in action many times: for example, the dishonest person who constantly suspects others of dishonesty, or the person who complains of being victimized and proceeds to take advantage of everyone and everything.

Part of this process has a magical giveaway quality: by projecting onto someone else something that I don't like about myself, I give it away, and supposedly no longer have to deal with it in myself.

When I find myself intolerant of what another person does, I do well to look for ways I do the same, perhaps in a disguised or more sophisticated way. The things I'm most intolerant of in others are often the things I'm most intolerant of in me.

Karen Horney noted that even love can be projected. Elaborating on her observations, Perls writes:

> If you are afraid to express "I hate you," you will soon imagine yourself being hated by the world, and likewise if you are too shy to say "I love you," you will find yourself expecting love from the world. . . .
>
> If unaccepted love is followed by disappointment, the painful experience makes [a person] shrink from yielding to his emotions. It is as if he had decided, "Let others do the loving: I won't run such a risk again." . . . [He] projects [his own] love, and consequently . . . conjures up visions of receiving just those affections which he suppresses in himself. (EHA, 242, 160)

The power in our projections

I project not only when I don't recognize something that exists in me, but also when I do acknowledge something in me but am afraid to express it. When I learn to express that part of me, I don't need to project it anymore.

When I've been projecting all my power and feeling manipulated, for example, I can start taking risks and asserting myself. Then I begin to feel my own power again.

Perls and his co-authors suggest that you can guess what another person is like, and *try on that way of being for yourself.* "Think yourself into the shoes of the aggressor, admirer, rejecter, foolhardy one," they suggest, "More often than not, the reversal will click" (222). How do you feel when you imagine yourself as that person? Do you touch a place in you that's real?

Doing this can be especially useful when you react very strongly to someone (for instance, when you feel afraid or helpless).

SELF-CONSCIOUSNESS

Self-consciousness is very different from self-awareness. Self-awareness is paying attention to what you do, and learning what you can from what you observe. Self-consciousness is attending just a little to what you do, and spending most of your time thinking that what you do is bad or wrong and worrying about what other people are thinking of you, or would think if they saw you.

When you first begin to practice self-awareness, it's easy to unknowingly slip over to self-consciousness, if your habit of self-consciousness is strong.

Perls suggests that when we feel self-conscious, we act as if we have no eyes. I'm so anxious about what you think of me that I see almost nothing about you. I've projected my eyes onto you, and from there I look back at myself, criticizing and belittling what I see.

We also act as if we have no ears, not hearing ourselves, but worrying about how others hear us. In Perls' words, "People expect the ears to be outside and they talk and expect someone to listen. But who listens?" (GTV, 36–37).

When I get caught up blindly in my mind, spinning around in vortexes of thought that take up almost all my attention, I have little energy left for what's going on outside of me.

I get embarrassed about not knowing what's going on so I pretend I know. Then I become self-conscious about what others think of me because I know I'm faking my way through the situation, and I'm afraid they might find me out.

I can begin to reverse this. The more energy I put into observing what's going on, the less energy I have to put into covering up. I can tell I'm coming out of one of the whirlpools in my mind when I begin to see and hear again.

With a group of people, try this:

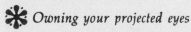 *Owning your projected eyes*

Clear a space so a person can walk all the way across the room. Half of the group stands on one side of the room, half on the opposite side.

One at a time, each of you walks from one end of the room to the other, stopping in the middle to say your name.

The others learn what they can about who you are by watching your walk and your body language, and listening to how you say your name.

Each of you pays attention to how you feel as you make this statement of yourself with all those eyes on you.

When everyone has done this, take some time to discuss how you felt walking across the room. Don't read on until you've finished your discussion.

. . .

Have you finished your discussion? Now each of you go back and walk across the room and speak your name one more time, with one difference.

This time, while you're walking, really look at the other people standing there. Find out all you can about them. See what they're doing, how they're standing, etc.

Do you feel any different? How? Again share your feelings with the others.

Next time you walk into a room and feel self-conscious, stop, take a deep slow breath, and feel your breathing and your whole body. Then, really look at and listen to the other people there, *learning all you can about them.*

As you get fully involved in doing that, your self-consciousness will diminish and maybe even disappear.

When you're concerned about how you're coming across to someone, and are afraid you've made a blunder, remember this: You've blown it in your own projected eyes—the eyes you've attributed to the other person. *That person doesn't see you through those eyes,* but through his or her own. Often the other person won't see you as blowing it at all, even when you think that's what you're doing. In fact, often the other person doesn't even see what you do. We're not so important in others' eyes as we think we are.

Keep alert for the next time you start to worry about what someone else is thinking of you. Now look carefully at that person. Have you been watching him or her closely? Thinking a lot about how stupid what he or she does and says seems?

I'll bet not. You've been too busy with your own concerns.

The same is very likely true for everyone around you. Do you see the joke? Each person is too busy wondering how *he or she* is coming across to have much time to pay attention to *you.*

Don't forget that everyone blows it a million times in a lifetime. That's how we learn. You don't have to—and couldn't possibly—do everything perfectly.

Sometimes you trip up on one thing after another. If you're willing to laugh at yourself and shrug your shoulders, very likely others will laugh *with* you instead of *at* you, and respect you too.

Actually, very few people like someone who seems to do everything just right. Faced with such "perfection," others feel bad by comparison. Most people have much more affection for someone who seems to be ordinary, doing the best he or she can, than for someone who comes on like Superman.

PROJECTION IN RELATIONSHIPS

Most of us continually guess what others are thinking and feeling, without checking those guesses out. We all try to read minds.

We read meanings into what others say and then act on the basis of those guesses. When our expectations aren't fulfilled, we accuse those persons of being dishonest. *They're not.* Maybe they didn't tell us what was happening in their heads, but then, we didn't ask.

At almost any point, I can start asking what's happening with you, even though I haven't been asking up until now.

The way I ask can be very important. In a marriage counseling situation, the husband became very irate when his wife asked, "Where are you now?" He thought she was probing and poking at him, attacking him, and implying, "You're being secretive."

"Is that how you feel?" I asked her.

"No," she replied. She began to look for a statement about herself that would reach her husband, and came up with "I need to hear you now."

He replied, "That feels good. I can respond to that and not feel probed at."

The same principle is equally important for parent and child, teacher and student.

We commonly project what we dislike or won't recognize in ourselves. When I project what I dislike in myself onto you, and then judge you harshly—and unjustly—for possessing that quality, I poison our relationship and hinder my own ability to grow.

If you feel jealous of your friend or spouse or lover, check out whether maybe *you'd* like to do a little lovemaking on the side, but haven't admitted it to yourself.

Projection is often involved when a person feels rejected. Unaware that they themselves are rejecting others, the projectors think that the others are rejecting them.

Now, of course, since the other person has rejected you, that person is an S.O.B. and you don't want anything to do with him or her. So you get everything you want. You get your separation from the other person, and you even get to feel like the Good Guy in the situation, because the other person did the rejecting.

If you think others don't want to be with you, *be attentive to how you push people away.* Look at how you say, "Leave me alone" . . . "Go away."

We also project what we admire.

A man who thinks he's weak may see all the women he's attracted to as strong, whether they really are or not. If he's uptight, he may see them as relaxed and easygoing. If he's in his head a lot, he may see them as simple and uncomplicated.

I had an awakening one day when a woman I felt attracted to "because of her warmth" (I perceived myself as cold in certain ways) said to me, "One of the things I like most about you is that you're such a *warm* person."

As I find out what I'm projecting, I get in touch with strengths within myself that I've been unaware of.

One day I meet an attractive woman. Before long I begin to realize that she's almost everything I've dreamed of. "I've found the perfect woman!"

I see a few virtues in her that fit with my image of an "ideal other." Then I explain away or blind myself to everything she does that doesn't fit that image.

Maybe I like a woman for her particular kinds of insecurities. That's okay. We all do it. But if I try to pretend that her crazy places don't exist, or that she's the incarnation of all truth and virtue, she may feel she has to live up to my fantasy. That makes it impossible for her to be herself. And that's a hell of a trip to lay on anyone.

I'll take you off the pedestal I put you on if you'll take me off the one you put me on. Then maybe we can have a relationship.

Transference and displacement

Sometimes we act toward a person as though he or she were someone from our past: a former spouse or lover, or parent or other authority figure.

When I do that with you, I see mostly the image I project on you, and see little of who you really are.

Freud called this *transference*. I transfer my way of relating to someone else onto you. A wife, for instance, may transfer some of her feelings toward her father onto her husband. Sexual feelings toward her husband get confused with sexual taboos toward her father, and she may be afraid of her own sexuality with her husband.

When I *overtly act* toward you in ways that were meant for someone else, it's called *displacement.*

Displacement of aggression is a common example. I do cruel things to you that are really meant for the big kids who used to make fun of me and beat me up when I was a little kid. I can't beat up father, but I can beat up my little brother. I'm afraid to talk back to my boss, but I can be nasty to my mate.

Checking our projections

I want to pick up all the messages I can that you're actually sending, and I don't want to mistake what's happening in me for messages from you.

To check out a projection directly, I ask you if what I'm guessing is so. For instance, I meet someone I want to make contact with, but she seems distant. If I assume this is because she doesn't like me, I may be losing a chance at a good friendship. Maybe her dog just died, and that's why she's far away. If I ask if something is bothering her, I may avoid misinterpreting her actions. Of course, maybe she doesn't like me.

When we're explicit with each other, we trim needless complications from our lives.

People easily get stuck on the implied messages—on the assumptions that are distortions.

"I know what you meant! . . . Don't try to tell me you didn't mean that!" . . . "You knew perfectly well what I wanted you to do!"

The whole thing can begin to feel Kafka-like. Suddenly I'm on trial. I don't know what I'm accused of, and my accusers are the judge and jury too.

I don't like to have to read your implications. I'm too often wrong. When you talk with me, I'd like you to assume that I can't read your mind at all. So you have to explain to me what you mean, clearly, directly, and simply, preferably with a concrete example.

If we expect something of each other, I'd like to have our contracts explicit:

"This is what I'm willing to give. This is what I want from you. These are my expectations. What are yours?"

When you've heard this from me, and I've heard it from you, we know where we stand. We don't have to guess, without ever really knowing.

A big reason many marriages hit the rocks is that each partner expects the other to read his or her mind.

"You should have *known!* You must not care for me very much if you didn't even know *that!*"

"But you never told me!"

"That doesn't *matter.* I shouldn't have to tell you a thing like *that.* You should just *understand!*"

You keep on refusing to tell me explicitly where you are, and at the same time you feel hurt and angry because I don't understand how you feel or what you want.

The defective logic here is: "You don't know where I am because you're not interested enough in me to really listen to me, so you must not love me."

In reality, I can love you but not be able to read your magical signs. If we both recognize that, you don't build up a lot of resentment about my misreading you, and I don't build up a lot of resentment about your never telling me what's happening with you.

If you haven't told the other person, don't expect him or her to understand.

✳ *Observing and guessing*

Sit facing another person. Make physical contact—touch knees, hold hands, or whatever.

First, *one of you takes five minutes to observe the other* and report your observations and guesses. Your observations are what you *see and hear:* for instance, "I see you scratching your face." Your guesses are what you *imagine about* your partner. These are your projections, identified as such: "I'm imagining that you feel sad," or "I'm guessing that you feel sad," or "You look sad to me—I'll own that."

So you might say, "You're sitting with your arms and legs crossed, and I'm imagining that you feel closed up and a little afraid."

Your partner corrects you whenever you confuse imaginings with observations. For example, "I see that you're very tired." "No. You *see* my eyelids drooping and my body slumping, and from this you *guess* that I'm very tired." Your partner does not give you feedback about whether your guesses are correct or not.

After five minutes, switch roles and repeat the exercise for another five minutes.

When you've both had your turn, you can take some time to talk about your experiences.

If you don't follow these instructions carefully, you'll probably fall into ordinary conversation and lose the value of this important exercise.

If you feel uneasy at first and can't think of much to say, it's all right to leave silences between your observations. If you have a hard time with this exercise, it will be especially valuable for you, so stay with it until you get through your difficulty and can distinguish easily between what you observe and what you imagine.

As you become able to tell the difference between what someone else sees you doing and what they guess about you, you'll be much less easily sucked in by the trips people lay on your head.

My first impression of a man I met recently was that he was on a heavy win/lose trip.

I kept alert for further information. Soon he compared my beard with someone else's which was longer. "He's got you beat," he said. There!—a piece of indirect evidence that fits with my first impression.

When I later talked with him about my impression of him as competitive, he agreed he was. The direct check confirmed the circumstantial evidence.

The better I get at carefully checking out my projections, the more I can rely on my intuition. My intuition is most trustworthy when I'm tuned in to all the cues that might give me information.

CENTERING LANGUAGE AND DISTANCING LANGUAGE

Fran's voice was lifeless as she droned on and on: "And then, you notice that the years are going by and you have a hard time being in meaningful contact with other people and it's just like you're in a bad dream. . . ."

Listen to her words: *You* notice that the years are going by; *you* have a hard time being in meaningful contact; it's like *you're* in a bad dream.

She really meant, "*I* notice; *I* have a hard time; it's like *I'm* in a bad dream."

Little wonder she was out of touch with other people. She wasn't even in touch with herself as the doer of what she did.

When I project what I do and see it as happening outside of me, I easily forget that I create and maintain the conditions of my life.

This is *alienation*—the feeling that I have no control over my own destiny, that I'm just manipulated from outside, a pawn moved by the hands of the unseen "they" who sit in seats of power.

This is the way things really are, so long as I project my power onto others. As I regain my sense of being the doer of what I do, I begin to find my freedom.

You can start using words that will help you get back some of the power you've been giving away. Keep an ear cocked for any time you use the word "you." Do you really mean *you*? Or do you mean *I*? Or at least *we*, though even that's often a substitute for what's really *I*.

"One" is usually also the projective form: "One thinks that . . ." means "I think that . . ." and so on.

In your everyday life, as you start to say *I* when that's what you mean, your speech will become simpler, clearer, and more direct. You'll start to feel some of your own power that you've been disowning.

You can also disown thoughts and feelings by using the word "it" or "it" expressions. In so doing, you make "things" out of your own behavior.

My "temper" possesses me. The temper is an *it*. So I say *it* possesses me, instead of *I feel angry*. I say a "compulsion" to scream enters my mind, instead of *I feel like screaming*. I say a "barrier" or "wall" separates me from other people, instead of *I push people away*, or *I cut myself off from them*. There is no wall between me and others, because keeping them away is a continuing active process.

Whenever you notice that you're using the word "it" or an "it" expression for something happening inside you, recast what you're saying and *become the doer*. Instead of "It occurred to me that . . . ," say "I remembered that . . ."

In one way of talking and thinking, you make yourself an *object*, *acted upon* by "things" inside you and outside you.

In the other way of talking and thinking, you're the *subject*: the doer, the thinker, the feeler. Your life is your own.

7 *Opening and Closing*

Emptiness

> The master Nan-in had a visitor who came to inquire about Zen. But instead of listening, the visitor kept talking about his own ideas.
> After a while, Nan-in served tea. He poured tea into his visitor's cup until it was full, then he kept on pouring.
> Finally, the visitor could not restrain himself.
> "Don't you see it's full?" he said. "You can't get any more in!"
> "Just so," replied Nan-in, stopping at last. "And like this cup, you are filled with your own ideas. How can you expect me to give you Zen unless you offer me an empty cup?" (P. Pauper Press)

We can be so busy that we have no time to be open to what's happening in us and around us. We need some spaces in between our activities and our thoughts.

Sometimes, you may come to places in your life where you feel empty and frustrated, where nothing seems to have much meaning for you. You may feel there's something wrong with you because you have no activity or direction.

There's nothing wrong.

In fact, these times when you're not full of activity can be worth a lot to you. They are times when you can take stock of what you're doing, what you need for yourself, and what changes you need to make in your life. They are times of many possibilities. You have a freedom then that you lack when you're moving in a direction.

A natural pause in a person's life is seldom an accident. Usually you create your pauses in some way, knowingly or not. The bind comes when you think you "should" be doing something else, instead of using the pause as a time for growth and exploration. When you have nothing to do is a good time to do your nothing.

When I put aside my preconceptions, and my old and well-worn ways of handling a problem, I can hear the problem tell me about itself and perhaps tell me its solution too.

To make space in our consciousness for the fuller awareness we want to develop, we must clear out some of our old concerns that are not important to us anymore. Zen Master Shunryu Suzuki comments:

> You should have a general house cleaning of your mind. You must take everything out of your room and clean it thoroughly. If it is necessary, you may bring everything back in again . . . one by one. . . . But if [certain things] are not necessary, there is no need to keep them.
>   . . . Before you put something in your room, it is necessary to take out something. If you do not, your room will become crowded with old, useless junk (111–12).

JUSTIFYING, DEFENDING, AND EXPLAINING

One morning I stopped at a gas station to clean my windshield.

"Jerry's *Friendly* Service" the sign on the station read.

I took a paper towel from my car and gave the windshield a squirt or two from the bottle on the gas pump.

A man came barreling out from inside the station.

"Don't you ever ask a person before you use his things?" he screamed.

"Sorry," I said, "I was only cleaning my windshield."

He got even madder then. "How would you like it if I just opened the door to your bus and took something and said, 'It's mine now'?" he shrieked. Then he started to lecture me, sounding as though he were virtue itself and I deserved twenty years in jail.

I got uptight too. In a voice as nasty as his own, I told him that his was the *unfriendliest* gas station I'd *ever* been in. Then I got in my car, slammed the door, and *peeled* out of his station.

I felt good, getting the last word.

Driving down the road, I thought about how stupid and selfish he was, how much he deserved to be told off, and how glad I was I had told him off. That's called *justifying*. I convince myself that what I did was "right," or the "only thing I could do."

When I justify, I'm trying to believe that my actions fit my self-image of being "always in the right," so I'm not apt to look honestly at what I do. I thereby lose the chance to see if I acted as wisely as I could.

I also close myself to experiencing what the other person's world is like for him or her.

Maybe what I did was stupid and ridiculous. That's okay. What's done is done. *The thing that counts is what I do next.*

To the degree that I'm justifying and explaining and defending what I did, I'm less present now, so I don't live as fully or as wisely at this moment.

I justify when I feel as if I can't just be the way I am and do what I do; I think I have to have a reason or an explanation for everything I say or do in case someone questions me.

Often as not, my explanations are distortions of what happened. I can seldom truly say "why" I do the things I do. Most often I just do what seems best at the time.

Have you ever watched certain parents with their children? "Annie, *why did you do that?* Tell me right now. I demand an explanation!"

Annie doesn't know. She doesn't know why she got angry, or stole something, or hit her little brother. If she does know, and tells the truth, she may very well get punished for it.

Since Mama or Papa demands an explanation, she thinks one up.

As time goes by, Annie learns that she may have to defend her actions against attack at any moment. She begins to have an explanation or justification for everything she does. Eventually she starts believing her own explanations.

With people of all ages, "Why did you do . . ." questions are almost always door-closers. Communications-breakers. They invite or even push the other person into defensive justifying and explaining.

An *accusation* is the worst of all. It's always a closer. It puts the other person in a category and treats him or her like an object.

Try this: For an entire day, instead of asking why you or anyone else did something, ask *"What* did you do?" Ask *"How* did you do it?" Ask "what" without implying "why," and without implying any judgment or accusation.

What difference do you find in the kind of communication that goes on?

Here's an exercise that can be very useful in learning about yourself.

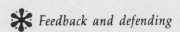 *Feedback and defending*

Sit in a circle with at least half a dozen other people.

Someone volunteers to be the "listener" first. All the others give that person feedback about how they perceive or react to him or her. Even people who have just met can do this, giving each other their first impressions.

You can tell the "listener" whatever you want to: what you see or hear right now as you observe him or her, what you have noticed in the past, what you guess about him or her, or how you feel about something he or she does. Be as specific as you can. This *feedback* can be really useful to the "listener." *A person can learn a lot from comments about specific behaviors, whereas general remarks are often useless and judgmental.*

The feedback continues until a minute or so has gone by in silence, or until the person says, "That's enough for me now."

Then the person who was the "listener" picks a new listener.

Here is the most important part: When you are "listener," notice how you want to explain yourself to people when they give you feedback. But you are not allowed to explain. The only thing you can say to a person who has given you feedback is "Thank you," and you *must* say "Thank you" each time a person says something even if you don't like what was said, unless it was said in a hostile or unfriendly way. (Then you might substitute, "I hear you," or "Got you.") The particular phrase "Thank you" is to remind you that whatever feedback a person gives you can be valuable to you.

When everyone has had a chance to be "listener," discuss what you experienced during the exercise.

───────────────────────────────

If you don't have a group to do the above exercise with, take a day to pay attention, on a moment-by-moment basis, to your process of defending, justifying, and explaining yourself. You may find that often when you're tempted to explain yourself, you don't need to say anything at all.

When we're heavily into justifying and explaining every action, stopping isn't easy, but it's possible.

My starting place for me in working on my own defensiveness was when I realized that I defended myself even against the idea that I might be defensive.

"You're really defensive, aren't you!" someone would say.

"*I am not!*" I replied. "I was only trying to tell you that . . ."

What do I defend myself against? Against anticipated punishment, naturally—bad things happening to me.

If the only bad thing is that I'd discover that I'm not like my image of myself, then what I need to do is to detach from that self-image.

The Sufi Sheikh Saadi of Shiraz tells this story: "A lout abused a man who patiently said: 'O you of bright prospects: I am worse even than you say. I know all my faults, while you do not know them.' " (Quoted in Shah, WS, 87)

I seldom find any use in denying another person's view of me. If you say I come across to you as self-righteous, or inconsiderate, or whatever, that's how I come across to you. When you tell me how you see me, I can explore with you what I do that contributes to your perceiving me that way.

When I notice that I'm explaining myself to another person, I do well to check out what I want from him or her. Odds are I want something. I hear myself asking for acceptance, consideration, or clarity, or perhaps only for an encouraging nod as I try to convince myself of this or that.

I seldom explain or defend or justify when I'm sure that something's really so. I mostly do it when I doubt.

The very process of explaining and justifying is itself almost always more harmful than the action being explained or justified. I don't have to waste my energy that way. When I feel tempted to defend myself, I can simply say, *"I hear you"* or *"Got you."*

The defending, the justifying, the explaining are all reactions. Someone pushes the right button in me and out comes my response. In that way, I'm not free. I'm not my own person.

You don't have to explain or justify or defend any way that you are. Just be, and know how you're being. You don't have to justify your existence. You're here.

OPENING UP AND CLOSING OFF

We all have a natural tendency to open up in situations where we feel secure and good. We know and allow others to know what's happening inside us. We trust others, and act in ways that make it easy for them to trust us.

When a situation is threatening or painful, we protect ourselves by closing up. We are wary about revealing ourselves to others, lest they use what we reveal against us.

To get a feel for the way you open and close, try this, right now.

✳ *Physical opening and closing*

Stand up and walk. As you walk, express closedness with your whole body, in whatever way you can. Let yourself feel completely closed toward people, toward everything. Don't let anyone or anything in.

Now relax and express openness as fully as you can with your whole body, first standing and then walking.

Switch back and forth between your open and closed body attitudes. How do they feel different, physically and emotionally?

What do you learn about how you express what's happening inside you?

No one is completely closed and no one is completely open. Each of us is closed in certain ways and open in others.

Closed means uptight and suspicious; open means relaxed and trusting. But closed also means safe and protected, and open also means vulnerable and risking. There are times when I need to be closed and times when I need to be open.

I don't want to give up my defenses. *I want to be able to use them when I need them,* and part of my defense system is to close up.

From where I am right now, I can handle certain kinds of stimulation and not others. I close myself to the ones that are too much for me now. I close myself to poison, when that's what someone wants to give me. I may even close off from doing things I sometimes like to do, if I'm tired or not in an appropriate place for them. Closing can be a way I take care of myself and gather my energy for when I need it. This works best when it goes hand in hand with a general openness that helps me see *where and how* I want to be open, and *where and how* I want to be closed.

When I don't have to protect myself, I'd rather be open. I feel better physically when I'm open. I learn more. I contact other people more easily. I feel more alive.

Chronic body tension and tightness are one of the most common sources of stress in our culture. Diseases and other harmful physical conditions are more likely to strike people who are under stress. Hemorrhoids, for instance, are more apt to afflict those who walk and sit with their sphincter muscles tightly contracted. The body is objecting in a clear manner to this physical way of keeping tightly closed.

Sometimes the signals from my body fit the present situation and sometimes not. I may close up now in a situation that reminds me of something that was painful in the past, even though the present state of affairs isn't really threatening.

In our everyday lives, opening and closing is intuitive and automatic. Often my intuitive response outruns my conscious awareness, and I learn what's happening with me when I notice how I've opened or closed myself to someone or something. My body gives me information that my head can use.

In my teaching, I've discovered that the class that doesn't go well is usually the class in which I haven't opened myself to where the students are, to their needs and directions.

When I'm willing to be open enough to explore how I'm closing myself and what I'm closing out, I can learn how I stop the flow of what's happening, or stop myself from going with what's happening.

Jourard writes,

> I am . . . ready to grow when I experience boredom, despair, depression, anxiety, or guilt. These emotions inform me that my goals and projects have lost meaning for me. . . .
>
> . . . If I do acknowledge these [all-is-not-well] signals, my choice is either to . . . let my changed being disclose itself to me, even when it hurts (it frequently does); or to decide to affirm the project of being the same (an impossible project, but one that many people try to live). If I decide to try to be the same, then I will repress my experience of all-is-not-well signals. I have resolved, really, to stop perceiving myself. (166)

In their old age, some people turn senile. Most often these are people who think they've wasted their lives, and they can't handle that. They've closed themselves off, bit by bit, from their experience until there is little left they dare perceive; they've disowned their own power, bit by bit, until there's little they allow themselves to do.

Other people grow wise as they grow old. They're the ones who stay open to what's happening in them and around them.

When I'm really open, I know it with an inner certainty. I feel no need to convince myself or anybody else of it.

When I'm closed, I may not realize it. After all, being open-minded is generally admired, and being admired may be more important to me than knowing how I am.

When I instantly respond, "I'm not like that!" I'm relatively closed. When I'm willing to take someone's remark about me and see how I am that way—or see what I do that makes me seem that way to others—I'm relatively open.

Check out your own reactions. If someone tells you something that doesn't seem to fit the way things are, do you reject it out of hand? Do you feel upset, or angry with the person who said it?

Or do you go into that person's way of looking at the world to better understand that different way of seeing things? Do you ask a person who mentions something you don't like to tell you in more detail what he or she means, and do you really listen to the explanation?

If I'm the One Who Knows, I can feel important, superior. The trouble is, the more I think I know, the less I'm free to learn.

Being open doesn't mean you have to give up your own views and agree that things are as another person sees them. It means accepting that another's way of looking at his or her world, even though you may not agree with it, may be best for that person now—and may even add a new dimension to your own understanding, if you let it.

Carl Rogers writes of openness toward our own experience: *"I find I am more effective when I can listen acceptantly to myself,* . . . realize that I *am* angry, . . . or that I feel very full of warmth and affection for this individual; or that I am bored and uninterested. . . . If I can accept [my real feelings], then I am also much more likely to be able to accept his feelings in response"* (OBP, 17, 18).

When I feel another person being closed toward me, I close up like a clam. I retreat. Even my body seems to pull away.

Yet, someone has to make the first move toward opening up communication when it's blocked. If I want to be in touch with the other person and I don't make that move, I don't feel so good when I go away.

✳ *The clam exercise*

In a group, get together with two other people you're either not too comfortable with or have the least contact with.

One of you close up physically, like a clam. Experience your closedness fully, as though you were saying to the other two people, "I hate your guts, and I'm going to deliberately keep away from you."

Their task is to get you to come out. What do they do? How do you feel in response, and what do you do?

How do you avoid coming out? At what point do you begin to let yourself come out? Which approaches do you respond to?

Then switch. Another person closes up and you coax him or her out.

When all three of you have been the "clam," take a few minutes to share your experiences.

When I feel that other people don't share enough of themselves with me, I can try sharing more of myself with them. Then they often begin to share more of themselves with me. Openness often begets openness. (Rokeach provides additional descriptive information about the open/ closed dimension of personality. See OCM, BAV.)

UNFINISHED SITUATIONS

> A monk told Joshu, "Please teach me."
> Joshu asked: "Have you eaten . . . ?"
> The monk replied: "I have eaten."
> Joshu said: "Then you had better wash your bowl."
> At that moment the monk was enlightened. (Reps, 96)

When I finish something I start out to do, or resolve a problem between me and another person, I feel good. Thoughts about unfinished business don't distract me while I'm doing other things.

Other times I leave something unfinished that I could finish. Perhaps a job half-done that I have to come back to, or a problem concerning someone that hangs over me like a black cloud every time I see that person. I don't feel so comfortable then. I think about the unfinished business when I'm doing other things, so I don't pay full attention to what I'm doing.

Kay and Warren have been divorced for three years. When Kay and I talk casually, she almost always mentions her past life with Warren. "He used to do this, he didn't do that," etc. She distracts herself from what's going on now by looking back to what went on in the past. That's a clue that she has a lot of unfinished business she's putting her energy into, and that she's not paying enough attention to what she could be doing for herself now.

Of course, we can't live without unfinished business. Life is a continuous flow between opening up new situations and closing those that have been open. I become hungry and I eat. I begin a project and I carry it through. I don't understand what someone says and I ask that person to explain.

The trouble comes when I don't eat, or stop the project in the middle even though I think I should complete it, or don't ask what the other person means and go away wondering and worrying.

This can be a source of chronic fatigue: I'm constantly trying to be in my present and my past at the same time, worrying about loose ends from the past at the same time I'm trying to live my life now.

We all sometimes use our unfinished business to distract ourselves from being aware of uncomfortable events and feelings. We can use our old unfinished situations to create still more unfinished situations in the present, by distracting ourselves from finishing what's happening now and leaving that unfinished too.

It's important to develop a sense of *when* the unfinished business is a distraction, and *when* it's the thing that's happening that I have to deal with.

At times, I'd like to tell another person of my love or my anger, but am afraid to. This kind of unfinished situation is at the heart of many people's problems with each other. In marriage and family counseling, people often find that they can give themselves permission to listen to each other's statements of love and anger, even though they had seldom succeeded in doing so before.

A lot of unfinished business comes from situations in my past that I never finished working through with friends, siblings, parents, former lovers, or others.

I may want to tie up my loose ends with you by telling you how I feel. If I'm afraid that you'll respond in a way that's frightening to me, I may stop myself, and leave those loose ends dangling.

We need to learn how to close our accounts. To finish the business before we leave a situation, instead of putting it off and telling ourselves we'll finish it "one of these days." And to be sensitive to when we don't feel closed with a situation.

I need to learn how to tell another person that I still feel opened-up on something between us. That I need closure.

Yet I also need to know when I've done all I can, when I don't have to keep a situation open any longer.

When I face a problem and do something about it, I free the energy that I've been putting into worry or into keeping the problem out of my awareness. Then I have that energy available for something else.

When I do these things, I leave fewer matters hanging. I have fewer complications. I feel more in touch with my life.

8 Talking and Listening

As I sat in a cafe the other day, I listened to two men talking at the next table.

Each was so intent on having *his* say, so impatient for the other to finish, that he hardly heard the other. They constantly interrupted and cut each other off. Neither one ever paused to think about anything the other had said before replying.

That reminded me of my long struggle with my own talking and not listening. At one time, I left little room for anyone else to speak if I wanted to say something. My voice was loud enough to ride over other people's comments and *I got my thing said.*

In so doing, I left myself little space to listen. I also defeated my own purpose, because when I cut others off, they were often so resentful that they didn't hear another word I said.

One evening in a therapy group, a scene from my past burst into my mind. I was nine or ten years old, sitting at the dinner table with my family. The adults talked and talked. I had to wait forever for my turn, clenching my fists and squirming to restrain myself. When at last my chance came, my words rushed out as fast as they could come: I had to say *everything* I wanted to say during my brief turn to speak. That emotional energy was so strong that my loud, rapid way of talking stayed with me for twenty years.

In the last few years, I've found that I don't always have to say something clever to be a worthwhile human being. I don't always have to be "the entertainer." Entertaining you is as much your responsibility as mine. I have two ears and only one mouth. Perhaps that's nature's way of telling me to listen more and talk less.

One way I can talk more clearly is by getting rid of "fillers" that can turn a simple comment into a torrent of words.

Some fillers are short, like "You know," "I mean," "Don't you think?" Others are long: "Well, I guess if I were really to look at it from that angle, I could see where that might make some kind of genuine sense in the particular situation at hand." I could rephrase that sentence, "That makes sense to me," and lose nothing.

Sometimes when I talk to you, I'm really talking out loud to myself. I don't expect you to listen to that part of what I'm saying. The trouble is, you don't know those are messages to me, and you listen to them along with the rest of what I say. You have to wade through all my words to find the ones that are meant for you.

But if I differentiate between what I want to say out loud and what I can leave as silent thoughts, then when I talk, I'm talking *to you*, and you can hear me much more easily.

One way I don't talk *to you* is by saying many of my words automatically, like programmed speeches coming off a reel of tape. I may get the center of the stage and a few crumbs of appreciation while I'm playing my tape for the eleventh time, but I seldom really contact anyone.

When I go through the check-out stand at the market, I might comment on the baseball team or the weather, while I'm thinking about something else entirely. By contrast, if I take a moment to really look at the checker, I may see something that's happening with him or her. Then I might say, "You look tired," or "I really like the necklace you're wearing." If my words touch a real place in the other person, we have a moment of genuine contact, and both of us feel good.

You may be a person who has no trouble keeping quiet. In many situations, you may even have a hard time saying what you think and feel. Perhaps you were punished or ridiculed for speaking out when you were a child, and have learned to keep your mouth shut.

If so, you can find someone who will listen sympathetically while you talk about things you feel a little afraid to talk about. Gradually you'll be able to speak about things that are even harder for you, and to speak to successively larger groups of people. (See pp. 197–98 in Chapter 18.)

Talking with others vs. pronouncements and pitches

Sometimes I bang my head against the wall trying to convince a person of something that he or she isn't ready to hear. When I notice that I'm doing that, I can stop. Then I can find out what's happening with that person, so I can talk to a place that's part of his or her experience.

When I broadcast *at* you like a radio announcer, I'm not speaking from a real place in me to a real place in you in a caring way. Instead, I treat you as an object that's conveniently there for me to talk to.

My tone of voice, my rhythm of speech, my lack of contact with where you are, or a feeling of distractedness may signal me that I'm talking *at* you. For instance, I may be saying something that's important to me, but that doesn't mean much to you. Once I notice that I'm talking *at* you, I can listen to where you are, make eye contact if I haven't been doing that, and start talking *with* you in a way that's real for both of us. As I do this, my voice and my whole manner become different, and I relax.

When three or more of us are together, I avoid speaking to anyone *about* someone else who's present. Instead, I make my statement *to* the person it's meant for. For instance, rather than saying, "Jean, I think Tim was unfair to you just then," I say, "Tim, I think you were unfair just then." This principle is called *"No gossiping."* Applying it can greatly increase directness and clarity.

When you talk *at* me, which you might do by broadcasting loudly, or by talking so softly that I have to strain to hear you, I imagine that you're using me. You're talking for yourself and not for me.

If you talk *with* me as though you want me to hear you, and you show me that you want my response, I feel important to you. You care.

One way I talk *at* you is by trying to *persuade* you to agree with me. I'm trying to sell you my point of view. "Whom are you trying to convince?" Perls used to ask when people talked this way. When the person really thought about it, he or she answered, "Myself."

I used to use sarcasm a lot. Eventually I began to notice that people often closed up and became defensive when I did so. Sarcasm too often hurts. Now I'm not so "clever" as I used to be, but I more often make real contact with people.

One way I can make real contact with you is by sharing my own feelings. When I speak of my hopes and fears, I show my own vulnerability. This helps assure you that I won't attack you for showing me the ways you're not so perfect or so certain of yourself. In this place where we're not protecting ourselves against each other's eyes and ears, we can more easily be real with one another.

Argument and exploration

Barbara and Phil, a couple in their late thirties, had moved out of suburbia and "onto the land." They were having a lot of trouble between them. They loved to argue, and each sought hard to win. Barbara could win certain arguments by pointing out to Phil what he'd done wrong on the land, and Phil could win others by reminding her of how inadequate she was at "roughing it." When one won an argument, the other often felt hurt, angry, and resentful.

With the help of a counselor, they realized that one person could make a point without this meaning that he or she "won" and the other person "lost." Phil could agree to help Barbara lay a piece of flooring without feeling that she "won" because he "gave in."

Each partner also came to appreciate what the other had learned to do, instead of blaming the other for not doing it better. They began to focus on what needed to be done rather than on why it hadn't been done before, or on how bad the other person was, or on "who won."

It was an eye-opener for me when, a few years ago, a friend said, "You know, you really don't like being contradicted." Naturally, my own self-image had been that I was open-minded and ready to listen to anything. I saw the truth in what she said, and realized that I had to be "right" in order to feel worthwhile as a person.

That taught me that in almost every argument, the underlying feelings are the most important thing happening. When someone who's arguing says, "I'm just being logical," it's *almost never true*. If I'm being logical, then from my point of view, you must be either stupid or stubbornly self-centered. You can hardly miss my message, and you're likely to feel hostile toward me in return.

Once I stop attacking you and start listening to where you are, *we can move from argument toward a process of exploration.*

When we explore, we listen to each other. I find out how you feel as well as what you think. Since we're not defending our own viewpoints we're free to look at many possible ways to meet our situation. We're not limited to either your idea or mine.

We can explore more easily when we share our experiences than when we throw opinions back and forth. Sharing experiences lets us touch in a more personal way and gives each of us new information.

It's especially important to avoid overpowering a child with argument. I can usually give a child a very logical and coherent argument as to why he or she should do what I want, and the kid is not likely to be able to come up with nearly as good an argument in reply. In that case, my reasoning isn't honest reasoning—it's an exercise in power and oppression.

Advising and analyzing

One way to give advice is by "providing answers," suggesting to people what they should do to solve their problems. A different way is by providing information that the person doesn't have.

Psychiatrist Eric Berne describes the game "Wooden Leg," in which someone asks for advice and then turns down every suggestion offered: "No, that won't work because . . . ," "No, that won't work either, because . . . ," etc. Here the person's request for advice is actually a way to get attention, rather than an attempt to solve the problem.

A person may also seek advice as a way to avoid responsibility for his or her decisions. If I tell you what to do and things go wrong, well, it wasn't your responsibility. But if things go right, you miss out on developing the trust in yourself that comes from standing on your own two feet. I sometimes reply to a direct request for advice with, "I hear you asking me to tell you what to do."

Other times when someone asks me for advice, I might tell what I'd probably do in that situation. This doesn't mean I think that the other person should do the same. That person must still make his or her own decision.

When I take the time to draw someone out, that person often comes up with his or her own answers.

Sometimes I still follow my impulse to advise people. After I've made my suggestion, the other person often falls silent and I notice a distant look on his or her face that tells me I'm way off the mark.

Then I can tell the other person that I've just realized that I don't yet fully understand his or her situation. I feed back what I think I've heard, and the person usually either says, "Yes," or tells me where I'm off the mark, and we go on from there. You can do the same thing.

The amazing thing is that almost always, even when my first response was insensitivity, if I show that I care and want to understand, the other person comes back out of the distant place he or she retreated into and makes contact with me again.

Giving information often has real value.

A P.E. instructor once told me, "If you choke up on the bat and stand this way, you'll probably hit for a higher average instead of striking out so often by trying to hit home runs."

I appreciated that information. He didn't tell me what to do; he just gave me a new alternative.

"Analyzing" another person *rarely* has any value for anyone. Overzealous psychology students sometimes have a disconcerting tendency to tell others "what's really going on with them."

If I'm constantly analyzing and interpreting your behavior, you're apt to get so self-conscious that you'll have a hard time acting spontaneously.

The more I try to analyze you, the less you're likely to let me see you, and the less I'm likely to understand your thoughts and feelings. When I'm not so busy analyzing you with my head, I can hear you with my heart.

Walt kept encouraging Brenda to talk to him but every time she told him her feelings, he'd reply, "That does not compute." After a while she began to give him only the kind of information he was asking for, which was thinking data he could handle through his computer, rather than feeling data.

Through counseling, Walt learned that he could comfortably respond to other people's feelings with his own. When he did, he stopped analyzing. At that point, Brenda said, "Walt, I feel so much better with you now! Before, you never heard me when I said how I felt. When I did talk about my feelings, I always came out feeling wrong when you got through analyzing me."

Now Walt is learning that in his business relationships also, he can deal with feelings, and not just profit and loss figures, where people are concerned.

Clear and concise—with spice

Writer Rasa Gustaitis reports that after trying unsuccessfully to engage Fritz Perls in chit-chat, she said, "You're impossible to communicate with."

"Communicate *what?*" was his reply.

When I hear myself chattering on, I check out whether people seem really interested in what I have to say.

Many people I know never pause when they're talking. They run each sentence into the next, stringing them together with "'and's" and "'but's" and "so's."

I have a hard time staying with such a person's line of thought for long. I need a moment to let the image evoked by a statement form in my mind.

Perls used to ask people who talk in run-on sentences to say "Period" after each sentence, and then breathe before starting another sentence. This is a difficult discipline, but the harder it is for you, the more valuable it will be if you stay with it.

PARALANGUAGE, INNER SPEECH, AND SILENCE

Sometimes I hear the voice in my mind repeating something clever that I "should have said." Or I hear myself rehearsing my reply to someone, instead of listening to what he or she is saying to me. Sometimes also I hear myself reinforcing my opinions and beliefs by repeating the same tired old ideas to myself over and over again.

After you've read this paragraph, stop reading for a few minutes and listen to your own inner talking. Listen to its rhythm and sound and to the kinds of words and phrases you use. Whom are you talking to? For what purpose? Do you badger and nag? Do you sound dogmatic or open-minded, confident or hesitating and uncertain? Are you figuring something out, or just babbling on? (Perls, Hefferline, and Goodman, 108)

Some people continually talk to themselves in ways that say, "I can't do anything right, I'm licked before I start," and so on.

If you do this, you can *move from bad-talking yourself into good-talking yourself.* You can say, "That was just a little setback. I can use my energy to do some good things for myself and for other people."

Ouspensky comments that the ability to be silent when necessary is an important part of self-mastery (NMU, 167).

Inner and outer silence go together. I can feel and sense physical and emotional events inside me much more easily when they don't have to compete against the chatter in my mind for my attention.

✳ Hearing your silence

Sit by yourself and become aware of your breathing. Now, as best you can, as you inhale, be aware of what's happening in you and around you without letting any words come into your mind. Then, as you exhale, listen to any words that have formed themselves in your mind.

Whenever a line of chatter starts up in your head, notice how this is different from the inner silence you've been experiencing. Then stop the chatter and return to the first part of the exercise.

Do this experiment for several minutes. Notice any changes in the way you feel as you do it.

As I discover my own silence, the quality of my waking consciousness undergoes a change. I begin to hear the quiet around me that's punctuated by the occasional sound of a shout or of a bus going by. I hear the spaces between the words when others talk to me, rather than only the words.

When in a group, some people are uncomfortable with silence. If half a minute passes without anyone talking, someone will jump in nervously with a comment to fill the space. This leaves people little time to sit with their thoughts.

The Tribal Council, an ancient social institution used by Indian peoples throughout North America to deal with important problems, can serve us too. It gives everyone a chance to be heard, and to hear what others have to say. It also insures that no one can dominate the conversation by his or her ability to put on a good show or shout others down.

In a Tribal Council, everyone sits in a circle and the ceremonial pipe is lighted and passed around. (A cup of herb tea or a ceremonial stick or other object can be used instead of a pipe.)

Then one person says, "I will speak," and starts to talk. No one else may say anything until this person ends with the words "I have spoken." Even if the speaker falls silent for several minutes in the middle of a statement, no one interrupts. This guarantees each person time to be in touch with his or her feelings, with no worry about others butting in.

When a person has finished speaking, the pipe or other ceremonial object goes around the circle. No one speaks. Everyone reflects.

Another person says, "I will speak," and makes his or her statement.

No one may speak a second time until everyone has spoken once. Often only one statement from each person is needed to reach a decision.

A simpler version of the Tribal Council is the "go-around." It can be a good way to start off a meeting: everyone makes contact and hears what other people are thinking and feeling.

Here there is no special ceremony. Each person in the circle says how he or she is feeling right now, or tells of a recent important experience, or speaks on some issue.

Then the person sitting to the right or left of him or her speaks, and so on around the circle.

This can go quickly, while the Tribal Council often takes a long time. In the go-around, each person may be limited to a minute or two. But be careful not to get so caught up in rehearsing your statement that you don't hear what others say.

One day I found a spot by a gentle brook that ran through a meadow. There was a miniature waterfall surrounded by some tall grass and horsetails. I sat there motionless for a long time.

Eventually tiny sounds and movements began to occur all around me. A dragonfly settled by my knee. A spider crawled down the bank, then scurried away. When I first sat down, the place was almost still. Now it teemed with life.

The same is often true of people. I can walk into a situation, be loud and active, and soon it's my scene. I can walk in and be quiet, and soon people forget about me and do things they never do when I dominate the situation.

Paralanguage

"He pressed her hands. There was nothing, of course, that one could say, no words, no consolations of philosophy—only this shared mystery of touch, only this communication from skin to skin of a flowing infinity," writes Aldous Huxley in his novel *Island* (329). These words speak of a kind of communication called "paralanguage." This includes touch, movement, gesture, eye contact, and the sound of the voice.

As another person speaks, listen. Some people use the same cadence or rhythm over and over again. Does the rhythm seem to carry any message? What is it?

Now, as you keep listening to the person's voice, begin to imagine music playing in the background. It may be rock, country music, precise chamber music, a symphony with great passion, dissonant modern music, or whatever else fits the sound of that person's voice right now.

Once you have a clear sense of the music that goes with the voice, try to think of a song title that fits it. Your title may well be the statement that the person is making.

As you hear yourself talk, does your voice fit the statement you're making? If not, can you make your music fit your message?

Listen in your mind as Perls describes some of the things he hears in people's voices:

Do you sing, or do you saw?
Do you stroke, or do you rasp?
Is your voice dead, or soaked in tears?
Are you machine-gunning me with the rapidity and explosiveness of each of your words? . . .
Do you take my breath away with the and-and-and of your anxiety? . . .
Do you torture me with mumbling low sounds in order to make me strain? . . .
Is your voice boomingly filling the room, leaving no place for anyone else?
Or are you whining, whining, whining, turning me into your wailing wall? . . .
Do you punish me with daggers of your Sunday-school teacher's finger-pointing screech? . . .
Or are you engulfing me in loving sound vibrations,

Melting me and turning on lush, embracing fantasies? . . .
. . . the sound is true—
Poison or nourishment.
And I dance to your music or I run away.
I cringe, or am attracted. (IOGP)

Body language

The way I move and hold my body can tell you how I feel right now, and it can tell you much about who I am. With one movement, one gesture, one position of my body, I can give you my anger or my love, my authority or my submission, my gentleness or my pain.

In your everyday contact with people, you can discover for yourself the meanings their gestures hold by noticing what ways of behaving fit what kinds of gestures. (Among recent books on body language, see Poiret; Fast.)

One way to observe others is to try to feel what it's like to be another person. Van Dusen describes this well:

> As a boy in San Francisco, I traveled everywhere on streetcars. . . .
> I designed a game that later proved useful. For example, an old lady gets on the streetcar and sits down. . . . I become her for a little while. I study everything about her, and reconstruct my world as this old woman.
>
> My tattered cloth shopping bag is precious; it contains food for a week. I put it between my legs to hold onto it. I have to hang on—these cars jerk so— . . . one slip and I would fall, breaking my bones. So noisy. So confusing. . . .
>
> Sometimes I would even try the person's movements—try the tremor of an aged hand that has so little power to grasp things.
>
> As an adult, this game was very useful to me in dull administrative meetings. (23–24)

Here's a way you can experience another person's rhythm and flow:

❋ Mirroring

Do this exercise without speaking at all. Sit behind another person. Both of you close your eyes and start rocking. Explore different rhythms of rocking, and find one that feels right for you.

Now open your eyes and pick up the movement of the person in front of you. Mirror that person's movement and body posture as closely as you can.

After several minutes, close your eyes again and go into your own rhythm. Feel the difference between your rhythm and the other person's.

Now, both of you turn around. You go into your own rhythm, and the person behind you will do everything you just did.

After a few minutes of this, stop and face each other. Now mirror each other face-to-face. Nonverbally decide who will begin to move and who will mirror, and when to shift back and forth. Try a mundane event, a magical event, a playful event.

Next time you get into a conversation, try this:

 Cameras

Imagine that you're a TV camera, and can turn the picture and sound on and off independently.

In your mind, "turn off the picture," and put all your attention into listening to the other's tone of voice, and to how he or she comes into and moves out of the conversation. *Ignore the specific content* of what the person is saying.

Then "turn off the audio," and direct all your attention to the other's posture, gestures, movements, and facial expressions—especially the areas around the eyes and mouth.

You can do this as an exercise with another person or persons by taking turns being the talker and the observer, the talker telling about something of interest to him or her.

After about ten minutes, the observers give the talkers their feedback about what they saw and heard. Then the talkers and the observers switch roles and repeat the process.

LISTENING

Communication is easier when what we're communicating fits with what's going on around us (Sears). We're likely to have a hard time talking about important ideas or deep feelings amid the noise and attractions of the county fair. And when we're at a party, I don't want to spend my time being a psychologist for you. I want to be there with you as me.

One important way I interfere with my ability to listen is through snap judgments. Once I make my snap judgment, I close myself to further information that might contradict it. So I feel sure I'm right, even though I may be terribly wrong.

I also stop listening by "knowing" what you're going to say before you say it, so I use my listening time preparing a reply instead of taking in your full meaning. I may cut you off and finish your sentences for you. When I let you finish them yourself, I'm often amazed at how different what you say is from what I was anticipating.

I may dispute some detail of what you say when that detail has nothing to do with your real meaning. I may, for example, take issue with the particular words you use, instead of listening for the meaning that comes through and around the words.

I'm especially apt to turn you off when what you're saying demands a deeper response from me than I'm willing to risk. I may not want to be as vulnerable as I'd have to be to deal with some emotionally charged area in myself or in our relationship.

My feelings can help me listen. I can tune in to what I'm feeling and then become aware of what in you may be triggering my feelings.

My feelings can also get in the way of my ability to listen. If I'm afraid or anxious, I may put so much energy into dealing with my fear that I have a hard time hearing anything. If I want you to like me, I may worry so much about how you're responding to me that I'm almost deaf to what you're saying.

You may use words that touch off my anger or anxiety, even though you mean no offense or threat. The words that trigger my feelings may just be part of your way of expressing yourself.

I can be aware of disagreeing with you and not always have to tell you so. Just being aware that I disagree is often enough.

For instance, I may disagree with something very minor that you've said, and I don't want to sidetrack you from your central theme.

I don't always have to listen. Suppose I'm exhausted or overstimulated. As you talk on and on, I may begin to feel irritated by each word, until I can't listen any more and just wish you'd shut up.

At such times I used to pretend to keep listening as I got more and more agitated and irritated and disagreeable. In time, I learned to handle such situations by saying something like "I need some silence. I'm too overloaded to talk any more right now." I can say something *about where I'm at* that implies no criticism of you.

Listening is a more active process than hearing. Of the many things I hear, I choose a few to listen to. It's important to me to be in touch with what I want to listen to and what I don't.

I can ask myself, "What's in it for me to listen?" "What am I learning?" "Does the other person really need a listener right now?" If I find no real value in listening, I can stop wasting my energy. I can more easily be there for you when you're saying something that you want me to hear if I don't waste my energy listening to crap neither one of us really cares about.

Sometimes while you're speaking, I think of something I "must" say. I may have a hard time holding off saying it until I've really heard what you're saying. I can get so distracted by my effort to hold off saying what I want to say that I scarcely hear you. That can lead to statements like "I'm sorry I interrupted you, but I was afraid I'd forget what I was going to say."

I more often have a hard time holding back my comments when I'm talking *at* you—trying to push a point or change your mind—than when I'm genuinely listening to and exploring with you.

I usually have faith that if I'm listening, I'll be able to say those things that seem so urgent. If they matter enough, even if I forget them now, they'll come up in my consciousness again and I'll say them the next time I see you.

Feedback and understanding

"Marian," said Carol, "I really felt hurt by the things you said this morning."

"Why, that's ridiculous, Carol. There's no reason for you to feel that way."

Notice how Marian responded to Carol's statement of feeling hurt not by showing understanding, or asking Carol to say more about how she felt, but by judging Carol's feelings: "Why, that's ridiculous."

All my talking to you contains two messages. Directly or indirectly, I want you to know how I feel and what I want. We almost all share a deep longing to be heard and understood. When I'm trying to say how I feel and the other person doesn't hear me, I sometimes feel hurt and angry—not so much at the situation itself as at not feeling cared about.

Elvira Madigan said, "Isn't that what love is—to borrow your loved one's eyes? To know the world as your loved one knows it, from inside her?"

When I try to understand what another person is feeling, I help that person open to self-understanding and change. When I let people know, in a way they can hear, that I really want to understand them, they have an easier time accepting themselves.

As I learn to hear not only what another person says, but also the personal meaning, the emotional flavor, the inner feeling of it, I am understanding *with* rather than understanding *about* that person.

When I say something to you, I need some response from you that assures me, "Yes, I heard you." That lets me know that I'm getting through, and makes it easier for me to talk to you.

The simplest feedback—a gesture, a nod, an "Uh huh"—is enough to tell me that you're paying attention and you think you're hearing me.

Carl Rogers suggests a feedback method that lets you *check out* whether you're hearing correctly. Thomas Gordon calls it "active listening," and says that adults find it useful in listening to children.

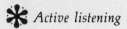 *Active listening*

Part I: Feeding back explicit content. Get together with one other person. For five minutes, one of you will talk and the other will listen. After every few sentences, the listener *repeats back what he or she heard the talker say.* This can be in the same words the talker used, or it can be in the listener's own words. The talker says either, "Yes, that's right," and continues, or corrects the listener's error, or adds what the listener left out. Then the listener feeds that part back. As soon as the talker is satisfied that the listener understands, he or she continues. This exercise may feel stiff and unnatural, but it's important to stay with it *for the full five minutes.* When five minutes are up, switch roles.

When you are the listener in either Part I or Part II, if the talker rushes on from sentence to sentence and leaves you no room to respond, say so.

After each part of the exercise, share your experiences.

Part II: Feeding back emotional meaning. For another five minutes each, do just as you did above, but this time, in your listening and feedback, focus on the *feeling that seems to you to come through and underlie the person's words.* If you find very little feeling in the person's words or tone of voice or posture or gestures, you might say something like "You don't seem to care very much or feel very deeply about what you're saying." Again the talker confirms or corrects the listener's impression.

Part III: Responding with your own feelings. Again the other person talks about a matter of personal interest or importance while you listen. You provide either kind of "active listening" feedback when it seems appropriate, and *tell how you feel in response to what the other person says and does.*

Again, after five minutes, switch roles. Then share what you experienced.

In everyday life, when you tell someone how you feel about what he or she says or does, it's very important to *specify the particular behavior your feelings are a response to.* This is what distinguishes helpful feedback from useless or even harmful feedback.

If I say, "I feel hostile toward you right now," you have nowhere to go with that. *I haven't mentioned any action on your part that I'm responding to.* But if I say, "I feel hostile toward you for criticizing Frank," or "I feel really wonderful when you hug me like that," I'm telling you how I feel about *something you do* that makes a difference to me.

When you and I have a hard time hearing each other, an impartial third party may be able to help. This third person listens carefully to each of us, and without any evaluation, tells what he or she hears each of us saying and feeling.

As you and I begin to feel heard and understood, we begin to hear and understand each other.

TALKING AND LISTENING IN RELATIONSHIP

We often prevent ourselves from saying many things we need to say to each other, because we're "waiting for the appropriate time." "I'll tell her tomorrow," I think to myself, or "I'll bring it up some other time." As these many small things build up, we get a big storehouse of "things that haven't been said," with a lot of anxiety and resentment attached to them.

The unsaid feeling or desire that needs to be shared may be simple, like "I love you," or "I wish you wouldn't make the tea so hot," or "I wish you wouldn't put your fingers in the peanut butter jar, because I don't know where they went before."

This kind of sharing is most effective if I make my statement *specific,* and you give me feedback that lets me know you've heard me clearly.

When I tell you that I'd like you to do something differently, I want to make my demand for a change *very concrete and clear-cut,* so that you know without any doubt whether or not you're doing what I've asked. Some things I can't ask from you. "I don't like your attitude" isn't a useful gripe, because it doesn't deal with any specific behavior.

If when either one of us feels upset about something the other person does, we deal with it openly and make whatever changes we need to (instead of having one more small source of constant aggravation), we move toward a more nurturing relationship.

Asking for a lot of changes all at once is called "overloading." I do better to ask for only one kind of change at a time. Instead of trying to solve an issue of "controlling versus being controlled" between us, for example, we can resolve a particular concrete way of behaving that's part of this broader issue. Then we can deal with another equally specific item.

THOU AND IT.   Martin Buber has distinguished between an "I-it" relationship and an "I-thou" relationship. When I relate to you as an "it," I treat you as an object that I care about only in terms of how I can use you to my own advantage. When I treat you as a "thou," I respect you. I care about you and what you want, as well as about me and what I want. We make real contact, even if our encounter lasts only a moment.

When I honor and respect another person in all his or her uniqueness, that person usually does the same for me.

III

Behavior and Change

9 *Conditioning*

In ancient China, some infants were placed in urns. They grew to be dwarves whose body-shapes were like the urns, freaks intentionally created to amuse those who had no better pastime.

Our patterns of social conditioning form a person's ways of thinking and feeling just as an urn can form a body. Every plant and every animal, by its nature, grows in certain ways and not in others. If movement in certain directions is blocked, a person's energy turns back on itself in twisted ways. I do this to myself when I choke off the ways I naturally grow.

We tend to be automatic about much of what we say, feel, think, and do. From our earliest days, the adults who cared for us conditioned us to act in certain ways and not in others. Often they didn't realize the impact of what they were doing; and it's unlikely that they thought of it as conditioning.

In your daily life, notice situations where you respond before you have a chance to think about what you want to do. Many of these habits contribute to our convenience and our safety, our survival and our growth. A person couldn't possibly play ping-pong if he or she had to think about every action. When my habits take care of routine matters, I can be alert to other things.

If I don't watch out, though, the very efficiency of my habits in routine matters could lead me to give up my responsibility for making choices to meet a particular situation. I get in trouble when I start letting my habits take care of matters that are important to me. Sometimes, without realizing it, I allow my habits to govern the contacts with other people that mean the most to me. It is as if I close my eyes and ears and mind. I *think* I choose; I *think* I act consciously; but I act in the service of habits meant to cope with other times and other places. Instead of those habits serving me, they rob me of my own humanity.

91

When I'm the master rather than the slave of my automatic action patterns, they serve my organic growth. I stay attuned to what I as a whole organism need and am feeling, and keep my ability to make real, nonautomatic contact with others.

✳ *Taking inventory of your habits*

Take an inventory of your habits. See which ones are useful and which ones you want to change. Do this with a pencil and paper.

What do you do habitually? Rapidly jot down as many of your habits as you can think of. Take about five minutes for this right now.

. . .

Finished? Now see how you feel about each of those habits. Next to each put a plus, a zero, or a minus, depending on whether your first feeling toward each habit is positive, neutral, or negative.

How many pluses did you mark down? Minuses? Do you tend to see your habits in a positive or negative light?

Which minuses are really harmful, and in what ways? What could you do to change them? Which minuses do you dislike even though they cause you no harm? Are the helpful habits as consistent as you'd like? How can you make them more so?

If you're with another person, after you've both done the inventory, discuss the questions above.

You may have had teachers who taught you as though they were programming a machine. Though some teachers helped you develop a sense of competence and love of learning, others very likely taught you fear and failure. Though some helped you find your own directions and make your own discoveries, others probably taught you to follow orders and not ask questions. If you had enough teachers who cared more about their authority than about your growth, you probably left school more a robot than when you entered.

To the degree that I've been conditioned in ways that block my process of organic growth, I act like a robot. Something happens near me and I respond. Immediate. Mechanical. No time for thought, no time for choice, between the stimulus and the response. I'm reacting entirely to preprogrammed instructions in my memory banks.

A robot might live with the illusion that it can choose, but all its choices are determined by a program someone else created.

To become a robot has one real reward: It's *easier* to be a robot than to be responsible. I sometimes feel sad when I've acted in a way that harms me or another person. A robot needn't bother with such thoughts and feelings. It need only respond to any situation as its program tells it to. It faces few hard choices.

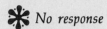 *No response*

Here's a way to get in touch with what happens when none of your conditioned expectations are being met and your habitual ways of responding have disappeared.

Sit facing another person. That person will talk to you for about five minutes on some subject of interest to him or her. You deliberately show no response at all. You do not speak or react with facial expressions or movements.

Now switch roles and repeat the process.

How do you feel when you talk and the other person shows no response? Afterward, share your experiences.

Perls and his colleagues suggest a way you can bring more aliveness into your day.

Notice some of your habits—the way you dress, the way you brush your teeth, the way you open or close a door. . . . If . . . some alternative seems just as good and has the advantage of offering variety, try to change. . . . Do you take pleasure in learning the new way? Or do you encounter strong resistances? . . . What happens if you watch someone perform a task similar to one of your own? Do you get annoyed, irritated, indignant at small variations from your own procedure? (GT, 120–21)

We can break out of our own patterns of childhood conditioning, and free ourselves from the cycle of automatically—without regard to whether they're helpful or harmful—passing these patterns on to our own children.

Sociologist Corinne Nydegger found that among the middle-class men she studied, those who became fathers later in life were less likely than younger men to try to fit their children into rigid molds, and more likely to encourage them to find their own directions. Parenthood to these men was something like a benevolent trusteeship, their function being one of promoting the autonomous development of their children, rather than shaping them.

In Samoa, this attitude seems to characterize parents of all ages. The Samoan people view a child's growth as an organic process, like the unfolding of a flower. In their view, children naturally tend to grow in a basically healthy direction, given the love, caring, and respect that they need.

CONDITIONING AND AWARENESS

Change involves learning new habits to take the place of old ones. First I try out my new way; then I practice it until it becomes habitual.

Change also involves developing more awareness of what's happening in me and around me. I start to act less automatically and more in tune with the unique aspects of what's happening.

For example, when people get angry with me, often it's not because of me but because of what's happening in them.

I was in a scene like that not long ago. I was on the job late at night and I needed a key that was kept in the boiler plant. The boiler plant supervisor's first reaction to me was one of irritation and hostility.

At first I wanted to respond with anger. Then I saw the tiredness in his face. "You look like you had a pretty rough day," I said sympathetically.

His jaw dropped. His whole manner changed. He relaxed and appreciated being understood. After a few words about his troubles in the shop, he was glad to help with what I needed.

Some kinds of change involve both learning new habits and developing greater awareness.

At a party, for instance, when I ask, "What do you do?" you might reply, "When?" To "How are things?" you could respond, "Which things?" Your response breaks through my stereotyped question and we have a chance to be more spontaneous and have fun with each other. When I want to, I can usually find a way to override the automatic stuff at almost any point in our conversation.

My ability to pay attention is itself a habit. I develop sensitivity to certain cues that tell me I'm not paying attention, and I respond by moving my attention back to where I want it.

The method of training for natural childbirth developed by Ivan Pavlov and his successors in Russia includes both conditioning and awareness. It is based on controlled breathing and directed attention. In the West it is called the Lamaze method, after Fernand Lamaze, who learned it in Moscow and Leningrad and brought it to Western Europe. Two excellent books describe this method in detail: Irwin Chabon's *Awake and Aware* and Suzanne Arms' *Immaculate Deception.*

Changing automatic patterns with the wrist counter

I used to have a habit of "persuasive talking." When I talked this way, trying to persuade my listener to agree with me, I was out of touch with myself and the other person. I talked *at* the person instead of *with* him or her.

"What are you trying to convince me for?" is the attitude persuasive talking often creates in the listener. He or she closes up, goes on guard, and becomes *less* likely to hear what is said than if the talker weren't coming on with the hard sell.

I wanted to stop talking this way. I tried paying attention to it and asked people to tell me when they noticed me doing it. A couple of months went by with no success. I talked persuasively as much as ever.

Then I got my first wrist counter. I started counting instances of persuasive talking and noted them on a graph. If I talked persuasively for five minutes solid I counted that as one instance, and counted once more for each additional five minutes.

In five weeks I was down from forty or fifty instances a day to five or six. My graph leveled off there, so I quit and went on to something else. Through awareness I changed my behavior and decreased the strength of that powerful habit.

You can use the wrist counter to reduce the frequency of almost any behavior that isn't maintained by strong reinforcers.

Define as clearly as you can what you want to stop doing. Click your counter once every time you do it. Keep a graph, and every day draw a line equal in length to the number of times you clicked the counter.

As the weeks go by, your lines are likely to get shorter and shorter. If not, it means you're probably getting something out of doing what you do.

Virginia Horowitz often hears people in her groups saying, in effect, "I'm afraid to change. If I do change, I may not get what I used to think I wanted."

How does change through awareness work?

Like this. When I start paying attention to some way I act, I experience as fully as I can how I feel acting that way. I want to know that place, even if it's painful. After I've changed, I may never have a chance to know it again as I can know it now.

At first I may not be aware for some time of when I act that way.

It may be the next day that I realize "Yesterday I . . . !" Before long, that realization comes only an hour or several hours afterward, instead of a day or even a week later.

Soon I start to pick up on what I've done only five or ten minutes afterward. I may begin to notice that I've just done "it" the instant I finish doing so. "Ha! I just . . ."

Two things are happening: My attention is more focused on that way of acting; and I'm beginning to feel less uptight about it, so I don't work so hard to stop myself from recognizing it.

Eventually I find myself aware of the act *as I'm performing it.* Then I can interrupt the old act right in the middle, and start to act differently. Ultimately I become better able to see where I'm going even before I start to do something.

Everything that's not too deeply buried passes through my awareness at some time. What I feel good doing, I keep on doing. What I don't feel so good doing, I look at more closely. In particular, I check whether I'm responding to an image of how I "ought" to be that doesn't fit who I am.

When I repeatedly stop myself from acting in an old habitual way, and act in alternative ways, my new pattern of responding starts to take the place of my old habit.

Reconditioning through awareness may work only if you feel better acting in the new way. Even if I know that in the long run, acting differently would be better for me, I'll probably keep acting in my old way if that brings me more immediate satisfaction than acting in the new way would.

This is the principle of *immediate reinforcement. An immediate result affects a person's behavior more than a delayed result.* A small immediate reward or punishment can affect the way a person acts more than a big one later on.

Another approach is to *consciously do* what I want to *stop* doing. R. K. Hall comments, "If you're not aware of something, and it breaks through into behavior only in a compulsive way, then behaving that way intentionally will often make the compulsion vanish."

Yates had people with nervous tics deliberately practice the tic in front of a mirror. This was very effective in reducing or getting rid of tics.

IMITATION

Zen Master Dogen once instructed: "According to an old Master: 'If you develop a close relationship with a good man, it is like walking in the fog or dew. Although you do not actually wet your garment, it gradually becomes damp' " (Dogen, 62–63).

Take a look at whom you spend time with. In time, you're going to become more like them. If that doesn't please you, find people who live the way you want to live. Who you're with is a big piece of the world you create for yourself.

In his statement, "Do unto others as you would have them do unto you," Jesus was saying in part that imitation is a basic principle of learning.

My acts say more than my words about who I am and what I want. When parents tell their children, "Do what I say and not what I do," they're fighting one of the main ways people learn. When my words and actions give you different messages, the odds are good that you'll take me at my actions.

A father once said to me: "I just don't know what to do about my son. He tortures the cat, beats up his playmates, and nothing I do seems to help. Every time I catch him at it, I whip the living daylights out of him, but it does no good at all."

Bandura and Walters found that aggressive boys were punished more by their fathers than were nonaggressive boys, and many studies have shown that after children watch someone in a movie act aggressively, they act more aggressively in their own play. The nonaggressive boys, the ones treated in a warmer, less punishing way, also liked their fathers better (Bandura, PBM; Bandura and Walters, SLP).

Reinforcement plays a role in imitation too. When a child gets rewarded for doing as someone else has done, he or she is more likely to act that way again.

A person also learns whether to do something he or she sees another person do by watching what happens to that person (Miller and Dollard; Bandura).

Modeling can be used to teach many things. For example, my fear can be reduced when I watch others comfortably handle a situation I'm afraid of. In one study of modeling, children who were afraid of dogs watched another child interact fearlessly with a friendly, harmless dog. After a few sessions of observing the model, these children were much more willing to come close to the dog than the children who hadn't watched the model play with it (Bandura).

When we work with modeling, we need to be careful who we choose for a model. For instance, students who get B's and C's usually make better models for failing students than A students do. The A student is too different, too hard to imitate. B and C students have an easier time being in touch with the failing student, and behave in a way the failing student can more readily match. So what do many schools do? They let only A students tutor.

We imitate each other in many kinds of everyday encounters. Without knowing it, I imitate the emotional tone I pick up from you.

If you come on in a hostile and aggressive way, I'm likely to be hostile and aggressive in return. If you come on warm and caring, I'm more likely to feel that way toward you.

A seeming exception to this is ways of acting that call out complementary roles. If you come on like Mama or Papa, I may respond like a child. Yet even with complementary roles, the emotional tone of both persons tends to be similar.

The fact that people imitate emotional tone explains how a person who's usually gentle and friendly and a person who's usually suspicious and hostile can interact with the very same people, yet live in totally different social worlds. One lives in a world of gentle, friendly people and the other in a world of suspicious, hostile people. Both worlds are real.

BLACK MAGIC AND ITS ALTERNATIVES

Gurdjieff speaks of black magic. He defines it as "the tendency to use people for some, even the best of aims, *without their knowledge and understanding*" (quoted in Ouspensky, ISM, 227).

When I try to affect the way another person acts, I like to be as explicit as I can about what I'm doing.

Parents who tell their children what patterns of reward and nonreward they're using protect those children from being conditioned by forces they know nothing of.

When I give parents suggestions about ways of handling problems with their children, I often recommend a negotiating session.

One parent—in this case let's imagine it's the mother—tells her son what she's unhappy about and what she's decided to try doing. Then she asks him how he feels about that, and what he wants from her in return. If she wants him to do something for her, it's only fair that he gets something out of it too. Otherwise it's her power trip. The parent and child bargain back and forth, and I mediate to make sure that neither one is bullying the other and that each one feels okay about the bargain.

We set up specific consequences for the times when either one doesn't follow through. For instance, the child may get some special privilege when the mother doesn't keep her end of the bargain. By fulfilling her part of the agreement, the mother gives the child a basis for trusting and respecting her.

In the long run, black magic is seldom helpful to the people it's used on. It breeds frustration and resentment. By contrast, change through awareness involves the consent and cooperation of the persons affected, and allows movement toward more open communication.

When you don't want to communicate in an open way, you've still got the option of telling me to go to hell.

"Hey, Charlie, you look like you had a hard day."

"Yeah. Don't make it any harder. Get lost."

BLACK MAGIC AND SOCIETY.   To the degree that you can see how I'm trying to control you, my power over you is weakened. Our best protection against being unwillingly manipulated by agents of government and business who would use the principles of conditioning against us is to understand those principles ourselves.

10 *Incentive*

We all try to get others to do what we want them to. If I don't know how to get you to act in ways I find rewarding, I may well feel frustrated and even pained. So in some ways, I influence your behavior and you influence mine. That's part of the reality of our lives.

The better I am at getting you to do what I want you to, the more careful I want to be that I don't rob you of your chance to think and feel and do in your own way, rather than in what I think should be your way.

We can know what we're asking and giving, and avoid the kind of manipulation in which I trick you into giving something you don't want to give. Then we learn to trust each other. Once we have mutual trust, I can feel good about deliberately giving you my power when I don't feel up to coping with something: "I'd appreciate it if you do this—I don't feel good about what I'm doing now."

❋ Manipulation and accommodation

You can do this either in a group or with one other person. Each of you takes out an object you value. When you're asked for your object, or you find that someone in the group (or your partner) has an object you'd like, one of you tries to manipulate the other into giving up the object.

The person being manipulated may either drive a hard bargain or make it easy for the manipulator to get the object he or she wants.

If you're doing this in a group, then move on to another person and try the opposite role, or see how your same role works with this different person.

What do you learn about your style of manipulating? Of accommodating to what the other person wants? Do you make the other person feel as though he or she is getting something of real value, or do you belittle what you're giving? As you interact, when and where do you tense up and tighten your body?

Reward and punishment

The *results* of what I do determine how likely I am to do that same thing again. Here's an example:

Father is in his easy chair, drinking beer and watching TV. In comes little Freddie.

"Daddy, I want some orange juice."

"Later." Daddy's eyes remain glued to the screen.

Freddie stands there for a half minute or so. Then, whining a little: "Daddy, *I want some orange juice.*"

"I told you *later,*" Daddy replies, his voice a little sharper. "Wait till the commercial. Can't you see I'm watching this program?"

A minute passes. Freddie's voice is now a whine: "Daddy, I'm *really thirsty.* I want some orange juice *right now.*"

Daddy, very irritated now, finally tears his eyes away from the TV and glares at Freddie. "Didn't you hear me? I told you I'll get it as soon as the commercial comes on. Now don't bother me!"

Freddie's voice immediately breaks into a loud screech—half-whine, half-cry. "But I'm really thirsty and I really want some orange juice and I can't get it and all I want is—"

"Oh, good grief! All right. I'll get it for you if you'll just shut up. How many times do I have to tell you not to whine like that?" With that, exasperated Daddy pushes back his chair and stalks into the kitchen.

The next day, Freddie's mother says to his father: "Henry, I'm utterly at my wit's end. All Freddie ever does is whine and wail anymore. I don't know what's gotten into that boy!"

"I don't know either," replies Henry. "And I'm sick and tired of it. I'm going to give him a real talking-to. And if that doesn't do it, maybe a whipping will."

When Freddie comes up and asks quietly, he gets no orange juice. No payoff. No reinforcement. When he whines, he gets what he wants. Mommy and Daddy are *teaching him to whine* by rewarding him when he does and failing to reward him when he behaves as they want him to. They're selectively reinforcing whining.

Giving Freddie a talking-to won't do any good. Neither will a whipping.

The only thing that will is giving him satisfaction when he asks quietly, instead of when he whines.

The word "reinforcement" in its general sense refers to both rewards and punishments.

"Reward" includes both *getting a positive reinforcer, or "goodie,"* and *escaping from a negative reinforcer, or "baddie"* (Behaviordelia).

"Punishment" includes both *getting hit with a baddie* and *losing a goodie.*

Once we understand the principles by which rewards and punishments operate, events that long have puzzled us start making sense. Here are the basic principles:

1) Any act that brings a reward tends to happen more often.

2) Any act that no longer brings the rewards it used to bring tends to happen less often. Eventually it doesn't happen anymore at all. This is called *extinction.*

3) Any act that is punished tends to be suppressed, often temporarily, but the potential to act in the punished way is still there.

As you develop your ability to see these three principles working in your everyday life and in the lives of those around you, you'll see and hear more, and move through your world more effectively. Behavioral psychologist John Krumboltz provides a number of interesting examples of such events.

According to behavioral psychologist B. F. Skinner, a positive reinforcer, or goodie, is "any event that increases the probability of a response" (SHB).

Positive reinforcement is usually, but not always, a "pleasant" event. Suppose I'm a schoolteacher. One kid in my room constantly disturbs everyone. Time and again I tell him, "Johnny, please be quieter." Every time I do, he obeys, but three minutes later, he's doing it again. Even expressing my anger does no good.

In all probability, getting attention, even though the attention seems like punishment, is a powerful positive reinforcer for him. For many children, any kind of attention is better than none at all. So when I pay attention to Johnny every time he makes a ruckus, I increase the odds that he'll make a ruckus in the future.

What can I do? I can ignore him when he acts up, and give him attention when he's involved in constructive learning: "Johnny, I really appreciate the way you've been working together with the other children for the past few minutes."

I can also recognize that if Johnny is after any kind of attention he can get, he probably needs more attention than he's been getting either at home or at school.

Studies have shown that most teachers give the children in their classes much more negative attention than positive attention. They criticize, condemn, belittle, and punish far more than they appreciate, praise, and reward. When asked to actually keep count, they find that their communication with the children is *primarily* negative communication. Many teachers are amazed and appalled to find out that they are much less likely to talk to a child when something good is happening. The same is true of many parents.

Without knowing that they were doing so, our friends, parents, and teachers often rewarded us for doing the very things they didn't want us to do.

Perhaps when you were a child you usually didn't get much cuddling or holding, but did get plenty of it every time you fell or stubbed your toe and cried a little. If so, you probably soon learned to cry a lot and get notably upset about even minor falls and bruises.

That sort of thing happens with hypochondriacs. Look how much attention they get when they're sick! Their illnesses take center stage. There's the story about the hypochondriac who finally died: on his tombstone was the inscription "See!"

Getting rid of a baddie can be just as rewarding as getting a goodie. When something I do gets rid of a baddie, I tend to do it more often.

If my first contact with a situation is frightening enough, I may be so afraid of it from then on that I avoid ever getting into it again. So if at some future time the situation stops being frightening, I'll never find out about it. I act like a rat that's been shocked in a certain place and is afraid ever to go near it again, even though the shock button may have since been turned off forever.

Do you know someone who has been "burned in love" and because of the pain is afraid to love again?

POSITIVE REINFORCEMENT

Appreciation is important to everyone. If my woman does something for me and I let her know I appreciate it, she'll be more likely to do it again. If I ignore her action, she'll be less likely to repeat it.

We often violate this basic principle. We mention things to people only when they're *not* doing what we want; we take their attempts to please us for granted.

I often feel a little angry or disappointed when I go to some special effort for someone and that person doesn't even notice it. "See if I ever do that again!" I think to myself.

When I don't mention something you do that feels good to me, my message is that when you do nice things for me, I act as though you don't exist. When you hurt me, I recognize you. Since you want to be recognized, you learn how to hurt me, instead of how to show your love and caring. As the days or months or years go by, we learn few ways to love and care for one another, and many ways to hurt each other, until our pain becomes so great that we scream our final curses and go our separate ways. Then one day, each of us finds someone else to do the same thing with again.

In marriage counseling, one of the partners in a couple that has been together for as long as twenty years will often say to the other, "I didn't know you enjoyed that." The other usually replies, "Well, I *expected* you to know that." "I *expect* you to know what I like" translates as "I want you to do good things for me, but I won't tell you how or when."

By cluing you in instead of expecting you to know, and giving you my appreciation when you do things I like, I'm telling you what you need to know to be good to me.

It's especially easy to forget to give children enough appreciation. It can seem simpler to just give them orders.

A mother may order her children to "pick up your clothes and don't leave them lying around" twenty-five times a day and get no results. If instead she gives out hugs and words of appreciation every time she notices that things are getting picked up even a little bit, she'll soon find that things get picked up regularly.

Some friends of mine taught their daughter to read using positive reinforcement. They began by giving her a raisin for every word she read. After a while, she was reading words fairly well. Then she had to start reading a whole sentence to get a raisin, so the task wouldn't seem too easy. Once she was doing well on sentences, they switched to a raisin for every page.

One Sunday morning the parents were awakened by their daughter's voice downstairs in the kitchen. Curious, they tiptoed downstairs and peeked into the kitchen. There sat their daughter at the table, a pile of raisins in front of her, reading aloud out of her book and taking a raisin after she finished each page!

Learning based on positive reinforcement leaves a person flexible and open to change. The person discovers (or rediscovers) that the world is basically a friendly place and that being alive feels good. He or she feels especially good acting in ways that have brought rewards in the past and being in situations in which rewards have come. The good feelings that go with something nice happening "rub off" on the person or on the situation in which these good things happen and on the activity that brings them about.

This process is called *secondary reinforcement.* An event that was originally neither pleasant nor unpleasant can, after it's been connected with a reward enough times, itself begin to feel good. In his novel *Island,* Aldous Huxley described this process:

> "Dr. Andrew picked up the idea . . . from a tribe in northern New Guinea. . . . Stroke the baby while you're feeding him; it doubles his pleasure. Then, while he's sucking and being caressed, introduce him to the animal or person you want him to love. Rub his body against theirs; let there be a warm physical contact between child and love object. At the same time repeat some word like 'good.' At first he'll understand only your tone of voice. Later on, when he learns to speak, he'll get the full meaning. . . ."
>
> "Pure Pavlov."
>
> "But Pavlov purely for a good purpose. Pavlov for friendliness and trust and compassion. Whereas you prefer to use Pavlov for brainwashing, Pavlov for selling cigarettes and vodka and patriotism. Pavlov for the benefit of dictators, generals, and tycoons." (221–22)

What is rewarding to me may not be rewarding to you; what is punishing to me may not be punishing to you. *Don't assume that because something is a reinforcer for you, it is for someone else too* (even though you may think it "ought" to be). Usually, the best way to find out what a person likes is to ask, even with young children.

What someone wants may depend not only on that person's general preferences, but also on what's happened to him or her lately. When I've just eaten, food is not much of a reinforcer for me. When I haven't had much loving for a while, a big hug and a warm smile are worth a lot.

By contrast, some people prefer to keep their relationships distant because they know how to relate by arguing and being hard, and they can pretty well predict how the other person will respond. A distant relationship doesn't demand a commitment to work their problems through. If you're nasty to me, I can dump your crap back on you and walk away, and feel good about walking away. If you're loving and gentle with me, I have a harder time walking away and feeling good about it. When I'm loving and gentle with you, I'm risking; I'm more vulnerable to feeling hurt by you.

Whenever I'm working with a family and someone says, "I want to straighten things out," I listen carefully to hear what that person *doesn't* want to straighten out. If you and I have some source of discontent with each other, there's something in it for both of us to have that happening—or it wouldn't be happening.

When we want to be warm and loving with each other, we've got to reward each other in concrete, direct ways. I've got to tell you what I want from you and when I want it. I've got to tell you when I'm feeling good with what you're doing, and show my appreciation by doing things for you that you like.

Even marriage counselors sometimes fall into the trap of getting sucked in by the problems in a relationship. The couple or family comes in and says, "We're having trouble with . . ." The counselor focuses on the trouble and forgets to find the good places they have together that they can work from.

If you and I don't spend some time developing the good things we have going for us, we can spend a lot of time mucking around in our problems and our pain, and we won't be spending much time in the sunshine.

Lasting change usually comes only when a new way of acting *works in dealing with the world.*

This is one reason our prisons are so ineffective. They do almost nothing to teach the people in them new skills and ways of acting that will help them once they get out.

Just one step at a time

Have you ever watched a parent get angry with a child who's trying to do something?

If I say to my daughter, "How many times do I have to tell you? You're all thumbs. Sometimes I wonder if you can do *anything* right!" it shakes her confidence in her own ability to do things. It makes it harder for her to develop a sense of competence in dealing with her world. Eventually she may conclude that she *can't* do anything, and no longer even want to try.

Without realizing it, I may have a psychological commitment to her being all thumbs. If she becomes competent, I can't feel so superior any more. So I teach her to be incompetent. She learns *my* lesson well.

The same is often true of a supervisor and his or her workers. If the workers get really good at their jobs, the supervisor's status might have less impact.

Were I your husband or wife, I could keep you dependent on me by keeping you from learning skills you need to make it on your own. Were I your parent, I could keep you dependent on me to nurture you, so that you'd never learn to nurture yourself—you'd continue to need me.

Instead of criticizing my daughter, I can give her some appreciation for what she's done so far. Then I can help her with something a little harder.

"Good. You've done well with that one. Now look—here's a little thing you can do to improve your next one."

I set *short-term* goals and give a lot of moment-to-moment support, reassurance, and appreciation. That way she learns that she *can* do things. She begins to feel competent and confident in her world.

At the beginning, I show her my appreciation every time she does a certain thing. She soon learns that the action that brings that goodie is different from all other actions. When she does that certain thing something nice happens, and when she does other things nothing special happens.

Through hearing my appreciation again and again, *she learns to appreciate herself.* She starts talking to herself the way I've talked to her. After a while I can begin to let more time go by between my statements of appreciation. As she comes to feel more confident and competent, she does things more and more often because she enjoys doing them, rather than because of my appreciation.

As experimental psychologist Harry Harlow has shown, we are all naturally active. We constantly express our innate drive to explore, to manipulate, and to do (unless it's been suppressed by the "don't touch anything, don't do this, don't do that" treatment).

At the point where a person gets good at a simple task, I can raise my criteria. I give appreciation now for something a little more difficult. It would cheapen my appreciation to give it for something too easily done.

If I'm trying to teach someone to do something a bit difficult, I reward him or her for closer and closer approximations to the goal. This teaching process is called *shaping*, or *successive approximation*. At any point I ask only that the learner do what he or she is capable of doing now. Yesterday I asked less, tomorrow I'll ask more. The important thing is *not to ask too much at once.* It does no good to go splat on your face: *A good way to get nothing is to ask for everything.* One step at a time you can get to places you could never reach in one big leap.

The timing of consequences

Intermittent reinforcement is when we reinforce a behavior *only sometimes* instead of every time it happens.

Behavior that's been rewarded only every now and then is hard to extinguish.

Suppose I'm a student. I may have one cold, rigid teacher who I know is always going to be deaf to me or bite my head off if I say anything. I never get rewarded for trying to communicate, so I clam up and forget it. That relationship is permanently on the blink.

I have another teacher who's great—almost always really there and tuned in. When she brushes me aside, I know she's in a bad place. With her I'm used to a constant schedule of positive reinforcement, so one nonreinforcement is enough. I'll sit back and wait until she's feeling better.

With a temperamental teacher who sometimes responds to me and sometimes doesn't, I've learned to expect my reinforcements on an intermittent schedule, so I might try communicating with her several times before I give up. If I've been getting a reward only occasionally, and I get nothing for a while, things may be normal. Nothing tells me for sure that things are any different than they ever were. I keep trying to communicate until I'm certain the rewards aren't coming anymore.

Reinforcement works best when it's in proportion to the difficulty or importance of the act. Not too much and not too little. Whether the reinforcement comes every time or only every now and then, it must always *follow* the behavior, the sooner the better. If it comes beforehand, it won't work.

The Premack Principle

Experimental psychologist David Premack has unearthed an extremely useful principle of behavior: The chance to do something that you often choose to do can be used to reinforce something that you seldom choose to do.

One fellow didn't like helping his son with reading and arithmetic. He felt that he "should" help but he seldom bothered, and felt resentful when he did. Then he decided he'd allow himself to ride his motorcycle for an hour after he'd helped his son with his studies for an hour. Now he had a real incentive. Soon he was helping regularly and feeling good about it. Before long the boy started doing better in school.

Behaviors we want to strengthen are almost always things we don't do as often as we'd like—"low-probability behaviors." All of us have some "high-probability behaviors" we could use as reinforcers. Interestingly enough, these are not always "pleasant."

One woman liked to paint in oils, but seldom took the time to do it. She didn't like housework, but felt that she "should" clean thoroughly each day, so she did. After cleaning, she was usually too tired to paint. Housework was a likely behavior, even though she found it unpleasant. Painting was an unlikely behavior, even though she liked to paint. So, taking time to paint could be reinforced by doing her housework afterward. She changed things around so that she painted first, and then did the housework. Soon she was painting regularly. The low-probability behavior was reinforced by doing the high-probability behavior afterward.

Since the consequence (opportunity to do housework) must follow the behavior to be affected (taking time to paint), the other way around wouldn't work.

The Premack Principle has another important implication: Almost any behavior can either be reinforced or be a reinforcer. The very act of eating, which can often serve to reinforce doing other things, is sometimes affected by other reinforcers. For instance:

"How pleased I am that you're eating well and enjoying your food," Mother says as her daughter finishes her dinner.

Before, dawdling over food was reinforced by the parent's attention—"Eat your dinner and don't play with your food." Of course, the child ate slower than anyone else. Now if she dawdles her mother ignores it.

Bribery and spoiling

Some people strongly object to the use of positive reinforcement, especially with children. "Why, that's just paying them off for behaving. That's bribery!"

Is it? Let's see.

Here's a typical situation involving what we'd call actual bribery: A woman and her little boy are in a store. He's crying and whining. "Listen," she says, "if you'll shut up and behave yourself for fifteen minutes, I'll get you an ice-cream cone."

What happens? For fifteen minutes he behaves, pouting and resentful. Then he gets his ice-cream cone, and soon he's back to crying and whining.

What's he learning? That he has to do what mother says for fifteen minutes, and then he gets a reward. He's probably also learning that misbehavior can pay off. From his viewpoint: "If I hassle Mommy enough, she'll give me an ice-cream cone to get me to stop for a while." His obnoxious behavior is often reinforced by attention and a bribe for temporary good behavior. Since the obnoxious behavior is positively reinforced, it becomes more frequent.

Compare this unwitting reinforcement of irritating behavior to reinforcement of desired behavior. In the same store, when a mother who's consciously using positive reinforcement likes the way her son is acting, she'll tell him *right then* how much she appreciates it. She knows that immediate rewards work better than delayed rewards, so she doesn't wait till they get out of the store. By rewarding desired acts immediately, she's rewarding a *specific behavior*, rather than *all* the behavior that occurred while they were in the store. The boy knows clearly and exactly what he's being rewarded for.

And every now and then, when he's behaving himself in a store, mother will surprise him with a special goodie. He learns that the odds on getting that goodie are better if he doesn't cause a ruckus than if he does.

With reinforcement, he learns to give his mother the same kind of respect and appreciation she's giving him; he learns to act often in ways that please her. With bribery, he learns to displease her except for short stretches of time, and to please her even then only grudgingly.

Some parents spoil their children. Spoiled children are used to getting everything they want. We spoil children by *giving them rewards regardless of what they do.* Since the rewards don't depend on their behavior, they can "misbehave" badly and still get whatever they want. Such children often grow up feeling that the world owes them a living. That's just one symptom of a graver problem: Since the children never have to face the consequences of what they do, they don't learn to take responsibility for the results of their actions.

A psychologist who has worked in several mental hospitals reports that in her experience, people who were spoiled as children seem to be the ones most likely to commit suicide as adults. Everything always came easy to them, so they never learned to face frustration. Now, frustration easily drives them to despair instead of to deeper thought and greater effort.

Some people, even when they understand how positive reinforcement differs from bribery and spoiling, still don't like it. A typical protest is: "It just doesn't seem right to me to pay someone off for doing something that he ought to do anyway."

". . . that he ought to do anyway." Think about that one. It usually means ". . . that I think he should be doing by now." Overlooked is the fact that he *hasn't learned to do it yet.* That puts him in quite a bind. It's like giving a child or worker a task he or she can't perform to your standards of perfection, and then getting angry because your standards weren't met.

There are some things a person can't learn until certain prior developmental steps have been taken. For example, there's no way I can toilet train a child before he has developed some control over his sphincter muscles. Parents who press and push can get their child toilet trained a little earlier than others, but not much.

Instead of asking the impossible, *start with the intermediate steps a person must master in order to be ready to do what you want done.*

Behaviordelia (a Michigan collective of behaviorally oriented psychologists and their friends) has a rule for this: *"Start where the . . . behavior is at.* Not where you think it should be. And the best way to find out is to . . . look and see. . . . [Often your] assumptions about what the behaver can already do . . . are wrong. Just because a student is in the sixth grade does not mean he can read at the sixth grade level" (9-11; 12-1).

I have found that *people who are most opposed to rewarding others for desired behavior are nearly always strong advocates of punishment.*

Parents who aren't willing even to try incentive programs with their children are perfectly willing to "give the little bastard a good belt to teach him a lesson."

Many of us were brought up on punishment-oriented discipline and we tend to repeat the same pattern.

Behavioral psychologists Tharp and Wetzel found that some parents time and again found ways to punish their children, even when this was strictly against the behavioral change plan. These parents wanted to punish their children more than they wanted to bring about the changes they said they were looking for. For them, punishing a child was a way they could feel their own power. It was also a way of expressing frustrations that weren't even related to the child. Having a problem with their child could serve as a diversion from confronting other problems they didn't want to face.

Those who'd rather use punishment than positive reinforcement seldom want to be treated that way by others. For themselves, they much prefer a bonus for good work to getting docked for sloppy work.

If I don't care enough to change in the ways I need to change in order to effectively reinforce the behavior I want from you, then you won't change. Why should you? There's nothing in it for you if you do.

I often work with a child, parent, and teacher to change the child's "problem behavior." Typically we work out a contract that involves all three of them. When someone breaks the contract, about 90 percent of the time it's one of the adults.

If I really want you to change, I have to be willing to change too.

POSITIVE REINFORCEMENT AND SOCIETY

B. F. Skinner's work suggests ways we can evolve a society based on understanding, love, caring, and appreciation in place of our present reliance on punishment, suspicion, suppression, and violence.

This means more than "permissiveness." Permissiveness is "leaving a person free to learn." That's a beginning, because a child raised "permissively" is free of many of the punishment-linked hangups that haunt the older generation. But it's not enough. Carried to an extreme, permissiveness means that each person has to rediscover the wheel for himself or herself.

The step beyond permissiveness is a caring guidance that respects and fosters the other person's independence. Such guidance means helping people explore new possibilities and develop their own potentialities in creative ways, through sharing time and space with them.

Behavior learned by positive reinforcement does not require surveillance. As a person does something that brings rewards, he or she usually comes to like the activity itself.

As parents begin to raise children by loving, caring, and positive reinforcement rather than by oppression, threat, and punishment, more and more of us will feel good when we help instead of hurt one another. We will less often cause, or want to cause, pain and injury. Out of caring we learn to feel; we will become more sensitive to others' needs, and we will provide for one another better. With all this happening, the police will have a smaller job. We will need less government control.

Once we understand how to bring up our children and relate to each other through positive reinforcement rather than punishment, no one will have to make us do it—we'll do it simply because it works and because we feel good with ourselves and with each other when we do.

11 Ending Unwanted Behavior

The "neurotic paradox"

In the early days of this century, Freud noticed that some of his patients acted over and over again in ways that were destructive to their social relationships, their work, and their hopes for happiness. Some observers have called this the "neurotic paradox."

Actually, there is no paradox. Once a way of acting has been learned, it needs a reward only now and then to keep it going. An act may be kept going by small immediate rewards even though bigger punishments follow later on.

One immediate reward I may be getting when I seem to be acting against my own self-interest is the reduction of anxiety.

If I'm a heavy drinker, I reach for the glass again to dull the anxiety that's hitting me right now, regardless of what might happen later. In my mind and body, the anxiety is still there, but I feel more comfortable *now*.

In the past, in certain situations where I felt anxious or afraid, I acted in ways that warded off the threat, or at least helped me feel less anxious. Today I may still act in those ways whenever I feel anxious, even though the old dangers may be gone. When I do, I feel less anxious, just like before.

Experimental psychologist Neal Miller trained rats to run from a white compartment into a black compartment to avoid shock. Then he turned off the shock, so that the rats didn't have to leave the white compartment anymore. But they never stuck around long enough to find that out, and kept running out of the white compartment just as before.

What kinds of situations in your own past were so frightening or painful that you avoid them even now? Some of them are probably no longer

113

threatening, but since you never get into them, your old fears and anxieties have no chance to extinguish.

Many of the techniques we use to reduce anxiety work by taking up our attention with meaningless actions. An administrator I know keeps himself busy compulsively arranging the top of his desk as a way to avoid feeling his anxiety.

When I distract myself with a thought that "obsesses me" or an action I repeat compulsively again and again, then I never really contact what I am anxious about. I avoid the source of my anxiety by mentally going somewhere else, so I never experience it fully. My anxiety has no chance to extinguish because I'm not really present in the anxiety-provoking situation, even if physically I seem to be.

PUNISHMENT AND ITS PROBLEMS

Punishment has some useful applications. Before we go on to those, let's look at some of the problems it can create when used unwisely.

As Skinner's co-worker William K. Estes showed in 1944, *suppression* of behavior is a central effect of punishment. The suppression is often only temporary, because the wish to act in the punished way is *still there,* but the person is *afraid* to follow through on his or her desire.

Look into your own life. What don't you do because you are afraid to? How many of your everyday thoughts are fears of bad things that might happen? How much diffuse apprehension do you carry around in your body in the form of muscular tenseness and tightness? These things are the legacy of punishment.

Suppose I'm a newborn infant. This world is a fascinating place to me. At first I'm free to explore everything I touch and smell and taste and see and hear.

Then one day I'm doing something for which I get severely punished. For instance, I may be touching my sexual organs. Mommy sees me, and with a shriek of horror—whack! *"Don't do that!"*

I learn that this part of my world is dangerous and painful. Probably I don't stop touching that part of my body, but now I sneak away and do it where Mommy can't find me. And now, whenever I explore my sexual organs or those of other children, I am afraid. Perhaps the fear of being punished is so great that I now feel uneasy about rubbing, touching, or massaging *any* part of my body except when I have to, as when I'm dressing, washing, or soothing a pain.

Sooner or later, the same thing happens with another thing I do. And another, and another. The part of my world that's full of beauty and delight gets smaller and smaller. Some of the other areas of my life become so painful I avoid them entirely; many others are frightening enough that I feel anxious when I get into them. Through my fears, I may block off so many areas of my life, and live within such narrow boundaries, that my flexibility and my openness are severely hindered.

 Your ways of punishing and feeling punished

If you're in a group setting, go around to each person and make two brief one-sentence statements: "I can punish you by . . ." and "You can punish me by . . ." Don't try to think up what you're going to say in advance.

Stop in front of the person, look at him or her, and say the first things that come to mind. Then discuss with the group your style of punishing and the kinds of events that cause you to feel punished. Several other group members might also want to do this. If you have no group available, do this by yourself as you go through your day. When you encounter someone, you can note to yourself how that person could punish you and how you might be punishing toward that person.

Past punishment

Some of the things I got punished for doing in the past are all right to do now. Certain behaviors often taught to children are not helpful for adults; and certain behaviors that most children aren't allowed make sense for adults.

If as a child I was punished when I disagreed with my parents, I learned that I must not "talk back." To some degree I generalized this to all authority. Now I may be tongue-tied and afraid to speak up with my boss or other authority, even when I really need to.

I may have grown up hearing, "Children are to be seen and not heard." Now I never know how to start a conversation. I'm very quiet and withdrawn until someone addresses me; then I know that it's okay for me to talk.

To the degree that I've introjected punishment, every time I even *think* of acting in the punished way, I actually punish myself right then by tensing up my body and talking harshly to myself inside my head.

Beneath the layers of punishment, my desire to act in the forbidden way lives on. Within me rages still the struggle between the side of me that wants to act in the forbidden way and the side that unites the recorded voice in my head that says, "You must not," with my own "I'm afraid." I may feel an impulse to lash out at my punisher, yet I stop myself from lashing out. Or my body mobilizes to run away, yet I stop myself from running away. I'm like two separate "me's" pushing at each other from opposite directions and vibrating with the tension. This is one way people get ulcers and high blood pressure.

In your everyday life, you can watch the effects of punishment on other people. With children, a supermarket or park is an ideal spot for this. Watch a parent scold or punish a child, especially when you don't think the child was doing anything so awful. *Now watch the child react.* How does he or she seem different to you than before punishment?

On the job, what do you notice about an employee who's just been chewed out by the boss?

Reward tells a person more about what to do than punishment.

A person who gets rewarded for doing something *learns what to do* to get a reward. A person who gets punished *learns only one thing he or she shouldn't do* to avoid punishment, and may still not know what's okay.

In our nervous systems, there are many interconnections. When you flip a switch to turn certain parts of you off, you turn other parts off too. Another way of saying this is that fear *generalizes* easily from one act or situation to another. If I punish my daughter for a particular act, I don't know for sure what I'm teaching her to fear. In her thinking, she may not separate her act from the situation she was punished in. From now on out, she may always be a little afraid of *situations* that resemble the one she was punished in. Or she may be afraid of *people who remind her of me.* She may be afraid to do what she was punished for even in times when and in places where it's okay to do so.

No one knows how to fully control and direct the effects of punishment. With positive reinforcement, my predictions about what will happen have a high probability of being right. With punishment, I can only guess and hope. Our penal systems show this all too clearly.

Some people like to have others slap them and beat them and knock them around. When they were children, they hardly ever got any warmth or attention except when they'd been physically abused.

A mother or father, angry at a child's crying, sometimes abuses the child and then feels guilty and cuddles or holds the youngster. Pleasure and pain become linked in the child's experience. He or she learns that loving is good only when it hurts, and carries this early learning through a lifetime.

In the sex-violence linkage that is so popular in pornographic literature, movies, and TV shows, we see the reflection of the sadistic and masochistic cravings that are the result of a punitively oriented society.

Since behavior that's maintained by the threat of punishment seldom becomes completely voluntary, someone has to keep checking on whether there's any misbehavior. This means that punishment-based control is often difficult to maintain.

Maintaining behavior by positive reinforcement is much easier. Often the person will offer evidence of how well he or she has behaved.

I'll never forget when my father was toilet training one of my little sisters by giving her lots of appreciation every time she pooped in the pot. One evening when we had company, my sister suddenly toddled into the middle of the room with the removable potty-bowl in her arms, held it out, and proudly showed us all her huge brown turd. She got the appreciation she wanted and deserved.

When I punish you, you don't have to buy my evaluation of what you do. You don't have to join me in punishing you. I may downgrade you, but you can still feel good about yourself. And as long as you don't buy my evaluation of you, you're free to choose to "do it" and risk punishment, or "not to do it" and not risk punishment.

How punishment affects the punisher

Punishment poisons the relationship between the punisher and the person punished.

When you punish me, suddenly, from where I stand, you're bad. A voice inside me says, "You may say you love me, you-who-speak-with-forked-tongue, but I've seen you be cruel to me. You've lost part of my trust. I know that there are things I can't say or do near you. You won't fool me again." The more you punish me, the less I am real with you.

To some degree, I may begin to conceal myself from everyone as I do from you. I become a little suspicious, a little closed, toward all of them. Yet you are the one I resent most.

A child who feels punished learns how to protect himself or herself, and also how to punish in return.

The parent wants to come close to the child in certain ways, and the child's response is, "No way—I'm not giving you any of that good stuff. I'm closing you out of my world."

As my child internalizes the punishment I give, he or she not only learns to punish himself or herself, but also picks up my ways of punishing, and finds ways to punish me by not giving me what I want. By refusing to do what I want done, and refusing to relate to me in any intimate way, he or she can feel some power. This most often comes into the open during the teen-age years.

McIntire writes of a teen-ager who was picked up by the police for vandalism:

> The mother stated that she could not guess where her daughter was when she was arrested. When asked where her daughter usually went on her nights out, she answered, "Oh, I don't know. She never talks to me." "When was the last time she told you about school or activities with her friends?" she was asked. "I can't even remember," she said. "Oh, yes, now I remember, she told me what one of those bad boys said about her figure—just as if she were proud of having boys think of her that way!" When asked what her reaction was, the mother answered with some pride, "Well, I told her that if I *ever* saw her with that boy again, I'd give her the whipping of her life!"
>
> What do you suppose the daughter learned from this little exchange with her mother? To leave some boys alone and not talk to them? Or to leave her mother alone and not talk to her? (81–82).

Out of enlightened self-interest, if I want a relationship of sharing and caring with you, I'll move toward open communication and reward-oriented discipline, and away from punishment-oriented discipline.

Perhaps I'm afraid of warmth and loving feelings. Then as the years go by, I may change. I may begin to want an open, loving relationship, and become more willing to risk being vulnerable. If I've closed you out, I'm going to have a tough time redefining what I want with you. It'll be hard for you to hear me, hard for you to believe me if you hear me, and hard for you to do anything about it if you hear me and believe me.

Many older people tell me that this situation is a central tragedy in their lives. Many younger people tell me of their parents' belated reaching-out, and say that it has come too late. Others tell me of reaching back to their parents and developing a relationship that's open and loving.

HOW TO USE PUNISHMENT

As we saw in the last chapter, what we think is punishment may sometimes act as a reward. Temper tantrums are a classic example. Any attention given to a tantrum usually reinforces it.

Almost always, the best way to deal with a tantrum is to ignore it.

Let the person have the tantrum. It'll help him or her to blow off steam. To try to force the person to bottle it up by giving or threatening punishment is the worst thing you can do. If you just let the person be and don't pay any special attention during or immediately after the tantrum, except for showing an understanding attitude toward his or her feelings, the tantrums will almost certainly become less frequent and less intense.

It's important to remember that almost all of us *need* to throw a tantrum now and then, even as adults. When I want to scream and jump up and down and pound the table, I feel much better after I've done exactly that. Then I'm less likely to pound *you*.

One kind of punishment that is often effective and that can even have constructive side effects, *if it's used in a loving way*, is *withdrawal of a positive reinforcer*.

Losing the use of something because I haven't taken care of it is a way I learn responsibility. I learn from the consequences of my actions. Children face this situation when they break their toys and get no new toys to replace them for a while, or when the toys they've left lying all over the place are put into a locked box for a week or so.

For this kind of punishment to be effective, there has to be a clear, immediate, and consistent relationship between abusing an item and losing the use of it. This is no place for intermittent or delayed reinforcement.

Punishment may be appropriate when stopping an unwanted behavior immediately is more important than getting rid of it for good, as, for instance, when someone is getting hurt or may get hurt by the behavior. If little Becky runs out in the street in front of cars, I may punish her for it until I teach her to feel good about staying on the curb. *This last step, to give her goodies for staying on the curb, is vitally important and too often overlooked* by those who mistakenly rely on punishment alone. When Becky goes out tomorrow afternoon and doesn't run into the street, I'll give her a lot of appreciation for staying on the curb.

Punishment can serve to suppress one way of acting while a new way is learned. Suppose that every time a certain event occurs, I respond in a particular way. I'd like to stop acting that way, but that event always triggers the same old response in me, and I seem unable to do anything about it.

Vicki wanted her son to stop whining; but whining, we found, was the only way he could reliably get her attention. Vicki agreed to immediately pay attention to him when he approached her in a more agreeable way.

When I saw them a week later, the boy complained, "She still ignores me a lot when I ask for something quietly." At that point, they struck a new bargain: Whenever she ignored him in spite of his quiet request (no fair whispering!), he could immediately say, "You're breaking our deal," and she'd have to pay him a twenty-five-cent fine on the spot. Giving out a lot of quarters was punishing to Vicki, and she quickly started paying more attention to her son. Her long-run reward, which kept her new behavior going, was having a much happier relationship with him.

Punishment is popular for two reasons: It usually gets the other person to *immediately* quit what he or she is doing; and it gives you the good feeling that comes with getting that anger out.

Experimental psychologist Nathan Azrin found that when he shocked a monkey, the monkey learned to pull a string that lowered a ball into the cage so he could belt it one.

A great danger is that the real reason for using punishment is not to change behavior but to even the score. If I'm going to use punishment, so far as I can I want to use it for particular behaviors with particular goals. This means punishing you *when you act in a certain way—not just when I feel angry.*

Sometimes you may push me so far that I really want to lash out. How far you can go with me depends on how tired or upset I am at the time.

I can tell you, "I'm feeling really mad at you right now. You better lay off, because if you push me, you're gonna get it."

When you learn to hear that statement, you need almost never draw my punishment. You learn to back off and give me space when I feel uptight. I must be careful to avoid "crying wolf" and use those signals *only when I really need them.*

Wendy and Jeff developed a signaling system that worked well for them. Wendy never used to let Jeff finish what he was saying. This was a source of constant irritation and they were both unhappy about it. They developed a signal that Jeff could use when he wanted her to stop and listen to him. When he put his left hand over his ear, Wendy was to stop at that point. If she didn't, he was to turn and walk out. This was very effective.

Naturally, if I want you to respect my statement that I can't handle any more of something from you right now, I also have to be willing to respect that kind of statement from you, whether you're a child or an adult. Demanding more from you than I'm willing to give to you breeds resentment.

WARNINGS. If I warn someone that punishment is coming and he or she doesn't lay off, that's warning enough. More than one warning conveys the message that I might not mean it. If you're accustomed to a lot of warning, you know that despite what I say you can do anything you please until you push me to my limit.

Effective punishment is governed by the rule that a specific unwanted behavior will have some unwanted consequence. This rule must be followed *consistently*.

Many chronically anxious people developed much of their anxiety through getting inconsistent punishment when they were children.

If a parent uses punishment, the child needs to know *in advance* exactly what's forbidden and be consistently punished *only for those things* if he or she does them. Children and adults alike can get along pretty well if they know explicitly which actions will bring punishment and which ones won't.

Suppose, by contrast, Lisa gets punished for actions she didn't know would lead to punishment. And suppose that when she does things she's been punished for before, sometimes she's punished and sometimes not. Soon she has no idea what will happen. The whole world begins to seem unpredictable and threatening. Any action might offend someone and bring punishment. The child may begin to feel a diffuse anxiety about doing almost anything.

A good rule of thumb is: Use punishment only when you can't think of anything else at all that might work. Instead of using punishment casually, like aspirin, we'd do better to treat it like a dangerous prescription drug. In his book on behavioral counseling, Krumboltz discusses a number of alternative approaches.

This is not so easy for those of us who grew up on punishment-oriented discipline. I feel sad at the way I sometimes—before I'm even aware of what I'm doing—lash out at others when it does no one any good. Unlearning old habits can be a long, slow process.

Punishment should be appropriate to the importance of the act. It's most effective when it doesn't threaten the person's self-esteem. The purpose is to change behavior, not to assassinate character.

A DISTURBING TREND.   I'm alarmed about an increase in the use of punishment under the name of "aversive control." Many of those who use it ignore or are ignorant of Skinner's careful demonstrations of its harmful side effects. See the movie or read the book *A Clockwork Orange* if you want a taste of aversive control.

Aversive control is such a dangerous tool that I would like to see it used only after all other alternatives have failed, when it is absolutely certain that no other known method will work.

When an aversive program is used—and there is *almost never* valid reason for such a program—the personality of the person who carries it out is of crucial importance. A nurturing and caring person is most likely to carry it out in ways that benefit the client. Naturally, those who are least nurturing and most punitive are the ones who tend to be most enthusiastic about aversive control.

A MORE EFFECTIVE WAY: EXTINCTION

Many unwanted ways of acting persist simply because they keep bringing rewards. Eliminate the rewards and these ways of acting cease. This is called *extinction*. Fear is extinguished when I confront the situation I'm afraid of and nothing bad happens. *Extinction is the basic way to get rid of unwanted behavior.*

If I'm afraid of dogs, and I let myself be around a lot of gentle, friendly dogs, soon I'm not afraid of dogs anymore. My fear of dogs is extinguished. Unless, that is, I'm getting a lot of secondary goodies, like attention, out of being afraid—for example, people soothing me with "Oh, it's all right, it's a good dog, it won't hurt you," etc.

Punishment prevents extinction. Conditions may change so that one of my old behaviors no longer brings rewards. If that way of acting is punished and suppressed, I have no chance to learn that I'll get no more goodies for it, so I keep on wanting to act that way.

Many children wail and fuss when it's time for them to go to bed. The parent need only say, "It's bedtime," and there's a barrage of crying and pleading to stay up "just a little while longer."

Sometimes the parent relents. Other times the child gets dragged into bed, only to begin a new round of crying and screaming. The parent may go in five or six times to tell him or her to go to sleep.

The child is reinforced for causing a scene by attention from the parents. Since the child only sometimes succeeds in getting to stay up or in getting the parent to come into the bedroom, the reinforcement is on an intermittent schedule—the kind that keeps behavior going longest.

In this situation, extinction typically works well. You put the child to bed with a hug and a moment of loving attention that tells him or her you really care, and also explain exactly what you're doing: "I'm going to sit with you and show you how much I love you while you're going to bed. Then I'm going to leave the room, but I'll come back in before I go to bed." After that, until you're on your way to bed, you don't come back in no matter how much fuss the child makes.

This simple extinction procedure works even better if you positively reinforce "going to bed quietly." First thing the next morning, you can tell the child how much you appreciate the way he or she went to bed, and maybe even whip up an especially nice surprise breakfast as a reward.

It's also *extremely important* for you to meet the child's need for attention at other times so that he or she feels loved and cared for. Taking fifteen minutes for a bedtime story each night or a little while each day to listen to your child tell about what's happening with him or her can often work wonders.

Things probably won't be a bed of roses when you first try extinction. In the going-to-bed situation, for instance, even after the bedtime story, conversation, or cuddling, the first two or three nights may be awful, with twice as much wailing as before. Children need to test limits.

When a well-learned action no longer brings the usual rewards, the person temporarily performs the actions more often and more vigorously, in hope of getting results. Outbursts of anger are also common.

If I put a coin in a machine and nothing comes out, I may get mad and pound the machine and call it names; and I may put another coin in and get even madder when there's no result. After that I'm likely to give up and quit putting money in.

With the bedtime scene, after a few heavy nights, things are likely to get better.

If the situation hasn't improved within a few weeks, then something else is going on. Perhaps a real fear of the dark, for instance. Then you might want to talk with a counselor.

If, after the child has learned to go to bed quietly, a relative or friend who doesn't know what's happening comes visiting and gives the kid attention for running a half-hearted version of "I wanna stay up," the whole magnificent act is likely to return in all its splendor. Intermittent reinforcement strikes again!

After a while, even if there hasn't been any reinforcement, a person may try out the old behavior again, to see if it will work now. The food machine was on the blink yesterday, but maybe it'll be okay today.

Psychologists call this eventual reappearance of behavior *spontaneous recovery.* The old way may pop up again several times before the person gives it up for good.

Sometimes, even when I think a behavior has been totally extinguished, there's one final return to it, a farewell orgy with this behavior that I'm about to leave behind. I don't need to think that all is lost, that I'll never be able to wrench myself away. This is not a "hello again," but a goodbye.

Extinction is most effective when, as one way of acting is being extinguished, an alternative way is being strengthened. Eventually the event that used to trigger the old way of acting triggers the new, alternative response instead.

This strengthening of the new behavior works best when it's impossible for the person to do the old thing while doing the new one. For example, the muscular and glandular activities that go with relaxation and those that go with fear *can't occur at the same time*. This procedure is called *substituting an incompatible behavior* for the old behavior.

Since the new behavior is weak, it should be reinforced *every time* it occurs. That way it gets strengthened rapidly while the old behavior is being extinguished.

Eventually the new way of acting becomes strong enough that the stimulus that used to trigger the old way now regularly triggers the new way instead.

One psychologist—I've forgotten who—had a grandmother who did nothing but bitch to all the members of her family about anything and everything. One of the woman's few pleasures was spending time with her family. But since she was such a drag to be around, most of her relatives didn't visit her or invite her over any too often.

The psychologist tried an experiment. First, for a time he recorded how much of her conversation was negative and critical.

Then he began ignoring her critical comments and paying a lot of attention to her other remarks. Whenever she started complaining, he looked out the window, cleaned his fingernails, and acted bored. But whenever she talked more pleasantly, he acted interested. He showed that what she was saying was important to him.

You can guess what happened. Soon she stopped griping and the times they spent together turned into good times.

But the rest of her relatives noticed no change. With them she continued to complain. So the psychologist let them in on what he was doing and asked them to do the same.

Before long the whole family began to notice a transformation in Grandma. She became more pleasant to be around. Everyone began to spend more time with her, and her life became fuller and happier. They had extinguished her critical, complaining behavior and strengthened more gracious behavior to take its place, to the benefit of all.

CONTRACTS FOR CHANGE.   I can make the process just described explicit by telling you what I like and don't like, and how I intend to respond to what you do. A contract for change is a useful way to get this kind of explicitness.

When I want to change some way I act, or want you to change some way you act, I say to you, "I want to change in this way, and you can help me by . . ." or "I want you to change in this way, and I'm willing to help you by . . ."

Then you make your statement in reply, accepting, rejecting, or modifying any part of my statement, and we negotiate until we reach an agreement.

For instance, I say, "I want you to stop digging into your food with your fingers. I'm willing to help you change by saying, 'Please don't' when I see you about to do it." You reply, "That's okay," or "I feel uncomfortable with that. But I hear that you want me to keep my fingers out of the food, and the way I'd like you to help me is by . . ."

The first item we negotiate is: "Do you want to change?" If you say, "No, I really don't want to change," then I make a personal reevaluation: How important is it for me? Can I live with what you do? Perhaps it's more important at some times than at others. I may be able to tolerate your fingers in the food if we're just hanging around, but really want you to keep them out if we're having a formal dinner party.

Our contract also specifies what I give you in return for your changing. Maybe you want me to look over and smile in appreciation when I see that you're using your spoon instead of your fingers. Or maybe that doesn't matter much to you, and there's something else you really want from me. So we each get something that's important to us. Social psychologist Harold H. Kelley has carried out a series of studies that show the great value of this approach.

Some kinds of change really *are* important to me. Other things you do may bug me because of my past conditioning, but may actually cause me no real difficulty. Often I see parents getting bugged at their children's natural curiosity and activity when the children aren't bothering anyone or anything. Equally often I see people get upset at things others do that cause no one any harm but are just expressions of those people's personal styles. Sometimes *I'm* the one who needs to change, by leaving you more space to be yourself.

IV

Awareness and Acceptance

12 *Attention*

Attention is the cutting edge of awareness. What I'm aware of depends not only on what's happening, but also on what I pay attention to.

You can develop the ability to know where your attention is, so that when you want to you can focus it on a particular place and bring it back there when you begin to drift. You can develop a sensitivity to emotionally charged thoughts and subtle tensions in your body that tell you when you're blocking off your awareness of something you may need to pay attention to. You can learn how to avoid being distracted when you genuinely don't want to be.

Gestalt psychologists speak of the "figure-ground phenomenon." I may drive down a street many times and never notice a certain mailbox. It's not important to me. It's part of the background or "ground" against which other things stand out.

Suppose I want to mail a letter. Now the mailbox leaps out at me. Suddenly it is the "figure," and everything else becomes the "ground."

Whatever I focus on becomes the figure, and other things fade into the less clearly defined background. One day I notice the sun, the breeze, the trees, the flowers. The next day I'm so wrapped up in my busy schedule that I'm oblivious to all these things.

✳ *As if for the first time*

As I continue to live on a street and get used to much of what it holds, I begin to see less of what's there. Many things on the street have become background and are no longer foreground "figures" for me.

129

Walk down a street you've never walked down before. Get a sense of how you pay attention to what's there.

Then return to your own old street with this same alertness. Deliberately find things you've never seen before—both large things and small details. Be alert for events you usually don't notice, or skim over. See how much you can discover that you never noticed before, or that you once saw but now no longer see.

===

Perls comments, "The pictures or sounds of the world do not enter us automatically, but *selectively*. We don't see; we *look for, search, scan* for something. We don't hear all the sounds of the world, we *listen*" (IOGP).

My interest creates the meaning I find in a situation. A mother may have a hearing loss and be sleeping three rooms away from her baby, but should the baby make an unusual cry, the mother is likely to awaken.

I can deaden myself by responding automatically instead of listening and searching. I find my aliveness as I learn to choose what I attend to.

Like a lens, my attention can capture just so much of what's going on and no more. I can be like a camera, turned outward toward other people, objects, and events. Or I can turn inward like a microscope, exposing all those dusty places that have so long and cleverly kept themselves hidden, waiting through the years for my maturing eyes and ears to learn to see and hear well enough to discover them.

If I'm doing one thing and my attention wants to go somewhere else, my energy is split three ways. Part of it goes to the task, part of it goes to the other place, and part of it goes into struggling to pay attention here. In a sense, the distraction is actually an *attraction* to the other place.

Unfinished business has a way of demanding my attention even when I've pushed it into a far corner of my awareness. It can lead to agitation, anxiety, and even a feeling of depression that seems to have no explanation.

Sometimes I'm in a situation where I have to keep my attention on what I'm doing even though I don't want to. At such times I can promise myself a definite future time to think about what my mind keeps drifting to, and then *keep that appointment with myself*. Knowing that I'll think about the matter fully then, I'm better able to pay attention now.

SELF-REMEMBERING

Gurdjieff describes a variation of the awareness continuum (see pp.

33–34) that involves silently reporting to myself what *I am doing*. He calls this process "self-remembering." When I remember myself, instead of seeing only a street, I'm involved in what I'm doing, and I'm also aware of myself as the doer (Ouspensky, ISM, 117–22,188).

Usually, the quieter and less distracting the situation, the more easily I can remember myself. It's hard to do amidst a great hubbub.

The divided attention of self-remembering is a way to know where my attention is, so I can attend to what I want to, instead of to whatever hooks my attention at any given moment.

We might call it "two-pointedness." The ability to attend in a two-pointed way is useful in its own right, and also makes it easier to move toward "one-pointedness." Zen masters speak of learning to live in a "one-pointed" way, with total attention on one thing at a time. For instance, when I watch a sunset, I'm just watching the sunset, and not doing anything else.

Our ordinary consciousness, however, is "many-pointed." As I watch the sunset, my attention is captured by first this thought and then that one. I'm lucky if a quarter of the time I'm actually looking at the sky.

With two-pointedness, I detail some of my attention to watch what the rest is doing. At first this noticing of what I'm doing with my attention is difficult. After a while it gets easier, just as learning to drive a car does.

Anything you do can be the content of your self-remembering. Your self-remembering might, for instance, include such awarenesses as "Now I'm thinking that I'm doing this experiment wrong, now I'm wondering if there's any value in this, now I'm tightening my arm and stomach muscles," etc.

As you get better at this, you can be more present with your activity when you're remembering yourself than when your attention is scattered in many different places, though not as present with it as when you're one-pointed.

The *Bhagavad-Gita* calls the process of self-remembering "the Witness." The Witness is that place within me that witnesses my actions, that knows that I'm doing what I'm doing as I do it. In most of us, the Witness is asleep. Through two-pointed attention we can awaken it. As we do, we strengthen our capacity to choose what we pay attention to.

Eventually this becomes more than an exercise. I start to be aware of my times of unawareness. I have an intuitive sense of when I'm focused and when I'm scattered, of when my consciousness is clear and when it's hazy. When I'm hazy, I don't try to do something that requires being clear. Noticing the different qualities and the feeling of my consciousness through the day, or through several days, is very entertaining.

Two-pointed consciousness can be misused. Watching myself as I do what I do can be a way of keeping myself from living fully—a way of keeping distant from my own experience.

I can be aware of myself without feeling that I'm looking on from the outside. I can look at what I do from the inside, from the middle of my experience. This was Zorba's way—living his fullness of love and laughter, and sometimes pain and sorrow. He was totally involved in his experience, yet almost always took a moment to notice where he was and shake his head in wonder at it all.

ATTENTION AND DISTRACTION

Distraction sometimes seems almost a law of life, doesn't it? The other day on my way home, I was thinking, "When I get home, I really want to go sit by the creek awhile and get myself together."

When I got home, I got caught up in what the people in my house were doing.

Twenty minutes later I remembered, "This isn't what I want to be doing now!" I pulled myself away and finally made it out the door and down to the creek.

I used to be pretty poor at paying attention to people when they talked with me. Time after time I'd realize that my mind had drifted away. Every couple of minutes I'd have to ask the other person to repeat something. If I didn't want to ask for a recap, I had to reconcile myself to missing part of what was said and try to "fake it" to continue the conversation.

When my attention is scattered, *I don't give myself the choice* of really listening carefully to the other person, even when that person is saying something I think is really important.

Even now I'm sometimes surprised at how much I've missed when I listen to a tape recording of a conversation between another person and me. I'm not always an accurate judge of how well I'm paying attention. If I want to make sure I'm hearing you, or that I'm being heard, I'd better doublecheck.

I want to feel free to ask you to repeat what you said if I didn't quite get it. I'm not always interested in what you're saying, but when I am, I want to make sure I hear you. And I want you to ask me to recap if you didn't quite get what I said. If we agree on these two things, we'll more often hear each other.

Even when we are distracted, we usually allow our attention to be batted around.

When I have something to gain, I have little trouble paying attention. Observe yourself: How easily are you distracted from an unpleasant task? From an enjoyable one?

One morning I was giving an exam. It was an important test to the students who were taking it. No sooner did we begin than some workmen started drilling outside, and kept it up for the whole exam period. Many students complained about the noise, so we gave the test again under quieter conditions.

There was no significant difference between the two test scores for any student. The noise had claimed a good part of my attention. But even though the students were disturbed by the noise, they were not distracted. The test was too important to them to let that happen.

When I'm clumsy, when I knock against something or break something, or hurt myself or say something stupid, almost always my attention is somewhere else.

A while back a ladder collapsed beneath me and I fell and broke my foot. I was aware as I was falling that my mind had been off wandering before I fell.

When I chop wood, I can easily see where my attention is. When I was splitting firewood yesterday, part of the time my attention was focused clearly on what I was doing. As I sat a log on end, I saw its size, its shape, its color, and the lichen growing on it. As I raised and swung the axe, I felt balanced and in tune with my movement. At those moments, every cut was straight and true.

Other times my attention wandered. Thoughts of this and that came drifting through my mind. Then I often split off just a piece of bark, or the axe twisted in my hand and I got no cut at all. No more than half my swings were good ones.

Here's a technique for calming and focusing your attention when you feel scattered or hurried:

✳ Just one thing at a time

Sometimes I notice that I'm hurrying, concerned to get on to the next thing, and not here with what I'm doing now. At such times, my mind and body are tense.

When I realize that I'm doing that, I stop what I'm doing and breathe deeply and slowly a few times.

Then I return to what I was doing but allow myself only one movement at a time. For instance, I won't both bend down and reach for something at the same time. I bend down, stop for an instant, then reach out. If it takes two hands, I reach with first one hand, then the other.

With my momentary stop after each movement, to see and feel where I am and note the next thing I'm going to do, I stop my hurried, automatic way of acting.

Doing things this way may feel strange to you at first, but the strangeness wears off as you learn to focus your attention on each moment of what you do as you do it.

Try this. Get up and do one simple thing, like taking something out of your pocket. Do this in your usual way and at your usual pace.

Now review in your mind what you just did.

Then perform exactly the same sequence of actions over again, *just one thing at a time.*

I've found it useful to do "just one thing at a time" with certain routine tasks, like unlocking and opening a door. By the time I've finished what I'm doing, my attention is right here in this moment, I'm no longer trying to get to what comes next. I don't feel hurried anymore.

Another way I can center myself is by focusing my "bare attention" on the sensations in my body. I can sense my body—and especially my legs and feet—as I move and stand, and move *consciously*, like a dancer. When I notice that my attention has wandered, I bring it back to my sensations. The ancient Chinese moving meditation called Tai Chi, now taught in many parts of the United States, involves this way of focusing attention. The same is true of hatha yoga when it's done slowly and consciously, feeling fully the stretching in each muscle. I can take the feeling hatha yoga gives me into other events of my day.

BOREDOM

Boredom is a way I deaden my life. It's a way I can torture and ultimately kill myself.

You've probably known old people who retired and died not long afterward, or died almost immediately after their spouses died. Other old people find interests that nourish and sustain them.

I feel bored when I try to pay attention to something I'm not interested in.

But whenever I feel bored, I can find something in the situation that interests me, I can change what's happening, I can drift off into the more interesting world of my own thoughts and fantasies, or I can get up and go. I don't have to poison myself by staying bored.

✳ What's missing?

Next time you feel bored, close your eyes and go into fantasy. In your mind, go somewhere you'd like to be right now.

Then open your eyes and come back from that somewhere. Look and listen here. Now close your eyes again, return to your fantasy, and look and listen there. Then come back again.

What did you find in your fantasy that's missing in your present event? Can you find any ways to bring the aliveness you found there back here? (Adapted from Perls)

When you and I are talking, if I'm not interested in what's happening, I can change it.

I do you no favor by pretending that I'm interested in what you're saying when I'm not. That poisons both of us. I'm listening because I think I "should," not because I want to. I feel dead or resentful as I listen, and you and I make little contact.

If I'm bored, you're most likely not so interested either. We can probably find something else to do or talk about that we'd both prefer. I can say, "I'm not with this right now. Let's talk about something I feel involved in too." Or I can suggest doing something else entirely.

If you allow me space to give you that kind of feedback, as long as I do it in a way that shows you that I care about you and am not criticizing you, we can have many good times with each other. If, in reply to my telling you I'm bored, you say, "You don't care about me, because you're bored with what I'm saying," you're telling me you don't want to know when I'm interested and when I'm not, so we'll probably often feel dead when we're together. Or you may be telling me you don't feel my caring for you, so I need to let you know I care.

In a group, when I say I'm bored, other people can say how they feel too. If enough of us are bored, we can all do something else. If I'm the only one, or almost the only one, then I find a way to enjoy some aspect of what's going on or I leave.

When I find myself in a dull meeting, I often listen to the voices, tune into each person's way of being there, and watch what happens in the group. There's always much more happening when people interact than just the content of the conversation.

Some things by their nature grab my interest more than others do. Yet I can interest myself more or less in anything or anybody.

Orage writes, "Who can read and understand everything about one person has the key to the knowledge of the race. Thus, to be bored by anybody is to fail to look for interest in him" (EA, 69).

People who are not like those I usually spend my time with are especially interesting to me when I let them be.

As I develop my ability to be interested in wherever I am and whomever I'm with, I'm less at the mercy of circumstance. The better I can entertain myself, the less I need to be entertained.

WE ALL NEED ATTENTION

Throughout our lives, we all need attention. And we need a lot of it when we're very young. Research shows that infants who don't get enough attention don't develop normally.

Children and adults alike usually prefer certain kinds of attention to others. Attention given in warmth and love and caring is best. But if a person can't get that, he or she may learn to do whatever will get a rise out of you. People who don't get enough attention often prefer unfriendly attention to no attention at all.

If you and I are in relationship, I may want you to pay attention to something that's important to me, even though it doesn't matter much to you.

But you forget. I feel angry, but you think I'm being unreasonable in wanting you to consider the matter important just because I do. Actually, I'm angry because you *forgot*. That's a way of not paying attention to me. If you often forget, you're telling me I'm not so important to you.

Making others invisible is a way of avoiding, of not dealing with, of putting other people down. It's a way of saying, "You're not important."

We often do this to children. A small girl walks into the store to buy something. Adults come in after her and get waited on while she's still standing there. This says to her, "You're not important. You don't matter." This is an issue many racial and ethnic minorities know all too well.

When I make you invisible, I'm telling you that you're nobody. That's a strong statement. When I acknowledge you and share a moment with you in some kind of exchange, I'm telling you you're important. I'm telling you I care.

13 This Time, This Place

Tanzan and Ekido were once traveling together down a muddy road. . . .

Coming around a bend, they met a lovely girl in a silk kimono and sash, unable to cross the intersection.

"Come on, girl," said Tanzan at once [and] carried her over the mud.

Ekido did not speak again until that night. . . . Then he no longer could restrain himself. "We monks don't go near females," he told Tanzan. . . . "Why did you do that?"

"I left the girl there," said Tanzan. "Are you still carrying her?" (Reps, 18).

When my wife and I first got married, we had some trouble in communication. She took many of my statements to mean what her former husband would have meant by them.

With some hard work, we realized that this was what was happening. She was still carrying her former husband, much as Ekido carried the girl all day.

Remember those lines Joan Baez sings? "Yesterday is gone, and tomorrow is blind; I live one day at a time."

Only this moment exists. The future and the past are dreams. Memory is a collection of old phonograph records and photographs.

The smell of a street I walked along five years ago, the taste and texture of a taco I bought at a vendor's stand—these things are vivid in my mind as I remember them, but they're not like the smells and tastes and touches I experience now.

When are you more alive? When you feel the breeze on your cheek, hear the wind through the trees, feel the kiss of warm lips on yours? Or when you drift among memories and anticipations of these things?

When you lose yourself in yesterdays and tomorrows, what happens then to your todays?

If instead of being here, I'm lost in dreams of what might be or might have been, I never feel quite satisfied. The food is never *quite* good enough, and I never get quite enough to eat. I can glut myself on every sensual gratification and every kind of entertainment, and it's never enough. I keep wanting *more*.

When I'm really here, even a small event can delight me and leave me feeling filled.

My present includes my remembering of many yesterdays. These are my roots. I draw on them for the lessons they hold and the good feelings I can find there. A good storyteller is full of yesterdays, and tells of them with such vitality that they come alive today.

My thoughts about tomorrow give me a sense of my directions and my expectations. Everyone needs some direction. Even learning to be here with myself and my experience without going anywhere can be a direction.

Good living in the now includes setting things up for good nows in the future. When I'm stuck in living *only* in the now, I'm not using what I learned in my past, and I'm not taking stock of where I am today in relation to where I want to be tomorrow. Taking stock of what I need to do for myself now is necessary if I'm going to do any planning for tomorrow.

My present moment is the *focal point* of past and future. It's the expression of all that has happened, and the place where I must apply my energy to affect what will be. Many of my memories of yesterday and thoughts about tomorrow have some message and meaning for my life in this moment.

At the same time, I want to be careful to avoid confusing my present event with yesterdays that are in some way similar to it.

THE PAST

"By trying to understand everything in terms of memory, the past, and words, we have . . . had our noses in the guidebook for most of our lives, and have never looked at the view," writes Alan Watts (WI, 99–100).

"What I said yesterday," Gandhi declared, "you can't go by. It's what I say today."

William Glasser notes that in schools, mental hospitals, jails, and juvenile homes, we often imprison people in their pasts. Everyone who works with a given person expects that person to act as the case history described him or her. Caught in those expectations, the person is indeed likely to act that way. So Glasser refuses to read case histories, and works in those areas where the person shows strength and promise.

My own experience is that most of the information that has been compiled about a person tells me almost nothing about his or her capacity to change. Yet our institutions make a fetish of collecting such information. The "historical approach" is sadly defective—and often totally mistaken—as a guide to understanding present and future behavior.

In many ways, I am a very different person now than I was ten years ago. I'm glad I'm not imprisoned in people's conceptions of me as I was then. There *are* specific incidents in my past that changed my life in important ways. But no one who has been collecting data about me knows which personal events and subjective experiences are the crucial ones.

In our relationships with each other, we can often and easily lock ourselves into the past.

I may have felt hurt or belittled by something you once did and I continue to feel angry with you even though you mean well now. Even though I've told you how I felt, I refuse to let the past event be past. I continue to blame you for it. In return, *you* get angry with *me* for continuing to blame you. The cycles of hurt and counterhurt, attack and counterattack, keep going.

By staying angry, I can keep you feeling guilty. This gives me a tool to control you. Every time I feel as though I might be losing with you in some way, I drag out what happened in the past. "Remember when you were so bad? Remember that? I remember it too. Don't think for a moment that I've forgotten it."

Out of your guilt, you say, "Oh, okay. I'll do what you say." But inside, you resent me, and our relationship stays closed and manipulative. So we both lose.

If you've done something that I still have strong feelings about, we need to deal with that unfinished business. I need to explicitly share how I feel with you without attacking you, and we need to deal with that and with whatever feelings you have about the matter until we reach an understanding.

Many cycles of blame and counterblame, hurt and counterhurt, are started by trivial events that of themselves cause us no real harm. Once I see the cycle, I can step outside it by stopping what I'm doing to keep it going, and let the other person know I'm hearing how he or she feels.

Some people spend years obsessed with things they did long ago. Their past mistakes dominate their present lives.

When I find myself dwelling on some past event, I wonder what unfinished thoughts and feelings I pushed out of my awareness at the time of the event. What valuable messages have those thoughts and feelings carried all these years, waiting for me to listen to them?

Beyond that, I learn from what I did that I want to do certain things again and not others.

We all make mistakes: we all act in ways that turn out badly. Mistakes result from bad information, faulty decision-making, or chance.

Driving along a road, I come to a fork. The right fork looks more interesting than the left one, so I take it. Five miles later, the road ends, and I have to go back and take the other fork. I did what made sense to me at the time, given the knowledge and understanding I had. With the same information, I'd do the same thing again.

The trouble comes when I feel that I'm "bad" and "wrong" and beat myself over the head for my mistake. A mistake is something to learn from—not an excuse for blaming and fault-finding.

When I feel upset about my mistakes, I'm more likely to make other mistakes. I'm also more likely to convince myself that certain things I've done weren't mistakes at all, even though they really were. That leaves me with poorer information to base future actions on.

My friend Antonio was a priest in Italy at a time when priests did not readily leave the church and marriage for priests was not even being considered. Antonio staged a false death, disappeared, and married the woman he loved.

Afterward he began to feel guilty and anxious about "what he had done to" the church, his family, and his friends. His guilt and anxiety worked on him and eventually poisoned his marriage. To punish himself for what he had done, he made many mistakes about things that were important to him. Two children later, he and his wife were divorced.

Antonio's snowball of anxiety, guilt, and mistakes threatened to destroy him. Recently, he has begun to drop his obsession with his past mistakes and develop a more positive attitude toward life. If he can get to the point where he no longer uses his past to punish himself in the present, he'll have a chance to live the rest of his life in a way he can feel good with.

An error or mistake is different from wrongdoing. Wrongdoing is when I act contrary to the way I know will be good for me or for you. Maybe it seems too hard to do what I know I need to do, so I don't bother. I mess myself up; I do myself wrong. Or I do something that messes you up, knowing somewhere inside me that I'm doing you wrong.

THE FUTURE

"A man in the house is worth two in the street," a love of mine once said. "No day comes back again. One inch of time is worth a foot of jade," wrote Zen Master Takuan.

Yet how many people spend almost their whole lives getting ready to put on their performances, instead of being here!

Another way of living is to let myself arrive here *first*. "Yes—here I am." *Now* I ask myself what I'm ready to do from where I am, rather than asking myself to be ready before I arrive.

If I must prepare for every little event, I have no spontaneity when it comes. I don't want to program myself so completely into my expected future that I can't respond creatively when things don't happen as I thought they would.

✳ No getting ready

Right now, ask yourself, "What can I do for myself that doesn't require any getting ready?"

You can get ready to the extent of putting on your shoes and socks, but no more than that. Or if you don't want to do even that, find something you can do to be good to yourself starting just as you are right now. See if you can think of several alternatives. Then do one of them.

If you think you'll be happy only when you achieve this or that, you may well wait forever. People who only look forward to the future hardly ever catch up with it. Somehow, when "later" comes, the good times it promised too often seem to be waiting in another "later" farther on.

Every tomorrow becomes today. If I'm looking at tomorrow, I may not see today when it gets here. I can live the way I want to live tomorrow only if I start to live that way today.

One way to start being here in each moment of my life is by developing a clear awareness of how my mind wanders from the here and now. When, moment by moment, I'm fully aware of what I'm doing that keeps me from being here, I'm here.

✳ I would live in today if . . .

This is an exercise to get in touch with how you keep yourself from doing what you want to do for yourself now. For instance, "If it weren't for my family, I'd . . ."

You and a partner (who, let's say, is a female) and two or three other people get together in a group. Your partner will talk to all of you as though you were members of her family, or other people who have an important influence on her. She assigns a role to each of you. You don't make any comments.

She says to each of you, "I would live in today if you would . . ." and finishes the sentence in a way that fits the relationship between you and her. She includes herself as one of the people she makes this statement to.

Alternatively, you can do this by yourself in your imagination or by writing out your statements.

My present fantasies about my future may not fit who I am when the future comes.

George grew up in a Navy family and was going to be a Navy pilot. His history gave him his fantasy of his future. He took this expectation with him through his childhood, his young adulthood, and the war in Vietnam.

He felt strongly that the Vietnam War was wrong and immoral, and also felt strongly that he had to become a Navy pilot. He entered the Naval Academy and began his training.

About halfway through, he had a breakdown. As he experienced his fantasy of being a Navy pilot coming true, he found that it didn't fit who he was then. He ultimately left Navy training, and is still working out some of his guilt feelings about doing that.

If my future is to nourish me, it has to grow out of what's happening with me now, and not only out of the programs and scripts I carry with me from my past.

Anxiety and the future

One way we trick ourselves into leaving the here and now is by pretending that we can do something about future events that we can't actually affect. Perls says,

> . . . anxiety is the gap between the *now* and the then. If you are in the now, you can't be anxious, because the excitement flows immediately into ongoing spontaneous activity. . . .
>
> . . . Usually, the anxiety is . . . concerned with the role we want to play. . . . "Will I get my approval?" "Will I get applause, or

will I get rotten eggs?" . . . To *realize* that [the rotten eggs are] not a catastrophe, but just an unpleasantness, is . . . part of waking up. (GTV, 3, 30–31)

When I feel anxious and I can't do anything about what's going to happen, I can take care of myself by becoming aware of what I'm doing.

If I'm anxious about getting up and talking before a group in three minutes, I can pay attention to how I experience that anxiety *now* in my breathing, my heartbeat, my stomach, my hands, my jaw, and my shoulders. As I become interested in those events, I'm likely to become less anxious.

 Stop!

Right now, *freeze—don't move your body*. In your frozen position, tune into the sensations in your body. Hold your position, even if you feel uncomfortable, until you check out all the events in your body you're aware of. "Right now I'm experiencing . . ."

Now move into a position that feels more comfortable. Be aware of what you experience as you do.

The way to be here is not to try to push the future out of your mind, but to pay attention to what's happening now. Trying not to think about the future is still thinking about the future. When I'm totally involved in this instant, time does not exist. There's only this moment, and now has no duration.

Krishnamurti comments, "Eternity is not continuity. That which endures is not eternal. Eternity is in the moment. Eternity is in the now" (FLF, 286).

Hurrying and slowing down

If I'm hurrying to get *there*, I'm not being *here*. My mind is filled with where I'm going, and I'm blind to where I am.

My hurried state exists not only in my mind, but in my body too—in my nerves and glandular secretions. So when I get where I'm going, I'll still feel hurried, and I won't be likely to function at my best.

Any time I'm anxious to get on to what's next, I'm not here in what

I'm doing now. When I feel a yearning to "move on," I first check to see whether there's something happening here that I'm not comfortable about—something that "moving on" will help me avoid.

By synchronizing your breathing with your walking, you can center yourself while you're carrying out your daily affairs. This is a valuable technique for getting out of your head and into what's happening around you. *Even while you're getting there, you can be here.*

✳ Walking and breathing

When you notice that you're hurrying, stop. Close your eyes and take one full breath—one slow complete cycle of inhaling and exhaling. Then begin to walk again, according to one of the following patterns. (A "full step" is a step with the left foot and a step with the right foot, so that in four full steps each foot touches the ground four times. We could call this eight half-steps.)

For walking at moderate speed: Take four full steps with each incoming breath, and four full steps with each outgoing breath. Pay careful attention to staying with this pattern.

For wandering slowly along and really seeing what's around you: Take two full steps with each incoming breath, and two with each outgoing breath. This will really slow you down.

For getting somewhere fast: Take three full steps with each incoming breath, and five full steps with each outgoing breath, regulating the amount of air you breathe in and out to fit this rhythm. This walk comes from Bali. It's a vigorous rhythm that will let you cover a lot of territory fast, while staying in touch with yourself and your surroundings.

Take a few minutes to try each of these walks right now.

In coordinating your walking and breathing, you need not limit yourself to the walking patterns described here. Shorter people sometimes find that three full steps suit them better than four. Find a comfortable rhythm that suits you. The main thing is to keep your walking and breathing synchronized. Each time you notice that they're not together anymore, stop completely and start off again with them together.

These ways of walking may help you appreciate Thoreau's comment:

A broad margin of leisure is as beautiful in a man's life as in a book . . . Nature never makes haste; her systems revolve at an even pace. The buds swell imperceptively, without hurry and confusion. . . .

Men say that a stitch in time saves nine, and so they take a thousand stitches today to save nine tomorrow. (From Chapter 8)

THE NOW

A man who had worked hard to become an attorney decided to run for city council. In talking among family and friends, his wife began introducing him as "Mr. Mayor," although he hadn't yet even been elected to the city council. When he objected, she dismissed his objection with "Well, you will be."

She never said, "Now is okay. What you're doing now is enough." She was always looking for the next place. She didn't deal with what *is*, and *didn't recognize* that she had the present and future mixed up.

When we don't realize that we're not in the present, we *may not have our present experience available to us.*

George was having trouble with his colleagues in a training program. Over and over he tried to assume roles of authority that fit his past but did not fit this situation of working with his peers. He acted like the boss and expected the others to act like subordinates, even though they were all equal in authority.

When he was forced to recognize what he was doing, he said, "Well, I need to see if I can stop being ambitious," and immediately looked forward to doing something in the *future*. He was *going to* stop being ambitious.

He *would not focus on* his *present* behavior—on what he was doing with himself and his peers right then in that training program. That left most of his present unavailable to his awareness.

This time (now) and this place (here) is the *only* time when and the *only* place where I can act. Even remembering the past and anticipating the future are *acts in the present*.

Among the ways I keep out of touch with what's happening here and now is naming. Once named, a thing need not be looked at anymore. It's got its category and that's that.

If something doesn't have a name, I have a harder time pretending I know what it is. I have to look at it to find out. Alfred North Whitehead comments, "In the Garden of Eden, Adam saw the animals before he named them; in the traditional system [of education] children named the animals before they saw them" (quoted in Watts, WI, 100).

Screening everything through my labels, categories, and classifications can be a way for me to avoid direct contact with experiences I feel afraid of.

Sometimes names and labels are useful. Other times I do better to forget the category, and experience the individual object or event as fully as I can. As Watts put it, "A menu is very useful, but it is no substitute for the dinner" (WI, 92).

When I get in touch with any way I feel—even if it's discomfort or fear or apprehension—I find richness there. I discover more of who I am.

One way I get into the now when I'm out of it is to find a way for my present situation to be interesting enough that I feel alive here. I ask myself, what here can I enjoy or learn from?

When I talk with another person, I sometimes pay attention to the effect of what I'm saying. Does it bring the two of us more fully into what's happening with us now, or does it take us into the there and then? If we're going into there and then, is that all right with me in this situation?

My times when I'm completely here are beautiful to me. At such times, there's nothing in my mind about what I've left undone—about what I need to get done to be on top of things. At those moments I'm not "on top of things"—neither am I "behind things." I'm just *with* things, however they are.

14 *Expectation and Uncertainty*

"But if I live in just the HERE & NOW won't there be chaos? . . . What if somebody wants to make an appointment to see me 3 weeks from now?"

". . . Write it down. That's HERE & NOW."

"Well, what happens 3 weeks from now?"

"3 weeks from NOW there's that appointment. Then: that is HERE & NOW." (Ram Dass and Lama Foundation BHN, Pt. 2; 23)

When you want to see me, I have some choices. I can make the appointment or not; I can keep it or not; if I'm not going to keep it, I can inform you or not.

Whatever I do, I can ask myself this: How much am I working from what I want to do, and how much from expectations of what others want me to do?

When you call me on the phone, you expect me to answer. If I don't answer and you know I'm home, you might feel rejected. Actually I might not want to talk to anyone. If we agree that it's okay to ignore the phone, both you and I can feel free to answer or not.

Some people get upset when I ignore a ringing phone. They look at me as though *something were wrong*. When I don't meet their expectations in this or other ways, they feel threatened—suddenly I seem to have some new kind of magic.

Some people answer the phone no matter what's going on. Two people are making love, the phone rings, and one of them struggles up to answer it.

When my phone is ringing, someone is making a demand on me. When I go along with demands that don't fit where I am, I'm not taking care of myself.

147

An expectation is a prediction that I think will probably come true. I expect that the bus will come, and that turning on the stove will make the water in the kettle boil.

Expectations rest on history. I've watched water come to a boil a thousand times. I've got pretty solid information about the boiling point. If I go up 10,000 feet, however, the water-boiling process changes, and so do my expectations about it.

My expectations also change when I go inside myself 10,000 feet. As I come to know my inner world, doors I didn't know existed open. The deeper inside myself I go, the less my actions will be as they were before I started on my journey.

People are almost sure to do some things the way I think they will. The grocer will certainly be willing to sell me a loaf of bread. As he gives me the bread and I pay him, we both fulfill each other's historical expectations.

In other cases I might have a hope, but not an expectation. A friend might tell me, "Maybe I'll have time to drop by this afternoon and maybe not."

But if she tells me, "I'll be there around five," and then doesn't come, I have an expectation that doesn't pan out. I may feel upset. With reason. If I'd known she wasn't going to come, I might have done something else I can't do now. We expect each other to do what we say we will.

If I feel upset because she didn't show up, I can tell her so, rather than just burning inside. Then I feel better, and she finds out what's happening with me as a result of what she did.

It's easy to keep on living in our expectations instead of in what happens. Dieters often do this. Suppose I expected to lose a certain number of pounds this week. I didn't fulfill that goal and feel terribly disappointed, even though I may actually have lost some weight. Out of my disappointment, I get anxious about not meeting my expectations. Out of my anxiety, I eat.

This kind of circle occurs in any area where my goals are too high and/or I have no alternative expectations available.

"Tomorrow I'm going to look for a job." Tomorrow comes, and for whatever reason, I don't. I'm so disappointed in myself and so busy defending my not having looked for a job that I get anxious and depressed. My energy goes into coping with my anxiety and depression, and isn't available to help me look for a job then either.

The more I put myself down for not living up to my expectations, the less likely those expectations are to be fruitful for me.

As long as I've moved in the direction I wanted to move in, even if only a little bit, that's progress.

I like to make few promises, and to keep the promises I make. My life is simpler when I do what I say I will.

It's especially important to keep promises to children. A small child just doesn't understand when I say that I'll take him or her to the zoo and then don't.

"But you promised . . ."

I can make up for my broken promise by going to the zoo next week. But if I often break my promises and don't make up for them, I can kill a child's aliveness. Why hope for something if it never happens? When I break a promise to a child, I teach him that he can't trust me and can't trust the world. I also teach him how to hedge his own promises, and wiggle out of his own commitments.

"I want to do it for you, and *if* everything works out, we will" is something children can understand. If not, they need to learn. And I'll do well to see that things don't "not work out" too often.

Think about how you feel even now, as an adult, when someone breaks a promise that's important to you.

With one woman I loved, I never knew whether she'd do what she said she would. When she lived in another town, every day for a week she said on the phone, "I'm coming to stay with you tomorrow," and then didn't come. After a few days I was climbing the walls.

I ran all kinds of trips: "She doesn't love me at all," and "I must be worthless," and "I want her so much," and "I hate her guts!" and "How can I be mad at her when she's so confused and unhappy?"

I was too afraid of losing her to make clear, explicit demands. (As I've discovered since then, my payoff for not making clear demands is that I never have to confront whether or not you'll meet my demands. If I'm scaring myself that you won't, I don't make the demands. But when I don't make my demands clear, I seldom get what I want. You never hear exactly what I'm asking and I never really hear your response.)

That week of broken promises taught me a lot about expectations, and about living with what happens. After a while I just sat looking at the sunsets. Whatever else happened, they were still beautiful.

I wasn't avoiding my intense disappointment, but I didn't *need* it to feel alive. Whenever I feel let-down, cheated, or misunderstood, I want to deal with the situation that's the root of those feelings. When there's nothing I can do, or am willing to do, I won't deny my feelings and say, "I'm not really disappointed." My disappointment is deep. But I don't need to hang on to it. Now, here's the sunset. . . .

Both you and I will always have some unmet expectations. I can accept what comes—"This is what's happening now"—feel however I feel about it, and go on from here.

I live in a fuller and richer world when I'm willing to enjoy the experiences that come, no matter what I was expecting. A *parallel experience* is something like the one I wanted, but not quite the same. A *counter experience* is very different, or even opposite to, what I expected. I can even seek out and create parallel and counter experiences instead of always doing the same kind of thing. In so doing, I avoid the deadliness of owning the same package of plans and expectations year after year. Instead of confining myself to a single narrow path, I can be open to many possibilities.

Ken Keyes, Jr., speaks of *addictions.* When I set *conditions* that others must meet, or *requirements* that things be a certain way in order to let myself feel happy, I am addicted. I have been conditioned, or through my repeated choices have conditioned myself, to insist that things must be "this certain way." I don't have to be that hard on myself. When I free myself from an addiction by dropping my requirement that things be a certain way, I open myself to parallel and counter experiences. I become able to enjoy myself in a wider range of situations.

The less I'm locked into my expectations, the more I'm available and alive to whatever happens, so the simplest events can be a source of joy and wonder.

Your expectations and mine

Sometimes I meet a person who seems interesting to me and interested in me. He or she says, "Let's get together sometime." I reply, "When?" If the person is evasive and says, "Well, sometime," or something else that suggests that his or her interest is only lukewarm, I back off. But if the person says, "Let's look at the calendar," or something similar, I'm willing to go with it.

When someone doesn't follow through on a commitment he or she has made to me, there's a piece of unfinished business in my mind. If the matter is unimportant, I throw it in the garbage can with all those other unfinished events that could clutter up my life if I let them. The garbage can is another way to finish them. If the matter is important, I find out what's happening with the other person, and do something to finish what needs to be finished.

Trust is a kind of expectation. We usually use the word to mean feeling confident that others won't act in ways that will hurt us, or hurt someone or something we care about. Life based on a network of mutual trust and caring is fundamentally different from life based on mutual mistrust and suspicion.

If you have a hard time trusting other people, probably your first step toward developing your ability to trust is *becoming trustworthy.* If you can't be trusted, and don't trust yourself, you won't trust others. As you learn to trust yourself, you'll become able to trust me, and better able to tell when you can trust me and when you can't.

I've found only one thing I can always trust another person to do: namely, *to do what seems to that person to be in his or her interest at the time*. The more I know about what is important to you, the more I know about what I can trust you to do.

According to one of Perls' best-known statements, I don't exist to fulfill your expectations, and you don't exist to fulfill mine" (GTV, 4).

I've seen people take those lines and blow their lives apart. It's easy to remember the first half of that comment and forget the second half. When misread this way, it goes, "I don't want you to expect from me, but I'm going to keep on expecting from you. I don't want to buy your trip, but I want you to buy mine."

A couple comes to me for counseling. The woman is extremely ambitious. She and her husband have worked hard to achieve their status and possessions. She has endless expectations for her husband, and expects him to live up to them.

But the man is changing. He says, "I'm not here to live up to your expectations," and walks out.

He expects her to go into a less striving way of life, but never tells her that. If he did, they might be able to negotiate their differences. Since there's no clear communication, the husband's "I'm not here to live up to your expectations" becomes a stopper—because he forgets that she's not here to live up to his.

If you and I want a relationship, we've got to deal with the expectations we both have and the places we're both unwilling to be bound by expectations. If we're only talking about what *I* want, we're stopped. Our relationship has nowhere to go.

It's important that the expectations in a relationship be explicit. "But you should *know* what I want" just doesn't make it.

✱ *I can give you; I want from you*

In a group, with everyone standing, each person seeks out each other person in the group for a brief interchange of not more than a couple of minutes. The two of you look silently at each other for a moment, and then each of you says to the other, "I can give you. . . ," and "I want from you . . ." Then you each find another person to do the same thing with.

When all the pairing off is completed, each of you discusses with the rest of the group the kinds of expectations you found you were placing on yourself and on other people, the kinds of expectations that others most typically placed on you, and what you do that encourages those kinds of experiences.

You can do this silently to yourself with people you meet in your everyday life.

When I act in a way that doesn't fit someone's expectations of me, that person may feel uncomfortable: "Can I trust you at all?"

I've met women seeking to develop their feminine identity who expect me to be always strong and "masculine," and feel uneasy if I move into one of my gentler and more receptive places. Similarly, many men feel threatened when a woman starts feeling strong and asserting herself by going after what she wants.

I value being able to be who I am with another person—confused and vulnerable, decisive and strong, or whatever. I sometimes seem inconsistent to others as I express different sides of who I am. The more you and I allow each other that inconsistency, without insisting that the other behave in predictable ways, the more room we have to change and grow, and the more deeply we can understand each other.

When I do what you expect, I may do it because you want me to or because I want to.

If you're my boss, you may want me to humble myself before you.

If you leave me other options, I can explore what happens in our relationship when I act in one of those other ways, even though you'd rather have me eat crow.

But perhaps the only response you'll accept from me is "Yes, boss." When I act any other way, you punish me or threaten to fire me. In order to survive, I may choose to act toward you in the way you're asking for. When I do, I want to recognize exactly how I'm pretending to be someone I'm not.

WORRYING AND WISHING

Catastrophic expectations

When something is important to you or me, and we don't know what will happen, fearful fantasies about it can come to dominate our minds.

I've seen it happen in myself. I become blind to what's happening in me and around me now. I touch the world only through the screen of worry that I weave around me. Perls calls this a *catastrophic expectation.*

"My love has had enough of me, and I'll be left alone. No one will ever love a wretch like me again!"

"My son has surely fallen in the street and been run over. And I'm such a rotten parent that even if he lives, he'll grow up to lead a miserable, unhappy life."

"I'm sure to lose my job. No one will ever hire me again."

There we sit, brooding on our morbid thoughts like a stewing hen on rotten eggs.

I remember times when I did little more than sit around waiting tensely for a letter or for the telephone to ring. That guaranteed that I stayed miserable, as my mind kept spinning in the vortex it was caught up in. My catastrophic expectation was a way I stopped myself from moving.

Instead of immobilizing myself, I can find ways to be alive. Even when I'm waiting for a letter or a call, I can be where I can get to the mailbox or answer the phone and still do something I enjoy doing.

A person who expects the worst can bring on the very thing he or she fears.

If a fantasied catastrophe dominates my mind, I have less attention for what's going on right now, so probably I'll act more stupidly than if I paid attention to what's actually happening.

And since people tend to act toward you in the way that you expect them to, show a person you expect the worst and you just might get it. (Show people you expect the best from them and you just might get that too.)

The person who goes in for a job interview with a sense of his or her own competence is apt to communicate that. He or she is more likely to get the job than someone with identical skills who doesn't expect to get it. It's like living out one's history of that moment. Say I have a history of being unsuccessful in interviews. I go in for another interview, and sure enough—look what I do for me!

Try to touch your fantasied catastrophe.
Try to touch the chair you're sitting on. What's the difference?
What does that tell you?

Bertrand Russell writes, "Both happiness and efficiency can be increased by . . . [thinking] about a matter adequately at the right time rather than inadequately at all times. When a difficult . . . decision has to be reached, . . . give the matter your best thought and make your decision; having made the decision, do not revise it unless some new fact comes to your knowledge" (72).

Russell notes that we often try to escape from worrisome matters by pushing them out of our minds and avoiding them entirely. That doesn't work. The matter's always waiting there to haunt us.

Russell suggests a different approach. Go into the very heart of your worry. Run your worst fear inside your head until you're sick of it. Imagine that the worst that could happen is happening.

When I squarely face the worst that could happen in a situation, I'm either prepared for whatever happens or I find that my "disaster" is not so overwhelming. Some of my "catastrophes" turn out to be strokes of good luck. They open new possibilities and new directions.

With the Sufi Attar, we can remember this tale:

A powerful king . . . one day felt himself confused and called the sages to him.

He said:

". . . Something impels me to look for a certain ring, one that will enable me to stabilize my state.

". . . And this ring must be one which, when I am unhappy, will make me joyful. At the same time, if I am happy and look upon it, I must be made sad."

The wise men consulted one another . . . and finally . . . devised [a ring] upon which was inscribed the legend: THIS, TOO, WILL PASS. (quoted in Shah, WS, 74)

Wishful thinking and the magician

People who indulge heavily in wishful thinking distort their expectations in a different direction from those who expect the worst.

"Maybe if I just ignore it, the problem will go away."

"I can fake it through."

"Tomorrow the money will come in the mail."

When I think this way, I don't do the work I need to do to make my wishes come true. I don't make adequate preparations or take reasonable precautions. I'm taken by surprise when events don't happen as I want them to. That kind of thinking gets in the way of dealing with my reality. And at times, of paying the rent!

On the other hand, sometimes my wishful thinking can bring out the magician in me. Then I find real sources of power inside me that I haven't been in touch with before. I may do things that neither I nor anyone I know would have guessed I could do. I move from wishful thinking, which, after all, is limited to thinking, into feeling and using my creative, productive magic by being willing to *do something* to turn my wishes into realities. Thereby I find faith in my own ability to create and do.

UNCERTAINTY

Everything comes of itself at the appointed time. This is the meaning of heaven and earth.(*I Ching*, 98)

Through the years I've accumulated possessions, sought security in relationships, and lived in tomorrows that promised what I thought I craved.

These are forms of *external* security. External security can be comforting. Its drawback is that if that's my only form of security, I'm likely to be afraid of losing it. So no matter *how* much external security I have, I never feel secure.

"You possess only whatever will not be lost in a shipwreck" said the Sufi El-Ghazali (quoted in Shah, WS, 57). As I develop my ability to depend on myself, I become better able to handle whatever situation I'm in. This is *internal* security. I begin to feel secure in a different way.

I've learned and experienced many valuable things from events that have not gone the way I wanted.

And when I get one thing I want, I sometimes lose another. When I found a place to live by a creek, I had to give up the view I had when I lived on a hill. As my friend Daniel Chadima says, "Creeks don't run on top of the hills."

If I knew with certainty that everything would go the way I wanted, I would have no future. The future is the dimension of possibilities. Without uncertainty, tomorrow would be no more than yesterdays already written, waiting to pass by.

When I don't act on what's important to me, I may be behaving either timidly or prudently. When I take a risk, I may be behaving either bravely or foolishly.

Gambling on something that's really important to me is acting bravely. Putting myself into jeopardy for values *you* say are important but that *I* don't feel are important to me is acting foolishly.

When I act foolishly or timidly, my life and world often seem hollow. When I act bravely, my life is sometimes joyful, sometimes painful, but always full.

"I won't spend tomorrow regretting the past for the chances that I didn't take," sings Kris Kristofferson. I've begun to pay attention to how I protect myself by rejecting high-risk situations. When I notice that I'm doing that, I sometimes consciously take risks that I might otherwise have avoided.

I'm more willing now, for instance, to go into a situation feeling uncertain and vulnerable, not well rehearsed and not knowing what response I'm going to come up with. Out of that uncertainty, I may do or discover something new.

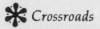 *Crossroads*

Make a list of important crossroads in your life that you've come to in the past year or so, and the choices that you've made.

Now, in fantasy, take the paths you *didn't* take at each crossroads. At a given crossroads there may be only one alternative or there may be several.

As you take your alternative paths, pay special attention to your physical sensations and your feelings.

How many of the alternatives you took were the high-risk ones, and how many were the low-risk ones? Many people find, after doing this exercise, that they consistently chose the paths that seemed the safest. (Adapted from Progoff)

In almost any situation, after I've done what I can, agents I do not control—and may not even know about—have their play. That's the Wheel of Fortune, the play of all the forces that affect us, the cosmic game of chance.

We can curse and fear the working of these unseen forces, or be ready to accept and work with what they bring, painful as that may sometimes be. The *I Ching* counsels:

> The superior man lets himself be guided; he does not go ahead blindly, but learns from the situation what is demanded of him and then follows this intimation from fate. . . .
>
> In times of . . . shock, presence of mind is all too easily lost; the individual overlooks all opportunities for action. . . . But if he allows the shocks of fate to induce movement within his mind, he will overcome these external blows with little effort. (12, 199)

I act more wisely when I'm not bound by the limits of my former understandings.

The farther in advance I plan a thing, the less I know where my head and heart will be when the time to do it comes. My long-range plans usually work out best when I leave them flexible and get down to the details only when the time to carry out the plans draws near.

No tomorrow

An ancient formula for living is to live each day as though it were the last day of your life.

That may in fact be true. As Don Juan Matus told Carlos Castaneda:

"Death is our eternal companion. . . . It has always been watching you. It always will until the day it taps you. . . .

"Death is the only wise adviser that we have. Whenever you feel . . . that everything is going wrong and you're about to be annihilated, turn to your death and ask if it is so. Your death will tell you that you're wrong; that nothing really matters outside its touch. Your death will tell you, 'I haven't touched you yet.' . . .

"This, whatever you're doing now, may be your last act on earth. . . . There is no power which could guarantee that you are going to live one more minute." (JI, 54, 55, 109)

I was once in a wartime situation where I felt that there was indeed no tomorrow. Suddenly everything seemed different. Every breath of cold wind on my cheek, every smell, everything my fingers touched, everything that came to my eyes, was absolutely pure, fresh, and beautiful. The very sky above me was part of my own being.

I had a great sadness about no tomorrow for myself. If my life was to end already, I had missed a lot. I wanted more. But I had given myself many good things.

Similarly, Joan Baez writes that as a teen-age girl, she fought constantly with her sister. Her friend Ira Sandperl suggested that each time they started fighting, she pretend that it was the last hour of her sister's life. Within several months, the fighting ended, and the two girls grew to love each other deeply (71).

As I remember that this day might be my last, an event that I hardly noticed before now seems miraculous, for I realize I may never experience it again. Then every minute is beautiful. Every morning I wake up in a new world.

15 As If

After Bankei had passed away, a blind man who lived near the master's temple told a friend: "Since I am blind, I cannot watch a person's face, so I must judge his character by the sound of his voice. Ordinarily when I hear someone congratulate another upon his happiness or success, I also hear a secret tone of envy. When condolence is expressed for the misfortune of another, I hear pleasure and satisfaction, as if the one condoling was really glad there was something left to gain in his own world.

"In all my experience, however, Bankei's voice was always sincere. Whenever he expressed happiness, I heard nothing but happiness, and whenever he expressed sorrow, sorrow was all I heard." (Reps, 30)

When I trust you to deal with me as I am, I let you know *who* I am. I act and speak in ways that fit what I'm thinking and feeling. I communicate clearly who I am and what I want.

Other times, I may act and speak *as if* I'm thinking and feeling something other than I am. In order to please and placate you, so that maybe you'll give me what I want, I act as I think you expect me to. My as-ifery is my theatre where I perform the role I hope will give you the impression I want you to have.

At any given time, I'm likely to have many arguments for choosing either to be real or to be as-if with you and with myself.

Our bodies can reveal a lot about our as-ifery. You can often see this clearly in children. The other day I saw a small boy go up to an adult. His body made an obvious statement. He stood stiffly. His hands were held straight down at his sides, where they couldn't get him in trouble. He had himself "under control." During the conversation, his as-if got away from him and he started fidgeting. But as soon as the adult brought this to his attention—"Be still and stop fidgeting"—his body again acted the as-if "I'm totally under control."

As I go through each day, I choose how much I'm willing to meet the demands and expectations of each person I encounter.

I go to a meeting. I'm expected to say something. If I don't feel like saying anything, I may keep silent, or say only that I don't feel like talking right then. But if I say something more—as if I felt like talking—I'm likely to feel resentful as I do.

Here's something you can try tomorrow morning:

✳ *Personal self and social self*

When you wake up and open your eyes, stop right there. Instead of getting into your expectations of what you need to do next, close your eyes again. Get in touch with yourself *as you are right then.*

Experience your breathing. Experience your body as you lie still. Then slowly move your hands all over your body. Sense where your bones are, where you ache, where you itch.

Your sense of yourself at that moment is your own. It doesn't include any other person, no matter who's in bed with you or who's waiting for you—in another room or an hour from now.

Now open your eyes. What do you have to get up and do for your world? What do you think it expects of you?

Out of my social expectations, I choose to go with certain personal as-ifs. If I have a meeting with the Director of This or That, and I know he or she expects people in my field to look "respectably well-dressed," I won't wear my jeans and sandals. I'll find some comfortable clothes I like that at least partly fit that person's expectations. I feel okay doing so because I'm choosing what I wear; I could wear my jeans and sandals if I really wanted to.

I'm resentful when I feel I have no choices. A man who is to appear in court may find that he not only has to pay for a lawyer, but also has to buy a new suit. For his lawyer tells him, "When you walk in wearing a dark suit and shirt and tie, you immediately reduce your sentence. Your clothes are saying, 'I'm like you, Judge.'" The price of *not* making that as-if statement is too high.

In one way of acting as-if, I'm aware that I'm doing so, and I take responsibility for it. In another, I forget my pretenses or push them out of my mind. I confuse my as-if with my reality. You and I might implicitly agree, without even consciously realizing that we're doing so: "I'll pretend not to see that you're gaming if you pretend not to see that I'm gaming."

When I'm in touch with who and what and where I am, I can refuse to enter your as-if world, and I can stop trying to hustle you to enter mine.

When I try to be only as you want me to be, I lose touch with my own experience and weaken my ability to take care of myself.

For instance, Alan had let a woman use his pen, and was waiting to get it back. He commented to Sally, who was standing nearby, "My whole life is like this. I want to leave now. I've asked her for the pen several times and she just goes on writing. I don't like what's happening, but I don't want to cause a scene and have people look at me. But I don't like the way my stomach feels when I stand here and do nothing."

Sally replied, "You either pretend you don't really care and endure the feeling in your stomach or risk the consequence of taking it back. It's your choice."

With that, Alan grabbed the pen and walked away feeling much better.

Hypocrisy means presenting a public front of seeming to act in the service of higher principles than I really am.

If I tell people that I gave some money to a good cause, in the hope that they'll think I'm simply generous, when I really made the donation because I wanted admiration or a tax write-off, I'm being hypocritical.

Jesus often spoke out against hypocrisy. His warnings against putting on a good appearance while leaving the inner self untouched have something to say to most of us.

The Nixon Administration scandals of the early 1970s revealed a whole structure built on a hypocritical as-ifery. Many people went along with the deceptions as if these things were all right with them. Yet when a few people started protesting "No, it's not all right," the whole structure toppled.

If I've been speaking and acting in as-if ways for so long that I've begun to forget which me is as-if and which is real, I need to notice when I'm being me and when I'm not.

A Hasidic tale makes the point. As a prank a very drunken peasant was brought into the palace and left only with priestly robes at his bedside. On awakening he recalled nothing of his past. He was attended and dressed with reverence and respect. However, he didn't recall being such a holy man. Soon he began to question: "Maybe I'm a drunken peasant dressed as a holy man, but what if the reverse is true and I'm a holy man who thinks he's a peasant?" When they brought him the holy prayerbook, he thought, "Aha! The moment of truth. Peasants can't read"—and he couldn't. But a new doubt appeared. How could he know for sure that all other holy men could read?

I don't have to stay locked into the script I wrote for myself last week. Living out the drama of my life in a creative and interesting way that fits where I am now takes less energy than acting as though I were the same day after day.

When I stuff my life into a restricted script, I have to pull out a lot of energy to bottle up the spontaneous flow of my life force When I let my energy flow naturally, I don't have to waste all that effort on stopping myself.

✳ *Flowing with the music*

Tune into how you feel right now. What kind of music would you like to hear? How fast or slow? What kind of rhythm?

Now put on some music that's different from that. Notice how you feel with it. Whether you feel good with the music or not, let its rhythm dominate you. Stand up and move or sway with that rhythm.

Then, find a way to feel your own rhythm, and move with it in a way that somehow also fits with the rhythm of the music.

Sometimes I feel good flowing with the music of the sounds and movements of people and events around me. Other times that music is different from my inner music, and I don't want to let it dominate me.

In certain situations, I can easily fall into my as-if ways. For instance, in restaurants, I used to be too embarrassed to ask to see a menu before I sat down, to see if I could afford what was on it. And then I'd be too embarrassed to get up and walk out if the items cost too much. So sometimes I paid more than I could afford by acting as if I was loaded.

Nowadays, if I'm in a restaurant and everyone else at my table is ordering the expensive items, I sometimes think I should order high too. But by dropping my as-ifery, I can order what I want, even if it's inexpensive.

My ability to act as-if can be useful. It can be a way of meeting you in ways you understand, rather than insisting that you meet me on my terms.

I may want to give you my warmth and affection. If I know you're uncomfortable with physical contact, instead of hugging you as I'd like to, I can show you my warmth and caring in a way you can feel comfortable with. When I do this, I'm acting as if this is my way of giving you my caring. When I'm willing to give to you or receive from you only on my terms, I don't leave space for us to contact each other.

BEING TRUE TO MYSELF

> Without any intentional, fancy way of adjusting yourself, to express yourself freely as you are is the most important thing to make yourself happy, and to make others happy. (S. Suzuki, 89)

Several years ago, I visited the classroom of my friend Susan, who taught retarded children. I was appalled at how poisonous Susan was in that situation. She was full of cold and punishing remarks, and seldom had a kind word for any child.

I could have pretended I'd noticed nothing unusual in order to "avoid damaging our relationship." Instead, I told her what I heard and saw, and of the sadness I felt both for her and for the children.

She heard what I said, and saw that she was taking her anger and frustration about her work out on the children. She decided to change her job at the end of the year, accepted the fact that she would be in that classroom until the year ended, and stopped punishing both the children and herself.

I heard and saw what I did only because Susan was willing to show me herself as she was in that situation, and didn't pretend that "all is well and everything's okay."

When I feel lonely, I don't want to pretend that I'm not. If I reveal my loneliness to you, there's at least a chance that we'll touch each other in a way that's real for both of us.

When I'm true to myself, speaking and acting in ways that fit what I think and feel, I usually feel better about what I do. I'm less likely to think, "I should have . . ." In the existential tradition, being true to myself is called "authenticity." Time after time in my everyday social relationships I meet someone, take care of our business, and walk away. Later I realize that I really felt good with that person. I could have taken a few moments to follow through, but I didn't. When I'm authentic, I can relate to someone as a person and not just as a role.

One thing that frightens me about being authentic with you is that I might be making myself vulnerable.

In a way, I'm safer when you're mystified by the cloaks, masks, and shadows of my as-ifery, for then you seldom know just where I am. You can't get at me easily, to zero in and harpoon me. Of course, if you can't find me, it's also hard for you to zero in and love me.

On the other hand, if I have reason to believe you'd use my openness to harm me, I may be true to myself by being closed with you.

In my work and in other areas of my life, I can ask myself, "How much room do I have to *be myself* in this situation? How much of the room I have do I use?"

I suspect that one reason for the high suicide rate among psychiatrists is that in traditional psychiatric practice, the psychiatrist is constantly living up to an image. The decoration of the office, the choice of a location, the way of responding to patients—all these are prescribed. Most important, traditional psychiatric training disciplines these specialists to keep their own feelings and responses out of the interaction with clients. For me, spending many hours a day with other people without ever sharing my own feelings would be extremely poisonous.

If, as the psychiatrist, I say, "What you're saying touches me deeply" or "I'm happy when I see you like this," I'm likely to feel better at the end of the day.

People who "go crazy" often feel no room to be themselves. They're caught among conflicting as-if demands—"I must act as if I'm this way, or this way, or this other way. None of these are ways I really am." If I'm such a person, every way I turn, I face some kind of punishment. I feel like I'm compressed into a black tunnel and I want to scream and climb the walls to get out of this unbearable situation.

At last, with nowhere else to go, I break through the top of the tunnel and into my crazy place. There at least I'm allowed to be crazy. I get a lot of leeway, because crazy is supposed to be unique and personal.

If you and I are in relationship, and we are authentic with each other, we may become very close. On the other hand, we may find that our authentic ways of being are in such a head-on clash that we can't get along without a lot of pretending.

In the long run, being real with each other is almost always better than pretending. In the short run, it may be painful. It may mean making major changes in what we ask of, accept from, and give to another person; or it may mean moving out of old relationships and into new ones.

In being true to myself, I don't want to limit your room to be true to yourself.

If I'm a "Jewish mother," or a "white knight," how much of my helpfulness is a demand that you be helpless?

If I give you warmth and caring, do I demand the same kind of warmth and caring from you whether you feel it right then or not?

In either case, am I demanding that you act as if you're the way I need you to be right then? Do I make it hard for you to be real with me?

If I can give you love and warmth, and also appreciate that you may not feel so warm and loving toward me right then, I'm letting you be yourself.

A few years ago, I realized that when I got angry with my children, I really wanted them to knuckle under and say, "Oh, I'm so sorry," so that I could be reassured that my anger was justified.

If I didn't get that penitence, I got madder and madder. I couldn't just be angry and be content with that.

When I need a certain response from you in order to justify my anger, I wonder about the realness of my anger. I wonder whether I'm acting as if I'm angry (or sad, or whatever) in order to manipulate you into doing what I want you to do.

Double messages often involve presenting myself as if I'm feeling different than I really do.

For example, I may want you to be close with me, but because I'm afraid of being hurt if you come close, I speak and act as if I don't want you to.

My game might be: "If this is important enough to you, you'll push. I'm dangling some goodies in front of you, and I'm putting up a wall. If you want me bad enough, come get me."

When I'm authentic, I'm saying where I am. When I'm concealing and manipulating, I'm testing where you are.

Marie says she wants a lasting relationship with a man. She has a habit of taking up with men who hang around her for a while and then wander on their way, taking her heart as they go. She can't understand why this happens again and again.

Marie's style of coming on to men is cool and offhand, as if she doesn't put much commitment into anything. Her double message is "I want you—I don't care about you." (That's a variation of the more universal "Come close—go away.") But once she and a man get into a relationship, she begins acting the way she genuinely feels, which means putting out a lot of caring and commitment, and expecting the same in return.

Little wonder she never gets it. Her as-if presentation of herself as cool and offhand attracts men who are looking for a temporary, casual relationship. They give her what she seems to be asking for.

Coming on cool is easier for her than saying "I really like you a lot." There's less risk of rejection. But Marie will probably do better if, somewhere along the line, she learns to risk telling how she really feels. She might start by saying, "I'm afraid of getting close to you, even though I want to," when that's the way she feels.

ROLE PLAYING AND CHANGE

Being true to myself may involve pretending. That's one of my choices too. For example, my relationship with you may be so important that if you want me to behave in certain as-if ways, I'll do it for you.

You may want me to go to a fancy restaurant with you and act as if I'm really into that, even though I'm not. I can put on my costume, go with you, and act as if there's nothing in the world I'd rather do. And because I really care for you, as long as you don't ask me to pretend too often or too much, I'll cooperate.

On one hand, there's a danger of getting locked into and blinded by my as-ifery. On the other, my ability to act as-if opens the door to a powerful tool of self-exploration. Like an actor, I can choose a role and then *be* that role, putting myself into it as completely as I can, trying to move and speak and act and think and feel in a way that fits that role. Then I'll have a pretty good idea of how it would be for me to be that way. Within rather wide limits, I can be anyone I can imagine being, do anything I can imagine doing.

The great Russian director Stanislavsky used this principle to teach acting. His actors learned to feel from the inside what it was like to be the characters they were portraying.

✳ *The magic theatre*

This exercise is done in a group.

For half an hour, all members of the group will stay within a particular room or other area.

As the session begins, go inside yourself and find a place that you'd like to try giving expression to. This may be an imitation of a way of being you've seen in someone else, or it may be some way of being you seldom express that is uniquely your own.

When you've found this place, whatever it is, stand up and walk around the room, and interact with other people, *being this person*.

If you have a hard time with the first personality you try, find another that you can get into more easily. Give yourself your full range of possibilities—gentle and caring, hard and angry, etc. The only prohibition is that you don't hurt yourself or anyone else.

If you think of some way of behaving that you feel embarrassed or uncomfortable about and want to avoid, that might be a good one to try on.

An easy way out is: "Usually I talk a lot so I'll sit quietly in the corner." That can be a real place or it can be a shuck. You're the only one who knows.

A way to stop yourself from getting into this is: "I feel silly doing it so I won't do it." You can get past that by giving yourself permission to be silly. You don't have to define being silly as not-okay.

Now look at what you did during the last half-hour. What doors opened up to you? What did you allow yourself to do that you seldom do? What ways of expressing yourself were closed to you in your role? When others pressed you to change, how did you go along with them, or how did you stay with your own place?

The role you chose to try out in fact exists in you. There are probably aspects of this role that can be valuable to you in your everyday living.

I've tried out many different roles in the magic theatre at different times, and each time it's shed new light for me on some dimension of who I am.

One way I can use the theatre is to explore my polarities. When I'm locked into a particular way of being, I try out its polar opposite. In doing so, I get a sense of the whole range of possibilities between those two opposites that are potentially available to me.

When I consciously act out one role or another in my everyday life, my performance can be entirely to please myself and perhaps get your applause, or it can be in some kind of communicative relationship with you. I can become involved in my performance to such an extent that I lose touch with you, or I can stay in contact with you, so that I not only enjoy myself in my performance, but am also in meaningful communication with you.

I can invite you into my drama, and if you're willing to join me there, we can make contact inside it. Or I can step into your drama and contact you there.

Anti-psychiatrist Ronald Laing warns about how we can *induce* each other to take on particular roles. In this process, instead of telling you what to do, I tell you what you *are*, and you unfortunately buy that (PF,

78-79). For instance, according to Laing, "A naughty child is a role in a particular family drama. . . . His parents tell him he *is* naughty, because he does not do what they tell him. . . . [Since] they define what he does *as* naughty . . . he learns that he *is* naughty and *how* to be naughty in his particular family." A variation on this is telling a third party, in front of the child, how the child "is" (PF, 80).

Induction goes a step beyond projection. "Suppose I projected my mother onto my wife," Laing continues. "She takes on the . . . value of my mother *for me*. That is projection. However, . . . I may or may not *induce* her to embody my mother. . . . Projection is done by one person as his *own* experience of the other. *Induction* is done by one person to *the other's* experience" (119).

To induce you to act like my mother, I communicate to you in both direct and subtle ways how I expect you to act, and then encourage, support, and otherwise reinforce you when you act in those ways. If, however, I recognize my induction process and think twice about it, I can start leaving you more space to be as you are.

THE DRAMA OF LIFE

I am a spectator to the drama of my life as well as the writer, producer, director, and star. Everyone I know is a supporting character in my play, or even a co-star of this scene or that one. Everyone I meet briefly or casually is a walk-on or an extra.

The play is almost always fascinating, for I seldom know just what I'll do, or how the other actors will respond.

When I take this view, I get a better sense of what my life looks like from the outside. Times of tragedy begin to be exactly that, to be known and experienced fully, rather than seeming like the end of everything, to be escaped at any cost.

If my play were nothing but cotton candy and peaches and cream, I would be shallow and dull. My struggles, my hard decisions, and my living through of painful events are all exciting and important learning experiences for me. My drama has times of comedy and times of tragedy. Both are part of who I am.

Each supporting character in my play is also the star of his or her own show. Just as that person is only a lesser character in my play, I am a lesser character in his or hers. I can appreciate that person's drama just as I appreciate my own.

I can even be silent and simply watch another person's play for a while. When I look at another person's whole show, appreciating it without judging—"This is what's happening now"—I'm less locked into my own viewpoints. I more easily understand someone else's way of experiencing the world.

People create many different kinds of scripts for their plays.

Eva went through tragedy after tragedy. Everything seemed to turn out disastrously for her. Then one day she realized that she was playing the role of "tragic heroine." At some deeply buried level of awareness, she *set things up* so they would turn out badly, and stayed away from experiences that promised to turn out well. Sadness and tragedy were what she wanted for herself at that point in her life.

Now she's got a new role that gives her room to be happier, and she is.

The events in my drama can have a great deal of power over me or just a little. It usually depends less on what happens *than on what I think* about what happens.

The central understanding in viewing life as a drama is that life is a journey. As sages have said throughout the ages, the point of life is the journey itself—not reaching a goal. If I'm obsessed with my idea about where I want to get, I'm not alive to what I could be experiencing along the way.

So here I am in Scene 7 of Act 2193. I don't know what's going to happen in this scene. It may be comic, it may be tragic; it may be pretty dull. This is my life. It is what it is.

Sometimes my sight is dimmed. I get locked into my old roles. I seek immediate gain or pleasure so intently that I neglect ways of being that help me learn and grow.

During my first year of teaching, I discovered that I was doing my job in ways that dulled me and kept me from growing. Much of the time I didn't enjoy my work. Then I discovered that when I wasn't having a good time, my students weren't either. Consequently, they weren't interested enough in what was happening to learn in ways that had meaning for them.

I had to play my role differently to stay alive inside. Now I don't lecture as much. Instead, I set up experiences for the students to go through and learn from. I try to be more a guide than a teacher. I feel more alive, my students feel more alive, and we all learn more.

We can sometimes be terribly serious about our dramas. But as Watts points out,

When human life is getting too hot, the Buddhas . . . say, . . . "You're crazy, you're playing the game too intensely." . . . Do all the things you do in life, but don't take it seriously. Do it as a game. Then everyone doesn't get guilty and uptight. That's Nirvana—to live in a let-go way.

It's so characteristic of our culture that we have to be *serious*. Even in our language and attitude: "Be serious." Don't laugh or smile. Don't have a good time. If the job isn't unpleasant, we must be doing it wrong.

Nick was on the board of directors of a well-known management consulting firm. The firm had been losing some of its bright young men to other companies. "Gentlemen," asked the chairman of the board at a meeting, "do any of you have any suggestions about what we might do?"

"I'd like to see us change the way we do things so we have fun in our work," offered Nick. "If people enjoy working here, they'll be less likely to leave."

The chairman's response, incredible as it sounds, was, "That's out of the question. I've slaved and strained all my life. I've *never* enjoyed my work, and there's no reason why anyone else in this company should have it any different." This is a true story from life's own theatre of the absurd.

You and I don't have to live that way. We *can* find ways to enjoy what we do. We can make problems into games, and play with them instead of sitting with knotted brows, creating a sense of oppressiveness about our tasks. I think we all need to recover the sense of playfulness toward life that has been numbed in most of us. This is part of what Jesus meant when he spoke of "becoming like a child again."

I felt both happy and sad as I read Art Hoppe's column one day. "If we all celebrated life," he wrote, "who could oppress or kill or hate his fellow man? My generation may reach for the stars from its armchairs, but it will never dance barefoot on the grass."

The heart of living lies in celebrating life as the exquisite absurdity it is. Confounded as it is by profound accidents, according to Virginia, my wife.

16 *Being*

Straight with Yourself

> Whenever a feeling is voiced with truth and frankness, . . . a mysterious and far-reaching influence is exerted. At first it acts on those who are inwardly receptive. But the circle grows larger and larger. . . . The effect is but the reflection of something that emanates from one's own heart. (*I Ching*, 237)

Occasionally I'm caught in the confusion of my conflicting thoughts and feelings and desires. I look for ways to put together everything that's happening with me and come up with what seems best for me to do or say.

Sometimes as I do this, I feel clear about what I'm doing and what motivates my actions. Other times I feel pretty foggy.

As I think about what I do, I'm straight with myself to the degree that what I tell myself about my feelings, thoughts, and actions matches what I know at deeper levels of my awareness.

I'm straight with you to the degree that I tell you what I think and feel, instead of pretending to think and feel otherwise.

I speak the truth to the extent that what I say corresponds to the event that I'm talking about. I may tell you something in all honesty, yet it may be untrue. For I may be mistaken about what I think I know. Or I may be dishonest as I speak to you, yet by accident be truthful. My tone of voice may reveal my true meaning, or my tongue may slip into words I didn't mean to say.

When I face facts, I can more easily separate the real from my illusions. "The facts are *always* friendly," writes Carl Rogers. "Every bit of evidence one can acquire, in any area, leads one that much closer to what is true" (OBP, 25).

Martha and her husband Charles had experienced a long, good marriage.

As they grew older, Martha began to want more contact with stimulating people and ideas. Charles felt threatened by this, and Martha kept telling herself that it wasn't really important to her. At last, however, she came to a point where she was no longer willing to deceive herself, and began going after what she wanted. When Charles found that she wasn't asking him to change the way he spent his time, he began to feel all right about Martha taking care of herself in the ways she needed to. Once they faced the facts about Martha's needs and feelings, their relationship became more comfortable for both of them.

When I'm straight with myself, I don't need to be afraid that some stray fact that comes along might threaten the web of fantasy I've spun to blind myself to something I don't want to see. I don't have to defend myself against perceiving anything that doesn't fit what I think of as my reality.

This was not so with Augie's mother. Augie grew up in the ghetto, and after he became an adult and moved away, his mother continued to live there. As Augie made his mark in the world—in the record business, he said—he began coming by to pick up his mother in a big, expensive car, bringing her elaborate gifts.

Some people whispered that Augie was in the rackets, but his mother would believe none of it. Yet she would constantly wring her hands as she sat smiling in Augie's fine limousine, looking around at the neighbors for their approval and perhaps for a little envy. She was always proud of how well her son had done, until the day Augie was killed by the mob. Even at that point, she refused to accept consciously any evidence of his involvement with the underworld.

I can become highly skilled in developing information to support my fantasies. I can look only at selected pieces of a whole truth; I can generalize a single instance to a wider range of events than it applies to.

I most often distort my perception in such ways when I don't take care of myself. That is, I trick myself or let myself be tricked into giving up what I need for my nourishment and growth. By distorting my reality, I avoid facing how I've hurt myself.

When I realize that I've confused or deceived myself in some way, I can be gentle with myself. I don't have to justify my self-deception. I did what I did. That's who I was then. Now I can find new ways of being.

When I discover something I haven't let myself see before, there may be pain in what I find. And I have to be willing to go through that pain to get to my good place. After that, I can *feel good* about being honest with myself in this new way. The more willing I am to allow myself this good feeling, the more likely I am to discover other things that I've kept hidden from myself.

I can get a lot of outside reinforcement for creating fantasies that lock me into where I am.

The people I live with and the institutions that affect me may be suspicious of change, and encourage me to continue to act in ways that they're accustomed to. They may view any risk I take in questioning some way I live or work as a criticism of themselves and the status quo. This may make it hard for me to change in ways that bring me closer to who I am.

When miniskirts first came into fashion, the administration of our local high school threatened to expel girls who wore them. Those teachers who objected to this policy were reprimanded. Two years later, when the fashion change had become widespread, many of the administrators were themselves wearing miniskirts.

I may have no idea how you'll respond to my attempts to change. If I want to, I can frighten myself about what you might do, and spend a lot of time trying to guess where you'll accept some risk-taking and where you'll reject it, instead of trying out new ways that feel good to me and dealing with what you do in response.

Tuning in to your own process

Many of my ways of being have been with me for a long time. In some cases, I've never really looked at their effects on me or on others.

For instance, I'm a habitual critic, and if you're around me, there's no chance for you to be right in what you say or do. I always find some way to have you be wrong. Yet I've never examined what this does to me, to you, or to our relationship.

When I consider this now, I see several effects: (1) Usually you feel lousy. (2) I have fewer friends than I'd have otherwise, because even though people might say, "Yeah, you really said it to him!" when I put someone down, the next minute they're on guard against being my next victim. (3) I don't feel good with myself, because I can't nourish myself by poisoning you, even if I get a momentary feeling of superiority from making you feel small. And (4) I cut myself off from hearing you, because if I heard you, I'd hear your pain at what I say and do to you. So I deaden the place in me that's like you, and reduce the chance of having whatever worthwhile relationship we might have had.

When I open myself to question what I do, I open up to alternative ways of responding. For instance, instead of criticizing you, I can support you and give you my appreciation.

During a marriage counseling session, Betty told Bill honestly about her disappointment in their sex life. Bill could have given her appreciation and support for her willingness to be honest, even though he was feeling hurt. He could have given her his resentment and anger at feeling betrayed for all the years she'd lied to him, saying everything was fine. Instead, he started accusing and criticizing her. Betty listened with her arms folded, legs crossed, jaws clamped shut, body immobile. Bill looked at her, saw her body message, and became aware of how he was punishing her honesty. He stopped abruptly and found that place in himself where he really did appreciate her willingness to be honest with him now.

✳ Truth buttons

Your body is usually more truthful than your thinking mind, so something that happens in your body can tell you what you're doing below the surface of your awareness.

Physical tension is a "truth button," as Gestalt Therapist Jim Simkin calls it, that everyone can use. When you feel your face or hands or stomach or sphincters getting tight, check out what's happening with you. Something may be going on that you haven't recognized.

Start to pay attention also to your characteristic physical or verbal mannerisms. These are often truth buttons.

(Several years ago I realized that anytime I began a question, "Just out of curiosity . . . ," it meant I was about to ask someone an important question. More recently, I've found that a helpless shrug of my shoulders often means I'm not exploring the options open to me as I face a problem.)

When you and I disagree about some matter, I may feel threatened by your questions or your point of view. Perhaps I get angry with you, using my anger to avoid dealing with what you say.

In such a situation, I want to feel my anger and be done with it. I don't want to use my lingering anger to keep me from listening to what you say or scare you into accepting what I say.

If I feel comfortable and confident as I disagree with you, the odds are better that I'm being honest with myself and you. I can see you as being wrong, and that's okay. I don't have to defend myself. I don't have to attack you.

I'm learning that my truth is only my own, and I must not persist in expecting others to automatically view my truth the way I do. They must seek their own truths. When I remember this, I feel less need to persuade.

Many decisions I've made were difficult because right and wrong were not clear-cut. The choices were never easy when I knew that either I or someone else would suffer in some way no matter what I decided.

Before buying my present house, I lived on a neighboring piece of land. The woods near the house, which the owner had been renting out, were littered with old autos, junk, and garbage. Day after day the hills rang with gunfire. I felt bad about those things.

When I bought the house, the people who lived there, who were basically good people, had to move out. I felt bad about forcing them to leave a place they liked, for I knew they'd be unlikely to find another place as lovely. At the same time, I was glad to change what was happening to that part of the forest. I struggled with my action both before and after I did it. I could find no clear-cut right or wrong there.

As I make a decision, I want to look carefully at the real events that are happening to me and others. I want to be careful not to let my wishes or beliefs or ideology blind me to important realities. I want to listen to my heart as well as to my head, and to the truth buttons that keep me honest with myself.

When I insist that everything I do is "right" and "good," I avoid facing the poisonous or destructive elements in what I do. When I insist that everything I do is "wrong" and "bad," I give myself no space to know the helpful, caring ways I am.

DECEPTION AND HONESTY WITH OTHERS

A beggar went to a door, asking for something to be given to him.
The owner answered, and said: "I am sorry, but there is nobody in."
"I don't want anybody," said the beggar, "I want food." (Hakim Jami, quoted in Shah, WS, 96)

Only you know the conditions of your life as you experience them. Only you can choose how you will meet them.

You may or may not compromise yourself in your work. As a clerk, a manager, a professional, you have a choice of serving people or serving the institution. As a salesman, for example, you may service people's needs, or you may talk them into buying things they can't afford. As a manager, you may care about your employees and their welfare, or you may care only about looking good to your superiors.

If I choose to cheat or steal rather than serve people, I want to be careful that I don't lie to myself about what I'm doing. I've known too many salesmen who began believing their own half-truths. Sartre writes, "It happens often enough that the lie begun in self-defense slips into self-deception" (quoted in Moustakas, C&C, 65). If I *know* that I deceive, at least I'm honest with myself.

Often we don't speak honestly even when we wish to, because we don't understand the ways in which we've so long misled ourselves.

I may want to feel important, to fit my image of "one who knows things." In trying to live up to this image, I think you expect me to be "expert" or "knowledgeable" or "all-powerful" in many areas. I feel inadequate in some way, and imagine that only if I know a lot will you respect me. Actually you may prefer that I not pretend to know more than I do.

Likewise, to the degree that I'm into hustling and conning, I don't really contact you. You exist for me only as an object I hope to use for my own benefit. When I get out of my con man, I have a chance to be real with you and let you be real with me.

Sometimes, out of our fear about how the other might respond, you and I mislead each other about what we're feeling. Here's an example of what can happen when we start having "things we mustn't talk about" in our relationship: "Ed . . . would pretend that everything was fine when it wasn't, as if any problem would disappear if you just refrained from looking at it. So a whole lot of things became taboo and I got this censorship setup in my head. Before I said anything I'd run it through my brain like film and censor it. The habit . . . got worse and worse until amost nothing was natural any more between us" (quoted in Gustaitis, 189).

Lowen and Levin describe the *double bind* we can easily get trapped in:

Telling the truth is a way of reaching for the pleasure of intimacy, as lovers well know. Telling a lie is an attempt to avoid punishment or pain. Therefore it is natural to want to tell the truth in situations of trust and to lie in situations of danger. . . .

It is when we feel we must lie to someone who trusts us and whom we like or love that we are trapped in what psychologists call a double bind. Whatever we do, we lose. This is what an unfaithful husband faces when he returns home to a wife he genuinely loves. He wants to restore his sense of closeness with her, but he knows that of course he cannot tell her where he has been and what he has done . . .

The liar . . . also . . . feels separated from himself. . . . He must monitor every thought before expressing it, fearful that a lapse of memory may betray him. He is indeed a divided man, constantly on guard—against himself. . . .

As long as we experience pain when we lie, however, we should take comfort from the fact. It is a sign that our emotions are alive. . . . What hurts is that we care. . . .

Dealing with pain . . . by deadening all feeling . . . proves to be the ultimate act of self-deception. . . . The deluded person . . . is sick and does not feel the fever. (116)

✳ The I-you game

With another person, carry on a conversation using only the two words "I" and "you."

You can use gestures and tones of voice to give these words any meaning you wish.

You can also do this in a group. After you've each had an "I-you conversation" with one other person for several minutes, you can walk around and communicate with anyone you meet, still using only the words "I" and "you."

In this game, sometimes the communication takes on an almost frightening clarity, and all deception becomes transparent.

I can be straight with you only to the extent that I know what's happening with me. If I'm not in touch with how I feel toward you, I'll have a hard time being straight with you. From my conscious mind I think and speak one way toward you, while from some deeper place, I send a different message with my voice, my body, or my actions.

I can listen for these *double messages* in what I say and do —the times when I say one thing and do another. Then I can go into myself to find out where that double message came from, and find out what's happening in me that I was not aware of.

Spitting in your face isn't honesty. Being straight with you doesn't mean always saying everything that comes to mind. Some people say things that needlessly hurt others, because "I have to be totally honest about everything."

If I say something that makes you feel small so I can feel big and

I say I'm "being honest," actually I'm being dishonest. I'm serving my image of myself rather than respecting you.

If I say something because I want to hurt or punish you, even if what I say is true, I'm not being honest, or candid, or frank—I'm being hostile.

I also do well to avoid making a big show of honesty. As Watts puts it, "It is big of me to be so sincere, to make a play for her by not pretending to be more than I am—unlike the other guys who say they love her for herself. I see that there is always something insincere about trying to be so sincere . . ." (JC, 46).

WHEN SILENCE IS ADVISABLE.   Would that I could always tell the truth. But to tell the truth is sometimes not so easy, even when I know it is the truth.

From time to time I'm among people whose views are very different from my own. If they're threatened by my views and committed to their own, perhaps the wisest thing for me to do is to keep my mouth shut.

In some situations, I may really get hurt if I'm straight about where I am. I don't want to put myself in that kind of situation too often, because I don't like having to be close-mouthed about my thoughts and feelings.

Honesty in society

Honesty is as important to a society as to a person, if that society is to nourish those who live within it. When a society turns away from looking at its values and processes, and from feeling what's happening within it, that society too easily endures injustice.

Sometimes you and I see clearly where people and other living beings are being harmed and where they are being helped—yet many of our leaders and other influential men try to convince us that we are mistaken in what we perceive.

In long sentences and complicated words, they tell us that only experts can understand these events that so offend us. Their reasoning is sometimes so clever that we conclude that we must have been mistaken.

Actually, almost every complicated issue can be explained simply enough for you and I to understand its details.

As I listen to the arguments of someone who tries to tell me that what I see is different than it seems to be, I ask myself, "What does this person get out of it if I believe what he or she wants me to?"

WHAT'S IN IT FOR ME

My payoff for deceiving you or myself

When I was an infant, I soon learned that I was punished when I acted in certain ways. I kept on acting in some of those ways, but learned to disguise the evidence.

If my child lies, there's a good chance that I punish him or her too much, and the lying is an attempt to avoid punishment. Or I may tell more than a few "little white lies" myself, so my child learns to do the same through imitation.

Whenever I deceive myself or you, I've got a payoff somewhere, unless I'm some kind of dummy. My deception gets me what I want or helps me avoid pain.

If I'm not straight with you or myself, I want to know exactly what I'm getting out of it. I want to know what it's costing me. Then I can decide whether it's worth it to me to keep on doing that.

I don't want to con myself about what I get and what I pay. If I'm deceiving no one but myself, I don't gain anything and I pay heavily. So I need still another self-deception to keep me from realizing how little I get for the price I pay. Very likely all I'm getting is a chance to hang on to my self-image. I may not even be getting that.

The fact that I'm sometimes not straight with myself or with you is no sign of "bad character." I need not condemn myself for it. Dishonesty is learned. It's a collection of habits of thought, feeling, and action. I develop those habits in part through my conditioning and in part through my choices about what I've wanted for myself.

For everyone beyond infancy, honesty is likewise an ability we must learn like any other. It's not something you inherently either have or don't have. Few of us know how to be completely honest even when we want to.

If I want to be more truthful with you or with myself, I can *do so* each time I'm aware that I have a choice.

Truthfulness and honesty

Whether I choose to be honest with you or lie to you, I want that choice to be my own, and not a response to what you or someone else is pressing me to do.

I remember the times I've prodded someone else to act dishonestly in order to ease my own discomfort about having been dishonest. So when you tell me not to be a jerk, not to pass up a chance to take advantage of some sucker, I suspect that you don't really care about me, but that you want my help in justifying some action of your own that you don't feel so good about.

When I've been living a lifestyle of running numbers and tricks on people, I find myself holding my breath and waiting to be caught or trying to be as invisible as possible. (If I don't breathe too loud, maybe nobody will hear me as they walk past. They won't see my tricks and my numbers.) This kind of anxiety can be a starting place for breathing problems like asthma and emphysema.

When I stop running my tricks on people, I start breathing freely again, because I don't care if my neighbor hears me breathe.

I remember the taxi driver who drove me around New York when I was a soldier just back from overseas. He took me on a wild goose chase to get to my destination. When I read him out for it, he apologized by saying, "Well, I figured if I didn't take it, somebody else would."

We talked as one person to another then, and he ended up not charging me for the trip. He had made a change toward confronting himself, and found a way to feel good with himself in the process.

What you did in the past doesn't matter. You don't need to keep raking yourself over the coals for your past actions. *What counts is what you do from now on out.*

"Truth calls to us, drawn by the innocent laughter of a child, or the kiss of a loved one," wrote Gibran (VM, 47).

V

Living with Feeling

17 *Feeling*

I need my laughter, and I need my tears. I need my anger, and I need my love.

Sometimes I lash out in anger at you or at myself. Then, when I've spent my anger, and I know you've heard me or I've heard myself clearly, I feel free to let that go, and move on. A Hebrew in ancient Egypt observed that the best Egyptian archers were the ones who knew how to hold tight, when to pull back, and when to let go.

Sometimes I cry about something I've lost, or about deeds I've done in thoughtlessness or anger. When I cry, I wash away the poison of the past and free myself to move on to another way of feeling.

As I have cried, so can I laugh. My joy can fill me, can make my body alive.

When I've rested from my dance and play, I love. I find that place where the trees and stars and I are one, and I want to nourish those around me as they've nourished me.

When I feel deeply and express my feelings as they are, I'm in touch with who I am.

✳ *Your ebb and flow of feeling*

Every moment has some kind of feeling-tone.

As you go through a day, occasionally remind yourself to notice what you're feeling right then. Take note of not only your strong feelings, but also your moods and subtle shifts of feeling. Do you feel bright and alert? A little muddy and not quite here? A vague sense of sadness that you can't connect with any specific event?

183

Notice how one feeling starts to fade away as you experience a new feeling taking form within you.

Be aware of *what you actually do feel,* rather than what you think you should feel. Notice when you think, "I shouldn't feel the way I feel." When are you annoyed or embarrassed, or surprised and delighted, that you feel as you do?

Before I became aware of the richness that lay buried in my ability to feel my life, I wanted to become "more rational." I used to get rid of feelings of discomfort by doing or thinking about something else, instead of tuning in to them to see what messages they held for me. I was like someone who goes to a psychologist to "get cured," thinking that means being able to go away and not feel anymore.

I didn't know then that in order to *think more clearly,* I also had to learn to *feel more clearly,* because thoughts and feelings are so intertwined.

Our emotions are sensitive instruments for living, often alerting us to important events in us and around us long before our rational minds have figured out what's happening. Try this:

✳️ Checking your feel-o-meter

Walk into a room. Look around. Listen to the sounds. Smell the smells. Pick up all the "vibes" you can.

Now pay attention to the feelings inside you. How do you feel in that room?

Next, if there are people in the room, tune in to them one at a time, and see what kind of feeling you experience in response to each person.

Now, so far as you can, notice what it is about the room and about each person that triggers the feelings you experience.

In her delightful children's book, Eda LeShan writes, "Sometimes knowing facts doesn't change a feeling. It may be a fact that every time Aunt Sue comes to visit, she brings you a present and hugs and kisses you. But . . . you have this funny feeling that she really doesn't like children so much. Feelings are just as important as facts, because they affect our lives just as much as facts, sometimes even more" (10).

Even though we may have learned to numb ourselves to them, all the feelings we've ever experienced are there and available for us to experience again. We don't lose our capacity to feel—we just put it in cold storage.

The flow of feeling

You may prefer not to feel a certain way because you're afraid you may get stuck in it, and be unable to feel other ways or think about other matters.

At other times, people may try to move you out of feeling a certain way when you're not ready to stop feeling that way yet. When I've not finished feeling sad or angry, I resent people telling me to "cheer up" or "calm down." My painful feelings are old friends just like my pleasant ones. I know that when I experience them fully, they'll give way to times when I feel good.

I don't need to go into certain ways of feeling. But I want to be careful: Am I consistently avoiding the same kind of places? Am I always giving myself the same kinds of reasons for shying away from those places in myself?

For my own growth, I need times of trial and difficulty as well as times of rest and easy sailing.

Bugental speaks of the *dominant emotional theme* in one's personality. As I listen to a person, one theme, one way of feeling, often starts to stand out.

Many of us are deaf and blind to our own dominant themes. When another person sympathetically voices an understanding of what I'm expressing, I can sometimes see my theme more easily.

I don't have to be committed to my most usual way of feeling. If I'm often sad, I don't have to hang on to my sadness. I can allow myself times to take delight in what's happening around me now. Then gradually my sadness, which today seems so overpowering, will start to take a smaller share of my awareness.

When I feel the same way in a wide variety of situations, it means that I'm missing a lot of what's happening in those situations. I look for and perceive only what I need in order to fit my own narrowed range of feeling to the situation. As I become aware of doing this, I can widen the range of feeling and events I allow myself.

We all have mixed feelings about people. Almost every child sometimes really hates his or her parents, however much he or she also loves them. I have many feelings about every person who is important to me.

When you feel angry or rejecting toward me, I can hurt myself by imagining that that's the only way you feel. I forget that you can get mad at me and still care about me, and that sometimes when you're mad at me, it's *because* you care about me.

When I have some strong feeling, that may be the only feeling I'm aware of, but my other feelings are still inside me, and in a few minutes or a few hours, I'm likely to feel one of those other ways.

Depression

When I'm depressed, I feel frustrated and bored with where I am and what I'm doing. Each new avenue I look into seems to lead nowhere. Every direction I think of trying seems dark and shrouded. Since no pathway I see looks promising, why try any of them?

The message of depression is that there's a place in me that wants life that I'm not giving life. People often get depressed when they are dissatisfied with their lives and need to make some kind of important change, though they may not know what that change might be.

The irony is that when I'm depressed, I feel no energy for finding out how to give life to the parts of me that are crying out to live. Instead of searching out new ways to meet my needs, I repeat my same old ineffective ways. With each path of involvement I try, I reinforce my illusion of helplessness by being unwilling to invest my energy in following through to a finishing point. I try five different projects and don't complete any of them.

The opposite of depression is excitement. I can open myself to my excitement by investing energy in any path that holds interest and promise for me.

When I stay with something that interests me, I start to come alive. By picking projects that are small enough for me to finish easily, I can feel excited about what I've done and about going on to something larger.

STOPPING FEELING

When Julie wants to, she can shut her feelings right off. Everyone in her family does that.

"How did you cut off the feeling?" therapist Robert K. Hall asked her one day when she almost got angry.

"I don't know," said Julie. "Somewhere I detached myself from that."

"That's the process to pay attention to," Hall replied.

Later in the same Gestalt session, he told another client, Terry, "You go into very touchy areas without feeling anything too much, put out enough to keep people's attention, and you do this all very well. It's a hard act to pull off. I'd call you very successful at it."

Terry replied, with hung head, "It's the only act I've got."

Howard came in for therapy because he had recurrent seizure-like tremors, and his doctor could find no physiological reason for them. He was an extremely depressed young man who locked up his anger tightly. He seldom let out his irritation even about minor things, like towels not being hung on the rack. In a counseling session one day, when he got close to expressing his anger toward his father, who threw him out of the house when he was sixteen, he cut himself off abruptly and his whole body went into the violent spasmodic tremor. The tremor turned out to be a muscular expression of his holding back the intense feelings that he wanted to express in words but was afraid to.

In almost every family and every group of people, certain ways of feeling are "acceptable" and certain others are "unacceptable." Think about your own family and friends. Are there certain feelings that they often show and encourage you to show, and others that they seldom show and discourage you from showing? What are the "unspoken rules" about showing feelings?

Our right to our own feelings

Those who taught us to block off our awareness of certain feelings sometimes no doubt thought that they were doing what was best for us:

"Don't cry. There's nothing to cry about, and it's ridiculous for you to be sad. Come on now, be happy."

"Now stop being angry with your mother and tell her that you love her."

When people said such things to me, I didn't stop feeling what I felt. But I could pretend to stop, and act *as if* I didn't feel as I really felt. So those feelings became the unspeakable, both to others and to me. Finally I began to think I didn't feel the way that was prohibited.

Likewise, when I tell you how to feel, unless you're strong enough to tell me to get off your back, I rob you of your opportunity to feel your own feelings. I'm asking you to tell yourself you feel only what *I* say you feel.

As I learn to recognize and accept my own feelings for what they are, I become less vulnerable to other people's ideas about how I "should feel." Instead of feeling guilty when I don't feel what you say or imply that I "should feel," I recognize that *you* don't like the way I feel.

As I come to live my own feelings more fully, I begin leaving others more space to have their own feelings. Instead of asking you to feel as I do, I begin to understand that you're a separate person, and appreciate you as you are, with your own feelings, values, and goals (Rogers, OBP, Chapter 16).

Our feelings are real even when we don't know why we feel as we do. *One way I can rob you of your feelings is by demanding that you have a reason that makes sense to me for feeling as you do, or else!* I can rob myself of my own feelings by demanding that I have a good reason for feeling as I do.

When I want to know more about what's happening with you, instead of "Why?" I can ask, "What are you feeling that way about?" If you don't want to answer, I can appreciate that you're feeling as you do, and that's enough.

Guilt, shame, and humiliation

Guilt, shame, and humiliation are all potent ways of stopping feeling. Let's say I'm a child who enjoys masturbating until adults tell me it's a shameful, dirty thing to do. I still like it, but others predict the very worst if I keep on. So now I feel guilty when I do it, because they expect me not to do it anymore.

Guilt is my feeling that I'm bad for doing what I'm doing, because my action is contrary to my image of how I'm expected to behave. Shame and humiliation are my feelings about myself when someone finds me out.

A "psychopath" not only lacks feelings of guilt and shame, but has also failed to develop means of self-regulation based on a genuine caring and affection for other people.

Guilt and shame and humiliation all include my anger toward you for stopping me from doing what I want to do. I may also be angry with you for making me feel small in front of others. Since I don't express my anger, it turns to resentment, or even hate. Hate is the extreme of resentment. In direct proportion to your success in causing me to feel guilty, ashamed, or humiliated, I resent or hate you. If I'm greatly afraid of losing your love or being otherwise punished, I may block out my awareness of my hatred or resentment.

✳ *A letter of resentment*

Write a letter to the person toward whom you feel resentment or hate. If that person has died, write the letter as though he or she is still here (and send it to the dead-letter office).

Tell that person how you feel manipulated with guilt, shame, and humiliation (or in other ways) and how you feel about that. Rant and rave and curse if you like. Include anything else that comes to mind that you want to tell that person now.

When you've finished, put the letter away. After a week has passed, read your letter. Send it or not, as you wish. (You may need to write many letters that you don't send.)

Once I've cleared out my resentment against you, I can more easily appreciate that you may have done the best you could, teaching me in the only way you knew. A true understanding of what you faced is more likely to grow in me once I get my bitter feelings toward you off my chest.

This process of "catharsis" works because I have said the "unsayable" and I continue to exist, and exist in relationship to you. I finish my unfinished business with you, and don't have to carry it around anymore. At the same time, I work through my fear of expressing the feelings I've held in, and develop my ability to express them.

If my parents dealt with me by using shame, guilt, and humiliation, after I confront them with my resentment—whether they're still alive or not—I'm less apt to displace my anger toward them by venting it on my children, using these same power tools of shame, guilt, and humiliation.

If you and I are in a close relationship and I feel guilty or ashamed about some ways I act toward you, I want to check whether I have any underlying resentments I need to tell you about.

I also want to make sure that I'm telling you *I resent* or *I feel angry* about these things, and that I don't slip into blaming and condemning you for doing them. If you start defending your actions as I express my resentments, this tells me that you're feeling attacked and aren't hearing me. I can point out that these are *my feelings*, and not condemnations, or I can skip it for now and try again when you're more open to listening to how I feel.

Those who taught us by guilt and shame and humiliation came through that same school themselves.

Yet, there are other ways of teaching. I can teach you by giving you my appreciation when you do what I ask you to, and by loving you and caring for you as a unique and beautiful person.

Sometimes just pointing out to you the consequences of your actions may be enough to get you to change your behavior, if you haven't thought about those consequences before.

When one feeling hides another

"Do you hide a spear within a smile?" the Zen master asks.

Some people get angry when in fact they feel like crying. Others cry when they're angry.

During arguments with her husband, Jeannie often feels angry with him, but instead of sounding angry, she starts crying. She was a "good girl" when she was a child. (Perls once commented, "Behind every 'good boy' or 'good girl' is a spiteful brat.") Jeannie is frightened of her anger. She doesn't take care of herself and she doesn't let her anger out, so she sits and whines, or breaks down into tears.

To be sure, when I'm angry with another person, if I look beneath the anger I almost always find that I feel hurt in some way. My anger is a defensive, protective response to my pain. I can learn to use my anger as a guide to find out where I feel hurt. However, I also want to keep my ability to express my anger. It's one of my ways of protecting myself.

Perhaps I'm afraid of my gentle, loving feelings. When I deny these places inside me, I may put that energy into other feelings—like anger or sadness. If I want to tell you that I love you but have a hard time saying that, I may get angry instead.

Some people were told, in effect, as they grew up, "You don't deserve to feel good about anything you do. It's wrong to feel good, bad to feel joy and love. You mustn't do that." Parents and other authorities seldom say this straight out, but often communicate it in many subtle ways.

When that happens, the potential for feeling and expressing joy and love can turn in on itself and become sadness or bitterness. If this has happened to me, I may fall in love with my own sadness, and sometimes my resentment too: It's called "feeling sorry for myself." But once I begin to smile and laugh and find out that no lightning bolt strikes me after all, I start to let go of my sadness.

Hanging on to feelings

One morning Bob and his son David had a heated argument. Bob ended up shouting at David, and went off to work red-faced and angry. His memory of the incident stayed with him all day. David forgot it. Bob came home that night feeling upset, and tried to "deal with" the morning encounter. David, in a cheerful mood, could hardly remember the issue or the event, and was surprised that his father even mentioned it.

Just as you and I may differ in how long we stay with one way of feeling before it gives way to another one, we also differ in how long it takes us to get in touch with our feelings. Some people are lucky enough to usually have a clear sense of how they feel right at the time of an event. By contrast, one friend of mine often doesn't have a clear sense of how she feels about something until a couple of days afterward.

We need to leave some space for each other's different rates of speed in getting in touch with our feelings and in moving from one feeling to another. I don't want to tell you that you shouldn't still feel sad because I don't feel sad anymore, or shouldn't feel anger toward me because my anger toward you has passed. On the other hand, if you get over your anger faster than I do, instead of my thinking this means that you're insensitive or that you don't care about me, I can be glad you finish with your anger toward me as quickly as you do.

At times I hang on to a feeling longer than is natural to me. That cuts me off from having other feelings as new events occur. When I get up on the wrong side of the bed, I don't have to stay there all day. When I insist on staying there, it's a signal that I need to look and see what source of discontent in my life I'm not dealing with.

I can hang on to any feeling. Hanging on to anger is especially common, because I can use my "justifiable" anger to punish you, even when the circumstances that called out my anger are long past.

Clinging to my anger gets me several things. I can feel self-righteous. At the same time I can avoid telling you clearly what I'm upset about if I'm not sure what I want to say to you. This avoidance is easier and safer for me than the hard work of getting clear about where I am right now and putting myself on the line to work things out with you.

Hanging on to being angry, or anxious and fearful, also keeps my veins filled with adrenalin, my muscles chronically constricted, and my digestive and glandular systems in a state of emergency readiness. This is hard on my body.

One way I can punish you is through silence about what's bugging me. I don't tell you I'm angry, but through my tone of voice, my movements, and my other signals, you can bet you'll get the message. And there's nothing you can do to make things right until I've punished you to my satisfaction. I work the poison of bottled-up anger out of my system by poisoning you in a thousand ways. This way of acting is called "passive-aggressive."

My friend Sarah writes,

When I'm on the receiving end of passive-aggressive anger. I want to totally close up. I tighten my stomach and tense my muscles as I wait for the boom to fall. Part of my punishment is the slow torture of waiting to be punished, breathing in the poison that hangs heavy in the air.

My mother got us conditioned to where if she raised her eyebrow, we knew we were going to "get it," but we didn't know when. Her tactic was to wait until I was in an especially vulnerable place. When I was a teen-ager, she'd wait until I wanted to do something really badly—go out on a date, for instance, and then say, "No, because of what you did last week," which hadn't been mentioned in the meantime.

Passive-aggressive behavior is passed from one generation to the next. If I've been severely punished for screaming and yelling, I learn that the only way I can get angry at another person is to be underhanded about it, to make that person suffer over a long period of time.

I can break the spell of passive-aggressive anger by confronting it, by recognizing what's happening and then telling the other person what I see: "If you have something to say to me, I'd like to hear it. I'll listen to your anger, but I won't stand for your slow poison."

When I'm on the receiving end of passive-aggressive anger, I get angry in return. If I suppress my anger instead of confronting the other person, at that point I victimize myself and become fifty per cent responsible for the continuation of the passive-aggressive process. I choose whether I succumb to my fear and keep quiet, or voice my own anger at being dumped on.

I also find that other people's ability to hook me with passive-aggressive behavior decreases directly as I give up my own passive-aggressive way of being.

DIRECT STATEMENTS AND SIGNALING

If we're clear enough in our relationship that we can often get what we want by asking each other for it directly, we leave the tremendous energy drain of manipulative games behind. We each begin to trust and be trusted, and as we do, we feel a great relief.

Sometimes you may want two things at once. You may ask me to be honest with you, yet not want to hear some of what I say in my honesty, and start to cry and be angry with me when I'm candid. Your tears may be your honest feeling, or a manipulation to shut me up, or a bit of both. I can respond to this double message either by using your anger and tears to shut myself up or, if being honest is important enough to both of us, by showing you that I care about the way you feel but continuing to be honest.

People are less often defensive when I tell them how I feel if I'm careful to express my feelings as my own feelings, and not as "facts" about them. In Rogers' words,

> To say . . . "What you are doing is all wrong," is likely to lead only to debate. But to say "I feel very much annoyed by what you're doing," is to state one fact about the speaker's feelings, a fact which no one can deny. . . . "You are to blame for my feelings of inadequacy" is a debatable point, but "I feel inadequate when you do thus and so" simply contributes a real fact about the relationship. (OBP, 319)

As I learn how to be direct and honest with you about how I feel and what I want, I also want you to be direct and honest with me. Then we create a place of trust that we can share.

When I go into a towering rage, my daughter says, "Wow! You sure sound crazy to me," but doesn't ask me to stop or to justify my feeling. If I get heavily into expressing affection and she feels smothered, her response is, "You sure are heavy in loving today." She doesn't try to stop me from being, but says how she experiences my being and where she is with it. She's learned that it's important for both of us that I say how I feel.

I can learn to read your signals even when they're not so clear. You may say to me, "Goddamn, look what a mess you made of things," when what you really mean is, "I'm very upset about what you did."

As I learn to hear what you're saying in your way, I become less likely to get hooked by the trappings of your manner of expression. I can listen to what you say, even if I can think of a clearer way of saying it.

I'm more likely to hear your meaning, and you mine, if we care about each other. I can more easily read my supervisor's signals when he says, "What the hell did you do with that piece of work?" if I know that he's also willing to say, "What a beautiful piece of work you did!"

We can also learn our signals to ourselves. When Noel gets frustrated and angry on a job, he puts down what he's working on and walks out of the shop. He's learned that getting a cup of tea or talking to someone for three or four minutes cools him off. When he returns, he usually feels much better, and can go right to the heart of the problem and sail through it.

My feelings give me signals about what I want to be doing now and whom I want to be with. They tell me what I need to do for myself. They help me know, appreciate, and enjoy who I am, and who you are.

18 *Working with Feeling*

By working with my feelings in certain ways, I can learn how to feel more pleasure and avoid unnecessary pain.

When I deaden my ability to feel, my payoff is that I feel less pain. The other side of the coin is that I also feel less pleasure—but I may never find that out. And in deadening my awareness of my painful feelings, I create *more* pain in the muscles of my body, for the way I block out my awareness of the pain that already exists in my muscles is to tighten up against it even more. Due to this chronic muscular tightening, certain places in my body never get the rest and relaxation they need.

When I start allowing my blocked-off feelings to flow freely once again, I release physical energy that I've kept locked up. I feel more alive in my body and my life.

Before I give a feeling full expression, I "look both ways." In one direction is my feeling itself; in the other is my environment.

I can get along without breaking into a belly laugh in the middle of a funeral. I can get along without shouting my anger at a timid soul who has a hard time handling intense feelings: this is the point where expressing myself can turn into selfish indulgence. *Rather than putting others on the defensive, I want to present my feelings in ways that they can accept and respond to with their own feelings.* I can find a way to express my feeling that suits the situation where I am. This is called "discretion."

As I open up my ability to feel, I keep my capacity to intellectually appreciate where I am. I can seldom accurately solve important problems confronting me on an emotional basis alone, any more than I can do so on an intellectual basis alone. My feelings and my rational mind can work together. When I'm faced with danger, for example, going completely into hysteria and panic leaves no room for rational problem-solving. I want my reason available to deal with the danger. At the same time, my feelings about the danger can bring forth the surge of my life force that I need to meet it. There are many stories of people performing incredible feats of strength and bravery when they've been afraid.

REOPENING CLOSED FEELINGS

Reopening closed feelings is a process different from the *cognitive* learning that most of us are used to. In this *affective* or emotional learning, change comes more through responding to situations with our feelings than through grasping them with our mind.

As I allow my previously blocked-off feelings into my awareness, they begin to seem less frightening, less overpowering. I become more able to say what I feel when I feel it, and I don't build up a backlog of unexpressed feelings that I inappropriately dump on whoever's available when I've reached "the last straw"and blow my lid.

I can start opening up to my feelings in one little area where I feel fairly safe, leaving scarier places for later on. As I become more comfortable with these easier-to-handle things I deal with first, the heavies start to seem less frightening.

I don't have to scare myself with "If I touch the lever, the sluice gates will open and I'll drown." Getting in touch with even those blocked-off feelings that I'm willing and ready to handle takes plenty of work and time.

One way I can find out how I'm feeling, when I'm not sure, is by paying attention to what I'm doing with my body. Here's a way to do this:

✳ The message of movement

Right now, stand up and walk around. Feel how you move, in your torso, your arms, your legs.

When you have a clear sense of how you're moving, *exaggerate* that movement as much as you can, whether it's a brisk, energetic movement or a draggy, heavy one. *Notice how you feel* as you move, and begin to *make sounds* that fit the way you feel. Continue to exaggerate your movements and make sounds for two or three minutes. When you've finished, ask yourself: "What's the message for me in what I've done?"

If you're working in a group, one person at a time walks around the middle of the room. The others give their impression of how he or she is moving, in just a word or two. The person then uses these comments as a basis for exaggeration.

We look now at four important kinds of feelings: fear, grief, anger, and joy. We will deal with other feelings in other chapters.

Some of our suggestions for working with feelings may seem very structured. We recommend that you try them as they're presented here. Then, as you integrate the principles underlying them into your life, you can discard the structures.

Fear

Fear is an exciting feeling, and the line between excitement and fear is sometimes thin. Think of how many people ride roller coasters and go to horror movies.

When I breathe deeply, I move toward being alive with my excitement. When I hold my breath, I move toward being paralyzed in my fear. "Breath is life," said Gurdjieff. When I feel excited or afraid, I try to remember to *breathe fully.*

I need and want some of my fears. They help me survive dangerous situations.

The fear I don't like is the kind that keeps my energy away from me. Any time I stop myself from feeling something, it's because I'm scared: At some point in the past, feeling that way brought me punishment and pain. We hang on to these old fears because we feel too uncomfortable when we move toward doing what we're afraid to do. When my present situation is really as dangerous as the past situation where I learned to be afraid, my fear has value. When it's not, as is usually the case, my fear is self-defeating.

If I get tongue-tied when I'm with an authority, I may be protecting myself against saying something that might get me clobbered. When I was a kid, I often got clobbered for what I said around people in authority. I learned to clam up. Similarly, I may clam up now, even when that's the worst thing I could do in the present situation.

The basic process for getting rid of fears from my past that don't fit my present is to do what I'm afraid to do, in situations where I'm pretty sure nothing bad will happen. As I act again and again in ways that resemble the way I'm afraid to act, and no harm comes to me, eventually my whole body learns that nothing bad will happen when I act that way. I stop tightening my muscles, holding my breath, slowing my digestion, and secreting adrenalin into my bloodstream. I can speed up this relearning by consciously relaxing my muscles and breathing deeply and fully whenever I feel a twinge of fear.

If my fear is strong, I want to be careful not to start right off doing something that's too much like what I'm afraid to do. Otherwise the whole force of my fear may come flooding through me so powerfully that I'm unable to do what I intended and feel reluctant to try again. Remembering the principle of shaping or successive approximation (see page 107), I begin with situations that are only a little like the one I fear, and gradually move to situations that are more like it.

The language of gesture may be tied in with my fears. When I was a child, I learned that small movements or subtle changes in voice tones—a raised hand, a turning away—contained direct statements of "I will hit you" or "I will leave you."

Now, in situations where you are not likely to leave me or hit me, your gestures may still trigger my old fears. If my own gestures make those same statements to you, I can learn new gestures that are less likely to trigger your and other people's fears.

In-Vivo Clearing.   Think through your fear until you can accurately describe a specific situation in which you'd expect to feel it at its maximum intensity. Write that situation down in precise detail. It might be either a situation you could put yourself into or one you're likely to happen into.

Now jot down a variety of other situations that are also related to that "most feared event," situations that you can either create for yourself or put yourself into. Think of some situations that are a lot like the most feared event, and others that are only a little like it, and hence are less frightening. Write each item on a separate strip of paper, so you can move them around easily.

When you've got a list of at least ten situations, or better yet fifteen or twenty, put them in an order that runs from the least to the most frightening. Check your ranking by having another person read off each situation as you sit or lie with your eyes closed. If you're ranked them correctly, you'll feel just a little more fear with each successive situation you imagine. If you feel less fear with one item than you felt with the previous one, reverse their order. If you notice a big jump in fear from one item to the next, think of one or two more items that will fit between these two, so that the increase in fear is small.

Then, as you can arrange the occasions to do so, *actually go through* each situation on your list, beginning with the easiest one and gradually moving toward the more frightening ones. You might sometimes want to go through a given kind of situation several times before moving to the next item on your list, or you might decide you can skip certain items.

The intermediate items you make up don't all have to be different. One woman who wanted to get over her fear of approaching strangers included such items as "Sit down with a group of several friends who are talking to someone I don't know"; "Sit down with one friend who is talking with someone I don't know"; "Sit down next to a stranger in a crowded cafe where there are hardly any seats left"; "Sit down next to a stranger in a cafe where there are still some vacant seats."

A man who wanted to get over his fear of talking in groups started out talking with one other person, then two persons, then three, working up to successively larger groups. He also distinguished among talking with children, talking with people of his own status, and talking with older male authority figures, according to how much fear he felt with each.

Before you go into a fearful situation, consciously relax your muscles and check to see that you're breathing regularly.

Imitation can also be useful in getting over fears. You can hang around with others who are good at doing what you have a hard time doing.

Finally, it's nice to have as an anchor the rational understanding that in most situations the worst that can happen in terms of your actual welfare is that you're no worse off than if you hadn't tried.

DESENSITIZATION.　A variation on in-vivo clearing is useful when your fear is so strong that you feel uncomfortable about actually doing things that are even remotely related to it. It's also useful for fears about things that happen with no action on your part, like fears of sudden loud noises.

First, make a list just as described above. Then lie down in a place where you feel secure and take at least ten minutes to relax each muscle in your body as completely as you can. Then imagine that you're lying on a sunny hillside or some other place where you feel very good and very happy.

Next, *vividly imagine* the least frightening item on your list. When you begin to feel afraid, remove your attention from the threatening item, go back to your relaxing scene, and relax your body again. When all tension is gone, again imagine being in the threatening situation. Continue this alternation until you remain relaxed and unafraid as you imagine the situation.

Then continue to the next item on your list. Doing three or four items a day, in a session lasting an hour or so, is plenty. Sometimes you may even need to devote a couple of daily sessions to a single item.

This procedure *works most effectively if you do it with a partner* who reads the scene for you to imagine from your list and gives you relaxation instructions whenever you hold up a finger indicating you feel any fear, or any tension in your body.

The main mistake to avoid is making the scenes on the list too general. They have to be *specific*, so that when the description is read, a particular scene comes immediately to mind. (For further details, see Joseph Wolpe's *The Practice of Behavior Therapy.)*

And remember—*it's all right to be afraid.* You don't have to be ashamed of your fears. In our own ways, we are all afraid.

Sadness and grief

"When you are sorrowful . . ." writes Gibran, "you are weeping for that which has been your delight" (P, 29).

When someone I love dies, I want to feel my grief fully, even if for me that means sitting back on my haunches and howling. At times like that, I don't need to feel any restraint on the intensity of my feelings. If I go through the depths of my sorrow, and then don't hang on to it, I can come out on the other side well and whole again.

If I've bought the idea that important events are not to be felt fully, I may find that I've suppressed my grief so deeply that I'm not aware of even any impulse to cry.

When I start to cry, and then tighten my throat and constrict my chest to stop myself, I feel choked, stopped up. I feel none of the deep cleansing and refreshing release that comes from crying fully.

Next time you feel an impulse to cry but don't, or start to cry and then stop, pay attention to your breathing and to your chest and throat. Now *intensify* your constriction of those areas. Hold your breath and tighten your throat. Try to cry through this tightening. What do you experience?

Now relax your chest and throat and breathe deeply and fully as you think about what you're sad about. What do you experience now?

After you've gone through this process several times, you're likely to gain greater voluntary control over your ability to cut off and reopen your crying and your feelings of sadness.

In our culture, men tend to be reluctant to cry, to speak of their sorrow, or to show it in other ways.

Actually, I can respect myself in my ability to grieve and feel my sadness fully. When I feel my anguish deeply, I'm not controlled, cautious, and fearful, stepping lightly and belittling areas of experience that I'm not comfortable with.

When someone I love dies, or we part ways, I may lose more than that person: I also face losing a part of myself that was called out by that person. So as I grieve, I want to offer that part of myself a chance to keep on living. Gordon Tappan describes a way to do this. Try it now:

✳ *Dialogues with someone who's gone*

Take a pen and paper, and give voice to the part or parts of yourself that came to life in the presence of someone who has passed out of your life. Then give that person a voice, allowing your thoughts and feelings to flow spontaneously onto the page and not worrying about whether that person would really say what you're putting in his or her mouth.

Pay special attention to any areas that were left unfinished between you and that person: anything that was left unsaid that needs to be said. Continue the dialogue until you've said all the things that seem important.

Now say goodbye.

Some people continue these dialogues for years, finding that in them they can express important parts of themselves for which they find no other outlet in their lives.

Anger

As children, we all had occasional temper tantrums. When we learned to inhibit our tantrums, many of us learned to stop all our anger. Somebody forgot to tell us that it was okay to be angry, but that some ways of being angry are more effective *and* less offensive than others.

Unexpressed anger becomes poisonous. It stops the coursing of the vital fluids of the body, and creates that familiar pinched look that traditionally accompanies the description of "the old maid" who has not allowed herself to feel anger at her life situation, anger that could provoke her to seek more aliveness in her existence.

In our culture, women are especially likely to have learned to stop their anger. It's considered by some to be "not nice," "not ladylike," to feel angry. At last this is changing.

When I hold back my anger because I'm afraid of what will happen if I express it, I feel resentful. If this resentment is strong enough, it turns to hate. Resentment and hate are both anger plus fear. Hate is the extreme of resentment.

Fran had been brutally raped and beaten. When she came to me, she was so afraid of men that she would not let herself express her strong sense of being violated. She had never allowed herself to scream and rage and mourn the event. When at last she was able to do that, she stopped projecting her hostility toward the man who had raped her onto every other man she met.

Put-downs often disguise anger. When I find myself being cold or cutting, I look to see who or what the source of my anger is.

When I disguise my anger in a put-down, I'm hoping that you'll hear my anger but not recognize it: I'll have said it to you and you'll know I've said it, but you won't be able to blame me for it.

So be appreciative when I give you my honest and direct anger. I'm giving you a gift: a real and important statement about me right now. I could poison you instead.

Almost everyone occasionally feels like screaming. Sometimes when I feel really frustrated, I go outside and scream as loud as I can until I feel better. Living in the country, I can scream anytime. In the city I often have to bottle it up, except when I'm driving in my car or when some kind of racket is sure to drown me out. I think every apartment building needs a soundproof "screaming room."

When we share our angry feelings with each other, we can find our way to a special kind of caring.

LeShan writes, "One day George's younger sister took his baseball cards without permission and left them out in the rain. When George found them the next day, he was so furious that he jumped up and down and yelled, . . . 'I hate you.' Nothing terrible happened. . . . George was finding out that he could get angry about things without really . . . hurting other people."

In his workshops, George Bach uses a ritual called "the haircut" that you can use to get your stored-up anger off your chest. It can short-circuit the destructive aspects of the fighting that, when done constructively, can have real value for a relationship.

"The haircut" is not meant to resolve problems between you, except the problem of not knowing each other's feelings. (Problem-solving rituals are discussed in Chapters 8 and 11.)

Let's say I want to give you a haircut. The first step is to get your permission. This takes away the feeling of being ambushed. If you don't want the haircut now, I ask "When?" and we agree on a time later in the day or within a day or two that suits us both. The "If I'm mad now, I've got to tell you now; I can't wait" statement is valid only if I'm mad about something you're *doing now,* or that I just found out about. If I want to give you my stored-up anger, I can store it a little longer until you're willing to listen. If this is a bad time for you, nothing I say is likely to lead to constructive change.

When the time for the haircut comes, we negotiate how long it may last, how far apart we stand or sit, and how high the person giving it stands in relation to the other. When a child gives a parent or teacher a haircut, the child might stand on a desk while the adult sits on the floor, to give the child confidence. Standing high above and physically near the person getting the haircut usually makes the person giving it feel more powerful. Both persons must feel okay about the agreed-upon height and distance. Time is also important. Some people are willing to listen to a haircut for only two or three minutes; others set no limit.

As the recipient, you state in advance if anything is off-limits, if any area of your life is so touchy or painful for you that you don't want the haircut to deal with it. But beware of "putting your beltline too high" so that you stop the person giving the haircut from dealing with matters that are important to him or her.

✳ *The haircut*

Say I'm giving you the haircut. We take the positions we've agreed upon. If there's a time limit, you have the watch.

I let loose with everything I'm angry about that I haven't been telling you: "I resent . . . ," "I accuse you of . . . ," "I'm angry with you for . . . ," and so on. I'm likely to feel best if I rant and rave and shout, getting my anger out in a way that fits how I feel. (I may start out quietly and need a couple of minutes to really get into my feelings.) If I "send a boy to do a man's job," as Thomas Gordon puts it, by giving you my anger in a quiet, restrained voice when I really feel like wringing your neck, I'll still feel like wringing your neck after I've told you what I'm angry about.

When I've finished, you don't answer back for at least a day. This gives you time to think about what I've said, and tells me that you're willing to listen because you care about me, and not because you want to blast me back. This is especially important when a child is giving an adult a haircut, or a person who is hesitant about expressing feeling gives a highly emotional person a haircut.

Sometimes when I'm very angry with you, I may feel like whomping you. The problem with hitting is that somebody may get hurt. Getting hit can also trigger feelings of intense rage or panic that go all the way back to early childhood, so that if I slap you around, your bitterness toward me may connect with a place so deep that you'll never forgive me.

When I'm so mad that words just won't do it, I can challenge you to a bataca—or pillow—fight. Batacas* are made especially for this: you can hit as hard as you want, and get a really solid, satisfying feeling when you land a good blow. The person you hit feels no pain at all. Lightweight pillows will do, but they're not as good.

So that both of you can feel completely safe, be sure to *adhere strictly* to the rules described below.

❋ The bataca fight

The smaller or weaker person says what he or she thinks is enough of a handicap to make the match equal. The more powerful person might have to use his or her left hand, or keep one foot rooted to a particular spot. Handicapping means that even a child and an adult can fight on equal terms: the adult might have to get down on his or her knees and also fight left-handed. After a handicap is agreed upon, it's a good idea to try a brief preliminary round to see if the handicap seems right.

Set a time limit for each round: thirty seconds is sometimes enough; two minutes is a very long round. Put the clock where you can see it. One of you calls the beginning and end of each round. *Either of you can end a round at any point by dropping his or her bataca or pillow:* this is a signal that the other person must stop *immediately. This rule is very important.* The head and genitals are off-limits: if either of you hits one of these areas, the other person gets three free hits. As you fight, make whatever sounds you feel like making. After each round, you can decide if you want another round.

There's no scorekeeping and no winner or loser—you just blast away at each other. To make sure the rules are followed, it's a good idea to have a neutral third person act as a timekeeper and referee the first few times you have a bataca or pillow fight.

---

*Batacas can be ordered from Bataca Products, Inc., Hanover, Mass. 02339.

If you have no bataca or pillow available, you can try *mock fighting*. Mock fighting involves growling, shrieking, and lunging at the other person as though you were actually fighting, but without making physical contact. This is known as "inviting somebody out to lunge."

FINISHING UNFINISHED ANGER.   You can also get free of any anger you still have toward a parent or any other person from your past. Find a beat-up old cushion and get something you can hit it with—e.g., a pillow or tennis racket or bataca.

Now imagine that the cushion you're going to hit is the person you still feel angry toward. Stand in front of the cushion and plant your feet a shoulders' width apart. Raise what you're hitting the cushion with over your head and hit the cushion as hard as you can, again and again. As you raise the object over your head, stand up on your toes, and as you swing down, come down on all parts of your foot, so that your foot ends up flat on the ground as you strike the cushion.

As you hit the cushion, say "This is for . . . and this is for . . . ," telling the person you're hitting everything you're angry with him or her for. You can curse and scream and say whatever you want. Breathe deeply and really yell. Since the person isn't actually present, nothing you say will hurt him or her.

If you stop yourself short and don't get fully into it, intensify and then relax your ways of tightening up and stopping yourself, just as you did with the exercise on expressing your grief.

When you feel spent, sit down in front of the cushion and tell the person you were hitting everything else you have to say to him or her.

You may have to do this several times on different occasions before you feel finished with your anger.

Laughter, joy, and joie de vivre

Johnny was a strange and interesting man. He knew how to be angry magnificently, but was fearful and embarrassed when he laughed. When he did laugh, for an instant his whole body would relax. Then he'd snap back into his protective stance with his shoulders up and his body tight and rigid.

With time, I learned that in his laughter Johnny felt terribly vulnerable. His father used to soften him up and get him laughing, and then attack him. Johnny began to expect that whenever he found himself feeling good he was being set up.

Laughter is so widely accepted that the restraints against it are more apt to be from the inside than from the outside. Somewhere in our past, someone may have said threateningly, "Don't make an exhibition. Stand still and behave yourself."

Have you ever been in a place where everybody was supposed to be feeling good, like at a church or family function, but if you *showed* your happy feelings with any kind of energy, the clamps got put on then and there?

Feeling good is allowing my energy to move, to flow and be free. If I stop myself from showing my good feelings, I stop the flow of my life force and I *actually don't feel as good*. I don't hurt anyone by enjoying myself. If someone takes offense as I express my good feelings, that's their problem.

✳ *Your space for feeling good*

In the course of your day, check out when and where you feel free to laugh, sing, dance, clap, and crack jokes, and when and where you don't. Are there places where some people wouldn't expect you to feel good, but where you feel good nonetheless? (Necrophilia is a dying art.)

How many of the places where you don't feel comfortable enjoying yourself could be comfortable to you if you tried?

HUMOR.   Many times I come through painful places in my life by finding moments when I can laugh at my situation, and find some lightness in my laughter.

I can't do this by going around my pain and pretending it's not here—I have to go through the pain to get to the other side. But as I go through it, I may find a way to make a joke or write a song about it. When I can laugh at myself in my difficult situations, I'm more open to new ideas and new approaches.

The other day I really got angry, picked up the dining-room table and bounced it like a checkerboard. Suddenly I realized what I was doing and saw how impressed my children were with my great rage as I jumped up and down as though I were going to move the universe. Then we all broke up laughing. That added something important to my anger that said, "I am my anger as I am my laughter and my love."

Marcel Proust, as he criticized some of the contradictions of the Church in France, also laughed and enjoyed the contradictions. I can likewise enjoy the contradictions in myself.

If my life were *only* absurd, it wouldn't be worth it to me. When it's so exquisitely absurd that I can only stand here breaking up with laughter at myself, its very absurdity is delightful.

UNHOOKING

Hitchhiking is taking somebody else's trip by borrowing his or her way of feeling in a particular situation. You come in tense and I respond by going into my own tension and uptightness. You come in laughing and relaxed, and I relax and feel comfortable with myself.

When you feel bad with yourself, I don't have to feel that way too. I can offer you comfort without having to feel what you're feeling.

Likewise, I can say to you, "I'm hurting," without asking you to hurt too. Often all I'm saying is, "Hold my hand—I'm afraid." If you join me with your terror, I don't need you.

When you stop to take me on your trip, I can go with you or not. Having my thumb out doesn't mean I'll take any ride that comes along. I can pay attention to where I want to go and what I want to experience along the way.

If I have no clear sense of where I want to go, I may be willing to go wherever you're going. The trouble there is that I may end up in places that I don't like at all and would never have chosen to go into. As I develop my ability to feel my life for myself, I'm less likely to depend on you to carry me along emotionally. I can stay with my own feeling place that's different from yours. When I can walk on my own two feet, I'm not dependent on my thumb, but I can still hitchhike when I choose to.

Unhooking is breaking the connection of automatic emotional responses to certain situations. It's not a way of avoiding feeling, but of giving myself space to have feelings that fit who I am in *this* situation, instead of borrowing someone else's feelings, or feeling as I used to in other situations that this one reminds me of.

You can become aware of how your feelings are hooked as you watch a movie or TV show, or listen to the radio. Pay attention to how you feel in response to what happens in the movie or program or commercial. Tune in to the sensations in your stomach and your muscles. Feel how you tighten and relax. Notice how the presentation is designed to manipulate your emotions, using music, lighting, and other cues to influence you. You can experiment with alternately allowing yourself to sink as fully as you can into a feeling that the presentation is triggering in you, and then withdrawing yourself from that feeling.

When I respond automatically to what you do, my response may or may not be to my advantage. You cry, and I feel guilty. You come on angry, and I knuckle under. You come on soft and loving, and I feel unwilling to tell you that I'm feeling angry about something you've done.

I can hook myself into a way of responding that doesn't fit where I am and what I need for myself.

When I'm responding from a hooked place, I often feel *caught*, so that nothing I do makes me or anybody else feel better. I find myself locked into my tight, frustrated feelings, and see no way to move along a different path.

Regardless of whom I'm with now, when I'm hooked I'm probably dealing with my unfinished feelings toward my mother or father, my brother or sister, or the kids next door.

Almost always, once I unhook from my automatic response, I have available another feeling that fits *this* situation better. I can choose how I want to act toward *you* now, instead of dealing with ghosts from my past.

When I unhook, I don't deny what I feel in response to your hook. If you come at me with anger, I may feel angry in response. Yet I may have enough awareness of what's happening in me that I have other responses available too. I may pick up that you're pushed out of shape, and say, "Hey, you look really upset. What's eating you?" One place in me is angry, *but that's not the only way I feel.*

We can also learn the ways we most often hook each other and stop acting in those ways. For instance, I am an articulate, well-read person. My hook is when, as that person, I start acting like a parent. When I become parent, I'm hooking you into becoming my child: "I know what's good for you, and I expect you to accept it."

As I drop my ways of hooking other people, I respond in a wider range of ways to a wider range of people. I can pick up haywire and disorganized messages without getting my own thoughts and feelings scrambled, and send out warm and caring vibrations in return. Then we all feel better.

Buddha said it long ago: "Hatred does not cease by hatred at any time. Hatred ceases by love. This is an unalterable law."

19 Energy Flow
in the Personality

"I feel so drained," I sometimes hear people say. "I have so little energy."

I can begin to discover how I waste and bottle up my energy, and learn how to find interest and excitement in areas of my life where I've been deadening myself. I can learn to go along with where my energy *is*, instead of getting upset because it isn't somewhere else.

Perls' concept of "holes in the personality" refers to areas where we don't allow our energy to flow.

When I don't look or listen, I don't see or hear; I act as though I have no eyes or ears. When I put all my energy into thinking and computing, I have no heart. When I'm scattered and distracted, I have no center.

Another way I lose energy is resisting what's going on around me, "opposing" or "setting myself against something."

Music I don't like may be playing in a situation where I can't turn it off. As I listen, I grit my teeth, furrow my brow, and think about how I dislike that music.

Sometimes I can stop this process and let myself flow with the rhythm and mood of the music instead of setting myself against it. Soon I start feeling good instead of irritated.

I can resist even the force of gravity, holding my chest and shoulders high and rigid, instead of letting my arms hang down and my shoulders move loosely with my body. When I do that, the muscles of my arms and neck and shoulders get tight and tired.

RESISTING AND AVOIDING

My life as it is confronts me with certain demands. Outside those matters, there is no "should" that says I have to deal with this or that immediately. I can deal with what feels right to me now. I can pick out something I can handle and work with that, rather than try to do too much and end up confused.

In the meantime, my ways of resisting or avoiding dealing with areas of my life that I don't feel ready to cope with now may keep me from being overwhelmed. They can help me handle the basic areas of my life that I need to deal with in order to survive at all. This sometimes happens naturally in all of us. It's a response to discomfort. When my discomfort is strong enough, and I have no other way to get rid of it, I block my painful feelings and the events around them out of my awareness. After all, who wants to be uncomfortable?

Unfortunately, these processes can also blind me to perceiving areas of myself that I *need* to deal with now.

As I learn how I avoid and resist, I can choose which ways I want to keep on doing that, and which ways I don't, because they cut off too much of my aliveness. When I park some way of resisting or avoiding on the shelf, I don't lose my capacity to use it, but I can choose when I want to use it and when I don't.

When I *avoid*, I look away from the issue. I let myself be sidetracked by my world of distracting events. Sometimes I'm aware that I'm avoiding and sometimes not.

At times I seem to be dealing with a matter when I'm really not. For example, I deal with an abstract idea related to the issue instead of with the specific issue, or I focus on some minor detail to distract myself from what's important about the matter.

Staff members of a local hospital spent most of a series of meetings talking about ways of dealing with patients. That was a real concern, but they were using it to avoid dealing with another matter that was also important to them: their own feelings of satisfaction and dissatisfaction in their work. They thought they "should" be concerned only about the patients, and that their personal satisfaction was not a legitimate issue. Finally they got out of that dichotomy by realizing that their feelings about their work affected their effectiveness with patients.

When I *resist*, I put something else between me and the issue. I block it out of my awareness and convince myself that it doesn't exist. I look at the event and see only the distracter I've put between me and it, or don't see anything there at all. When I go to the extreme of saying, "There's nothing there for me to deal with," or "I never do that," I'm resisting in the way Freud called *denial*. I *deny* that anything important is happening to me.

Not long ago, a boy and I were talking about his parents. Then, all of a sudden, he was making noises and shoving another kid, and the matter he'd been talking about seemed forgotten. As we talked, we'd gotten close to an area that was frightening for him: getting involved with the other kid was the boy's way of blocking his feelings out of his awareness.

Another way I can distract myself is with a surge of vague, mixed-up feelings that confuse me. My thinking gets slow and muddy, all my energy goes into coping with the way I feel, and I don't see the issue other people say is there.

Here's a way to explore some feelings that many of us often resist or avoid dealing with:

 Secrets

We all have our secrets. We may think these things we are ashamed or embarrassed about are so awful that other people might want nothing more to do with us if they knew about them.

Here's something you can do with others. It works best with eight to twelve people.

Identical pieces of paper are passed out to everyone. Each person thinks of something he or she has seldom or never revealed to anyone—some carefully guarded secret. Each person briefly describes it on the piece of paper, which is then folded and put in a hat. The pieces of paper are shuffled, and each person draws one out. (If anyone gets his or her own, he or she and several other people put back the ones they got and draw again.)

Each of you talks about the secret you've drawn as if it were *your own*, telling how you feel having a secret like that. Others can ask questions if they want.

No one ever finds out whose secret belongs to whom. *Do not under any circumstances or in any way make fun of anyone else's secret.* The temptation to do this can be strong, especially if a secret touches off anxiety, or the whole procedure takes a long time.

When you say to me, "I think you're not dealing with something," *in a nonjudgmental way,* you're also saying, ". . . and that's okay, as long as you know it's there, and that you have the choice to deal with it or not." Your implicit demand is that I be aware of what I'm not dealing with, not that I deal with it.

When I resist even that awareness, the main thing is not to force myself to stop resisting—which is impossible—but to *get to know the process* I use to keep myself from discerning the place that frightens me. *The resistance itself becomes the center of my work:* The important event is not what I'm trying to do, but how I interfere with doing it.

When I try a way of behaving that's new for me, for instance, and suddenly find that I'm giggling and chattering instead of doing what I meant to do, the laughing and chattering is how I'm stopping myself from experiencing the feelings and thoughts that come as I try the new way.

I can also ask myself, "What's in it for me not to take care of the matter I'm resisting dealing with? Is the gain for me in not dealing with what's out there worth the cost?"

I may do something a thousand times and still be unwilling to perceive it, if my payoff for keeping it out of my awareness is strong enough.

I've seen parents who are always saying "Just a minute" to their children. Perhaps two hours later, if at all, the parent responds to the child's request. This happens thousands upon thousands of times in the child's experience. The child soon learns how unimportant he or she is in the parent's eyes.

In the counseling situation, the child wails, "You always say, 'Just a minute,' *and then you forget about me.*"

"I don't do that!" the parent replies indignantly.

Until the parent is willing to deal with his or her resistance to recognizing how little importance he or she gives the child's demands, the situation will continue.

Often my payoff for resisting and avoiding is that it keeps me from recognizing something that might threaten my self-image.

INHIBITIONS. Having an "inhibition" is a way I resist feeling my power and ability. I'm "inhibited" when I don't do something I'd like to do because I'm afraid of someone's disapproval. When I stop scaring myself, I begin to have my energy available to act.

✳ Wish and inhibition

With another person, make a statement of what you'd like to do, right now in this place, but that you stop yourself from doing. "Here and now I want to . . ." You may be stopping yourself from *doing* something, or from *saying* something you'd like to say, but are reluctant to. (The latter is called "withholding.")

The other person replies by telling you why you shouldn't do what you're stopping yourself from doing.

How well does that person's prohibition fit your own inhibition? How is it different from what you say to yourself? Tell the other person, "Yes, that hits it on the head," or "No, that isn't it," or "That's part of it, but there's more."

If you can say, "No, that isn't it," then somewhere you have a statement of what it is.

Some common methods of resisting and avoiding

DISTRACTIONS   A way I can distract myself from feeling uncomfortable is by *jumping from one thing to another.*

When I feel embarrassed, I may scan for some event that can distract me from my feelings. I do this without knowing it. Then my attention jumps to that distraction, blocking out my thoughts and feelings about having acted in the way I don't feel good about. All this happens in an instant.

When I notice some kind of apparently unconnected chatter or nonsense come through my head with a lot of force, for instance, I look for what's behind or underneath my self-interruption. I usually find something that I feel uncomfortable about.

By jumping from one thing to another I can avoid dealing with my problems with another person.

You and I may need to deal seriously with matters that are important to us both. But as soon as one of us gets touched in a sensitive place, he or she brings up something distractive. Then one of us will find still another new issue to distract us from the second one as soon as it gets touchy. Or I may crack a joke and then forget what we were dealing with, or suddenly have to go to the toilet.

Distraction works especially well in groups, since every person brings in sources of distraction. I attend meetings in which hardly anything gets done. We have important things to do, but we consistently move on to something else before finishing the previous matter. When the meeting is over, I find myself thinking, "We spent two hours in there and we didn't finish *anything.*" For this to happen, we have to tacitly agree to let ourselves be distracted.

In a counseling interview or group, a client gets the counselor or group leader interested in one problem and then moves on to another one. The person never stays with anything long enough to finish it, yet isn't aware of doing this. He or she sends up a continuing scatter of balloons, let loose one at a time. Each one is interesting in its own right—but collectively they keep the person distracted and unable to finish anything. Then he or she may complain, "We never get anything done." By attacking the counselor, the person resists looking at how he or she avoids doing anything.

When a person says, *"Let's move on,"* in a counseling situation, it nearly always means he or she feels uncomfortable with what's happening right now.

So whenever I hear that, I doublecheck: "Do you feel finished with what we've been dealing with—ready to close the books on it?" Almost invariably the response is "No, I guess I've still got some work to do with that."

When I've dealt fully with some matter, I don't need to "move on." Something else will appear spontaneously in my awareness to replace it.

GENERALIZING. When I generalize, I can stay global and broad, and avoid focusing on the specific event that I'm not dealing with.

Generalization is seductive, because what I say may sound important when I spout fancy-sounding general principles. But I'm not likely to touch the heart of anything of real concern to either you or me if I don't go from our general principles back to specific events.

You and I help each other mutually avoid by accepting and encouraging each other's generalizations. Our generalizations are often *failures to discriminate* among different specific events. We can implicitly agree to act as though our generalizations are specifics, with concrete meaning. Once we do that, we can do a beautiful job of avoiding, and talk for hours without touching specific concerns important to either of us.

RATIONALIZATION. Freud used the term *rationalization* for the process of resisting an experience by substituting logic for feeling when one's feelings are what's really happening. In other words, everything has to "make sense" according to ideas I already hold. I don't allow myself permission to be illogical or unreasonable, or to act in ways that don't fit my old "shoulds" or my self-image.

My payoff in putting all that effort into staying out of touch with my real feelings, my real motives, my real intuitions, and my real awareness, is that I avoid facing my contradictions and my own fears about what would happen if people found out how I truly feel.

Once I realize that *it's okay for contradictions to exist in me*, I can start to notice when and where I rationalize, and see if that's what I really want to do.

WHEN ONE FEELING HIDES ANOTHER. I can use one feeling to mask another that I don't want to feel too deeply, or even recognize. I might, for instance, joke about something that's frightening to me. In the paratroops, I was the funniest guy you ever heard. I'd look around and see some of the men on my plane trembling with terror. I knew that same terror. My way of handling it was to get terribly funny—sometimes so funny that by the time we had to jump we'd all been laughing so hard that our eyes were watering. We'd forgotten our fear for at least a little while.

On the other hand, sometimes I find it best not to *have* to be funny when I'm afraid. Humor is often an expression of feeling helpless about a situation. When I find myself being funny when I'm anxious, I can check on myself: "Am I really as helpless as my humor suggests?"

I want to be especially careful when I joke about another person. That can cut me off from making real contact with that person, and often leaves him or her feeling bad.

At times I can avoid dealing with something by getting irritated or angry about it.

More often, my irritation or anger is a straightforward response to what you do, or to what I do, or to the present situation.

But when I'm angry about past history—my own or in general, like rehashing the Civil War—I'm probably using my anger to resist being in touch with something that's going on in me or in you right now. The same is true when I'm angry about some consideration like "What will happen if . . . ?"

My irritation or anger about an event in some other time and place is likely to provoke anger from you in return. The fight or tense exchange that follows blocks out all awareness of the current event that I wanted to avoid.

Just as anger can mask grief, crying can mask anger. By suppressing my anger toward you, I make myself powerless. The difference is often that tears that nourish don't sting. When my crying leaves me feeling cleansed, refreshed, and awakened, my crying is nourishing. When my tears come out of a place that hides another place, my eyes burn and my tears have a salty sting. This kind of crying can distract me from feeling my anger, or can be a way I avoid contact with you or manipulate you so you respond, "Oh, poor baby—I'm so bad! What can I do to make everything all right?"

MEETING AN IMPASSE

Many times I've wanted to make contact with another person but have stopped myself. I imagine that if I approach the person, he or she will laugh at me or turn away coldly. Other people may notice us and think badly of me too. At that moment, I don't feel strong enough to risk that put-down. The point where I stop myself from doing something that I want to do, because I'm afraid of what might happen, is an impasse.

I face many impasses. In some of these dilemmas I keep myself from doing what I want to do, whereas in others I want to stop doing something but keep on doing it. In still others I want to meet situations in a way different from my accustomed way, but I don't know of any alternative. Perls states:

> The impasse occurs originally when a child cannot get the support from the environment, but cannot yet provide its own support. At that moment of impasse, the child starts to mobilize the environment by playing phony roles, playing stupid, playing helpless, playing weak, flattering, and all the roles that we use in order to manipulate our environment. (GTV, 36)

In my impasse, I have one leg in the past—my experience through the history of my life—and one leg in the future—my still uncertain vision of where I want to go.

Straddling the opposing forces of the fear that ties me to my past and the hope that beckons me toward my future, I'm stuck, stopped, immobilized. I'm refusing to act in my old way, but I can't act easily in my new way yet.

For example, as a child I often found myself deciding whether to obey or defy the adults around me when they wanted me to act in ways that violated what I felt. Sometimes I obeyed them, and sometimes I defied them and rebelled. Later I generalized these ways of acting to include my relations with other authorities. I obeyed them and held them high or defied them and put them down. I seldom met them face to face.

Now I want to leave those ways behind. Yet sometimes when I meet an authority, I come to an impasse that causes me to fall back on my child-to-parent ways. So I'm in an in-between place, moving out of my old ways but not yet knowing what I'll do instead. I feel confused.

Confusion is an excellent distracter. When I'm confused, I don't see anything clearly—especially not what I want to avoid seeing.

To relieve my confusion, I can ask, "What are the conflicting things I want out of the situation? What do I want to avoid?"

When I'm confused about *what you're saying*, I can pretend I understand, stay confused, and not deal with your remarks. Or I can ask you to clarify. "Will you say that again another way?"

When I start exploring my confusion, I often find that I want two different things but can't have both.

The situation is like that of a woman torn between two lovers. "Which one shall I choose?" she wonders. Psychologist Kurt Lewin calls this an *approach-approach conflict.*

On the other hand, the woman may feel attracted to a certain man, but also be afraid of him. This is an *approach-avoidance conflict.*

Or she may have two lovers and strongly like and dislike certain things about each of them. This is a *double approach-avoidance conflict.*

Approach-approach conflicts are usually the easiest to resolve. Once the woman starts to lean a little bit toward one lover, she starts thinking more and more about his good points, and less and less about the good points of the other one. Soon she has convinced herself that this one is much better.

The other kinds of conflicts are harder to resolve, because the closer we get to something we dislike, the worse it seems, so we back away again. Once we're at a distance, what we dislike doesn't seem so bad, and what we like looks pretty good, so we move in again. Thus, we alternate between the opposing forces of advancing and retreating. A lot of life is like this.

An impasse is often a double approach-avoidance conflict. I dislike my old way, but it's easy. I'm attracted by the new way I see beckoning, but it's scary and uncertain.

An impasse is a crucial point in growth. At this point, actively or by default, I choose whether to be alive, to move forward into a yet-shadowy land of challenge and uncertainty, or to retreat to the familiar land of my well-worn ways, and in a sense to die. When my impasse involves something that's of great importance to me, and I can't get what I need for my growth now by staying with my old way, I face an *existential crisis.*

Moving through an impasse

I can move out of an impasse by focusing on what I'm doing right now. How am I keeping myself stuck and dead? What do I have to do to unstick myself and find my aliveness? I can also use the principle of shaping (see page 107) so that I don't demand too much of myself at once.

The *dialogue* can be a useful tool to help me explore what I want to do:

❋ The dialogue

Many people find that they can do this exercise most easily with pen and paper.

First identify yourself completely with one of your two opposing forces—the pushing-forward force or the holding-back force. Become totally that point of view in your mind and feelings, and *write to* the opposing force, noting everything you can about how you feel and what you think right then. (E.g., as your pushing-forward force, you might write, "I will give you no peace as long as you stay where you are. I want the freedom to . . . , etc." As your holding-back force, you might write, "I get many things I want very easily here, such as . . .")

Then switch. Become the opposing force. Give yourself time to sink into this other thinking-feeling place.

Now write a reply to the you who just spoke. Describe what's happening with you at the present instant.

Continue the written conversation, switching back and forth between the opposing voices whenever you feel ready to. *Stay with short statements* in your exchange—no more than a few lines. Sometimes one-line statements are the most valuable. Avoid rambling monologues that take you away from the confrontation between the opposing forces.

If you don't like to write, you can do the same thing talking out loud. Arrange two chairs facing each other. Identify each chair as one side of the dialogue. Make your statements out loud, switching back and forth between the two chairs.

(If you live with other people, you can warn them in advance about what you're going to do, so they won't think you're going nuts as you talk back and forth. You can even show them these instructions: "Look—it says right here in the book to do this. So let's have no crappy comments.")

Or you can close your eyes and do your dialogue inside your head.

A sometimes frightening aspect of working through an impasse is that when I give up my old way before I have a clear sense of my new way, I may spend some time in limbo.

The first time Perls worked with me, he quickly brought me to an impasse where my showman self didn't work for me.

I was sometimes so busy acting that I didn't tune in enough to important places in other people and in myself. I didn't know what my alternative would be, so I felt anxious when I stopped myself from "performing."

When I quit worrying about where I was going and started paying attention to my present experience, my anxiety dropped off rapidly.

Often when I have moved through an impasse and into a new way of behaving, I go back to check out the old behavior before leaving it completely, just to make sure it's still there and still available. This is part of a normal process of development; it's not something to fall into despair and lose heart about. First, it reassures me that I can still use my old ways when I need them—I haven't "burned my bridges behind me." Second, it's a means of testing my new-found strength. I feel stronger when I know I can cross the bridge again and continue on my new road.

LAYERS OF ENERGY

Pain and Frustration in the Change Process.   Reverend James Walker writes, "The therapist provides enough support to encourage the person to risk the pain of growth, and enough frustration of usual means of flight from pain, that the true self can be reborn" (105).

Thus, as Perls points out, any counselor who wants to be *helpful*, to give the person answers, to make things easy for him or her, is doomed from the start. I have to do my own hard work. Someone else can only point the way.

This doesn't mean I want to seek pain and make a virtue out of it. I can look for ways of growing that are not so painful, and I can recognize that the pain I feel is part of growth, or is a signal that there's some way I can grow.

Much of the pain involved in growing is due to the very act of holding back, of not doing what I want to do.*

The Cliché Layer of the Personality.   Perls views the personality as consisting of several layers. At the surface is the "cliché layer." Walker describes it well: "The *cliché layer* consists of the tokens of relationship that we take for granted, such as saying, 'good morning,' shaking hands, and various other forms of limited relationship. . . . These tokens *can* be leads or openings into more meaningful contact . . . setting the stage for deeper relations. Or they can be ways of setting limits to our relationships" (94–95).

Often even if a stranger asks me, "How are you?" I can feel a moment of real contact when I respond from where I am.

"How ya doing?"

"Tired."

"Wow, me too," the person replies with a sigh, and relaxes. Shortly,

---

*At some point in your growth process, you may find consultation with a professionally trained counselor to be helpful to you. To find a good counselor, ask around among friends who have used such services, call the mental health facility or growth center in your community, check with the psychology or psychiatry department of your local educational institution, or ask your community worker or clergyman. In choosing such an advisor, *trust your feelings* about anyone you consider seeing. The most competent person in the world won't be worth much to you if you don't feel good about him or her.

we go our separate ways, yet in that brief exchange, something real passed between us.

Other times I may not *want* to contact you. I see in your eyes and hear in your voice that you're interested in me only for what you can get from me, or I'm preoccupied and don't want to deal with anyone, or, for whatever reason, I want to keep my relationship with you on the surface. Just talking about the weather feels right to me then. But I want to be sure I don't lock myself into that place. I want to be able to speak from deeper levels of who I am, moving into my cliché layer only when that's where I want to be.

THE ROLES AND GAMES LAYER.   Below the cliché layer lies my world of as-if, where I pretend so that I can get what I want. I may play my roles and games in constructive ways, by respecting you and being honest with myself, in order to get things done. Or I may use them in ways that blind me to who I am and stop me from making real contact with you or anyone else.

I run into problems when I forget that my role is a role, that my game is a game. My mask sticks to my face, and I forget who I am beneath it. Then, in Walker's words, "We no longer play seductive, playboy, little lady, and little man; we 'become' the seductress, the Don Juan, the frightened or frigid little lady, the timid or impotent little man, the very important person, and so on. We are always onstage, and the real self rarely if ever emerges from behind the mask" (95).

When I identify so completely with my social self that I push away my deeper thoughts and feelings, I deaden my personal self. When I break through my social self, at first I may feel as though I'm in a void, with no ground beneath my feet. This place where I've dropped my ways of acting that don't come from who I really am is what Perls calls the "death layer."

From implosion to explosion

Sometimes I feel unable to carry out tasks, to cope with other people, or even to amuse myself. In these circumstances I may feel bored, lonely, even worthless. Or I may suppress my feelings so completely that I feel flat and desolate, an emotional wasteland.

This "death layer," "implosion layer," or "anti-existence layer" is where I hold myself in, deadening my senses and putting my brakes on. I turn my energy in on itself, and *implode* (opposite of explode).

There's one place I can always find this energy I keep locked up: my body. When I am tight and tense, I can be sure I have some imploded energy.

The more tightly I lock up my energy, the more likely I am to resent others who seem to be living fully. I can be poisonous toward you in my self-righteous determination to compel you to act in ways I approve of—"for your own good," of course. When I feel resentful about what I see you doing, immediately I ask myself whom or what you are harming. If the answer is "Nobody," then I know I have something to deal with in myself. If the answer is "Nobody but yourself," that's your business.

As I stay in touch with my death layer, I find that my personal self still exists. But I may be frightened of my inner thoughts and feelings to which I've been a stranger for so long. To feel comfortable with them again will take time.

Once those suppressed parts of me start to be active again, I begin to feel their energy, and the energy that kept them bottled up. This newly unleashed life force starts to demand that I give it expression. This is a crucial place—one where I've seen people mess themselves up by saying, "I want to be who I really am—I'm finished with my phony social self!" and throwing their whole social living situation overboard—family, home, everything. For some people this can be right. For others it's not, and in retrospect, they find that they have lost something of great worth. Just as I don't have to do everything for you and neglect myself, neither do I have to do everything for myself and neglect you.

Being for me involves me in my caring for you. Caring for you is part of my being for me.

When I go into and stay in touch with my implosion layer, I learn to feel how I bind my muscles, and how I deaden my body and make it heavy as I move.

When I contact long-suppressed feelings that lie deep inside me, I may *explode* out of my death layer into a wild display of my grief or anger or joy—or even orgasm if I've inhibited my sexual energy and kept myself tight and tense while making love.

Ernie had told me many times that he really loved his mother—now dead—and felt only contempt for his father. But one day, in a dialogue with himself, he unearthed a deep resentment toward his mother for the way she'd blamed him for most of her troubles. When he realized the depth of his resentment, he truly exploded into his anger, and told "her" all the things he felt toward her that he'd so long suppressed.

In that same session, Ernie realized that his contempt toward his father was borrowed from his mother, and discovered that he was genuinely fond of the old man.

VI

Events in the Mind

20 *Thinking*

In the words of an old Zen saying: "When an ordinary man attains knowledge, he is a sage; when a sage attains understanding, he is an ordinary man" (Miura and Sasaki, 121).

As an infant, I learned that there was a "me" and a "not-me." I began to know that my hunger was me, and the source of satisfaction a not-me. I experienced this difference before I learned language, before I could think in words and sentences. In this way, my *knowing* process began to develop.

My knowing process became distorted, however, when I was rewarded for learning information that has no real meaning or value for me, or was punished for failing to learn it. Many of our schools operate this way, rather than working with the child's natural knowing process. As Fromm describes it, the students' "time and energy are taken up by learning more and more facts so that there is little left for thinking. . . . 'Information' alone can be just as much of an obstacle to thinking as the lack of it" (EFF, 248).

As I come to see how the facts in my life relate to each other, I begin to develop *understanding*. Understanding is perceiving relationships among facts that are important to me. As I develop understanding, I become able to use my knowledge. I lose my blind worship of the facts themselves.

The Sufi El-Ghazali commented that the real object of education is the stimulation of an inner consciousness (Shah, S, 149–50). As my understanding deepens, I can move toward *wisdom*. I do this to the degree that, in each situation where I am, *I strive consciously to understand how life in that situation can be nourishing for me and for the other people there.*

Continuing along the path of wisdom, at last a person begins to experience something that's greater than the sum of all his or her knowledge, understanding, and wisdom.

At that stage one experiences the sense of beauty and deep trans-personal love that through the ages has defied man's attempts to define it. Most of us have known brief flickers of this state of consciousness. When I feel that way, I am centered in my world, and my life itself is a statement of the art of living.

Learning to think clearly is an important step on the path that leads to wisdom. In this chapter, we consider ways to do this, through developing our processes of knowing and understanding.

CONCEPT AND REALITY

The meaning of truth

Words sometimes block more than they reveal. They can prevent a true look.

According to phenomenologist Merleau-Ponty, beneath our thought there lies a "first opening" on things without which there could be no productive thought. This "first opening" is our contact with the thing or event itself, unencumbered by ideas about it. As Zen Master Mumon put it:

> In spring, hundreds of flowers; in
> autumn, a harvest moon;
> In summer, a refreshing breeze; in winter,
> snow will accompany you.
> If useless things do not hang in your
> mind, any season is a good season for you. (Reps, 106)

When I reach out and touch a new blade of springtime grass, I know the truth of that blade of grass. For me, this is truth: to experience a thing or event directly, so that I know it as it actually is.

I am unlikely to ever know the *whole* truth of it. Someone else may see or hear or touch a thing in a different way than I do, and know another side of it. The truth of a pancake lies not just in the eating of it, but also in the preparation of it. Consider the very expression "to see something in a different light." A field of grass looks different in the soft, warm light of sunset than it does in the brightness of midday. Truth exists in each of these experiences.

I consider an idea, statement, or concept to be true *to the degree that it helps me accurately experience the thing or event it represents.*

Zen sayings abound to remind us that no statement or concept is identical to what it is telling us about: "The instant you speak about a thing you miss the mark"; "Better to see the face than hear the name";

and Soseki's haiku, "Butterfly, these words from my brush are not flowers, only their shadows" (Miura and Sasaki, 98, 104).

The closest I can come to speaking truth is to cough or burp, because my cough or burp is the event itself, and not a statement about the event.

Our concepts are almost always in some measure arbitrary, depending, as they do, on the way we group events to suit our purposes.

We must learn to tailor our concepts to fit reality, instead of trying to stuff reality into our concepts. A concept is most useful when it points at specific aspects of our experience for us to pay attention to. Thinking and direct awareness are equally important.

Another dimension of truth lies in considering when my words and actions are true to who I am, and when they are not.

I want to be aware of when and where I find truth in what I do, and when and where I don't.

When I act in ways that are not so true to who I am, I want to be sure that I'm doing it to fulfill values that are central in my life. I may be more "diplomatic," for instance, and in a sense be less true to me, in order to derive some value that is important to me. When I do this, though, I'm cautious: I don't want to sell out something I really care about.

And if I want to have a lasting influence, says the *I Ching*, I must live my truth as well as speak it: "Words must be supported by one's entire conduct. If words and conduct are not in accord and not consistent, they will have no effect" (144–45).

CONCRETE AND ABSTRACT

❋ *A word and what it represents*

One at a time, read the words listed below. After each word, close your eyes for fifteen to twenty seconds and allow all the images and associations it evokes to swim into your mind. Then open your eyes and repeat the process with the next word on the list. Covering up all the words except the one you're going to read may help you focus on just one word at a time. Or do this in a group and have one person read the words, at appropriate intervals, to everyone else.

Here's a list of words you can use (or you can make your own list; it's best to stick to nouns):

tree	home	justice	freedom
mother	travel	work	love

If you do this in a group, take a few minutes to share some of your word associations. If not, imagine the variety of responses you would get to each word from ten different people. The exact meaning of any word is unique to the person who uses it.

The word "woman" is much more abstract than the name "Sharon Marian Adams." If I say "Sharon" to you, and we both know her, the image that comes into your mind is likely to be at least a little like the one that comes into mine. If I say, "woman," the images evoked in us may be utterly different. If I say, "person," the images will be even more diverse. And if I say, "living being" when I really mean Sharon, you and I are likely to have a hard time communicating. *Each of these terms is more abstract than the preceding one.*

When you ask me what something means, and I reply with an equally abstract or even more abstract statement, you still don't know what specific events I'm talking about. Politicians are skillful at taking a question they don't want to answer and raising it to the next level of abstraction. We really know what we mean only when we come down out of the clouds of abstraction and anchor our feet on the ground with a concrete example of what a word or concept means.

Listen as Perls skillfully guides a woman from her abstract statement to her concrete event:

> F [Perls]: . . . So let's have the dream.
> M: . . . I'm with my sister, and—and we have a lot of fun together.
> P: In the dream? /M: Yeah./ What kind of fun?
> M: We talk together, we do things together, we—
> P: What do you do together? You see, I can't understand abstract language. I must have something real to work with.
> M: We—we escape together, we—
> P: You escape together.
> M: We escape from people, and—
> P: I don't understand the word "people." From whom do you escape?
> M: From my parents.(GTV, 132–33)

The ability to think and converse on an abstract level is important. Without it, we would have, as semanticist Wendell Johnson says, a basketful of information but no idea where to go with it. Through abstraction, we connect our facts and consider their implications.

Johnson raises the question of why we find some writers and speakers interesting and others dull. Matters of style and charisma aside, Johnson notes that "dull" writers and speakers often remain locked into just one level of abstraction. Either they stay so abstract that we never find out quite what they're talking about or they stay at the level of detailed description without ever tying their facts together and considering their implications, so that we ask, "So what?" Interesting writers and speakers, suggests Johnson, tend to play up and down the levels of abstraction as a harpist moves up and down the strings of the harp. In writing and talking, then, we need to look for the implications that our facts suggest, and continually check our inferences against any information that might serve to test them (276–82).

We easily get into trouble when we forget that we're dealing with abstractions, and act as though they were concrete things and events. For instance, two men may argue about the question "Is it the nature of women to stay home and care for children, or is it their nature to want to go out and have a career?" *without realizing that there is no answer to their question.* When we move from "women" as an abstraction to individual women, we find that it really is Sharon Adams' nature to want to stay home with the kids, and it really is Mary Camden's nature to want a career.

When you and I disagree, it's likely that we've stated our disagreement in an abstract, general way. We can clarify what we're talking about if I give you a particular instance of what I said abstractly before, and you do the same.

I can use my abstractions to avoid important personal events that I feel uncomfortable about.

For instance, you tell me about something that made you feel terribly lonely. I reply, "Yes, I read an article about loneliness the other day. It said that . . ." In responding that way, I've *generalized,* perhaps because I feel threatened by your loneliness. I've moved from your specific event to the abstraction of "loneliness." We never make the contact we might have made if I'd responded to your *event.*

We've all seen what can happen when we get caught up in abstractions. We've seen in the horrors of Vietnam how we began thinking of an entire nation as the abstraction "enemies" and forgot that it was filled with individual people. We've seen how a fine, good person is released from prison and is turned down for job after job, because prospective employers don't see him or her as a person, but only as an occupant of the abstract category "ex-con" or "criminal."

Most of us sometimes behave as though certain words were the things they represent. If you've had a brutal and terrifying experience in prison, you may pale at the very word "prison." If you had harsh toilet training, you may get upset at the very word "shit," and forbid your own child to say it.

Semanticist Alfred Korzybski reminds us that no matter how good a map we make, it still is not the land it represents. His classic statement that *"the map is not the territory, and the word is not the thing"* is a basic principle of clear thinking.

SUBJECTIVE AND OBJECTIVE

"Now, let's be objective about what's happening here" is a statement that often commands instant respect.

By "objectivity" we usually mean being unbiased. This frequently includes being "emotionally neutral" about the matter in question. It may include gathering as much evidence and factual information about the matter as we can, and taking into account all the differing viewpoints available.

In my own life, I can try to be objective about myself and what I do by asking for feedback, and listening to other people as they tell me what they see me doing and how they feel about my actions.

Still we can never be completely objective about anything. Seldom do I feel completely neutral about anything that's important to me. To fit the ideal of being "totally objective," I'd have to become someone who doesn't participate in life at all, but only observes.

Even a physicist in a laboratory is never completely objective. No matter how precise the measuring instruments are, ultimately the physicist must look at those instruments from a subjective standpoint, from *within himself or herself.* The instruments themselves are no more than technological extensions of the physicist's own way of seeing the world.

Even the meaning of a word is subjective. A word by itself means nothing. It is only *I* who mean something by it. What I mean by it tomorrow, in a given context and a given situation, may be different from what I mean by it now.

I come closest to objectivity when I realize that all I can know for sure is "This is what I am experiencing." I am actually most objective when I *describe what I am experiencing as my experience and as nothing more than that.*

A "fact" is a piece of information that several of us agree is so.

A person who stays open to what's happening is willing to consider the possibility that his or her idea about something may be wrong. A person who is firmly convinced that he or she "always looks only at the facts" is usually more concerned with his or her self-image as a "fact-minded person" than with finding out what's happening.

Wearing a mask of "objectivity" is a handy way to avoid taking responsibility for my creation of my view of my world. I may do this by saying that I'm "just being logical" when actually I'm emotionally involved in what I'm saying. The trouble with all this is that as I do it, I *block off my awareness of what I'm feeling and doing,* and thereby lose some of my power to affect my world. When "objectivity" is my absolute stance in the world, I'm asking myself to put a premium value on being a "voyeur" in life.

If I really want to be open to the facts, I have to be willing to see my biases and what they mean to me. Then I can see past them.

DUALISM, POLARITIES, AND RELATIVITY

> Abide not with dualism,
> Carefully avoid pursuing it;
> As soon as you have right and wrong,
> Confusion ensues, and Mind* is lost.
>   (Shinjin-no-Mei, quoted in D.T. Suzuki, 78)

Most of us are accustomed to thinking in "either-or" terms: things are either "this" or "that." "Is the water hot or cold?" "Is she tall or short?" "This is true and that is false." "We're good and they're bad." This way of thinking is called *dualism.*

Most things in this world don't come in twos at all. People aren't "tall" or "short"—they're countless different heights. "Tall" and "short" are abstractions in our heads. Most things and events fall along a continuum of similarity to each other, like degrees on a thermometer.

Speaking of something in either-or terms may badly distort it, yet once I've accepted the either-or assumption, I see the matter only in that distorted way. Someone asks me, "Is it this or is it that?" and without thinking I try to answer in those terms, without reflecting that it *may not be either "this" or "that."*

Many questions cannot be answered in the terms in which they're put, especially when they ask for an either-or answer. When I avoid the trap of dualism, I can often respond to someone with a deeper understanding than a dualistic attitude permits. When another person says something, instead of jumping to a conclusion—"That's so!" or "That's not so!"—I can consider "How is it so, and to what degree is it so in that way?"

*In this context, Suzuki notes, "the Mind = the Way = the One = Emptiness."

There's usually *some* degree of truth, however small it may be, in anything a person says. Ed says to me, "The factory I work in is a horrible place." I may know that the factory pays well, is safe and clean and quiet, and is owned by a generous man. I resist the temptation to reply, "I'm sorry, but you're wrong," and instead ask, "What don't you like about it?" Ed tells me that he feels powerless there. All the decisions are made at the top; the workers have no voice. Ed wants some say in how his part of the shop is run. As I listen, I learn something I might have missed if I'd replied, "You're wrong."

Similarly, *if you and I want to work out some trouble we have in our relationship, we'll both have to give up the idea that one of us is right and the other wrong.*

Polarities

For years I put on a front of being always strong and capable. I seldom let myself be gentle or soft or weak. The former qualities are considered typically "masculine" in our culture, and the latter ones typically "feminine." Jung calls the "masculine" ways of being *animus*, and the "feminine" ones *anima*. Both are important parts of every person's thinking, but we may try to express only one of these sides and suppress the other one. Be assured that both will surface in some way.

During my childhood and teen-age years, I was afraid of being called a "sissy," and so, through a process Freud calls *overcompensation*, I overdeveloped those areas where I felt the greatest doubts about myself, and denied the existence of those aspects of myself I was afraid might be attacked, belittled, or ridiculed.

I've realized that always having to seem strong was a drain on my energy. I never gave myself a chance to feel weak or to cry, even when the urge to do so was intense. By never letting down my "strong-man" front, I refused to open myself to the kind of deep sharing that can come when we reveal our weakness and our vulnerability to each other.

When I'm *only* tough and assertive and powerful, I'm very one-sided. But, when I'm *also* gentle and receptive and vulnerable, I'm a fuller and deeper person, both to others and to myself.

The opposite side of this polarity is getting stuck in helplessness. When Diane saw me recently, she was unwilling to do some things for herself toward changing her life. "I just can't," she said. She had spent her life being pushed in a wheelchair. She had the opportunity to get a battery-driven chair.

"What's in it for you to be so weak and helpless?" I asked.

"I can manipulate people that way," she replied. "They say, 'Oh, poor baby,' and take care of me, and I get what I want and I don't have to think and do for myself. But I'm getting tired of doing that. I never learn to take care of myself."

According to an ancient Chinese saying, "Things that oppose each other also complement each other." In each side of a polarity there is some value and some drawback. Mao writes eloquently on this in *On Contradiction.*

As I think about any aspect of myself and my world, I can carefully consider the value as well as the drawbacks in the side of the polarity I reject, and at the drawbacks as well as the advantages in the side I accept. Then I move out of the stuck place that I'm in when I cling to one end of the polarity and negate the other end. And what seemed to be a contradiction takes on a whole new meaning. Out of my contradiction, I find my creativity.

Discovering your center, out of your experience of your extremes, is what Buddha called "the middle way."

Buddha was born a prince. As a young man he indulged himself in all the luxuries his father's palaces and pleasure gardens offered. Then one day he renounced his royal position and set off as a wandering beggar to seek enlightenment. He tried countless forms of asceticism, and became widely known for the tortures he put his body through. Years later he concluded that they were bringing him no nearer to enlightenment, and abandoned them.

Buddha learned something about who he was from each of these extremes, the hedonistic and the ascetic, and out of that experience, found a "middle way" that suited him. He avoided the dualism of clinging to the midway point and shunning the extremes, for he had found his "middle way" through an experience of extremes.

My friend Lillian shows how polarities can be integrated. She was angry about her tendency to become "mother" in all her relationships with people. With time, she also came to know the "little girl who needs to be taken care of" inside her. At first she disliked both her "mother" and her "little girl." Eventually she found that the mothering she could give her "little girl" could be nourishing; and her "little girl" 's aliveness made being "mother" a delightful and creative experience. Lillian's integration of these opposites improved her ability to relate to other people in ways both she and they felt good about.

As I integrate my opposites, my consciousness expands to include parts of me that I've been unaware of. As this happens, I become less often driven by unknown forces.

I also lose my compulsive need to find in other people those things that are missing in me. For example, as I've come to know the gentler parts of my own personality, I've begun to lose my need for a woman who is a "poor damsel in distress" so I can be a "white knight" and come riding in on my charger to save her.

✳ Reversals

Here's a way to work with your own polarities. Think of a situation in which you can imagine yourself acting and feeling the opposite of the way you habitually do. If you love your parents, imagine circumstances in which you could hate them. If someone bullies you, imagine circumstances in which you could bully that person. Experience your fantasy fully. Be alert for any resistance you feel when you begin to become anxious, afraid, or disgusted, and are tempted to stop.

When your fantasy has played itself out, consider what source of your own power you find in *each side* of the polarity. Consider also what you don't like that might come from clinging to either side of the polarity. (Adapted from Perls, Hefferline, and Goodman, 52–53)

Relativity and ethics

No truth, no event, no object has an absolute and isolated existence. Every state of being or way of acting exists *in relation* to some particular set of conditions.

I think more clearly when I use concepts that encourage relative thinking. I like words like *helpful* and *harmful, constructive* and *destructive.* Those words point toward specific events.

The question "Helpful or harmful to whom, or to what?" presents itself. "When? Where? How? Under what circumstances? In what ways? How do I know?"

When we use words like "right and wrong," "good and bad," "true and false," we seldom ask those questions. If we don't ask and answer them, we get caught in absolutes that may have little relation to the real people and events that we're concerned with.

CLEARING OTHER MIND-WEEDS

Almost every source of information has a viewpoint. When I listen to others, or get information from the media, I try to distinguish between the actual information I get and what the source wants me to believe. Even information that's accurate may be biased, if only the facts that support one point of view are given. I look to see what's *not* said about a matter as well as what *is* said.

Logic and illogic

Logic is a set of rules designed to make our statements consistent with each other. Logic doesn't measure truth, though illogic can measure untruth. My statement may be entirely logical, and yet totally distort the real event. Suppose I show you a yellow pear and say, "All yellow fruits are apples. This is a yellow fruit. Therefore, this is an apple." My reasoning follows the rules of logic, but my conclusion is false, because my assumption that all yellow fruits are apples is false.

"Aristotelian logic" divides events into mutually exclusive categories. It holds that if something has some characteristic, it cannot at the same time not have that characteristic.

The dualistic, "either-or" thought pattern of Aristotelian logic can cause us to think that ideas which seem to be contradictory cannot all be valid. For example, I cannot both love you and hate you. I must love *or* hate.

Another kind of logic is *paradoxical logic* (Suzuki, Fromm, and DeMartino), which shows how ideas that appear to be or are contradictory may also all be true. Paradoxical logic works because our ideas leave out many aspects of the real events that underlie them. The omitted parts of the real events may all be valid, even though the ideas we use to talk about those events may seem to contradict each other.

Certain kinds of illogic are neon arrows that tell us that someone's trying to confuse us so that we'll accept a statement that has little truth.

The *argumentum ad hominem* is an attack on the person. "You stink!" "You're too inexperienced to know anything about that." "Nothing you say can be true, because you're a hippie pervert who never takes baths."

The *argumentum ad verecundiam* involves shaming and appealing to morality. "What kind of a person are you to say a thing like that, anyway?" "Any good upstanding American can see that . . . ," etc.

The *argumentum baculinum* is based on fear and runs essentially, "Believe me or I'll hit you," or "A lightning bolt will strike you if you don't believe me."

The *argumentum ad crumenam* promises a payoff. "I'll pay you if you believe me," or "Good things will happen to you if you believe me."

(And then there's the *argumentum ad nauseum* that says, "I'll keep talking to you until you agree with me.")

Another kind of statement that can confuse us takes the form "A politician is a politician," or "Business is business." The statement *sounds* all right. The underlying meaning, however, is that all politicians are alike, or all ways of doing business are basically the same (and therefore I'm justified in exploiting you).

As Korzybski points out, any statement of this kind is *almost always false.* John Kennedy and Dwight Eisenhower were both politicians, but they were certainly unalike.

Someone might, of course, reply, "The exception only proves the rule!" This absurd statement is a way of saying, "Facts don't count." The person's abstract idea of "politicians" or "business" remains unchanged despite his or her experience. The saying really means, "The exception *tests* the rule," using the word "prove" in its older sense.

QUESTION AND STATEMENT.   Many of us often put our statements in the form of questions. Doing this allows me to remain safe and to avoid putting myself on the line. If I say, "What are you doing that for?" when I really mean, "I don't like what you're doing," I provoke you to defend yourself, but we never deal with my dislike of what you're doing.

This is especially true of the question "Why?" A "why" is often an attack on the other person: "Why are you sitting there with your chin in your hands?" "Why aren't you answering me?" This pushes the other person into defending. The real meaning in the examples above may be, "I wish you'd help me with this work I'm doing," and "I feel anxious when you don't answer me."

Try this: *Go through at least half a day without asking any questions. Make every question into a statement.* When others query you, see if you can detect which questions are real. Resist any temptation to reply to a question by defending or justifying, and instead respond to the underlying statement you think you hear. "I think I hear you saying that you feel . . ." Or you can explicitly say, "I'd like to hear your statement."

Sometimes, of course, questions really *are* questions. I may ask "why?" when I want to understand what's going on or what I'm doing.

Even though asking "why?" can help me understand myself, it usually does little to help me change my behavior. The idea that it does is an error we inherited from Freud. Insight is only a starting point. When I'm caught up in figuring out *why* I'm doing what I'm doing, I'm not aware of *what* I'm doing at this moment, and that's the key to change.

Next time you're tempted to ask "why?" ask "how?" or "what?" instead. Rather than "Why do you think you do that?" ask "Specifically, *what* do you do? *How* are you doing it?" As you ask and try to answer these questions, note how different your experience is than when you ask "why?"

Linear and lateral thinking

The left hemisphere of the brain, which controls the right side of the face and body, regulates the kinds of thinking that most intelligence tests measure: logical reasoning and the ability to manipulate verbal and numerical concepts.

The right hemisphere of the brain, which controls the left side of the face and body, is the side that regulates spatial, artistic, creative, and intuitive mental tasks. This is the side of our brain that can grasp a situation in its entirety, without grappling and figuring (Ornstein, 51–53).

Some people think mostly in a linear, organized, analytical way. Others think in intuitive flashes, in images that sometimes seem scattered and with no clear relation to each other so that one never quite knows what might pop out next. Edward DeBono calls this "lateral" thinking.

Our culture tends to prize linear thinking and be suspicious of lateral thinking. Yet, lateral thinking is a source of great creativity. As we learn to accept both these sides of our experience, we become better able to accept ourselves as unified wholes.

George Prince describes how we can avoid the trap of immediately judging every idea as either "good" or "bad," and open our minds to lateral thinking:

✳ *Brainstorming*

Get a group together and pick out some problem you'd like to solve. Divide your meeting into two parts. In the first part, criticism of any idea is forbidden. Everyone is free to toss in any ideas, no matter how crazy, wild, and impractical some of them may seem. People can also offer spin-offs from others' ideas, elaborating on or adding to the originals in any way they wish. During this process, if anyone criticizes an idea, others gently remind them that criticism is reserved for later on. One person writes down all the ideas that are suggested.

Then, after the flow of ideas has stopped, the group moves into a phase of evaluation. Now, as you each bring out the faults in the ideas that have been suggested, avoid being strictly negative and try to find ways to make each idea work. Cure the weaknesses if you can. Abandon your attachment to "your" idea and your opposition to "someone else's" idea, and try to find ways to make each idea work regardless of who suggested it. Then you may find yourselves with several good ideas to choose from. (Adapted from Prince)

21 Believing and Valuing

Buddha asked each of his followers to believe nothing until he or she had personally experienced it. His teaching was not a dogma, but a method to be experimented with (Saddhatissa, BW, 37). He had little patience for discussing matters which could not be tested out and which had no practical application. Kelen writes,

> A monk . . . suddenly realized that there were some gaps in his knowledge: "[Buddha] has never explained to me whether the world is eternal or not eternal, finite or infinite, and whether the soul is the same as the body."
>
> He paid Buddha a visit and put his questions. Buddha [replied], "Anyone who waited for me to . . . explain these matters . . . would die before I did. . . . You are like a man pierced by an arrow, and . . . he says, 'I won't have this arrow pulled out until I know who shot me and . . . what his family name is, and where he comes from; and whether he is tall or short . . . and what his bow was made of'. . . . You'd be dead before you knew all of this.
>
> "The religious life does not depend on [the matters you ask about]; therefore I have not explained these. Suffering have I explained; and the cause of suffering, . . . and the Path that leads to the destruction of suffering. For this is useful, this is concerned with the principle of the religious life" (126-27)

I believe that the sun will come up again tomorrow. I believe that if I take a certain road, I'll get to town. These beliefs are expectations that grow out of my direct experience in knowing my world.

Some things I believe because other people tell me that they're so. An astronomer tells me that a planet we call Pluto revolves around the sun. I've never seen this planet, but I believe that it exists because I trust the methods of astronomers.

237

We can call the beliefs I've just described "rational beliefs." *Rational belief is belief supported by available evidence.* We can also distinguish *"blind belief,"* which is belief in the absence of evidence, and *"irrational belief,"* which is belief contrary to available evidence.

With blind belief, we could make a case for or against our own belief, but it would be only speculation. With irrational belief, we turn a closed mind toward the facts we have at hand.

Dogmatism includes both blind belief and irrational belief. Dogmatically-held beliefs are not based on personal experience. I argue for something because others tell me it is so or not so and I believe them, even though neither they nor I have personally checked it out. This can be a deadening process, because dogmatically-held beliefs seldom fit a person's experience exactly. So I wind up distorting my experience to fit my beliefs. Thus I become increasingly less able to break through my beliefs and actually touch and taste and smell and hear and see the world that is potentially there for me.

Mind-binding leads to energy-binding. By keeping my belief system closed, I restrict myself physically as well as mentally. I stop exploring.

When I watch people who are not so locked into their belief systems, I frequently see them moving their hands around, looking, touching, and exploring. Those who are tightly locked into their belief systems more often tend to keep their hands to themselves and their eyes straight ahead.

I've been punished for saying certain things and for not saying others. The emotional blocks that resulted from these experiences can control the direction of my reasoning, so that my beliefs are usually emotionally consistent with my fears, rather than with what clear reasoning and an unbiased look at the evidence would lead me to conclude.

Notice when someone, in the media especially, tries to make you afraid of, or stir up your anger toward, any individual or group. This has been a basic step in almost every war in history, and almost every repressive move against those who disagree with the powers-that-be.

We get acceptance and praise from other people when we say we agree with their beliefs, beliefs that may be mistaken. Our rewards for clear thinking come most often from success in dealing with our world. Those rewards are often more delayed than is the social pressure for accepting inaccurate beliefs. We may end up believing blindly and irrationally because of what it gets us in the short run, even though we suffer in the long run.

Experimental psychologist Milton Rokeach has shown that we usually know much more about what we believe than about what we don't believe, and that this tendency is stronger the more tightly we hold to our beliefs (OCM).

The process works like this: If I let myself find out about those things I don't believe, I might find some value in them. Then I'll have to question the beliefs and disbeliefs I already hold. By staying ignorant about anything I don't already agree with, I can avoid changing.

On the other hand, by finding out more about the things I don't believe, I can open up to growth and learning.

Don Juan told Carlos Castaneda that our reality is merely one of many descriptions of the way things are. But we take this "reality" so much for granted that we hardly ever question it (JI, 9, 14, 299).

My Miwok Indian colleague David Peri was trained as a shaman, a healer. "The ordinary people of my tribe have many beliefs," he once told me, "but the shaman's path of learning includes strict training to *believe nothing,* to accept only what we have experienced for ourselves. Only thus can we avoid falling into superstition, and be sure we do not fool ourselves. I was taught that the most important thing of all is to know what I do not know."

Mary, who was listening, asked, "Then have you no respect for people's convictions?"

"I have no respect for convictions in and of themselves. I have seen many people cling tightly to convictions that are destructive and stupid. I do not respect that."

"Then do you hold nothing sacred?"

"On the contrary, I hold *everything* sacred. I hold my knowing of the world so sacred that I take every chance to make it more accurate, to bring it closer to truth. Refusal to question some contradiction in my understanding of reality means that I do not respect my view of things *enough.* A view that I have questioned mercilessly merits far more reverence than one that I have never challenged."

Faith

Faith, as I use the word, has nothing to do with belief. When I embrace another human being in warmth and love, when I feel life all around me and feel the warm sun on me, I have faith that life is good.

My faith is my affirmation. It is my "yes" to the universe, the world, my fellow human beings, and my own life of tears and laughter. It is my "yes" to myself, in my hard times as in my easy times.

Having faith means knowing that even my times of doubt and despair are not only all right, but are a necessary questioning of the way I live my life. Sometimes I need to question intensely to keep growing. From these times come some of my deepest insights and revaluings. Life without doubt is stagnation, a deadened Pollyanna's dream.

Jesus understood all this, and lived it. At times he doubted, but his faith was deeper than his doubt. He declared that through your faith, you can be saved, just as Moses had faith that he could lead his people through the wilderness. Most of us want to be saved from our continuing despair and self-negation, from feelings of being cut off from ourselves and from others.

To the degree that we find our faith in ourselves and in life, we free ourselves from these dark fears and apprehensions. When I feel my faith in me, in you, and in our world, I feel full and good, and the sun is in my heart.

ATTITUDES

A feeling is a momentary event. When a tendency to feel a certain way toward something or someone persists over a period of time, we call it an *attitude*. When an attitude is linked with an idea or belief, it becomes an *opinion*. An opinion, as we define it here, involves both thinking and feeling.

My attitude toward something or someone can vary from moment to moment and from day to day. And it's a matter of degrees. My favoring or disfavoring may range from very slight to very strong.

Actually, favoring and disfavoring, feeling "positive" or "negative," are quite broad categories. To be more specific, imagine the body postures that go with each of the following variations of a "negative" attitude: "a chip on the shoulder," "too big for his britches," "a timid attitude," "a fearful attitude." Begin to notice the attitude you see people express in their postures and movements.

Experimental psychologists like Heider, Festinger, Osgood, and Newcomb have shown that we usually feel more comfortable when our attitudes seem to us to be *consistent* with each other than when they don't.

We also feel more comfortable when our *beliefs* are consistent, and when our beliefs and attitudes are consistent with each other. In one experiment, for example, Rosenberg showed that when people were hypnotized and induced to change their *feelings* about U.S. foreign policy, they changed some of their *beliefs* about it too. Advertisers use this technique.

When I notice that some of my attitudes or beliefs don't fit together too well, I wonder whether one of them might be mistaken. That starts me moving to clear up what I don't understand.

Likewise, if I like and respect you, I may feel uncomfortable when you and I think or feel differently about some matter. I expect you to think and feel as I do about important issues, yet we disagree about this one. That discomfort may provoke us to search for some way we can agree with each other.

We may, for instance, feel differently about a certain political candidate. As we talk, we discover that you favor his proposals for education, while I dislike his views on labor. As you explain his proposals for education, I find that they sound all right to me, and you discover that you don't like his views on labor any more than I do. Our attitudes are really about *different things.* When we move from our more abstract "attitudes toward Candidate X" to our more concrete attitudes toward specific proposals, we achieve consistency and also learn something.

Other times, even when we get specific, we still disagree. Then I may adopt a let-it-be attitude. You and I differ on this matter, but we can still enjoy each other. I may still feel a little uncomfortable about our disagreement, but I can recognize that discomfort, and live with it.

My drive to achieve consistency can get me into trouble. If my desire for my beliefs and attitudes to feel consistent is stronger than my desire for clarity, my clarity may suffer.

If a matter is linked with something I strongly dislike, I may automatically be against it. Politicians often use this trick. In the United States, for many years some politicians who couldn't get elected on the basis of their own abilities and programs accused their opponents of "associating with Communists."

Social psychologist Edward E. Sampson, drawing on the work of Fritz Heider and Theodore Newcomb, mentions several things we almost all sometimes do to keep our attitudes consistent.

I may *repress* a belief or attitude that seems inconsistent with another one that is more important to me.

I may *distract myself* from being aware of something that's inconsistent with an attitude that's important to me. Kurt Lewin calls this "leaving the field": I may physically get up and go, or I may psychologically depart by daydreaming or picking up a magazine.

I may *distort my perception.* Most of us tend to like people who are like us and to dislike people who are different from us. So if I like you, I may see you as more similar to me than you actually are. If I dislike you, I may see you as more different from me than you actually are. I might, for example, misperceive any actual likeness in our attitudes. ("She really means something very different from what I mean.")

If I like you and our attitudes about Rebecca differ, I may begin to *change my attitude toward her* so that it's more consistent with yours. ("Actually Rebecca doesn't seem so bad after all.") Or I may *change my attitude toward you.* ("How could I ever have liked someone who thinks the way you do?") Or I may try to *persuade you to agree with me* so that our attitudes will be similar.

Osgood and Tannenbaum have shown that when someone makes his or her attitudes toward two different people or things more consistent, that person tends to change both attitudes toward some middle point, with the attitude that's held most strongly changing least. Thus, a barely known politician might benefit by loudly proclaiming his allegiance to Motherhood. If I'm neutral toward the politician and highly in favor of Motherhood, I may start to like the politician, and my attitude toward Motherhood won't change much.

Leon Festinger studied situations where people hold an attitude or belief that's inconsistent with some *action* they take. He found that most people want to think they did the most intelligent thing, and will go to great lengths to avoid thinking they did something stupid.

Thus if I do something that harms another person, I may make myself dislike that person in order to justify my act in my own eyes. A man may exploit his workers, then rationalize his action by viewing them as "ignorant, shiftless, and good for nothing."

It's when we feel we have a choice that we justify our actions in this way. Arthur Cohen paid people to write an essay supporting a position they disagreed with. Those who were paid very little later agreed more with what they wrote than those who were paid a lot. Presumably, since they couldn't say, "I sold out for the money," they made up other reasons to convince themselves that writing the essay was worthwhile.

And Brehm and Cohen found that after children chose one of two toys they had rated as equally attractive, their liking for the toy they selected went up, and their liking for the other one went down.

The lesson I draw from all this is that I want to be careful that my self-image of being someone who acts intelligently doesn't keep me from seeing my world clearly. Some of my attitudes *are* inconsistent with each other, or with some of my beliefs or actions, and that's all right. I'd rather admit that I didn't do the best thing than deceive myself in a way that will cause me trouble later on.

PREJUDICE

Prejudice is an attitude that I hold strongly and resist changing. Sampson writes of an experience with his own prejudice:

During 1965 I had the opportunity to spend a year in [Southern California's Orange County]. I began house hunting with a noticeable chip on my shoulder. I just knew that when "they" heard I was from Berkeley, they would cringe and color me Moscow red.

I finally found a house I wanted to rent. . . . The owner and I chatted amicably. In the yard next door a man was watering his lawn. My new landlord looked at him, looked at me, and said with a little laugh in his voice, "He's a Bircher". . . . My luck. The house I pick to live in for a year has as its neighbor a member of the ultraconservative John Birch Society. . . .

I treated this neighbor rather coldly. . . . My house had a swimming pool; he and his wife had none. Would I invite them to use mine? Hell no!

Even I mellow eventually. About three months before I was to leave Southern California my neighbor and I got into a friendly conversation. He happened to mention at one point that he was a butcher. I nodded. About five minutes later it hit me. *Butcher . . . Bircher.* What a fool I was! All along it all had fit together so neatly. . . . Who would ever have expected to hear butcher down there in Bircher country? (150–51)

Sampson's story is not unusual. Each of us has one like it. We are all prejudiced.

The less prejudiced I am, the more likely I am to be willing to look into myself and discover the prejudices I do have. As I come to know my prejudices, I can stop myself short of translating them into action.

One kind of prejudice we all share is prejudices about ourselves. "I can't do this"; "I don't know how to do that"; "Intellectuals like me aren't supposed to be able to fix cars, or fix washing machines," etc.

Prejudice is a *way* of thinking, feeling, and acting. The more prejudiced I am toward people and events "out there" in my world, the more prejudiced I'm likely to be toward myself.

So I tend to apply to myself my prejudices about people and things in general. For instance, if I hold prejudices like "A man doesn't cry, and a man doesn't sew," I stop myself from crying when I need to, and from mending my clothes. Likewise, a woman who thinks, "A woman doesn't get angry or do repair work," bottles up her anger, and feels incapable of repairing a lamp.

My prejudice may take the form of feeling hostile toward an entire group of people. When I do that, I respond to any member of that group as a "group member" rather than as a unique individual (Allport). I may prejudge a member of the group without ever having met that person, and without knowing anything about her or him. When I'm prejudiced *in favor of* a person or group, I'm likely to refuse to perceive or believe anything unfavorable about that person or group, and I may act in ways that give them special advantages.

I'm likely to be stingy with goods or services toward members of any group I feel prejudiced against. I'll certainly be stingy with my affection. When I favor other people or groups at the expense of those against whom I'm prejudiced, I *discriminate*.

Being the object of discrimination is usually a punishing experience, one that can engrave deep feelings in a person. People who have lived through years of prejudice and discrimination share feelings and experiences that others will never fully understand.

Some prejudices are tied in with *scapegoating*. Scapegoating is dumping the blame for my troubles on someone who has had little or no part in creating them.

For many years I always managed to have at least one scapegoat. But I didn't realize I was scapegoating until I was a college freshman and made my English teacher my victim. I told all my friends how awful he was. Later I painfully realized that he was a man of integrity, and that I had been most unjust.

I may still seek a scapegoat when things are going badly for me. But now at least I *know when I'm doing it*, and can usually run the drama in my head, instead of acting it out.

As you work to get in touch with your own prejudice, you may find that much of it is a projection of what you won't face in yourself. Reverend John Sanford writes: "Total rejection of another is a characteristic occurrence when someone else is carrying the burden of our own [shadow side]. A person who is carrying the burden of our projections is no longer human to us" (114, 115, 121, 148).

Nietzsche adds, "[Some] are proud of their handful of justice and commit outrages against all things for its sake, till the world is drowned in their injustice" (207).

When I'm prejudiced toward any group, I create a deadness inside me toward all the members of that group. The more such spots of deadness I have, the less I am alive. When I meet someone from that group, I pay little attention to that person as an individual, and learn almost nothing about him or her.

The more often I meet a member of that group as a unique human being, with the same basic concerns I have, the better I feel with myself and my life.

VALUING

Infants have a natural sense of what helps living and growing and feeling good, and what does not.

They positively value food, and negatively value hunger. But when they are full, they negatively value food. The infant "values security," writes Rogers, "and the holding and caressing which seems to communicate security." The infant "values new experience for his or her own sake," and is endlessly curious and forever exploring. Pain, bitter tastes, and sudden loud noises are all negatively valued.

"Unlike many of us," Rogers continues, "he *knows* what he likes and dislikes. . . . He is not at this point influenced by what his parents think he should prefer, or by what the church says, or by the opinion of the latest 'expert' in the field, or by the persuasive talents of an advertising firm. . . . He would laugh at our concern over values, if he could understand it. How could anyone fail to know what he liked and disliked, what was good for him and what was not?" (PTP, 6–8)

As the infant grows, those around him command him to accept their fixed values in place of his own organic valuing process. "*We* know what is good for you. *You* do not."

"But I don't like canned string beans, Daddy."

"Don't be silly. These string beans are delicious." Daddy *negates the child's experience of the world, then defines the world for the child.*

Daddy's statement implies that there is a "true" and "false" about the deliciousness of canned string beans. With *beliefs* there *can* be a true or false.

But *I value what I value*, and there's no external criterion for that. When people tell me, "You don't know what's good," they're really saying that they value something differently than I do.

We can all learn to pay attention to *what we actually do value*. A relationship or family can be a perpetual process of discovery, formulating new "rules of the game" as it goes along, based on what its members value at any given time.

I *actively value* something to the degree that I'm willing to *put my energy into doing something about it.*

My valuing process shows itself in my interests, preferences, decisions, and actions. I see most clearly what I value when I look at how I spend my time, money, and energy.

Owning an inexpensive but reliable car is a statement that I value transportation highly. Owning an expensive car is a statement that I value impressing other people, value thinking of myself as "a person so important that he owns an expensive car," or value certain costly performance and comfort features.

Marty says he values peace and social justice, but so long as I've known him, I've never seen him put any energy or resources into those directions.

He spends most of his spare time sitting home reading mystery novels. I'm willing to say that he values reading mystery novels more highly than he values peace and social justice.

On the other hand, Marty does at least *say* that he values peace and social justice. We can call these *cognitive values*. When he begins to do something about them, they become *active values*. What a person *does* is what counts most.

Here's a way to compare your own values:

 Cognitive and active valuing

Fold a blank sheet of paper down the middle. At the top of the left-hand side, write "cognitive values." List, in the order that they come to you, the dozen or so things that you consider to be your most important values. Then look over your list and rank the items, putting a "1" by the one you consider most important, a "2" by the one next most important, and so on. Do this before you read on.
. . .
Now turn the paper over and write "active values" at the top. Jot down, as specifically as possible, how you spend most of your time, money, and energy. Then rank these items according to how much you put into each. Be honest with yourself.

Now compare your active values and your cognitive values. What do you discover?

The more your cognitive values and active values go in the same direction, the more at peace with yourself you're likely to be.

I can confuse myself if I value dualistically. If I say, "You don't love me because you don't spend enough time with me," I'm creating an either-or situation. The question is not really "Do you value me or not?" but rather "How much do you value me, and in what ways?"

What I value and how much I value it changes from moment to moment, and from one period of my life to another. At one time in my own life, the shiny and bright and new and big formed the keystone of my value system. Other things are more important to me now.

I want to be careful that I don't become so obsessed with one thing that I forget to value other areas of my life. I need these other areas to add balance to my life, or I become "unbalanced." When I become unbalanced in this way, I can often steady myself by remembering the simple things in life. Then I might plant a tree, visit a friend, or reach over to touch a loved one. I don't want to become so caught up in my great projects that I forget these things. ·

22 *Images*

Imagery is the stuff of creation, of stories and poetry, of music and a brush on canvas. It can be a beautiful and fascinating world to explore and understand. It's also the everyday stuff out of which we create our lives, each moment and each day.

My image process is helpful when I want to keep some distance from what's happening in me and around me. I can use my ability to fantasize to avoid being overwhelmed by my pain or my fear. In the ghetto where I grew up, whenever we kids were singing and dancing in the street our fantasy became our reality, and we lost sight of the garbage lying all around us.

In my daydreams and my silent conversations with myself, the world in my mind is as much my reality as the environment around me. If I'm here-and-now in my fantasy, rather than distracted by it, it can be a rich place for me. The important thing is that I know I'm in my fantasy, and can choose to come out of it when I wish. By paying attention to what I'm doing with my fantasies, I can develop my ability to move into or out of my imagination, as fits the occasion. When I really nourish myself in my fantasy, I may be able to come back out of it and confront something I've been avoiding in myself or my environment.

How images can work against us

I used to buy records thinking that there were certain kinds of records I "should" have. I had an image of a "proper" record collection. Finally I realized how crazy that was, and began to buy only records that I really liked to listen to.

During my teens and early twenties, I saw most of my relationships

248

with women through veils of fantasy. I had grandiose ideas of how attractive I was to women, even though these fantasies were far from my actual experience. I had equally distorted fantasies of the women with whom I had relationships. Each one at first appeared to be the Golden Goddess of my Dreams. When I looked at her, I saw only the image I projected on her, and nothing about who she really was. I was more committed to my image than to the real person.

I had a special fondness for relationships by mail. That gave me still more room to live in my world of imagination, instead of being with a living, breathing person, with all her human frailties.

One woman and I lived through two years of a relationship that was sometimes like the screaming, clawing blindness of "Divorce Court" on TV. At last I went away to Chile, sighing with relief as we parted.

In Chile I was lonely. As the months went by, I began remembering the good times we'd had, and I created a new image of her in my mind. As I did, I passed up opportunities to form relationships with some lovely Chilean women I knew. By letter my old flame and I resolved to meet when I returned, and try it once again. Five minutes after we'd met, we knew it was a mistake. My old feelings were as strong as ever.

Even that didn't end the story. Back in the States, again my imagination ran away with me, this time filling my mind with the virtues of a girl I'd known in Chile. "I must make her mine," I thought. (Can you *believe* this?)

After one more relationship by mail, I borrowed the considerable sum of money that a ticket cost and flew back to South America. Naturally, that affair didn't pan out either. Only then did I finally learn my lesson about relationships by mail.

The process of relating to an image of the other person, rather than to the other as he or she is, is at the root of many problems in relationships. At first, each person finds ways to avoid seeing how the other doesn't fit the image in his or her mind. When the image finally crumbles, and the two stand naked to each other's gaze, they find—sometimes too late —that who they wanted isn't who they've got.

IMAGES AND EXPECTATIONS. When you say one thing and I expect you to say something else, I may hear what I expect rather than what you're saying. Then I respond as if you'd said what I expected.

That leaves you wondering. "What do I do now? I'm not getting a response that fits anything I'm saying."

For example, we may have a problem in our relationship, and I expect you to say, "Look, I've got nothing with you, so forget it." You may in fact be saying, "Maybe we can work this through. Here are some places we can explore." But I don't hear that, so we *don't* have anywhere to explore.

Or it can work the other way around. You may be saying, "I don't want to be with you anymore," and I'm expecting you to say, "Maybe we can still make it," so I keep trying with you instead of putting my energy into other places that have more to offer me.

I may try to force you or persuade you to fit my image of the way you "ought" to be.

Almost all of us at one time or another put this kind of social pressure on each other, in both trivial and important matters.

Instead of giving in to that kind of pressure, I can stay with my own sense of what I want for myself. Then I'm dealing with myself according to my own image instead of yours.

THE SELF-IMAGE

"If we renew, until they become a continuity, [our] moments of the knowledge of what we are not, we may find ourselves, all of a sudden, knowing who in fact we are," writes Aldous Huxley (42).

My self-image is a picture of myself that I carry in my mind. If I grow up among people who encourage me to be as I choose to be, the self-image I develop is flexible. As I change, I constantly reweave my image of who I am. When you try to deal with me as I once was, I can say, "I'm not the same as when you knew me before. Here's how I've changed."

If I grow up among people who punish me when I act contrary to their views of how I should be, my self-image is likely to become rigid. I may go through my life believing in pictures of myself that others can see are nothing like me at all.

✳ Image reversal

Finish the sentence "I am now . . ." by letting some image of yourself as you are at this moment come into your mind.

Now, reverse that image. Whatever appears in your mind will do—you don't have to get an exact opposite.

Now ask yourself, "How flexible was I? How much did I lock myself into a particular image?"

To my detriment, I may extend my self-image to involve too many other things. For instance, I see myself as "the kind of person who owns a horse," or as "the kind of person who would never care about wearing expensive clothes." I may identify with some belief or way of looking at the world, and take an attack on that belief as an attack on me. I sometimes think of my self-image as a bubble that gets bigger and bigger as it takes in more and more. The bigger the bubble gets, the easier it can be popped. If my bubble is big enough, I can feel threatened almost anywhere.

The less I'm in touch with who I really am, the more easily I'm threatened by anything that suggests I'm not the way I think I am. So I turn my finest angle to the camera. What I can't admire, I don't see.

For example, I may like to think of myself as "consistent." So even though I act in ways that contradict each other, I refuse to see any contradiction.

Yet at last there comes a point where, for some reason, I can no longer do this. Up to a point, I can avoid, but even God had to face it and flood it.

When I size up someone I've just met, I can be attuned to that person's image of himself or herself and of the surrounding world as it affects him or her. From that I get some feeling about how the person is likely to act in various situations.

The image I present to others

My image of myself affects what I make available for you to perceive. For example, I see myself as "important," and by coming on that way I'm asking you to respond to me as "important."

❋ The "presenting self"

Get together with a person you have some image of but haven't had a lot of contact with.

Let's say I'm that person and that I have, or pretend to have, something of great importance to me in my pocket. It could be a rabbit's foot, a key to my house, a picture of someone I love. I take it out and show it to you (actually or pretending) as a way of telling you something about who I am. By showing myself to you as I want you to know me, I'm giving you my "presenting self."

Then you do the same.

After this exchange, each of us tells what we know about the other now that we didn't know before.

You can do this in your daily life, noticing how you actually do present yourself to others.

In my daydreams and my daily life, I can lose time and energy trying to make myself "look good." I plaster my life with pictures of a temple so no one will know I'm really a merry-go-round.

The other day, Sally and I were talking and I guessed at her meaning. She replied, "No, not any of those. I was just talking to hear myself talk."

I don't have to keep up the image of being always sensible and intelligent. How refreshing! "No, I was just babbling. It didn't mean anything."

Acting as my image of myself prescribes

A very bright friend of mine went all the way through school thinking of himself as a "C student." Despite his ability, he always found a way to make sure he didn't get a better grade than that.

Most of us have ideas like that about what we can and can't do. I can't do some things only because I've never put time and effort into learning them. But my self-image tells me I "can't do those things," so I live within the narrow limits I've created for myself.

Psychologist Prescott Lecky studied a group of students who spelled badly. These people had no lack of ability—they spelled foreign languages as well as anyone. But in their own minds, they were "poor spellers." When they tried to spell in English, their every act conspired to uphold that self-concept.

Lecky found that the poor speller "expects his defect to be condoned and treated sympathetically . . . in effect he has his hand out, begging for indulgence."

So Lecky did a clever thing. He found an image that was more important to the students than their "poor-speller" image. That was an image of themselves as self-reliant and independent (178–80).

Lecky showed his students how those two pictures of themselves clashed head-on. When they saw the contradiction, many of the "poor spellers" started spelling better fast.

Idealized images of how I want to be

My image of how I want to be can be a starting point for change.

At first glance, the process seems straightforward. I often behave in some way I'd rather not. I see another way of acting I like more. So I try to act that way.

The danger here is that as I start checking my experiences against an idealized image of how I ought to be, I can lose sight of who I am.

I may set my ideals so high that I have little chance of reaching them. This is the way of the perfectionist. As I protect myself against being criticized for not having high ideals, I condemn myself to unending self-torture for never living up to my ideals.

Ideals can bring anxiety too. Once I have an ideal, there's a "right" way to be and all other ways are "wrong." All the anxiety that goes with my fear of being wrong starts dragging around with me.

Having an ideal and trying to meet it can also be a stop sign that brings constructive thought to a halt. Since I know how I'm "supposed" to be, I don't need to be alert and question anymore.

On the other hand, I can imitate some special quality I find in another person without having to act just like that person.

I can move in the direction of behaving in a way I admire without worrying about reaching any particular final way. That leaves me free to find my own expression of my new way.

A friend of mine has a special quality of "egolessness" in his relations with other people. He doesn't get upset at comments that most people would get defensive about. When someone says things he could interpret as put-downs, he tunes in to the central meaning he hears coming from that person, and speaks to the heart of the person's concern. The garbage that most of us would get upset about doesn't faze him.

I was greatly impressed by this quality when I first met him. Since then I've worked on that dimension of myself. Sometimes I can do that same thing now. My way of doing it is different from his way, but it suits who I am. And since I'm not trying to fit a rigid ideal, I don't have to be angry with myself when I do respond defensively.

SUCCESS AND FAILURE

For most of us, success and failure are important parts of our self-images.

Perhaps you've failed time and again at whatever you've tried, and conclude that you can't succeed at *anything*.

If so, a central fact is that you're *very successful at failing*.

If I'm successful at failing, I know one thing for sure: I get some kind of satisfaction—some *secondary gain*—out of failure. "I actually fail" is the central event. I don't get the primary goodies I would if I succeeded. But I'm notably successful in getting secondary gains like your sympathy—"Aw, what a shame. Well, you tried, and you're a good fella. Keep trying. Keep plugging."

If, when I fail, I get support and warmth from you that I don't get at other times, I may learn to fail in order to get those goodies.

When I consistently fail, I get another thing out of failing too: predictability. I know what to do to fail, what circumstances to do it in, how I'll respond to my failure, and what my secondary gains from other people will be. I face little uncertainty.

Often the kid who drops out of school is saying, "I know how to fail. I can do that well." If I'm that kid, one trouble I have in changing is that I'm afraid I'll be faced with doing something I won't do as well— something I'll be just average at, or maybe even worse than average. So I carefully guard my image of myself as a "failure," and tune out anyone who tries to get me thinking differently.

If I'm really successful at failing, I must have some kind of talent. The odds are good that if I decide to, I can start succeeding at other things too. To do that, I need to develop other ways to get the gains I get by failing.

I need to listen for the ways I ask for and eat up sympathy when I fail, so I can stop doing that and instead ask for appreciation when I succeed. And I need to develop ways of getting what I want from other people that don't involve hurting or punishing myself.

Finding your talents for success

The first step away from failure is to explore your strengths. What do you like to do? What do you actually spend your time doing?

As I listen to you tell me how you're failing, I may notice that you speak well and easily. You tell me you spend a lot of time shooting the breeze with the guys on the street or with the women in the laundromat. Okay, let's see how you can get paid for that.

A good talker might do well in public relations, or promotional work, or sales. Or as a radio announcer or a youth worker—the person who talks to kids who hang out on the street and helps them with their problems. Or a teacher—not the I-lecture-and-you-listen type, but the person who can really rap back and forth, who makes a room full of people come alive. If you work in a factory, check out the union. You might become shop steward.

Even if you see nowhere to go right now, you've done something by getting your energy together to explore. Sometimes it takes time to find your way. What counts is that *you're moving in the direction you want to move in.*

❋ *Appreciating your competence*

Find some everyday activity you do often and easily. Like pouring yourself a cup of tea, or unlocking and opening a door. Pay attention as you do it, and do it with special ease and style.

Then congratulate yourself on how well you did it. "Good! I really did that well!"

Take a few moments right now for some everyday activities. Put down this book, tie your shoelaces—do several things like that. Give yourself plenty of appreciation for doing those things so well and so successfully.

Throughout the rest of today, notice the many things in your daily life you do well.

Maybe you exchange a few pleasant words with the clerk at the store as you make a purchase. As you turn away—"I did that well." *Find where you are typically successful,* and give yourself lots of *immediate, moment-by-moment appreciation* for doing those little things so well.

Next, begin watching for things you sometimes succeed and sometimes fail at. For instance, perhaps you don't always or even often do or say little things to help other people feel good. Give yourself *extra* appreciation for succeeding at these things.

Pay special attention when you get into failure-talk inside your head. Notice the body position you go into when you feel like a failure. Exaggerate it. Do it to the point where you feel ridiculous (to get fully in touch with what you do). Now, out loud, talk your failure-talk to yourself, exaggerating that too. Take as long as you need to really hear what you're doing to yourself.

After you've explored these ways you make yourself feel like a failure, you can do something else. From then on, whenever you notice that you're in your "failure posture," move into a posture that lets you feel good in your body. When you notice failure-talk inside your head, cancel the rest of it and put your attention somewhere more worthwhile for you.

If you want to be more successful in a certain area of your life, pick something *specific* that you want to do.

Many people spend so much time generalizing their problems that they never get down to working on specific things. "My problem is self-confidence. I can't do anything different now, because self-confidence takes time to get."

Statements of confidence and support from other people can do a lot to help you feel competent and successful. Belittling and put-downs from others make it easier for you to feel like a failure.

Part of the way I can keep up my image of myself as a failure is to stay away from people who give me support for my competence. When I hear appreciation for the way I've done something, I can refuse to believe it.

The more willing I am to use the statements of support I get, and to stay away from people who belittle me, the more easily I can move toward feeling capable of standing on my own two feet.

Feelings of inferiority and striving for superiority

Alfred Adler, one of the pioneers of modern psychology, wrote at length about feelings of inferiority and superiority.

In many of his patients he observed a process he called "striving for superiority" that originates in a feeling of *inferiority*.

If I'm a child, I *am* inferior in many ways compared to the adults around me. If those adults help me to do so, I can feel delight with myself as I am now—I don't have to compare myself to anyone. But if adults and other children think they have to make me feel small in order for them to feel big, they will tell and show me in many ways that they're superior.

As I grow in size and strength, I begin to imitate their ways. I step on others and make them feel small so I can feel superior by comparison. Years after those who made me feel inferior are in the grave, I may still be trying to get back at them by making someone else feel small. Thus I keep the vicious cycle going.

Many books and movies have shown the brutality with which some people kick and elbow aside others standing in their way so they can climb the ladders of "success" in government or business.

This kind of "success," spawned by the drive to be "superior," seldom brings much happiness, for the striving never ends. There is always someone else to whom I feel inferior, whom I must surpass to feel superior. And as I gain power, my lust for power grows, for the more people I control, the more superior I can feel. And once on top of the ladder, there's nowhere to go but down.

Thus, there is no resting place. Nowhere on the ladder of superiority do I find peace with myself. Nowhere do I find love or happiness. These things are outside the dualistic game of superior and inferior.

I can step outside that game. I can start appreciating myself as I am, so I don't crave to feel superior to another.

I can pay attention to the cues inside myself that tell me I'm about to put you down so I can feel superior, and *stop myself from doing so*. Then I can look you in the eye as an equal, as one person to another, and maybe even share some warmth and caring.

Success and failure in my own terms

Suppose I have a job that fits everyone's image of success. "Look at what a great job he has," they say.

But I don't like what I'm doing. There's something else I'd rather do.

I may face pressure from people who think I'm crazy to give up that "great job" to do something that pays less or has less prestige but is what I want to do.

If I'm in touch with who I am and where I want to go, I can withstand that pressure—and maybe even, without knowing it, serve as an example to someone who's facing the same struggle.

A close friend of mine gave up his job as professor of anthropology and became an electrical repairman. The job suits him better and he's glad he changed.

I can start to define "success" in *my own way* instead of someone else's. Striving for superiority is reaching for success in someone else's terms. I can stop trying to get promoted to a job that has more prestige but that involves work I don't like as much as what I'm doing now. I can start making the decisions that will help me lead the life I want to lead and help me feel good with myself, instead of the ones that will make me seem successful in other people's eyes.

Some of my colleagues in other universities can't understand my "lack of success." They wonder, "Why haven't you written professional papers?" "Why aren't you Chairman of . . . ?" and so on. In their terms I'm a failure.

They've accepted a standard definition of success that's widely shared in our profession. The pressure to accept that definition is strong. I accepted it myself until I began to understand how I was poisoning myself by trying to live a life that was not my own.

Now I do work I like. I feel good about what I'm doing. I'm very successful *in my own terms.*

Parents are often a source of feelings of success and failure. I may feel successful as an electrician, but to Mommy, who always wanted me to be a doctor, I'm a failure.

I could buy her judgment and *feel* like a failure. But there's another way I can deal with these parent-messages. I can hear the implied message that I have the skills or the intelligence to be what she wanted me to be.

I think here of my experience counseling young men who refused to be drafted into military service. Often the man who came in for counseling was from a military family. Sometimes he had been thrown out of his home because his family wouldn't tolerate that kind of contradiction.

Yet how often, as I listened to the young man talk about his family, I heard some suggestion that said, "Find your own way." The young man was not successful in his parents' overt terms, but he was successful in terms of the implicit statement that said, "Do what you have to do for yourself."

My father was a failure in most people's eyes. When we finally got enough money together to open a small fruit store, the business made money only when my mother ran the store.

My father refused to act in ways that would lead to success. When some kids asked, "Can we have a few cherries?" he gave them the cherries. Other kids heard what he'd done and came in, and he gave them cherries too. Soon he'd given away a whole lug. He said, "Children should have cherries."

My mother blew her lid at that. To her and to many people in my family, my father was a hopeless failure. To me, his success as a nurturing human being was more important than making money, if that meant his becoming someone else.

Unfortunately, he saw himself as a failure. So much of the feedback from his small world said, "You're a failure," that he bought that evaluation. But he wouldn't stop what he was doing. He still said, "This is who I am."

LIMITS

Moving past limits

I sometimes have to narrow down the number of choices I consider, so I don't become confused by too many alternatives.

My problems come when I forget that I set these limits, or accept the limits someone else imposes on me, and think that the options I see are the only ones open to me.

As I find out how I give up my power, and learn to stop doing that, I can move past limits that have been the boundaries of my life.

When I push against my limits, I'm surprised at how many mountains turn out to be mole hills. I'm also surprised at how much strength I have to climb the mountains that are really mountains.

✳ *Expanding your life-space*

Think of a place in your locality where you've either never been or where you've been but didn't feel at ease. (When somebody says, "Let's go to . . . ," you say, "Who, me?")

Now, *actually go to that place.* Act as you want to act there—perhaps in a way you've never acted before. Pay attention to the kinds of responses those surroundings trigger in you.

Moving past my limits means considering new possibilities. It may also mean giving up something I value in order to get something that's even more important to me.

In moving beyond one of my limits, I take a risk. The risk may be no more than that of having my feelings hurt, but when I don't feel good about myself, even that risk can be frightening.

Taking a risk does not mean acting stupidly. If I'm on the fourteenth floor, I won't test the limits of gravity by walking out the window. That's not taking a risk—it's being stupid. In that situation, I *know* what the limits are.

When I don't know what the limits are, I can find ways to test them that won't harm me or other people.

One limit that's important for many of us is the fear that others "won't like what I do," or "won't like me." So I bend over backward not to offend you. I do things I don't want to do to please or impress you. Your whim becomes my limit.

I can break through this limit by learning to do what I feel good doing. As long as I'm neither causing you injury nor belittling you, if you don't like what I do, that's *your* problem.

Living with limits

As I change in ways that help me move past certain limits, I also want to live comfortably with those limits that feel right to me.

Discipline is one kind of limit. Letting my energy go in all directions is a way I can avoid going far in any direction. Discipline means channeling my energies along certain paths. When I do this, I can achieve goals that are important to me.

Economy sets another limit on my actions. If I spend my resources heedlessly, I soon have nothing left. By contrast the *I Ching* reminds us that "if we live economically in normal times, we are prepared for times of want" (231).

Time sets its limits too. Some things can be made to happen quickly. Others by their nature happen slowly. Some events are over all too soon. As the *I Ching* puts it, "Whatever endures can be created only gradually by long-continued work and careful reflection. . . . He who demands too much at once . . . ends by succeeding in nothing" (127).

When I remember this, I don't lose heart when the going is slow. I can feel good about working in a way that feels right to me, even though results don't come overnight.

CONFRONTING OBSTACLES. When an obstacle blocks my path or threatens an enterprise I want to carry out, I do better to stop and assess the situation than to push blindly forward. Once I have a clear view of the forces at work, I may find a way around the obstacle.

Sometimes when I pause to understand an obstacle, I realize that what I'd planned to do doesn't fit the situation. It may not be right for me or for other people who are affected, or may conflict with more powerful forces that are at work. In any case, I can withdraw from that project and do something else.

Living through difficult situations is an important way I learn, if I use my eyes and ears, my reason and my imagination, and stay in touch with my heart and my intuition.

Out of such learning can grow strength and wisdom. Out of this strength and wisdom comes the power to move past obstacles that would once have stopped me easily.

23 *Dreams and Fantasy**

On the Malay Peninsula, a people called the Senoi created a way of living that centered on their dreams. Upon awakening each morning, members of the tribe consulted their dreams for messages.

If a person dreamed of feeling angry toward someone, or of hurting or killing that person, he or she immediately shared the dream with the person, and then the two of them resolved the tensions between them. Members of a family shared their dreams upon awakening, and then worked on problems the dream revealed. People of the tribe gathered daily to discuss the new understandings that grew out of their dreams. When someone reported an especially interesting dream, other members of the tribe might say, "Go back into your dream tonight and see if you can bring back a new dance, or a new teaching, for us."

Drawing on the wisdom of their dreams, the "primitive" Senoi people created a democratic society in which mental illness, crime, and conflict were unknown. Like many artists in our own culture, they also used their dreams as a source of creative inspiration.(Stewart; C. Hall)

Perls views a dream as an *existential message*, a statement about something that is important in a person's life. He says, "I believe that any single dream contains the essential message about our existence."

Throughout the ages, dreams have suggested new directions, new possibilities, and answers to important problems. Dreams can tell me what I need to do that I'm not doing, and what I'm doing that I need to stop

---

*We are deeply indebted to our friend and colleague Gordon Tappan for his many important contributions to this chapter.

261

doing. I may want something consciously, and then my dream life says, "No, you don't."

"To unlock the doors behind one's eyes and go into the chambers of the heart and soul is a frightful and awesome experience!" comments psychiatrist Ernest Rossi's client Davina.

Dreams unlock these doors. Our dreams, which Freud called "the royal road to the unconscious," reveal the themes and dramas that are active in our lives, or that lie bubbling below the surface of our everyday awareness.

My dreams come from a source within me that is deeper than my conscious intentions. They speak of who I truly am, and what I truly want, rather than of who I think I am and what I think I want. They are a side of me that complements, and often struggles with, my reasoning mind.

My dreams are my inner guide. In my daily life, I may neglect my deeper needs, so I can act in ways that fit what my society prescribes for me. But if I listen to my dreams, I find a place in me that's concerned about my own growth and development.

My dreams also tell me how I can finish unfinished business in my life. Sometimes I find them to be rehearsals for my performance in the theatre of my life.

As I work with a dream, living with it in many different situations, I begin to know the less developed parts of who I am, parts I've ignored or neglected. Thereby I move toward wholeness.

Jung declares that dreams compensate for things that are missing in our conscious lives. They express parts of us that we allow no other outlet.

Many women in our culture, for example, have learned everything about how to run a household, but very little about their own inner nature. Increasing numbers of women are finding that living a culturally standardized role of housekeeper, wife, and mother is not enough for them. Something important is missing. They want to feel their creativity in the arts, trades, professions, and other areas traditionally reserved for men.

As I find out what's missing in my life now, and find ways to express that dimension of myself, I discover what I need for the next step in my growth.

Jung's follower Ira Progoff suggests that we are like wells, each of us unique in our own way, but at the bottom tapping a common stream that connects us all. We are all loving, bitchy, bawdy, sorrowful, afraid, and all the other things that every human being has been since the first day man and woman walked this earth. Our instinctive readiness to act in certain ways takes unique forms in each of us. These personal forms are all expressions of the old forms that have been with us for eons, forms that grow out of the primal energy that Jung called the *collective unconscious*.

As I create my dream, I draw on the events of my daily life, and on all the forms and energies available to me from the collective unconscious we all share. Thus, my dreams are not only my own inner creation, but are also expressions of themes that have been important to human beings in all times and all places.

Remembering dreams

Perhaps you have a hard time remembering your dreams. Many people are seldom aware of having dreamed, but we can all learn to remember our dreams.

Keeping a *dream log* is a great help. Keep a large notebook and a pen by your bed. In the morning, *as soon as* you're awake enough to write, even though you may still be groggy, write down your dream from beginning to end, with as many specific details as you can remember. If you recall only a tiny fragment of a dream, write down that fragment. It is often enough to work with.

When you feel resistant to writing down a dream—"It's too much trouble—I'd rather just lie here"—make a special effort. The dreams I'm most reluctant to write down are often the most important ones.

A friend of mine described having a dream, waking up, writing it on a pad beside his bed, and going back to sleep. Upon awakening, he couldn't remember the dream. Gleefully he turned to his pad, only to discover that it was totally blank. He had dreamed the whole sequence!

If you don't remember any dream when you wake up, write down the first two or three things you think of. Pretty soon they'll turn into dreams. Using an alarm clock to wake up can also help, because the alarm often interrupts a dream so that it's especially vivid and easy to remember.

Sometimes when you wake up at an exciting place in your dream, try *continuing to dream* in your half-awake state of consciousness instead of stopping the dream by waking up fully.

If you don't *do* anything with your dreams, of course, there's no point in remembering them. When you work actively with them, you're likely to remember them more often and more easily.

The times when I'm busy with my important affairs and "can't spare the time" to consult my dreams are often the times when consulting them would be most valuable to me.

CHARACTERISTICS OF DREAMS

My dreams state my feelings about myself, about others, and about my world as it seems to me. My dreams don't tell me how anything outside me "actually is," but they say a great deal about my world of reality *as I experience it.*

A dream has its own inner logic, which is very different from the kind of logic our waking minds are used to. As a result, the messages in our dreams may seem contradictory and confusing until we learn how to understand and work with them.

 This is my existence

Tell your dream to another person in the first-person present tense, as if you were having the dream right now: "As I enter the run-down room, several people are talking to each other. No one looks at me. I feel invisible, and queasy in my stomach." You may want to close your eyes as you describe the dream, so you can re-experience it as vividly as possible. *Be sure to mention how you feel* at each point in the dream: "I feel invisible, and queasy in my stomach." These statements of feeling, often overlooked, are crucially important in working with dreams.

After each brief statement about the dream, add the words *"This is my existence."* "As I enter the run-down room, several people are talking to each other. No one looks at me. *This is my existence.* I feel invisible, and queasy in my stomach. *This is my existence."* And so on.

When you've finished, discuss your thoughts and feelings about the dream with the other person.

If you're alone, you can do the exercise out loud to yourself.

A *series* of dreams with similar themes often points to some message that's struggling to be heard. The theme that runs through the dream series typically deals with something that's important in your life right now.

For several months I dreamed of doing something wrong, and having to go back and fix it. One night, for instance, I was a bus driver. I turned onto the wrong road without realizing it, and someone from a nearby house came after me in a pickup truck to tell me. Then I turned around, went back, and got on the right road. Another time I had to deliver an important message. First I took it to the wrong man. Then I got my message back, recognized my mistake, and finally delivered it to the right person. This series of dreams told me that I needed to slow down and pay more attention to what I was doing, so I could do things right the first time.

Even more dramatic is the *repetitive* or *recurrent dream*. If something comes up again and again, says Perls, it means that some problem that hasn't been dealt with is asking for your attention. Often these repetitive dreams are nightmares that show how you frustrate yourself.

Nightmares, scary parts of dreams that aren't nightmares, and frightening daytime fantasies often contain direct messages to me about something I'm leaving unfinished, or am in some way not dealing with, in my daily life. Often they point to a fear of moving ahead in some area of my growth.

Being *defeated* by a frightening image, suggests Rossi, may mean that some aspect of who I am is being overwhelmed. *Successfully confronting* a threatening force may mean that I'm developing a neglected aspect of myself (74).

Most people, when troubled by nightmares, want to suppress them or get rid of them. Actually, that's the worst thing you can do. It's like ripping out a warning light when it flashes. The frightening forces that nightmares represent are sometimes me getting angry with myself when I've tried to tell myself something over and over and refuse to listen. "If you won't listen to me one way, I'll scare you into listening." My nightmare dramatizes and exaggerates what I've been trying to say to myself, but haven't paid attention to.

Some dreams contain *transformations*. A block of ice melts into a puddle. An airplane changes into a bird. An old man turns into a young woman.

Rossi suggests that slowly evolving transformations, like the growth of a plant or the coming of dawn, tend to reflect long-term trends of personality growth. Transformations that seem sensible and familiar usually reflect evolutionary changes in a person's life or personality. Transformations that seem absurd or are sudden or abrupt may mean that the person faces a crucial situation that he or she needs to deal with immediately.

Rossi also suggests that ugly, harmful, or otherwise unpleasant transformations signal a blockage of the growth process that the dreamer needs to pay attention to, whereas transformations that seem pleasant or beautiful represent constructive, desirable changes in a person's way of living and being (149–50).

One of my own dreams captured an important change in me through an image of a man who had a line down the left side of his face, as though on one side of the line something new had replaced what was there before, but the old and new sides had not completely grown together yet.

Sometimes people have dreams in which they appear older than they are. Rossi suggests that such dreams often show what the person will be like later in life *if* certain developmental trends in that person's life continue (135). Such a dream may show me how I will be if I follow some new direction that has opened up for me. These dreams often occur when a person is at a point where choices are available. Having such a dream alerts me to look carefully at the directions I'm moving in, to see which ones I want to stay with and which ones I want to change.

In some dreams I'm an observer, while in others I'm an active participant. In still others, I'm both. Being only a watcher, and therefore uninvolved, may be a message to me that I'm reluctant to venture and risk. That limits the fullness of my life.

Being both a participant and an observer may mean I'm breaking through old understandings to a deeper level of awareness. Rossi reports a dream in which a woman experienced herself as a building and also as an observer watching as the building, which represented part of her old self, fell over.

Rossi also writes of *healing dreams* (166). In a healing dream, or a series of such dreams, I handle a painful situation from my past in a more effective way than I originally did.

As this healing process completes itself, the old painful situation takes a different place in my life than it had before. It loses some, or even all, of its painfulness, and may even become a resource I can draw upon as I seek to understand the experiences of others. I may also have healing dreams about my present emotional or physical problems.

When I'm grappling with some issue, I can *program myself to think about it.* As I go to sleep, I tell myself over and over what I want to dream about. The insights that come from these consciously initiated dreams are often just as valuable as those from dreams that occur spontaneously.

The shadow side

I may not want to look at something in my dream, for within my dream lie sides of me that I've rejected. I've built part of my self-image on the idea that "*this* part of who I am is good, and I have to keep the other part, the bad stuff, out." I feel afraid that if others see my "bad side," they'll want nothing more to do with me.

Sam comments, "In my family, I took on the 'good boy' role and my brother, the 'bad boy' role." Sam pushed his "bad boy" into his shadow side, while his brother pushed his "good boy" into his. Now each of them is beginning to re-own the parts of himself that he suppressed.

If you ever feel you're a prisoner in your own jail cell, as many people sometimes do, it probably means that you keep important parts of yourself locked up and don't allow them expression. Here's a way to start exploring those parts of you:

✳ *The prisoner*

Sit back and close your eyes. Let the image of a jail cell come into your imagination. The person in the cell will say or do something to let you know who he or she is. Then imagine opening the cell door and letting that person out. Watch to see what that person, who is part of your shadow side, does when set free.

As that aspect of yourself, what do you do immediately? What do you do after you've settled down from that first flush of new-found freedom?

If there's more than one person in your cell, find out how each of them is you.

You may want to return to your jail cell from time to time to see who's there. And in your dreams, you can find parts of your shadow side that you keep locked in even deeper dungeons. These parts of you can add richness and vitality to your life.

Coming to terms with aggressive, hostile impulses is important. Otherwise we project these impulses onto others, and then try to destroy those others because *they* are "evil," as in the Inquisition, Naziism, Stalinism, and fanatical anti-Communism.

In my own life, I've found that the destructive power in my dreams is greatest when I feel most powerless. As I find ways to feel my power, the violence in my dreams dies down.

Even when we don't recognize what's going on there, our shadow side can dominate our conscious actions, as a submerged boulder dominates the wave patterns on the surface of a pool in a stream.

A refusal to confront some area of my own experience is a kind of death: "No, I'll live my life only on my idealized terms." Being unwilling to face myself as I am is death to a part of who I am.

As I learn to live with and channel the energy from the "dark side" of my own nature, I open up to new sources of aliveness and creativity.

GESTALT DREAM WORK

Everything in my dream, maintains Perls, expresses some part of who I am. Different parts of me come through as different characters or objects in my dream. A policeman, a thief, the bridge they're running across, and the river flowing beneath the bridge are all aspects of who I am.

Occasionally, someone toward whom I have conflicting feelings, or with whom I need to work something through, appears in my dreams. This tells me that I may need to deal with that real-life situation.

From Perls' point of view, that person also represents some dimension of myself. After I've dealt with the specific issue that centers on that person, I can continue onward to explore the side of me that person personifies. When I do this, I often find that the crucial battle is with myself, rather than with the other person as I first imagined.

I can work with my dreams to *re-own* the fragmented, projected parts of myself, and *re-own* the hidden power and potential my dreams reveal. In so doing, I move toward an *integration* of parts of myself that I've compartmentalized and blocked off from one another (GTV, 67).

Perls describes a technique you can use by yourself to work with your dreams. The first step is to master the technique of "identification." Try this:

✳ Identification

Close your eyes, and in your imagination, transform yourself into an automobile. *Be* the car. Notice specific details about the car you become, and how you feel as that car.

Now, in the same way, become a six-month-old baby.

Now become the mother of that baby.

Now again become the baby.

Now the mother again.

Now become who you are today.

(Adapted from GTV, 68)

In your imagination, you've just "lived" the experience of being an automobile, a six-month-old baby, and the baby's mother. In a similar way, you can bring a dream back to life, reliving it in your imagination as if it were happening now.

Consult your dream log and make a list of *all* the details in the dream you want to work with. "Get every person, every thing, every mood," says Perls,

> and then work on these to *become* each one of them. Ham it up, and really transform yourself into each of the different items. . . .
>
> . . . Let them have encounters between them. . . . Have a dialogue between the two opposing parts and you will find—especially if you get the correct opposites—that they always start out fighting each other, . . . until we come to an . . . appreciation of differences, . . . a oneness and integration of the two opposing forces. Then the civil war is finished, and your energies are ready for your struggles with the world. (GTV, 69)

Your dialogues may be in your imagination, on paper, or out loud using the double-chair technique (see pp. 216–217). As one character or thing, you may find it useful to tell the person or thing with whom you're in dialogue *what you are to him or her or it.*

You may not have time to work with every part of your dream. In that case, you can tell your dream to someone or relive it in your imagination in the first-person present tense, like in the "This is my existence" exercise, and stay alert for any emotional charge or feeling of tensing up as you relive the dream. Those places in the dream where you feel some charge are likely to be the ones that connect with important issues in your present life, or important places where you can grow.

Notice what's *missing* in your dream as well as what's present. In a dark and somber dream, warmth and color are missing. When I see my face in a mirror, my body is missing. In some dreams, what's missing is obvious: a house has no roof, or no foundation. A woman has no breasts, or a bicycle no wheels. What's missing can tell me something important about what's missing in my life now, or about a "hole in my personality" where I need to develop some aspect of who I am.

In the following dream, we see how one of Perls' clients moves toward a greater gentleness with herself and a deeper understanding of her life. This person was working out loud, but you can work in the same way in fantasy or written dialogue. Notice that "L" takes the part of the license plate and the lake, but does not engage in active dialogue, becoming the license plate talking *to* the lake and then becoming the lake replying to the license plate. Sometimes, as in this example, identification alone is enough. More often dialogue is needed to bring out the full value of the dream.

F [Perls]: Will you please play the license plate.
L: I am an old license plate, thrown in the bottom of a lake. . . .

I'm no value . . . I'm outdated . . . and I'm just thrown on the rubbish heap. . . .

F: Well, how do you feel about this?

L: . . . I don't like being a license plate—useless. . . .

F: Okeh, now play the lake.

L: I'm a lake . . . I'm drying up, and disappearing, soaking into the earth . . . (with a touch of surprise) *dying*. . . . But when I soak into the earth, I become part of the earth—so maybe I water the surrounding area, so . . . even in my bed, flowers can grow. . . .

F: You get the existential message?

L: Yes. . . . I can paint . . . I can create beauty. I can no longer reproduce . . . but I . . . I water the earth, and give life. . . .

F: You see the contrast: On the surface, you find . . . the license plate, the artificial you—but then when you go deeper, you find the apparent death of the lake is actually fertility.(GTV, 81–82)

Through our dreams, we can find again the aliveness that we've been suppressing. This is especially true of power. As children, many of us were forced to suppress our power because the adults around us didn't want competition. *They* wanted to be powerful, and demanded that we be weak so we wouldn't threaten them. All that power is still there, hidden, waiting for us to tap it and use it in our lives.

DREAM GROUPS

Gordon Tappan has developed a way for a group of people to work together on their dreams, without anyone in the group having any professional expertise in dream work. Dream groups work best when the same group of people meets weekly over a period of several months. This allows deep sharing and trust to develop. There has to be a fairly high level of trust among the people to begin with, however, or the group will never get off the ground.

"After a few weeks with a group," says Tappan, "I've sometimes gotten such a sense of each person's process that it seemed like each dream a person reported was the only dream the person could have had at that time."

A dream group is based on *sharing*. Just as with Gestalt dream work, there is *no interpretation*, no attempt to "figure out the meaning" of a dream or "tell what the dream means." Interpretation is a way to kill something that's alive.

Here's the process, in Tappan's words:

❉ *The dream group*

One person tells a dream in the first-person present tense, reliving it as fully as possible while telling it and describing all the details he or she can remember.

At the same time, each other member of the group, with closed eyes, "dreams" the same dream along with the person who is talking. Each person's "dream" has different details, but they all deal with the same basic events.

Then a group member shares *how the dream just described is for him or her.* If you're the dreamer and I'm the group member, I tell you what I think and how I feel as I experience your dream. I'm not "trying to help you"—I'm exploring what your dream means to me. As I do this, if something in your dream really connects with something in my own life, it's fair game for me to explore in myself whatever it kicks off. This means that I'm as vulnerable as you are. I don't stand back and stare at you and your dream from a distance.

Any person in the group can borrow your dream and work with it as his or her own.

As you hear each person's response to your dream, you can hear where that response touches something in you—"Yes, that's really true for me too!"—and where it doesn't—"No, that's yours. It's different for me." Or if your response is too strong—"No! That's bullshit!"—you may stumble across something important.

If you treat each other with gentleness and caring, a dream group can be a magical experience of people sharing at a very deep level.

Through the dream group, your dream can live more fully within you. By staying away from analyzing and playing junior psychologist, you can avoid the model of *"This* is what the dream means. This is the 'right answer.'" When we assume that there is no one right answer, then instead of a single narrow channel, there are many different directions and possibilities.

We can follow the flow of energy in the group and roam freely. We can laugh and play as we explore and discover. There's no advantage to making our exploration a heavy, serious thing that leaves us cramped and constricted.

When the energy in the group begins to sag, that's the time to leave a dream. Or the person who produced the dream can say, "I've had enough," at any point.

SYMBOLS

A dream reflects a network of ideas and experiences in the dreamer's life, and there is often a special value in exploring it as a whole.

On the other hand, certain events in your dream may have special power for you. These are worth exploring in extra depth. Treating important dream events as *symbols* is one way to do this, especially when a dream makes no sense to you at first.

Sometimes the symbols in a dream are right out front and bigger than life. Last year Sally was thinking about going to Europe for the summer, but could not quite decide whether she wanted to go or not. One night in a dream, she saw a giant theatre marquee, brilliantly lit up, with the words "DO NOT GO TO EUROPE" emblazoned across it.

In ways like that, my dreams can tell me about a decision that I've already made at a deeper level, while with my conscious mind I still think I'm struggling over it. If I pay attention to what I'm saying to myself in my dream, I hear my decision and I can stop playing games with myself and with anyone else involved.

By and large, the language of dream symbols is an individual one, not a universal one as many "dream interpreters" have claimed. Anyone who says he or she can tell you what a certain symbol in your dream "means" is mistaken.

However, some dream symbols can be universal. They arise out of experiences that are common to us all. They often, though not always, have similar meanings for many of the people in whose dreams they appear. Jung has given the name *archetypes* to these shared symbols that we all have the potential to experience. An archetype has no content; it is an instinctive potential to experience and respond in certain ways. The content of an archetype is learned through our individual experience.

Though you and I may experience the same archetype, the specific form it takes may be quite different in each of us, and the value each of us finds in exploring that archetype is likely to be more different still. You and I may both dream of a child. Yet as we explore what that symbol sets off in us, I may get in touch with how I make myself dependent on others and refuse to take responsibility for my own life, while you discover ways to open yourself to a more spontaneous and less programmed way of living with yourself and your world. The "child archetype" usually points to some kind of unrealized potential within the dreamer, but that potential can be very different for different people.

Here's a way to work with your own dream symbols:

✳ *Symbolic equivalents*

Imagine a movie screen. Take an important event or symbol from your dream and project it on the screen.

Then clear the screen and allow another scene or symbol that for you is somehow equivalent to the one from your dream to flash itself on the screen. Allow whatever it is to come spontaneously—don't try to force yourself to come up with a scene that "makes sense" to you as an equivalent to your dream, for this would hinder the free flow of your fantasy process.

Then, rapidly, one after another, flash other "symbolic equivalents" of your dream on the screen. If you're doing this with another person or a group, report the scenes in your mind aloud as you experience them, so the other person(s) can imagine them along with you.

What does this process tell you about the existential message of your dream?

This "symbolic equivalents" technique can be applied to other events in your life besides dreams.

A dream symbol may mean I'm in touch with the potential it represents, or it may mean I'm not in touch with it and would do well to contact that potential in myself.

The key to working with symbols is to *open myself to everything within me that's connected with that symbol,* and see what comes. The moment a symbol attracts my attention, I can be sure it holds some promise for me. And ultimately, as I work with it, it will become part of my own experience. Likewise, when I get another person to talk about my dream symbols, I soon find out what life is about for him or her.

Polarities are as important in working with dream symbols as they are in dream dialogues. Tappan comments,

> When I dream of being an eagle, my first feeling may be one of flying, soaring, feeling at one with my own body and with the air around me. Then I want to experience what's *in contrast with* that. I open myself to the shadow side of my eagle nature, to see what's the reverse of my first impression. I find myself diving from the

sky, clawing and screaming as I strike and carry off my helpless prey.

Then I explore the polarity within each side of this main polarity. My flying and soaring can also have to do with being flighty, being inflated, having no real substance, being out of touch with the ground. My clawing and striking can also be strength, expressing my confidence in my ability to take care of myself without *having* to claw and strike.

Experiencing both the "positive" and "negative" sides of a dream helps me find my potential and power in dreams that are not so pleasant, and helps me stay alert to the pitfalls and dangers that are present in even the most positive, growth-oriented paths.

You can read more about dreaming in Ann Faraday's *The Dream Game* or Jung's *Dreams*.

FANTASY AND IMAGINATION

Waking fantasy is another way to explore our experience.

Sally comments, "My whole living life, day by day, used to be cradled in a fantasy. That was the only way I knew how to cope with my existence. While I was a housewife, I had a skeletal existence—getting up, doing my chores, smiling mechanically. I could operate as an apparently normal, well-adjusted person on about one-sixteenth of my mental capacity. I put all the rest of my mental energy into fantasy, not realizing that my fantasies held the key to many kinds of creativity."

Fantasies can be especially important to children. LeShan writes,

[Louis's] desk was near the window, and he loved to sit and let his mind wander as he looked at the trees and the sky. His second-grade teacher wasn't very happy about it. She thought Louis ought to be concentrating on his workbook. . . . One day he decided to write a composition about his daydreaming. It was a story about how brave Louis was—how he saved other people just like Superman. He was the strongest and wisest man in the world. His mother said, "That's a very important story, especially for a little boy who has four older brothers and three older sisters!" In his daydreams, Louis could forget how much he hated being the youngest and littlest in his family. (55)

Psychologist and educator George Brown tells how classrooms of children can come alive when children share and talk about their daydreams and fantasies. Even children who have always hated to write compositions often jump right in when they go through a guided daydream (see pp. 276–278) and then are asked to write a composition about it.

✳ The existential message

When you find yourself in a fantasy, describe it in *one sentence*. Or make a one-sentence summary of a dream you've had.

Now take a look: What does that one-sentence label mean to you? Does it say anything about how you're living or not living your life at this moment? If so, that's the existential message of your fantasy or dream.

Getting lost in too many words can destroy the essence of the existential statement. That's the value of the one-sentence summary.

You can work with your waking fantasies in all the ways we talked about working with dreams, and in other ways as well.

Jung developed a method of working with fantasy that he called *active imagination*. I sit or lie down, close my eyes, and think of something important to me. Then I give up conscious control, and let whatever happens happen. Sometimes I get an unfolding story, sometimes just one scene. The key is to let what comes come, no matter how outrageous or obscene. When I allow myself to imagine and explore awful possibilities in this way, those energies are less likely to burst through uncontrollably in situations where I might actually cause some harm to myself or someone else. I can enter into dialogue with the strange and frightening beings of my imagination and see what messages they hold for me.

Here Jung describes how active imagination works:
A chain of fantasy ideas develops and gradually takes on a dramatic character: *the passive process becomes an action.* At first it consists of projected figures, and these images are observed like scenes in the theatre. . . . There is a marked tendency simply to enjoy this interior entertainment and leave it at that. Then, of course, there is no real progress but only endless variations on the same theme. . . . If the observer understands that his own drama is being performed on this inner stage, he . . . will notice, as the actors appear, . . . that they all have some purposeful relationship to his conscious situation, that he is being addressed by the unconscious. (PJ, 295)

I may be afraid of what may happen if I let myself flow freely with my fantasy, and struggle furiously to stop something that wants to happen in my fantasy from happening. A breakthrough often comes when I *let it happen*—when I let myself go ahead and fall into the dark pit I'm so afraid of, or let the wall I'm trying to hold up fall over on me.

On the other hand, if I'm often passive in my life, and reluctant to do things for myself, in my fantasy I may need to fight, climb, struggle, and forge ahead.

Stories and guided daydreams

I can view life as a story and process rather than as a linear, goal-directed movement. Tappan suggests one way to do this:

✳ *A story from pictures*

Thumb through a magazine or book with many pictures in it and find three or four pictures, each with one or more people in it, that you really like.

Now, in your mind, arrange the pictures in some kind of order. If it's an old magazine, you can cut them out and set them in front of you.

Now, *write a fairy tale or other story based on the pictures.* Take at least fifteen minutes to do this. (If you prefer, you can tell your story to another person, making it up as you go along, instead of writing it.)

When you're done, share your story with another person or a group of people, and listen to what your story touches off in them. Each other person also shares a story.

Of course, your story is about you and your life. You can do this again and again, whenever you think it may be helpful.

Desoille, Leuner, and Assagioli have developed a technique to encourage exploration through fantasy that we will call the "guided daydream."

Instructions for several guided daydreams are presented here, the first one in detail, the others more briefly. With each one, *read through the description, then close your eyes and imagine everything that was described, taking as little or as much time as you need.*

If possible, immediately after you've finished a guided daydream, tell it to another person in the first-person present tense. This retelling can help bring out important details and events in your fantasy.

House.   Walking along, you come upon a house. Look it over carefully. Walk around it. Now find a way to enter. Wander through the house, looking at and feeling each room. Then imagine that you *are* the house, and are each of its rooms in turn. Have a dialogue with the you who entered the house, telling how you feel *as* each room, and how you feel as yourself being in each room. (Some architects I know use this technique with clients as they develop house plans. The people are more satisfied, and there are fewer major changes during construction. Can you think of ways to use guided fantasy in your own work, using the ones that follow or creating your own?)

Going into the Depths.   You find a cave that leads far down through many caverns into the depths of the earth. In one of the caverns you find an object that has great value to you. At last you enter a cavern that contains a deep, clear pool of water. You dive into the pool, which is illuminated by some unseen source of light, and explore what you find there.

Climbing a Mountain.   Down in the valley, you search for and ultimately find something you want for a journey. Taking it with you, you ascend a nearby mountain, making your way through difficult obstacles. Notice what the obstacles are, what the mountain is like, and how you feel there.

Journey into the Desert.   Ahead of you in the desert is an ancient pyramid of green stone. You enter it and look around. The walls dissolve away, and all the characters and events of some problem or choice that is important to you surround you. Free of distraction, imagine what will happen if you follow a certain path. What path do you choose? Then become a person or thing affected by your decision, and explore the impact of your decision on that person or thing. (Who or what did you avoid as you did this?) Now, in the same way, imagine what happens if you follow a different path. Do this for each important alternative choice that occurs to you.

Pool and Wise Person.   You walk along a path through the middle of a forest. Notice what you see. You come upon a small meadow with a pool of water in the middle of it. When you look into it, you see a reflection of yourself. Then you look up, and a wise man or woman is standing on the other side of the pool looking at you. By speaking or acting, the wise person communicates some message to you.

Bon voyage.

Many oppressed peoples hear the majority culture's fantasies about themselves from so many sides that they begin to accept them: "I am lazy, I am irresponsible," etc. And members of the majority culture accept fantasies about themselves that leave them no room for their individuality.

Whether we are members of oppressed groups or members of the majority culture, our own dreams and fantasies can help us get a sense of our own directions, our own power. We can create our own dreams of where we want to go, dreams that grow out of our desires to nourish ourselves and care for one another, rather than out of the desires of industrial and financial czars to have us act in ways that will guarantee them the greatest possible profits, or the desires of those who hold power to have us act in ways that will perpetuate that power.

VII

Synthesis

24 *Centering*

If you stand very still in the heart of the woods, you will hear many wonderful things—the snap of a twig and the wind and the trees and the whirr of invisible wings. If you stand very still in the turmoil of life, and wait for the voice from within, you will be led down the quiet pathways of wisdom and peace in a world of chaos and din. . . . You will draw from the silence the things that you need.

(Author unknown)

The silence will also draw from you—and sometimes demand from you—the things you have to give, both to others and to yourself.

Charlene was a psychology intern under my supervision. She was bright and capable, and used every moment to learn as much as possible. She worked six days a week and studied on the seventh day.

As the weeks went on, I could see her losing touch with herself as she collected so much from outside herself. With all this running around, she began feeling as though bits and pieces of her were flung all over the map. Not pulled together into any kind of understandable whole, she was too scattered to work effectively with people.

Finally I said to her, "You need to stop and give yourself time to connect with your own centeredness, so that when you arrive somewhere with somebody, you're there."

When I take time to center myself before entering a situation or starting to talk with someone, often I then speak and act from a deeper place in me. I'm more in touch with myself and more in touch with you or with my task.

To find my own center, I sometimes need to be alone. I need space to find out what I feel and think, and what I want for myself now. I get tired of bouncing off other people. I need then to go off by myself, or disconnect my phone and put a sign on my door that says, "I need *me* now."

Here's an effective way to center yourself in the middle of your daily life. Teachers tell me it's a lifesaver when they're about to be driven right up the wall by a classroom of active kids, and people in the business world say it helps them get a sense of perspective when they need it most. You can do this just about anywhere.

✳ Physical centering

Stand with your feet pointed forward, shoulder width apart. Unlock your knees so that your legs are flexed. Close your eyes, and from your feet—not from your waist—begin to move as far in a clockwise direction as you can without falling over. Move slowly, with one full inhalation and exhalation each time you go around in a circle, exhaling as you go through the front half of your circle and inhaling as you go through the back half.

When you've fully tuned in to the rhythm of your circular movement, gradually make your circle smaller, continuing to coordinate your breathing and movement, until your circle becomes very tiny. Be sure your head is erect and that your shoulders are loose.

Now stop at the center of your circle, where you are perfectly centered in relation to gravity. Check this by moving slightly forward, then back, then to the right and left, then back to the place of perfect balance, your knees still slightly flexed. Then take three deep, slow breaths. As you do, feel any tension that's left in your mind and body flow out with your outgoing breath, and a sense of complete well-being flow in with your incoming breath.

Once you can center yourself in this way, there's a shortcut you can use when you need to. Close your eyes and go directly to where you think your physical center is. Check to be sure you really are centered with gravity by moving slightly in each direction, and then take your deep, slow breaths.

You can also center while you're sitting. If you're on a chair, sit well forward so that you don't touch the back when you're at the rear of your circle. If you're on the floor, sit cross-legged, double over a pillow or cushion, and sit on the forward edge of it (not in the middle) so that your knees are tilted slightly downward and you can keep your spine erect easily. Otherwise you'll probably have to lean forward uncomfortably to stay upright. (When I sit on the floor and have no cushion, I often take off my shoes and sit on them.)

Quiet time with yourself

Robert was struggling with whether or not to get a divorce. He appeared constantly harassed and unsettled, and said, "I can't seem to get any perspective on it."

"How much time each day do you sit with your thoughts and feelings, free of any distractions?" I asked him.

"None," he replied. "As soon as I get home I turn on the TV, and it's on until I go to bed. Whenever I'm not watching it or doing something else, I read a paper or a magazine."

"Try sitting quietly with yourself for half an hour each day with no TV, no radio, no magazines, no distraction of any kind," I suggested.

When he returned a week later, he said that in just those seven days, giving himself that time had made a big difference.

Without any fancy name for it, Robert had taken half an hour each day for unstructured meditation. Such times when we are with ourselves without *doing* anything are an essential part of being in touch with our center.

I don't go into those quiet, empty times with a program: "I must deal with this thing"; or "I must solve this stuff." I may *have* things I need to deal with; I may have unfinished business that I've neglected. If these things come up, I deal with them. If not, I just live fully in the moment, experiencing myself as I am right here right now. This is my time to be with myself and do whatever I do, with no distractions and no program. It's a time to *get out* of the programmed character of so much of my daily life. I can focus on the feeling, the "texture," the "color" of my experience of me and of this place at this moment in my life.

If I always have a lot to deal with when I sit down, it means I'm not giving myself enough quiet time to keep current with my life.

Taking this time each day—at least ten minutes, and preferably half an hour, or even more, if you have that kind of time—to feel and listen to yourself quietly is the essential element in meditation.

CALMING AND FOCUSING PROCESSES

Certain specialized forms of meditation provide other specific benefits. They help me be more directly in touch with what I'm doing with my mind and body. They strengthen my ability to focus my attention where I want to and to avoid distracting myself. They improve my ability to think clearly and deal with problems effectively. They can reduce my mental clutter and make it easier for me to give "bare attention" to what I need to deal with.

In recent years, "meditation" has become a big thing in certain circles, while to others, the word has a certain "mystical" and vaguely suspect feeling about it. Acutally, it's an extremely practical, down-to-earth process that anyone can use.

Some people have picked up the idea that, by meditating, they can "raise their consciousness" and can thereby become only loving and giving persons. They want nothing to do with "base" feelings like anger and hate and agitation. This attitude leads to what Tibetan Buddhist teacher Trungpa calls "spiritual materialism," which is actually our old friend judgment in disguise. I start thinking some people are "higher" and others "lower." I worship those who are more "spiritually advanced" and feel contemptuous toward those who are less so. I'm apt to either be self-right-eous about how advanced my own consciousness is or be critical of myself "because my consciousness is so low," and have a hard time appreciating myself as I am.

When I let myself recognize only the ways of thinking and feeling in myself that I think reflect "higher consciousness," I become half a person, cut off from my fullness as a feeling being. I lose much of my spontaneity, my power, and my potential. If you've been confronting this problem, you probably need to put more energy into getting in touch with your feelings, at least for now.

An opposite danger is becoming attached to mucking around in my painful feelings so constantly that I seldom get out of them. I may do this because I haven't developed alternative ways to feel alive. In any case, I need to find out what messages those feelings hold for me, and then put my energy in other places.

You may think, "I'd *like* to try a meditative practice, but I can't spare the time."

In one sense, you're right. You may have to make some changes in your life routine to create a time and place where you can sit undisturbed for half an hour each day, or even for ten minutes. You may have to make some adjustments in your social life. If you meditate first thing in the morning, which for many people is the best time, you may have to get up earlier.

In another sense, you don't sacrifice or give up anything. Through meditating, you'll see more clearly what you need to do and what you don't. You'll probably spend less energy on things you don't need; you'll do less useless scurrying around. Your life is likely to become more efficient, so that you can do less and accomplish more. You're likely to get back more time than you invest.

Once you've started meditating regularly, you may sometimes think, "My meditation is not good. I must not be doing it right."

As long as you're taking time to sit quietly with yourself, *everything you do is right*. Staying aware of what you're doing, whatever that may be, is the important thing. If you're judging what you do as you meditate, pay attention to how you judge yourself.

Each different approach to meditation has its merits. You can learn to trust your intuitive sense of what you need for you at any given time.

The idea that any one way is better than others is an error. Trouble begins when someone has the idea "My way is better than your way." The best way is the one you need for yourself right now.

Posturing your mind

Sit on the forward edge of a cushion as described earlier. Lay the sole of your right foot along your left thigh, and then your left leg on top of your right, so that your left sole touches your right thigh. (Or you may find the reverse more comfortable: left leg below, right leg on top.) This is called the "half-lotus" position. If this is hard for you—and some people's knees just aren't built to lie down flat—you can sit in a simple cross-legged position, or sit upright on a chair, without touching the back of the chair. If your legs are very flexible, you can lay each foot over the top of the opposite thigh in the "full-lotus" posture.

Now center yourself as described in the "physical centering" exercise. When you're centered, pull your head backward in relation to your body so that your ears are approximately in line with your shoulders, and your gaze is slightly downward.

You can lay your hands in your lap or on your legs. One position is to lay your left hand, palm up, on your right hand, so that your left fingertips touch the spot where your right fingers and palm connect. Then touch your thumbtips, so that your thumbs and first fingers form an oval. This is called a "mudra."

Alternatively, lay your hands palms up on your knees. Then slide them up toward your waist until you find the place that feels comfortable. Now start with them by your waist and slide them down toward your knees until you feel comfortable. Now find the place somewhere between the two places you just found that feels most comfortable. Touch the thumb and first finger of each hand together.

Holding this posture is not so easy. Your back may get tired. Your legs may hurt. Your body is likely to slump as your mind drifts, and you'll eventually have to bring yourself back into the proper posture. The straight-spine position is important because it not only allows you to breathe fully most easily but also stimulates the nervous system in a way that helps you stay alert. Zen Master S. Suzuki writes, "To take this posture itself is the purpose of our practice. When you have this posture, you have the right state of mind, so there is no need to try to attain some special state. . . . If you slump, . . . your mind will be wandering . . . ; you will not be in your body" (26–27).

When you find yourself slumping, you can pay attention to how you feel in the position you've moved into. Sit that way for as long as you want to, continuing to be aware of the sensations in your body as you do. Then when you're ready to, sit upright again.

As you sit, be aware of your breathing. Try this now:

✳ Following your breath

Continue to breathe normally just as you have been. Center your awareness in your chest and feel your breathing and the movement of your body from the inside as you breathe. Let your breathing be your consciousness.

Notice how shallow or deep your breathing is, how tense or relaxed your chest, and whether you are breathing with your stomach, your chest, or both.

When your breath is halting and irregular, and when you momentarily stop breathing entirely, just notice that. When you remember to, check to see what you were thinking of a moment before that might have provoked the tinge of anxiety that caused you to stop breathing regularly.

If you don't try to control or direct your breath, but stay aware of it, eventually it will slow down and become more regular and rhythmic by itself.

As you pay attention to your breathing, various ideas will come into your mind. Each time you notice an idea beginning to form, you have the choice of thinking about it or of keeping your attention on your breathing.

Often you'll find that your attention has drifted away from your breathing. When this happens, take note of where it has drifted to and ask yourself whether that's an important matter for you to think about. If so, you can jot down a word or two in the pocket notebook you keep beside you when you meditate (if that's not distracting for you), and then return your attention to your breathing. If not, pick up your attention from wherever it's drifted to and bring it back to your breathing. Or if you want to think about an important matter right then, instead of saving it until later, you can go ahead and do that. With time and practice, you can develop the ability to pick up your attention and bring it back to your breathing or other object of concentration each time it drifts away.

When you first begin "breath following," your mind is likely to be much more centered toward the end of your meditation period than toward the beginning. The thought you give to a problem at that time is likely to be more focused and clearer than it would be earlier in your meditation, or at other times during the day. When you set aside a matter with a promise to yourself to think about it later, however, it's important to keep that promise. Otherwise you won't believe your next promise to yourself. You have to know you really will think about the matter later in order to be able to set it aside now.

Eventually you'll get better at setting something aside for the time being, in order to stay with your present experience. Once you've developed that ability, then you may want to give yourself more room to contemplate important matters when they come up in your mind, knowing that you'll return to focusing on your breath when you've thought about them fully.

You may want to try a special breathing pattern called "the circulation of the light" in the ancient Chinese text *The Secret of the Golden Flower* (30–45). Here we'll call it more simply "figure-8 breathing."

You can do this in a sitting or standing position after you've learned it, but you can learn it most easily lying on the floor (a bed would be too comfortable). Put on some background music if you like. (Horn's "Inside," Erik Satie's piano compositions, and Koto music for Zen meditation are excellent for this.)

❊ Figure-8 breathing

Lying on your back on the floor with your arms by your sides, imagine that you're inside a large number "8." The middle of the "8" is at your waist. Your head and torso are inside the top loop, and your legs and feet are inside the bottom one.

Do not try to adjust your breathing in any special way. Just *imagine* the pattern of breathing described here, and allow your breathing to match itself gradually to this pattern.

Imagine that your breath enters your body through your navel, filling your stomach with air, as in belly breathing. Then it passes from your navel to your spine and moves upward along your back until it reaches the very top of the "8" somewhere at a point far out above your head. At this point your lungs are totally inflated, and for a moment you feel motionless.

Then as you exhale, imagine your breath moving down along your face and chest and stomach to complete the top loop of the "8," going into your body at your waist again, emerging through your anus and going down along the back of your legs to reach another point of motionlessness far beyond your feet, at which point you've completely exhaled. Then your breath returns up along the front of your legs and enters your navel again, and so on.

To help yourself stay in the here-and-now rather than drifting into fantasy, you can touch the thumb and first or middle finger of each hand together as you exhale and separate them a fraction of an inch as you inhale. This can also help you keep from drifting off in other forms of meditation.

Once you've mastered the figure-8 pattern, return to straight up-and-down breathing, then go back to figure-8 breathing. Be aware of how they feel different.

When you finish meditating, grasp your right wrist behind your back with your left hand, and slowly bend forward as far as you can or until your head touches the floor. Let any tightness in your body go so you can drop forward a little farther, but don't try to push forward with your muscles.

This bow is a sign of respect to everything around you that has shared your meditation time with you. If you're sitting in a lotus or cross-legged position as you do this, it's called the "Yogic Seal." Many people find it painful after just a few moments when they first try it, while those who have been doing it for a long time greatly enjoy it and hold it for five minutes or more.

If your feet are asleep after you've finished meditating, you can massage them and shake them before you try to stand. Once you're standing, you may want to stretch to limber up your body.

Difficulties at the beginning*

A formal meditation like "following your breath" is more demanding, more difficult, and at first, not so pleasant as the simpler "quiet time" meditation.

When I first began to meditate, I went through several months when I often felt uncomfortable as I meditated. (Some people get through that period in much less time, but almost everyone experiences some discom-

---

*At some point during your experience with the meditative process, you may want to consult a qualified teacher of meditation. For a referral, contact your local recreation department, Asian institute, Zen center, or the activities office of a junior college, college, or university.

fort.) Over and over I was bombarded by strong urges to get up, to walk around—to do *anything* except keep sitting there.

What was happening? In everyday life, when I feel uncomfortable in my body, I move in a way that gives me relief. When I feel anxious, I often do something that distracts me from what I feel uncomfortable about.

But when I sit in meditation, I can't distract myself so easily from my discomfort. One stimulus after another from my body and my mind triggers uncomfortable feelings in me, and my response to each one is the same: continue to sit, and feel whatever I feel.

Soon I begin to have available the new response of "continuing to sit and do nothing." I can choose to act in this new way of doing nothing, whereas before I had available only my one automatic way. Through my discipline, I gain freedom.

As I experience painful feelings I've kept out of my awareness, I learn to live with them more easily, and they come to be less painful. If I feel like crying or laughing or screaming, I can allow myself to cry or laugh or scream if I seldom express these feelings; or I can be aware of my impulse but stop short of giving way to it if I express such feelings often and easily.

When my discomfort is physical, like pain in my legs or back as I keep on sitting, I can work with my awareness of my pain. "Exactly where do I feel it? What is its character and size and shape? Does it change and move, or stay the same?" I can do this kind of exploration with an itch, a tingle, or a soreness in my muscle at any time and any place. Naturally, *I answer these questions through direct awareness rather than with words.*

I can experiment with moving my attention back and forth from my pain to my object of concentration. As I do this, I alternately make one my "figure" and the other one a distant "ground" (see pp. 129–30).

We can affect the "figure" and "ground" in our awareness by the way we focus our eyes. Try this experiment:

✳ Eye-focusing

Set some object like a candle or a vase at least six feet away from you. (If you're doing this in a group, sit in a circle and put the object in the center.)

Hold your finger about six inches in front of your nose and focus your eyes on it. Then, as you continue to focus, also notice the object you've put off in the distance. Probably you'll see *two* objects. If not, be sure you're really *looking* at your finger.

Once you see the two objects, move your finger closer to your nose and then farther away, noticing what happens to the "two" objects as you do. With practice, you'll be able to adjust your focus wherever you wish.

Some people find that they can keep their attention attuned to following their breath more easily when they unfocus their eyes and let everything go hazy as they inhale, and focus sharply as they exhale, or vice versa.

One day when I was counting my breaths as described below (page 291), I felt extremely uncomfortable. Each breath seemed endless, and I badly wanted to get up from where I was sitting. With every breath I counted, I was glad to be one breath nearer to the end of my meditation period.

Then suddenly, I felt as though I had broken through a barrier into a totally new space. I felt myself breathe each breath and count each number, and I was completely *with* each breath, my discomfort and wish to finish totally forgotten. I was *here* instead of trying to get *there*. Each breath was all that existed, a moment of eternity. With continued practice, this state of consciousness became easier to attain.

Another difficulty is that of getting bored or falling asleep. If you fall asleep, that's okay. When you wake up, just straighten back up into your sitting posture. If you don't want to do that, move into "quiet time" meditation.

Nondirective meditation

Nondirective meditation involves letting your mind move freely just as in "quiet time" meditation. The difference is that in nondirective meditation, you sit in the formal meditating position.

Krishnamurti suggests that, as you meditate, you try to be aware of every thought and feeling, noting your experience without judging it. This is much like the "awareness continuum" and "self-remembering" techniques (see pp. 33–34 and 131–32).

This is likely to be the most effective form of meditation for you if you have a strong tendency to direct and control things. In the passive awareness of this meditative state, we can learn to live with the people and things around us as they are, without thinking we have to change them to suit us.

Maharishi Mahesh Yogi's "Transcendental Meditation," or "TM," is a variety of nondirective meditation. It involves repeating a word or phrase called a "mantra" silently to yourself over and over again. You return your mind to your mantra when your attention is not attracted somewhere else. Some Indian teachers of mantra meditation, including Maharishi Mahesh Yogi, conduct an "initiation ceremony" in which they give each person a particular mantra. For some people this seems most helpful. Others, like Baba Ram Dass, report excellent results with mantras that people choose for themselves. Actually, you can use anything that feels right to you as a mantra—even a few words from a song or an advertising jingle. You may want to choose a word or phrase that has some personal importance for you—perhaps something from your own religious tradition, or a Sanskrit mantra like "Aum mani padme aum."

Some people prefer to intone their mantra in correlation with the rhythm of their breathing, while others do not relate it to their breathing at all. You can experiment to find out what works for you.

You may have your own way of centering that has something in common with the kinds of meditation described here. For example, when my friend Mike goes fishing, he gets completely absorbed in each moment of what he does. As the fly hits the water, that moment is all that exists for him. Mike is centered in each instant *of his experience of fishing.*

Concentration techniques

"Quiet time" is the least structured meditation we've described. "Non-directive meditation" is a little more structured, and "Breath following" is somewhat more structured still.

Many people find that one of these techniques suits them very well. Others like a little more direction.

In general, the more harried, hassled, and distracted I feel, the more demanding the meditative technique I need to slow and center myself. When I'm fairly centered to begin with, I can use a very simple meditation.

When I give my mind a demanding meditative technique to be busy with, it's as though it takes my thoughts and feelings that are darting in every direction and starts them moving in a circle. And as they begin to revolve around the common center of my meditation, my breathing deepens and my heartbeat slows.

Concentration practices are an excellent method for developing your ability to focus your attention and hold it where you want it.

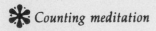 *Counting meditation*

As you follow your breath, silently count one number on each inhalation, leaving your exhalation empty to experience yourself and your surroundings. Count "1" on your first inhalation, "2" on your second, and so on up to "10." Then take one completely empty breath, and begin at "1" again.

When you notice that you've lost count and drifted off, return to the last number you remember. If you've lost track of where you drifted away, start over again.

You may want to close your eyes and visualize each number and hear it in your head as you count. If you have a hard time seeing the number in your mind, try seeing just the top edge of it at first, and gradually you're likely to be able to see more and more of it. Let each number remind you to feel your breath.

One small addition to counting meditation may help you to focus your attention. On your outgoing breath, silently count "1" each time, until you get to 10. If you have your eyes closed, you might visualize it as a subscript down in the right-hand corner of your visual field. After you've taken your empty breath and are ready to start counting from 1 to 10 again, count "2" on every exhalation, indicating that you're on your second series of ten, and so on.

Zen monk Kwong Sensei suggests an alternative counting meditation in which you count "1" on your outgoing breath, "2" on your incoming breath, "3" on your next outgoing breath, and so on.

Word-passage meditation

Eknath Easwaran, of the Blue Mountain Meditation Center, suggests a variation on counting meditation using a passage of words instead of numbers. If you meditate in this way at the beginning of the day, the saying that you make the object of your meditation is likely to stay with you throughout the day. Then you can relate the events of the day to it. You may want to keep the same passage for several days or even weeks, or you may want to choose a new passage each day. Choose one of not more than about ten words, one that has real meaning for you.

As you continue with this kind of meditation, the understandings embodied in the sayings you choose are likely to become part of your life. Lao-tzu is a fine source of such sayings, and many of the sayings of various other sages and psychologists that are quoted in this book can also serve this purpose.

In this word-passage meditation, first memorize the saying or passage, then say one word to yourself on each incoming breath, just as with the numbers in "counting meditation." For instance, I might read Fujimoto

Roshi's comments on developing a "mirror mind" through the process of meditation:

> The function of the mirror is to reflect what is before it. . . . It remains quiet in spite of the activity of the reflections. . . . A mirror state of mind is difficult to attain, so as we proceed, we must remain aware of our limitations.

This idea of the mirror mind is important. Many persons, when they first begin to meditate, complain about distractions. Barking dogs, vehicle noises, people entering the room—all these seem distracting. The concept of the mirror mind teaches us to *be aware of these events as they are*—they're not just distractions, they're things we notice as part of our meditation. "So this is what's happening now!"

I might select the first sentence of Fujimoto Roshi's statement for meditation. Using the counting-meditation technique, I can see the words (instead of numbers) in my mind, and I can also use subscript numbers on my exhalation.

One common misunderstanding is the idea that concentration means pushing things you don't want to think about out of your mind. Actually, that's impossible, because if you're trying to "not think about" something, you're still thinking about it.

Rather, concentration involves really focusing on what you *do* want to pay attention to. If your attention wanders elsewhere, that's okay. Just bring it back to where you want it. It's easy.

Contemplation, or reflective meditation

Meditation is a good time to think about difficult issues in your life and about qualities you'd like to develop in yourself.

When you think about a problem, you might want to start with a guided daydream, like the "Journey into the Desert" (see page 277).

Then begin to follow or count your breath, or intone your mantra, and keep an awareness of your problem in your mind. Don't "force yourself" to think about it—just let everything about it that wants to come into your mind come in. If you sometimes want to let go of your object of concentration to follow a thought about the problem, that's all right too.

Kwong Sensei told me to try thinking of myself as a mountain, great and immovable, when I sit in meditation. A few nights ago I did that. The night was cold. Great gales blew. Trees bent far over and creaked, and one or two fell crashing to the earth. I went down to the creek to sit.

Gradually I began to be the mountain. With my eyes closed, the sound of the rushing waters became the sound of my own waters, streams gushing forth from me. There I sat, majestic, unmoved and immovable, capped with snow and covered with forests. I felt infinitely strong, and at the same time felt infinite compassion for all the creatures and other beings that graced my slopes.

A FINAL WORD. You'll probably do best to find one or two ways of centering and stay with these for a while. That usually works better than jumping around from method to method.

Stories of people meditating are full of tales of breaking up in laughter and delight. You can't be centered if you're too grave, for that leads to a ponderous one-sidedness. An important benefit of centering practices is developing this lightheartedness, this ability to laugh at yourself when you notice yourself being very serious. Being centered in my own experience includes living fully in my joy, my laughter, and my delight.

Don't look for miracles and visions in your meditation. When you have unusual experiences, jot them down and leave them for later, to work with in ways described in Chapter 23.

There are miracles enough in your body and your environment at every moment, if you but see and feel them. The veins in a leaf, the shifts in the patterns of sunlight and shadows in just a few minutes as the earth turns—these everyday events are miracles enough.

25 *Wholeness*

"I have no idea why I did it—something just came over me."

"I'm not myself at all today." (I wonder who I am?)

"Often I do things I don't really want to, but I can't seem to help myself."

"I want so many different things I don't know *what* I want."

These comments show that, in a sense, each of us is like a collection of different people living together in one body. When I think of myself in this way, as a "cast of characters," I understand a little more about why I do or don't do certain things. Each of my characters has some function in my life, and something to say about who I am. Gurdjieff calls these characters "small I's" and Roberto Assagioli calls them "sub-personalities."

Some of these characters from the theatre of my life have only walk-on roles in my existence. They walk on stage and walk off. Others are on stage for longer periods of time. Some are major and enduring parts of who I am.

Some of my characters, if I let them, would fill up my existence and let none of the others in. When this happens to me, I become locked into one way, or at most a few ways, of being.

At times, certain of my characters seem to be fighting for control. First one character jumps into my driver's seat and uses my mind and body to express itself, then another pushes it out and takes over. Sometimes even after one character gains control I don't just relax and be what I am at that moment. Other characters try to push it out and take over, so that I'm in conflict about what I'm doing even while I do it. My hang-loose, easygoing character has me down at the beach to have a good time, but my compulsively responsible character keeps telling me about

295

the work I need to be doing. This is a way I can both sabotage and torture myself.

When there's a "palace revolution" going on in me, I need to be aware of it. If that revolution is going to bring some kind of change, I need to be aware that *I* am doing something to change how and who I am. I am the director of my revolution, and the characters in it are all mine. When they're in conflict, I need to hear what each one has to say. As I listen to each statement, I can ask myself whether the revolution I'm causing is likely to lead to the kind of change that will bring me closer to being the whole person I want to be.

When one of my characters has a lot of energy, I may commit some act that has long-term effects that are not what I want, but that I have to live with. By confronting my mistakes and dealing with them from my centered place where I see my wholeness, I'm less apt to repeat those mistakes.

I have perhaps a dozen characters who play central roles in the drama of my life.

One of them is my "Star," my performer—juggling firebrands and eating apples at the same time. Another is my talkative, articulate character who's always ready to rap. Then there's my "Pusher," who can push me to work very hard for long hours and never give me any rest. And my hang-loose, easygoing self who's into having a good time now (his favorite word is "mañana"). And my quiet, listening, intuitive self who's tuned in to what's happening with other people.

Among my central characters, too, is "El Patron." El Patron is my guiding, directing, controlling self. He can be arrogant and authoritarian.

El Patron was born in my distant past, and for years he didn't change much. Recently El Patron has begun to learn and grow. He's discovered that he doesn't have to have the stage all to himself. When one of my other characters walks on, El Patron can be in relationship with that part of me. He can be lighthearted and laugh with the saucy lady in me that likes to flirt and giggle. He doesn't have to say, "Oh, but that's not El Patron who directs, organizes, and is responsible for his own life and the lives of others."

Many of us have our equivalent of El Patron. If, as a business executive, I wake up in the morning anxious about my business, El Patron wakes up with me. He's anxious about what's going to happen as I get dressed, and anxious as I eat breakfast. He doesn't let me feel the tingle of cold water splashing on my face. He doesn't let in the kid who smells the hot cereal at breakfast. I'm locked into being El Patron.

Or my El Patron may come from a world view that says, "Play it cool, don't get involved. Don't worry about *anything*." That El Patron may deaden so much of my energy that I often have a hard time even getting out of bed.

If I want to move toward wholeness, my El Patron has to make room for my other characters.

✳ *Recognizing your characters*

Look through an old magazine that you don't want anymore. Each time you see a picture that touches you strongly in some way—attracts you, repels you, arouses your curiosity, etc.—cut it out and lay it aside, until you have fifteen or twenty pictures.

Now lay your pictures out on the floor. Each one represents a side of you. Some of these may be parts of you that were important in the past; others are parts that you are struggling with or trying to express now. Many of these are likely to be characters that are important parts of your life. You may want to give some of them names.

Arrange your pictures so that the nearness of certain ones to others shows which parts of you are most clearly in contact.

Now check whether you've omitted any important dimensions of who you are. If so, find another picture—or even a trinket or other object—that can represent each of those missing parts, and put it where it belongs in the display.

If you're doing this exercise in a group—three to eight people works best—after about half an hour, when all of you have finished, everyone will gather around to look at your creation. As you explain it to them, tell how each picture or item is you, and say a little about what's happening in that area of your life. Others can ask you questions at any point.

When you're done, go around with everyone else and listen as each person in turn describes himself or herself through the pictures. (If there are more than about eight of you, you can separate into two or more groups so that it doesn't take forever.)

After you've finished, you may want to take cardboard and glue and make your pictures into a collage. Watching how these change through time can be interesting.

At certain times in my past, I turned away from looking at certain characters in me, because recognizing those parts of myself was painful. When any of us do this, says Rossi, "We unwittingly set the stage for feelings of inadequacy and inferiority. The more rigidly we define ourselves the less likely we are able to cope with the infinite variety of life" (9).

As I recognize and re-own a part of myself I've disowned, I become able to channel and use my power effectively.

Some of our actions grow out of parts of ourselves we've turned away from. Others reflect parts of us that are newly emerging. We can scare ourselves when we behave, think, or feel in ways that we don't see as being us. "That's not like me."

You don't have to scare yourself when you are "not like you." Rather, you can ask: "How is this not like me, and what would I do in this event to be like me?" You can explore those places in yourself that feel strange to you, to find new areas of your own potential that you can draw on.

If I see myself as a growing organic being, I'm not locked into my past events that led me to this moment. I can use what I've learned from those events, and also trust the totality of my present reactions, even though some of them may seem quite unlike me. Out of my unfamiliar new responses can grow new characters, new dimensions of myself that more fully express who I am today.

Wholeness means that instead of fighting with one another, the different parts of who I am become old friends. As I come to know and care for them, and am able to move in and out of them more consciously and less automatically, I become less likely to think and act in contradictory ways, or to act in ways that don't fit the situation.

Sometimes I'm more in touch with myself that way than at other times. As I teach my class, for instance, Don Juan* walks on stage. When I'm in touch with myself, I can use my Don Juan's element of play and seduction to make whatever I'm teaching more personal and more meaningful. On the other hand, if I lose myself in becoming the player and seducer, I'm likely to lose my effectiveness as a teacher.

The reverse is also true. If my teacher comes in and takes over when Don Juan is appropriate, things get equally screwed up. It's part of what's often called male chauvinism when a man decides he's going to teach his woman how to make love better. If he does it out of his teacher place, rather than out of his loving, caring place, he's likely to mess up the relationship thoroughly.

Even when I'm inconsistent, I'm inconsistent in ways that are consistent with me. You are inconsistent in ways that are consistent with you. Seldom will you and I be inconsistent in the very same ways.

For example, Vivian announces to a group at the beginning of the

*The Spanish libertine; not Castaneda's teacher.

evening, "I want to work on my shyness. I'm going to make a real effort to speak out in the group tonight." Then she says nothing for the rest of the night. Her words and actions are inconsistent in a way that's consistent with who she is. When I'm invited somewhere as a consultant, I may say to myself, "I'm going to go in and be very quiet and participate only when I'm asked for an opinion." Nevertheless, I may find many things I want to say, and—unasked—say them. For both Vivian and me, it would be inconsistent of us to follow through with the intentions we stated.

Locking ourselves in

When we get totally caught up in one or another of our characters without realizing that we're doing so, we lose all sense of perspective on what we're doing. Then we have no alternatives available.

Irma is so committed to her "poor me" character that even when she's given goodies, she finds ways to turn them into put-downs and losses. That's how she related to her parents, and she carries that way of being into all her other relationships.

Gurdjieff calls this "identification" with the character. To avoid confusion with the Freudian meaning of "identification," here we'll use the word "cubbyholing" for the process of getting locked into just one character, one of our many potential ways of being.

When I get cubbyholed in one of my characters, if I flash for even an instant that that's where I am, I can remember that *that's only a small part of me, and I am much more than that.* For example, I seldom experience any strong feeling in complete isolation. For an instant I may feel I'm only my anger, but actually I also experience a something I call passion behind that anger.

That passion is my energy. There's passion in my anger, passion in my loving, and passion in my grief. I may also feel hurt when I'm angry, jealous when I'm sad, or feel even more complex combinations of emotion.

As I learn to acknowledge my various feelings when they come more than one at a time, I have more of who I am available to me. I can be angry and compassionate at the same time: I can be angry with you at this instant, yet understand that the whole situation cannot be other than it is, and that you had to act the way you did.

Louise's husband had been drinking heavily for five years. Recently, Louise said, "I've had enough," and walked out the door.

That jolted her husband into starting to work seriously with Alcoholics Anonymous and to make some real changes in himself. He asked Louise to come to a session with me. As I listened, essentially I heard him asking Louise to start all over again.

Louise's trouble saying yes is not that she doesn't love him now, but that she has such a heavy investment in being angry with him that she feeds her anger to the point where it blocks out her other feelings. In part, she's using her anger to justify having left him. Louise won't be ready to try again until she's willing to contact her other feelings.

When I feel angry with you, or loving toward you, or any other way, if I can also tell you what else I feel toward you, we're more likely to be able to work things out.

Sometimes when I'm extremely angry with my children, I don't look at them at all. I close my eyes or turn my head away or look at the ceiling. That way I stay with only my anger. I'm less likely to see something in them that might touch other ways of feeling in me.

My other option is to look at them while I talk to them. When I do that, I'm more likely to let in my compassion and love for them at the same time that I feel my anger. I don't undo my anger. I still own and express it. But I'm more available to work out with them what my anger means for me, and what I want from them.

I suspect that sometimes when I keep my other feelings out of my awareness, someone or something else is involved in my anger. Instead of expressing my anger directly to that source, I express it to the person I'm talking to.

A word of caution here: Saying to yourself, "I'm more than this feeling I have right now" can be a way of disowning and staying out of touch with that feeling. When you can consciously express that feeling, and have developed a real awareness of how you take yourself into and out of it, that's a good time to begin learning to experience and express other dimensions of yourself.

Working toward being able to move freely and consciously among my characters reminds me of the creek I live by. Each autumn I clear out logjams that built up the previous winter, so the water can flow through freely. Otherwise the banks cave in around the logjams.

In a like way, my body gets into trouble when the circulatory passages block up, and the blood can't flow freely through the body. It's important for our life energy to be able to flow throughout the entire personality in a similar way.

INTEGRATING SOME IMPORTANT ASPECTS OF OURSELVES

"Parent," "adult," and "child"

Psychiatrist Eric Berne has described three important characters we all have inside us: child, parent, and adult.

As children, we are curious, spontaneous, and full of wonder. In our untrained, impulsive, and expressive earliest days, we have few "shoulds." When I am my *natural child* I delight in the sensuous feeling of lying in the sun, of walking barefoot, of cool water splashing in my face. I'm likely to feel warm and loving when you do what I want, and angry, frustrated, and rebellious when you don't.

I think here of Gene Kelly in the movie "Singing in the Rain." Singing and dancing, he jumps, skips, and splashes through the water in the gutter, with an absolute child's delight.

Before I learn not to ask certain questions, I am curious about and interested in everything. As my *creative child* (Berne's "little professor"), I figure out how things work and how to get what I want. I see many things adults often overlook, and I understand things that many adults don't want to understand. My guesses about my world are often wrong, but through them I learn and grow; and when they're right, they sometimes contain great wisdom.

My *adapted* child has learned certain ways to avoid punishment and get rewards. I may go along with the demands on me or I may run away from them. I become a "compliant child" (the "good boy" or "good girl") who does everything I'm told to do; a "withdrawn child" who is distant and unresponsive; or a "rebellious child" who says no to almost everything.

Beware of the trap that caught one man who came to see me. He had learned the language of Berne's psychology, but used it to avoid taking responsibility for his actions instead of using it to grow. Whenever he was messing up his relationship with another person, he would actually say the words, "This is my adapted child," as though in saying them, everything else got cleared up. But he stopped there, and never went on to work anything out with the person.

Our parents present us with a range of behaviors. Out of those, we select the ones we want to imitate. We also make choices about ways we don't want to act. For instance, Robin's mother always talks in a loud, harsh voice. From her earliest years, Robin has disliked that voice and has chosen to talk more quietly. We select what we wish from our parents' behaviors and attitudes to enlarge, enrich, and justify the characters we've chosen to make part of our lives.

If my parent gave a lot of orders, punished me often, and was cold and distant, then when I'm in my parent character I'm likely to behave similarly toward others. This is the *judgmental parent*.

If my parent was nurturing, caring for me with love and concern, my parent place is likely to have some of those same characteristics. This is the *nurturing parent*.

If my parent smothered me with so much affection and protectiveness that I had a hard time learning to stand on my own feet, I may try to do too much for you and not give you enough space to be yourself. This is the *overprotective* parent.

My "adult" comes out of my experience with my world when I am not too anxious to think clearly and act effectively. I learn by experiencing the consequences of what I do. My adult includes two parts.

My *rational adult* is that part of me that has learned to deal with myself and my world as effectively as I can on the basis of the information I have available.

My *emotional adult* is that part of me that has learned to accept and live with my feelings as they are, without being thrown out of kilter by what I'm feeling. This kind of learning takes place when I'm free to feel as I do. Since most of us don't have this freedom as we grow up, we're slow to mature emotionally. Many of us never fully develop our emotional adult. When children are free to feel as they do, the emotional adult develops right along with the rational adult.

You might want to try the "Recognizing your characters" exercise again (see page 297), paying attention to these parent, adult, and child places in you.

Anima and animus

Jung drew attention to the importance of integrating the "masculine" and "feminine" sides of our character, as part of our movement toward wholeness.

He gave the name *animus* to what he viewed as "masculine" consciousness and behavior: aggressing, achieving, creating, rational, problem-solving—outgoing, penetrating energy. He used *anima* to refer to "feminine" consciousness and behavior: receptive, nurturing, soft, intuitive, drawing on the depths of the inner world and the unconscious.

Every man and woman *needs a balance of anima and animus characteristics*. If I limit myself to one of these sides of me, I cut myself off from half my potential as a person.

Few of us have an even development of these aspects of our character. In a balanced personality, anima and animus characteristics intertwine in each of the areas of a person's life. If you feel lopsided in either direction, you can develop the complementary side.

Power and control

Imagine that you and I are at a control panel inside a vehicle. Each of us has charge of certain instruments and levers. You're responsible for control and I'm responsible for power. You decide where we go and the route we take. I decide how much energy we have to get there: when we move and how fast we go. Control is a statement of direction. Power is a statement of energy to move.

In my life, I may have enough control over my behavior to do something, go somewhere, and be something. But I also have to find the energy to get from here to there. Or I may have a lot of energy to go somewhere, but the controlling place inside me wants to close down. Then I fight myself. My struggle is likely to show up in physical symptoms like backaches, ulcers, and high blood pressure.

I can use my control in at least two very different ways. *Compulsive control* is clamping-down that directs and channels energy in a narrow way. I push and squeeze all my power into certain places, even though I have energy to go to other places.

Centered control comes from a deeper contact with myself. When I'm in touch with what I need for me, and what other people around me need for them, I can channel energy in directions that meet those needs.

The paradox of control is that *the more compulsively I control, the more likely I am to go out of control* and the less able I am to genuinely meet my own changing needs and the needs of those around me. This is frequently an occupational hazard for politicians.

We've all seen people compulsively grabbing after political or economic power and control. We've all seen others, and even ourselves, compulsively trying to control in our everyday contact with other people. When a person values power and control above all else, is unwilling to give up any of that power to others, and is busy grabbing after still more and more power, that person has lost control. Deposed politicians are often victims of their own compulsive control.

As I work toward developing a genuine sense of my needs, I develop my ability to control myself in centered ways. I become better able to use the options and alternatives in my life.

My first needs are that I have food, warmth, shelter, and good health. Given these, I need space and time to be in touch with myself and to contact other people in a way that's real for both—or all—of us. I need to exercise my capacity to be curious, to explore and create and do. I need contact with my natural world in a way that lets me draw on it for renewal and refreshment. I need to exercise and move my body. And I need to feel good about myself and about the way others view me. Abraham Maslow discusses these needs in greater detail in *Toward a Psychology of Being*.

To the degree that I'm meeting these needs, I have the power to give up my compulsive control. So long as I'm not meeting them, my power goes into compulsive control. This is overcompensation in Freud's classic sense. Not finding the kind of regeneration that comes from meeting my needs, I feel powerless. *Feeling internally powerless, I try to grab hold of external power in a way that lets me create an image of being powerful in my eyes and in the eyes of others.*

When I have centered control, I am spontaneous. I trust what I will do with my power. When I clamp down tightly with my compulsive control, I'm afraid of what I might do with my power, so I don't let myself be spontaneous.

DEVELOPING OUR UNDERDEVELOPED SIDES

CREATIVITY. "I like to hear an event like a musician, touch it like a painter, feel it like a sculptor, read it like a writer, taste it like a chef," says my friend O'Rich.

Jung commented that creativity typically comes from developing the undeveloped sides of the self rather than from accentuating the developed sides.

Creativity exists when we find new ways of understanding relationships and relating to the world of things. Creativity can occur at the easel, at the kitchen table, or at an insurance man's desk. Creativity is a process of finding new ways and new sources of energy; of using as much of me as I'm familiar with, and reaching out to use resources I haven't used before.

Doing something I've never done before is a creative act, though countless others have done it before me. A child tying his or her shoelace for the first time is creating. Learning how to copy something someone else has made is creating.

Just as there's a creativity of imitation, there's a creativity of perceiving and using the world in new forms, like using windmills to generate electricity or finding special ways of expressing the world at the easel or in music. That kind of creativity grows out of the "sense of wonder"—the ability to enter a situation and see it "as if for the first time." Opening myself to new possibilities develops my creativity in experiencing the world.

A person who relates to the world mostly by thinking may seldom be aware of his or her feelings. The feeler may have a hard time keeping a sense of perspective. An intuiter may not be so good at getting things done in the world, while a doer may plunge blindly ahead with little awareness or thought of what he or she is doing. "Extraverted," outward-going people who have an easy time making casual contact with others often fail to develop their inner resources fully, while those who are "introverted" neglect the outward-going parts of themselves.

When I want to develop one of my underdeveloped sides, I may begin by using the kind of energy I already have plenty of. Suppose that thinking is my overdeveloped side, and I want to develop my feeling side more fully. The question facing me is, "How do I get from thinking over to feeling?"

Obviously, I can use my thinking. That's my most immediate power source. I don't have to be put out with myself: "Hey, I'm still doing a mind trip!" I hear people say, "Wow, I just ran a head trip!" as though some great sin has been committed. At the same time you're learning to tap new energy sources inside you, you can know and be with energy sources you already have.

THE MEDICINE WHEEL.   The Cheyenne, Crow, and Sioux tribes of Plains Indians guided their lives by the ancient teaching of the Medicine Wheel. In his compellingly beautiful book, *Seven Arrows*, Hyemeyohsts Storm writes,

> To the North on the Medicine Wheel is found Wisdom. . . . The South is the place of Innocence and Trust, and for perceiving closely our nature of heart. . . . The West is the Looks-Within place, which speaks of the Introspective nature of man. . . . The East . . . is the Place of Illumination, where we can see things clearly far and wide. . . .
>
> To Touch and Feel is to Experience. Many people live out their entire lives without ever really Touching or being Touched by anything. These people live within a world of mind and imagination that may move them sometimes to joy, tears, happiness or sorrow. But these people . . . do not live and become one with life. . . .
>
> Each person is a unique Living Medicine Wheel, powerful beyond imagination, that has been limited and placed upon this earth to Touch, Experience and Learn. (6, 7)

Each of us has a "Beginning Gift" that corresponds to one of the directions on the Wheel. To become whole, we must visit the other places on the Wheel, and learn what each offers. As we do, we become able to make our decisions within the Balance of the Four Directions. Storm continues.

> A person with the Beginning Gift of the Mind must always try to include his Heart in his decisions. When he does this, he begins to turn upon the Medicine Wheel. A man can live out his entire

life without ever finding more than what was already within him as his Beginning Gift, but if he wishes to Grow he must become a Seeker and Seek for himself the other Ways. (8)

As I move toward wholeness, I become open to caring about and sharing deeply with many different kinds of people, since I don't have to have particular qualities in them to complement missing parts of me.

On the other hand, deliberately looking for certain qualities in others can help me get in touch with those same places in myself.

As I come to know many dimensions of myself, I can more fully share your experiences of this world we share. To the degree that I can feel my own joy and sorrow I can feel your joy and sorrow as well.

26 *Be Good To Yourself*

Do you ask for what you want? Or do you sit around hoping others will know what you want and give it to you? Do you hug someone when you need a hug? Or do you stand there afraid to find out whether anyone's willing to hug you or not?

Some people ask for support by telling me how bad they are. They want me to say, "Oh, I don't think you're bad. I think you've got a lot going for you." Or they want me to guess what other kind of support they're looking for.

If you're not willing to ask directly for what you want, the odds are you won't get it. When you ask, you may get it or you may not, but you've established your strength and your caring for yourself and others by asking. It's never too late to start learning to ask for what you want.

You don't have to brood about why you haven't been good to yourself in the past. Instead, you can ask yourself, "How am I stopping myself from getting what I want, and how can I be good to myself now?"

Part of doing this is paying attention to how you don't allow yourself the goodies people give you: "I'm really not that good; I don't deserve that."

Carol did this when she decided to have her parents sit in with us at her counseling session. Her father opened by saying, "Carol, I'm really happy with the way I'm seeing who you are and how you are." He intended to give her a positive, supportive statement. She translated it, "You're judging and evaluating me."

Notice also how you sabotage yourself: "I don't think I'm going to be able to do this." This means you're not really going to try—or, sometimes, that you don't want to do it.

307

ASSERTION.   If I'm so timid that I seldom get what I want, or so aggressive and belligerent that I often offend people and turn them off, I can learn to express myself more effectively. Asserting myself is asking for what I want, or acting to get what I want, in a way that respects the other person. As Alberti and Emmons point out, it's the middle way between timid holding-back and inconsiderate tromping on other people's toes.

I might feel afraid that if I assert myself by saying that I'd like to share some time with you, you'll "reject" me.

If I feel worthless and you turn me down, I figure it's "because I'm not good enough." The better I feel about myself, the less subject I am to feeling "rejected."

Actually, no one can reject me. Others can only say that they want to do something else right now. That's a statement about *them*, not me.

Last night I was sitting in a cafe with a lovely lady. We were getting tired and ready to go home. I said, "I'll gladly come home with you if you invite me." She laughed and said, "No thanks, but I'm glad you asked," and we both felt good as we parted. I'd made my statement in a way that made it easy for her to feel at ease with whatever reply she wanted to make.

In ways like that, gradually I'm learning to say what I need to say for me. In your own situations in your life, you can learn to say what you need to say for you.

When I pay attention to what's happening where I am, I can usually sense how much room I have to assert myself in the situation I'm in.

Kids are often amazingly good at sensing how far they can go. When my son went to the orthopedist, the guy started putting him down for his long hair.

My son took it and took it. Finally he got fed up and said essentially, "Listen, I came here for my bones, not my hair. When I want to deal with my hair, I'll go to the barber."

The doctor did a double take and incoherently sputtered more or less, "You can't talk to me that way here in my church," and then shut up.

Do you say no when you feel no? Or, in order to be "nice," do you often agree to do something even when you don't want to, knowing you'll feel resentful and unhappy about doing it?

Try this:

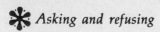 *Asking and refusing*

Sit facing another person.

Ask the person for something, or to do something. It can be as simple as asking for an ashtray, or it can involve something that's important for both of you.

When you've asked, the other person says no.

Ask again, in any way you think might get you what you want.

The other person *must* refuse your request at least three times, and may then continue to refuse for as long as he or she cares to. The person doesn't ever have to give you what you're asking for unless you put it in a way that causes him or her to feel like saying yes.

As you ask, pay attention to how you try to get the other person to say yes. How do you feel as you ask? How do you feel when you're refused?

Then switch roles and repeat the procedure. How does the other person try to get you to say yes? How do you refuse, and how do you feel as you refuse?

When you're done, talk with the other person about what happened between you.

Mary Ann came in with a dream about a mouse that had been sneaking around and biting her toes. For me, her dream tied in with a "mousy" quality I noticed in her voice and bearing.

In her dream encounter with her mouse, Mary Ann started off disowning her mouse, saying it had nothing to do with her. As she explored her dream, however, she began to get in touch with her "mousy" way of handling her world, a world that she wanted to be more assertive with. Her mousiness was her way of being "nice" while going after what she wanted.

As Mary Ann became aware of how she used her mousiness, her mouse became a more handsome, more powerful *rat*. She discovered ways to use the strength of her rat as a friendly, assertive place for herself and others without having it be a sneaky, backhandedly aggressive place.

GIVING MYSELF WHAT I NEED.   What are you *not* giving yourself, or giving yourself enough of, that you need? (And what are you giving yourself that you'd be better off without?)

I've always got something good that I can give myself, if I'm willing to. And a Pollyanna I'm not. I hate getting stuck in traffic, and sometimes get angry when I do. But I also know that wherever I am—even in a morass of concrete and steel—it's a chance to look out at the people in the cars around me. I seldom do that at other times. I still resent getting stuck in traffic, but I can do something good for myself while I'm there.

To be "self-sacrificing" when I don't want to be is no service to others, because I feel resentful toward them in the process.

Once I was visiting my son in the hospital. In the ward was a badly burned child who'd been there a long time. He was calling the nurse, but she was tied up with another patient and had been going at a hectic pace. She was clearly in need of a few moments by herself. She heard the child call, looked at him, saw that he wasn't in pain or danger, and said, "Georgie, *I need me now*."

The boy totally understood. She didn't need to say, "I'll be there in a little while," or anything like that. He knew where she was coming from.

When I come on clearly and directly with where I am, others usually respect me, and often feel attracted to me.

ALONENESS. I need times to be alone with myself. Even the best company is good only so long. I need my own time to assimilate what's happened in the time that you and I have spent together. I need time to find my own center, to be with myself in a way where I'm not bouncing off other people and responding to their demands on me. We all need both the dimension of being with people and the dimension of being with ourselves.

Aloneness need not mean physical distance. I can be on a bus or subway filled with people, or at a desk in a crowded library, and still find the solitude I need. What's crucial is that no one is making demands on me, and I feel no need to make demands on anyone else.

In our culture, we easily fall prey to the myth that "you should always have somebody to be with." The alone person is seen as alien, weird, "not a team player." We introject this subtle social pressure and think there's something wrong with us when we're alone. Then we feel *lonely*, and our time alone is painful instead of nourishing. (In *Loneliness*, Moustakas deals in depth with this experience we all sometimes share.)

Aloneness is a time when I feel no need to be with other people. At those times, I have time leisurely to explore my surroundings and my inner world—time to think lofty thoughts or pick my nose.

Times when I'm alone but preoccupied with "needing other people," or worried about what others think of me, or would think if they saw me, aren't really being alone at all.

I suspect that almost everyone needs to run away from home now and then. Children certainly sometimes need a place to run away to for a while. There's no need for parents to get upset about this. It doesn't mean you're failing as a parent—it just means your child needs a change of scenery.

One group of families I know has an arrangement in which any child can run away to any other house for a few days, and it works out beautifully. The parents, too, get vacations when their children run away.

Most adults I know sometimes need to run away by themselves too, to be away from spouse, lover, family, everyone. I certainly do. When I go away for a couple of days and get a hotel or motel room where no one knows me, or camp out in the wilderness, I have space to be with myself in a way that I seldom have at other times. If I want, I can be with other people, but I don't have to respond to any expectations about who I am. I come back refreshed.

TOUCHING AND THE BODY.   One of the most important ways we nourish each other is through touching and being touched. Most of us need more hugging and touching and cuddling than we give and get. Infants in institutions who don't get touched enough in caring ways sometimes actually die; and when I don't get touched enough, I at least wither a little.

We need to hold each other. We need to feel a pat on the back for a job well done, and feel someone cradle our head from time to time. I suspect that if every person on this earth got four long, warm, caring hugs each day, there would soon be no more war. I think we often touch with our fists because we're afraid to touch with open hands and hearts.

Luckily, fear of touching is often a fairly easy fear to get past, because touching feels so good. A few years ago I used to walk around with my hands always straight down at my sides, so I "wouldn't intrude into other people's space." I started hanging around with people who were touching and hugging all the time, and my old inhibitions started to dissolve.

Our bodies also need to be touched in deeper ways, to soothe and relax our tensions, and to break up the hard knots where we keep our muscles chronically tight. Massage is such a valuable and beautiful way of giving and receiving that I'm amazed that it's not a skill that we all learn as we grow up.

You may want to read a good book on massage. You may want to go to a professional masseur or masseuse and ask that person what he or she is doing when something feels especially good, so you can learn to do it too. There are many different kinds of massage, all valuable. You and your friends can learn from different sources and exchange what you've learned. And without any special training at all, you can start to learn massage by rubbing and kneading another person's muscles, and asking that person to tell you whenever something feels good or doesn't feel so good, and when you should use more pressure or less.

Being good to our bodies is a major part of being good to ourselves. Yoga, bioenergetics, breathing and body awareness exercises, Tai Chi, deep-muscle massage, athletics, exercise programs, exercise in daily life, a healthy diet—all these are ways we can be good to our bodies. If there's a recreation department, growth center, or adult education center near you, it probably has workshops or courses in how to be good to your body.

The bibliography at the back of this book includes a number of books on massage, Yoga, and other techniques to bring your body more alive.

In the midst of my daily life, I can take ten or five or even two spare minutes to feel where and how my body wants to stretch and move and then do what my body tells me.

Try this:

 Stretching

Stand up. Stretch slowly, and feel your muscles from the inside, as fully as you can. Move your body in ways that you seldom move it in. Notice where you're tight, then stretch in ways that release that tension. "Shake out" your arm or leg or foot or any part of your body where there's tightness you can release by shaking.

If someone feels uptight about you doing your stretching exercises while you're at a bus stop or waiting in line, just smile and tell them it's good for you. (I've even stood on my head in an optometrist's waiting room.)

People who are hunched up when they're old got that way by hunching when they were younger, until their muscles literally stuck together and locked into that position. Watch people of all ages, and you'll see the shapes they're molding their bodies into.

If you pay attention to and listen to your body, you're likely to stand straighter, be more limber, and feel better physically until the end of your days.

My signaling system

Every now and then, I feel a little freaky. I jump out of my skin at small disturbances and see things all out of proportion to their real importance.

This feeling is a "truth button," a warning signal that holds an important message for me. Often it means that I'm too scattered and distracted;

that I need to immediately drop everything I can and be with myself. I need some time to be quiet, to center myself, and to think through all the matters I'm involved in, so that I have a clear sense of where I am.

At other times, that freaky feeling is a signal that I need to use my energies in some way other than the way I'm using them now. My freakiness comes from stopping my energy from flowing as it wants to flow.

The times when I disregard this warning and plunge ahead with what I've been doing are the times when I most often fall ill. My body itself puts the brakes on and *forces* me to stop for a while. I've finally learned that, instead of getting sick, I can heed that early warning signal. I can take a day of sick leave from work when I really need a "mental health day." Sometimes even an hour's break from my usual routine can help.

Even in my demanding everyday activities, I don't have to rush around. I can be here with this moment.

So often the thought "I'm late, I have to hurry" need no more than flit through my head, and I begin responding with subtle emergency reactions in my body. I tighten my stomach and tense my muscles slightly. I experience a slight sinking feeling and an alert wariness. Over time, these things create actual physical stress.

I've begun to realize that no one else is so much more important to me than I am that I'm willing to push myself to high blood pressure and ulcers for their sake. I can remember my centering and slowing-down techniques, and recall this anonymous prayer I once saw on a plaque:

Slow me down, lord.
Ease the pounding of my heart by the quieting of my mind.
Steady my hurried pace with a vision of the eternal reach of time.
Give me, amid the confusion of the day, the calmness of the everlasting hills. . . .
Teach me the art of taking minute vacations—of slowing down to look at a flower, to chat with a friend, to pat a dog, to read a few lines from a good book, . . . and inspire me to send my roots into the soil of life's enduring values.

You may have times in your life when you "go crazy." Most of us do—some of us in an extreme enough way that we need some time in our local mental health center to get ourselves together again, others of us in less extreme ways that we handle by ourselves.

My crazy times are important times in my life. They're strong messages, with red lights flashing and bells ringing, that I need to make certain changes in the way I live my life. I ignore such messages at my peril.

My crazy places are potentially nourishing places. In them, I find understandings and sources of energy that I seldom tap at other times. By going far out there, where it's easier for me to listen to the depths of who I am, I get back into my center here.

Laing has found that when people who have "gone crazy" are given support and nurturing conditions, they often work through things that are important to them during their altered state of consciousness. According to Laing, people given this kind of therapeutic help have a much higher recovery rate than people who are given heavy doses of suppressive drugs and treated as though there's "something wrong" with them.

In our daily lives, we often handle symptoms of minor craziness by suppressing them with tranquilizers or other drugs. This is usually the worst thing we could do. *When I have such a symptom, I want to really experience myself, and pay attention to what I'm telling me.*

I can find out how I'm violating my own inner nature, stop doing that, and start giving myself what I need that I'm not getting.

Spontaneity

When I'm spontaneous, my words and actions respond uniquely to *this* moment, *this* situation. I don't need to think of what to do or how to do it—I just *do* it. Spontaneity is letting-happen, rather than deliberate, thought-out action.

Allowing myself to act spontaneously is especially helpful if I tend to inhibit my acts and censor my words. So many of us labor under heavy prescriptions of what we *shouldn't* do, even when we want to. We have nameless fears of awful consequences "if I act like I really feel like acting" or "if I show myself as I really am."

Many people have trouble speaking in groups. Typically, they sabotage themselves by having some image of how they have to say things; they have plenty to say, but "don't know how to say it." Instead of trying to speak in some special way, you can say whatever comes into your mind, and trust it to be a genuine expression of you now.

"Learning to be spontaneous" may sound like a contradiction. Think of it, then, as unlearning our ways of being contrived and manipulative. The function of spontaneous self-expression is to express yourself, not to influence the other. Sometimes your self-expression has an impact, and sometimes not.

Spontaneity is not the opposite of self-discipline; it is the opposite of inhibition. True spontaneity can go hand in hand with self-disciplined learning. In one sense, spontaneity takes the utmost discipline—the discipline of tuning in to what I really feel like doing, learning how to do it, and doing it, despite my fears. I have to trust myself and others to allow myself that discipline. It's much easier to take the built-in socially conditioned and approved way that I usually take.

Spontaneity does not mean doing anything I please, regardless of the consequences to me or others.

I can use the word to lend respectability to self-indulgence. I can use it to justify lack of consideration. I can use it to justify stepping on other people to get what I want. Then "spontaneity" becomes an excuse through which I evade responsibility for "accidentally" harming others.

Sometimes my need is not for greater spontaneity, but for enjoying and appreciating my spontaneity, and appreciating how I nourish myself with my spontaneity.

Other times—usually when I would profit most by acting more spontaneously—I don't allow myself to see the need to flow freely. I convince myself that my studied, careful, fearful ways of acting are the only ways available to me.

If I've minimized such fears in myself, and easily act or speak spontaneously, then there is often value in taking pause to choose what I want to do and how I want to do it.

NATURAL CYCLES

To every thing there is a season, and a time to every purpose under the heaven:

A time to be born, and a time to die; a time to plant, and a time to pluck up that which is planted; . . .

A time to weep, and a time to laugh; a time to mourn, and a time to dance; . . .

A time to get, and a time to lose; a time to keep, and a time to cast away. . . . (Eccles. 3:1–6)

In one sense, my life is a journey from one point to others, some points near, some points far, and all different. In another sense, my life is a series of cycles, of wave forms, of returning again to events that are like events I've known before but that I experience in a different way each time.

Every woman knows her cyclical nature well. She feels the changes in her body as she moves into, through, and out of her menstrual cycle.

All of us, women and men alike, move through other biological cycles, or "biorhythms." We all have mood, or feeling, cycles. When I'm on the upswing of my cycle, it's easy for me to feel good and alive. When I'm on the downswing, it's easy for me to feel gloomy and unhappy.

We also move through cycles of mental sharpness. Every teacher has seen the same child come in one day and solve problems in an instant, and come in another day and be unable to understand the question.

We move through activity cycles too. At the peak of my activity cycle, I have great energy and zest for life. At the bottom, I can hardly get out of bed. In his book on biorhythms, *Is This Your Day?*, George Thommen describes these cycles in detail, and suggests ways of using them. Gay Gaer Luce also discusses biorhythms in *Body Time*.

People living in close relationship sometimes find that their cycles bump into each other. This can be true for couples, for roommates, and for families. We can make things easier on ourselves by allowing a little extra space for each other at such times, as when one person is very energetic and the other wants to take it easy, or one feels happy and the other feels down.

I don't have to get angry with myself because I'm not always so energetic, or happy, or mentally sharp. When I feel foggy and drifty, I can *be* foggy and drifty, and that's okay.

When I'm aware of where I am in the cycles of my own life, I can act more wisely. I don't set forth on something new when I need to draw in my energies. I don't keep working on the same old thing long beyond my time for new beginnings.

Times and transitions in our lives

The *I Ching*, or *Book of Changes*, has provided important insights to people of many times and places, speaks of the cycles in human affairs.

When I run into obstacles, the *I Ching* says, my trouble may be a message that I'm trying to do something that's beyond my ability at the present time, or that I'm trying to act or change in ways that don't fit who I am.

Instead of obstinately staying with a certain course "come hell or high water," I can keep alert to all the forces at play. Then I'm more likely to see when an undertaking is getting into trouble, and I can take steps to deal with what's happening. I'm also more likely to see when an undertaking is apt to turn out badly. Then I can make a wise retreat, withdrawing my energy from the project in a way that insures that no one will suffer as I do so.

When a Japanese firm with over a thousand employees recently became aware that bankruptcy was inevitable, it spent the last of its resources in a successful effort to find other jobs for every one of its workers.

I may meet an obstruction because the forces in me and around me are such that this is not the right moment to act. There are difficulties to be surmounted, but I need to surmount them with intelligence, discrimination, and patience, rather than try to blast through them. Thus I can avoid needless conflict.

Just as we all face obstacles, so also each of us lives through times when the conditions of our life are dark and painful.

When I'm in the midst of troubling and difficult conditions, I can look around and ask, "What can I do to change all this?" I may find something I can do, and do it.

Or I may find that I'm creating my own trouble and dark times, so that I carry them with me everywhere. Then I can ask, "What changes do I need to make in the way I am with myself and other people, *whatever* the conditions I find myself in?"

Eventually my hard times always end, and better times return. Like springtime of the year, my life has its new beginnings. My old projects and my resistances to trying something new have fallen by the wayside, and I'm ready to forge ahead. This is my time of great creative energy. The *I Ching* says, "It is a good thing to hesitate so long as the time for action has not come, but no longer. Once the obstacles to action have been removed, anxious hesitation is a mistake. . . . We must work with determination and perseverance to make full use of the propitiousness of the time. . . . Spring does not last forever" (79, 233).

Sometimes in my life and my undertakings, everything goes well. The energies from within me and the circumstances outside me seem to flow together in a natural way. Even my mistakes turn out right.

Such times are temporary, so I do well to live fully in them while they're here. At the same time, I don't want to become careless and neglectful in my undertakings and relationships. Small problems I could gloss over may signal deeper currents that I need to pay attention to. If I attend to them, I'm likely to stay in my time of abundance and delight for a longer time.

PAIN AND SUFFERING

Times of pain and suffering are part of the natural cycle of life. Events like death, divorce, illness, separation from loved ones, and failure in our enterprises are part of the natural cycles we all experience.

There are two things I don't need when I'm into my hard and painful places. One is to convince myself that I'm bad and that's why I'm suffering so.

The other is for someone to tell me that I don't have it so bad, and have no good reason to feel the way I feel.

What I do need is to find ways to handle my suffering without being destroyed by it.

Distraught with grief, a woman whose only son had died came to Buddha wanting the boy's life restored. "Bring me a mustard seed from a household where no one has died," said Buddha, "and I will bring him to life again."

The woman searched and searched, through village after village. In every house, a child or parent or brother or sister or husband or wife or grandparent or friend had died. The woman found no mustard seed that would do, but as she searched, everyone she met listened to her story, and in turn told her stories of their own grief and suffering. She began to realize, "I'm not the only one. This woman I'm talking to who has tears in her eyes—it's her loss too. I don't feel so alone in my grief."

She recognized her place in the natural cycle of life and learned to perceive death within the context of life.

Through all his days, the focus of Buddha's teaching was that we can find ways to reduce our suffering. *About a third of our suffering is inevitable,* he said, *but we ourselves create the rest of it.* We can learn to stop doing that.

"I belong to this realm of tears and beauty, the earth," says "Red" Thomas. As I learn to accept the suffering I do experience, as I realize that pain and hardship are part of what it is to be a human being, my suffering becomes gentler; not less intense, but in a real way all right.

Life is hard enough as it is. I don't need the extra suffering of thinking, "I *shouldn't* be suffering right now. There's something wrong with me."

Many of us grew up being told over and over by our cultural myths that we were supposed to end up living in a fairy-tale kingdom where we know nothing but happiness forever and ever. Life isn't like that. So when we experience sadness as well as joy, pain as well as pleasure, we oppress ourselves by thinking that our life "is not the way it should be."

If it were possible for me to live through none of the hard and painful sides of human experience, I'd be living on the surface and out of touch with the depths of life. But if I knew only the hard and painful sides, I'd be running to the surface of existence, frantically keeping out of touch with the depths that offered me nothing but pain and hard times. Life is the whole thing, and I don't want to live only half of it.

Living through the pain that is an inevitable part of my life is, of course, different from *neurotic suffering,* which is living off suffering, loving it, getting our goodies from it, and refusing to also know the lighter sides of life.

To be tuned in to the pain that others feel is part of wisdom. I need to be sensitive to the times when I cause others pain, so that I see and feel the ways that I'm "the bad guy," and do not delude myself with a banner of self-righteousness. Sometimes I still act uncaringly in the service of ancient habits. To the degree that I'm willing to perceive the pain that these actions cause others, I can invest the time and work it takes to learn to act in other ways.

Much of our pain centers around losing or being afraid of losing something or someone we value, such as job, mate, money, esteem. I want what *was* to continue, instead of living with what *is*. Or I'm afraid of losing what is, instead of being willing to live with whatever will be.

On one hand, I want space to experience fully my feelings about my loss or prospective loss, and to listen to the messages they hold about what I need to do for myself. Perhaps I need something similar to what I've lost, or perhaps I need to open new dimensions in my life so that I don't depend so much on what I'm so afraid of losing.

On the other hand, I can learn to appreciate each thing or event in my life when it's here, and each next thing or event as it comes.

When my suffering is so intense that I'm really on the ragged edge, I often find comfort in doing something very simple, like scrubbing floors or washing windows. This is especially so when my hard times center on a feeling of the worthlessness of my life.

"Dust thou art, and to dust thou shalt return," the Old Testament says. We start out as nothing and end as nothing. Yet somewhere in my existence, there can be moments when I shine brightly for me and those around me. We can all find those moments in our lives.

DESIRE AND HAPPINESS

Desire is a fundamental part of life. When I'm hungry, I want food. When I'm cold, I want warmth.

When I want, I have options. When I need, I'm more limited. When I'm hungry, I can wait to eat, but when I'm starving, I have very little room to wait. The difference between wanting and needing is that when I have needs and don't fulfill them, in some sense I'll suffer real damage.

My needs can be physical or psychological. I may need affection so desperately that I can't exist as myself if I don't get it. When I *want* a certain person to care about me, however, it's something I would *like* to have, but if I have to, I can survive as myself by finding other ways to nourish myself.

When I'm concerned only with my survival, I have less room to think about you. When I'm dealing with my desires, I have room to think about who you are, and what you have to give and what you don't.

I may be ruthless and inconsiderate of others to get what I *think* I need. For example, a successful businessman who still feels so inadequate and has such strong unmet ego needs that every business encounter seems like a matter of survival for him is apt to be ruthless and unavailable to conciliation and compromise. He may think he has to "come out on top" in every deal regardless of the personal cost to him and others.

When I get clear about the difference between what I need to survive, and what I want in order to be fulfilled or happy, I can take a look at how my ways of getting what I want affect my life.

As I desire, so I live, say the *Upanishads.* I hear my desires in my longings, my wishes, and my dreams. My deep driving desire is a central organizing force in my life. I can examine each of my desires carefully to see if it has intrinsic meaning for me. Will fulfilling that desire help me feel better with myself and my life? As I get clear about what my most important desires really are, I can evaluate which among my lesser wants also lead me toward fulfilling my central desires, and which ones lead me away from doing so.

Many outside influences try to create this or that desire in us. I may begin to want something that has no real value for me because of all the messages I'm getting from other people or from advertising. I start thinking I'm missing something. (As an experiment, go over to your cupboard and see what you have on your shelves that you haven't used more than once since the day you bought it.)

When I feel "wants" that are really "shoulds," I may not realize that they're someone else's "should-wants" instead of my own wants. A woman friend of mine says, "I used to think I wanted to have a baby, but it was really a should. Maybe I'll want one someday, but not at this point in my life."

I may get so caught in my habitual likes and dislikes that I stop venturing, stop trying new things that might bring me deeper satisfaction. During my teen-age years and early adulthood, I did this with food, people, music, and other areas of living. I refused to touch things I didn't already know I liked. That limited me severely. Then I began to try things I thought I disliked, and new worlds of experience began to open up for me.

For many centuries the philosophies of India were concerned with "stopping desire." As a young man, Buddha knew all the pleasures of the princely life. But no matter how much he had, he always wanted more. At last he listened to the wise men of his time: "The root of your troubles," they said, "is not the lack of objects you desire—it is desiring itself."

After trying every avenue to root out his desires, at last Buddha concluded, according to philosopher and historian A. J. Bahm, "that not only did excessive desire end in defeat, but excessive desire for freedom from desire also ended in frustration" (37).

I don't get rid of a want by replacing it with another want—"I want to be rid of this ridiculous desire."

I can learn, through my experience, which of my desires have a real chance of being fulfilled and which do not. Then I can put my energy into working toward ends that I have a chance of attaining.

It's also possible for me to feel good with myself even when I don't attain my goals. I can find happiness in fulfilling those desires I do fulfill, and also in *working toward* those important objectives that I don't attain. Then at least I know that I've done what I could.

Greed and craving are distortions of desire. In greed and craving, I relinquish most of my consideration for anybody else in my existence. Having some—or *more*—of whatever it is becomes such an important end in itself that everywhere I look, what I "must have" is the only thing I see.

This is an insatiable, self-designed torture trap. Both greed and craving find an endless field of conquest, and leave me endlessly dissatisfied.

What I'm greedy for is probably a red-herring substitute for something else. If I feel good with myself, and feel the caring I need from other people, I'm less likely to be greedy.

I don't have to want to be different than I am.

The other day my car was stuck in the mud. At last we got it out; then, as I backed down the long road, I got stuck again. I was in a hurry, feeling hassled and uptight to begin with. The second time I got stuck was the last straw. I got out of my car, jumped up and down, beat the ground with my shovel, and screamed and shook my fists at the sky. My emotional age at that point was about two.

At the same time, I could appreciate the exquisite absurdity of what I was doing. I could see the comedy of that moment in my life for what it was. I could laugh with myself while I was tearing my hair out. I didn't have to put myself down and tell myself I "shouldn't" feel upset, as I would have several years ago. I could give myself room to want to get where I was going, and to want to not be stuck even though I was stuck, without torturing myself by thinking that I "shouldn't have those desires."

As Kwong Sensei points out, if I'm the fourth horse on the team, instead of trying to be first horse, I can be the best fourth horse I can. Then I *am* the first horse. I don't have to sit waiting to be something I'm not, instead of living now.

27 *Being and Sharing*

Giving and receiving

Julie wanted very much to have a child. When Wendy was born, Julie was generous with her milk, her holding and stroking, and her other ways of caring. These gifts helped Wendy grow and blossom, and she felt good about herself and her world from the very start. As she received Julie's nourishing care, she learned not only about receiving, but also about giving.

Deborah thought she wanted a child, but really didn't. She was always busy with other things, even after Ginny was born. Ginny often didn't get enough to eat, or enough love and caring. She sensed her mother's coldness, and within the first few months of life, developed a "basic mistrust": "Life is hostile; the struggle isn't worth it, because basically I won't get what I want." Many years later, Ginny is still haunted by a nagging fear that she "won't get enough." She's learning to be more generous to both herself and others, but she still has a hard time giving, because she's afraid this would take away from the little she has, and a hard time receiving, because she feels "undeserving."

Review your own history of getting. Not so much from whom you've received, but *what* you've received, and in what ways each thing was nourishing or poisonous to you. What are you getting that nourishes and poisons you now? Take a few minutes to do this before you read on.

Then do the same thing for your history of giving. How have the things you've given nourished and poisoned you and other people? How does what you're giving now nourish and poison you and others?

Also notice *how* you take in people, experiences, and things as well as food. Do you nibble or do you shovel it in? Are you impatient to get? Do you take everything that's offered, or do you sample, and accept only certain things?

Sometimes I'm greedy, demanding more than I need of some things, or more than others want to give, because I'm not getting enough of the things that are really important to me.

Other times I'm stingy, not giving what I could spare. Depending on what's being asked, and on my own energy and state of mind, giving up almost anything at all can sometimes seem painful.

By desperately trying to get, I may push people away, and make it even harder for me to get what I need. When I feel too needy, too grabby, people sometimes get scared. They think I only want to take their energy, and will give them nothing in return.

At times like those, I may have to forget my pain for a little while and *give* the very thing I need to get. Giving it seems to open me to getting it.

Once I was in agony over the crumbling of a love affair. I hungered for a lot of caring and comforting. A friend came in distraught about events in her life—in no position to listen to or comfort me. I pulled myself far enough out of my own pain to listen to her, and shared her sorrow and frustration. When we'd finished talking, we felt a deep closeness with each other, and I realized that, in some strange way, she had also comforted me.

When I'm demanding something from another person, I sometimes find that I'm stopping myself from finding it within me. By contrast, when I insist on finding everything within myself, I want to look at how I stop myself from getting outside support. What's in it for me to insist on doing it all by myself? As I consider all this, I can open myself to get what I need from many sources, both inside me and outside me.

The idea that any one person can fill all his or her spouse's or lover's or children's needs is a big source of trouble in many of our relationships. No one can be all things to everyone. Each of us needs a variety of different kinds of relationships with different people.

You may think you always have to give something in order to be liked. "If I don't give something, nobody will want to be with me." For many years, I felt uncomfortable in new social situations, and thought I had to be "the entertainer." Finally I learned that I don't have to carry that burden. By shedding my "entertainer" role, I can be with you in a way that's entertaining for both of us.

If I think I have to give in order to be liked, I'm apt to resent you, and take away with one hand while I give with the other. By paying attention to how I do this, I can learn how to give without taking away.

So, too, with receiving. If I feel uncomfortable about taking something you offer me, I'd better turn it down. I feel best when I take no more or less than I want to take, and give no more or less than I want to give. This Hasidic tale is a good commentary on the act of over-giving. One day an old, poor Jew lost his one prize possession—his snuff box. Sadly he walked into the forest near his village seeking consolation. There he saw a beautiful goat with long horns that swept the sky, clearly a holy goat. Gently the goat asked him why he was so sad. On being told the reason, the goat invited him to take a piece of his horn and make himself a new snuff box. He did so and it became a curiosity for all the villagers. Under duress he told them where he got the material for the snuff box. One by one they went to the goat, and asked for and were given some of the goat's horn. Soon the horns were gone and could no longer sweep the sky so that the stars could shine down more brightly.

When you take and take and I'm not feeling good about it, I start to feel ripped off. Then I need to take care of myself. At the least I need to tell you what I want in return. If you don't respond to that in a way I feel good with, I'm likely to set very clear limits on what I'm willing to give you, or even go away from where you are or ask you to spend less time where I am.

I may poison myself and our relationship when you don't give me what I haven't told you I want. Thus, on one hand, it's important for me to be able to say clearly what I want and expect in return for what I give. Sometimes all I want is your appreciation, but I'd better tell you when I want more. And if I'm not hearing your appreciation and that's important to me, I can tell you that.

On the other hand, my giving feels best to me when I can avoid getting locked into thinking, "What do I get out of it?" People get into trouble when "I'm afraid you're getting more than I am" becomes central in their relationship.

In our *sharing* of ourselves and what we have, my giving is receiving, and my receiving is giving. At such times, giving is its own reward. We can be with each other in this moment in a way we will never forget, even if we were never to meet again.

"The measure you give is the measure you will receive, with something more besides," said Jesus (Mark 4:34). Sharing with love and caring comes when I give freely of myself and what I have, and you do the same. We both end up having more than we need and don't have to worry about who's getting more. If you trust me and you want more, you'll tell me, and vice versa.

In any important relationship, there are things I appreciate. If our relationship has much depth, there are also things I resent. In my uneasiness and my fear, I may convince myself that I have no resentments against you. Telling you of my resentments is as much a gift as telling you of my appreciations. Sharing these two kinds of feelings opens up communication and leads toward clarity and trust.

✳ *Appreciations and resentments*

In a situation where you both feel comfortable, face the other person. Tell him or her all the things you appreciate, and then all the things you resent. (Beware the old devil of justifying and defending.) Then the other person does the same. *Don't discuss* what you just said to each other. After a day or two, when you've both had time to reflect, you may want to discuss your thoughts and feelings about what you said.

In a group where you've all known one another for some time, you may need several hours for the exercise. During that time, each of you seeks out each other person in the group and shares your appreciations and resentments. Or, everyone can sit in a circle while one person at a time goes around to each other person, stands in front of him or her, and makes statements of appreciation and resentment. When one person has gone all the way around the circle, the next person does the same thing, and so on until everyone has gone around. Either of these ways of sharing can be a fine way to end a class or group.

Service

It's easy to remember only our rights and forget our responsibilities. I am not here only to be fed. I must feed you back.

American Indian Chief Rolling Thunder says, "If you want to get high, go out and find an old lady who needs groceries and get her a bag of groceries and bring them to her. You can be plenty high by just helping your brother or sister in time of need."

Naturally, I want to be sure that I'm helping you get what you value, and not what I think you should value. I want you to be happy in your own way, not in the way I think you should be happy.

Sometimes a policeman or waitress or nurse gives me, in a caring way, something I need. Even though it's "in the line of duty," their caring makes what they give important to me. As they do their work, they find room to be people too.

By contrast, when we accept the role of being only a function, we become depersonalized for other people as well as for ourselves.

As a parent, I don't have to be only a cook, chauffeur, housekeeper, credit manager, and so on.

As an employee of a public service institution like a utility company, a commercial enterprise, or a government agency, I also don't have to act as though I am no more than the role I play. I'm not just an extension of the institution. I can give myself room to be the real person I am. In so doing, I find ways to feel good with my work and my relationship with the people I meet in my work. People may approach me as though I were the institution, but I don't have to accept that. In remaining personal, I best fulfill my job for the organization, the people I deal with, and myself.

Recently I contacted a representative of the local electric company to put in electric service for an experimental music school I was opening. The man's immediate response was that, because it was not a residence, he would have to charge me the higher, business rate.

I described the nonprofit character and financial limitations of the school, and the need to keep the costs low so that poor children with talent could attend. I said to him directly, "Please look at your regulations and try to find a way you can allow me to pay the lower, residential fee." He hesitated a moment, then said, "Okay, I'll call you back."

In about an hour he phoned back. The joy in the man's voice was in complete contrast to the deadness of his voice before. He sounded like a kid who suddenly got himself an extra lollipop. "I found a way! I got it! We can do it!" He was totally delighted with himself at being able to meet a real human need that he could hear and understand.

Livelihood

Work is an important way of giving.

Many people in this world are doing some weird and crazy things in their work. I used to work as a salesman, selling people things they didn't want and couldn't afford. Some people I know, and even respect in other ways, are actually arranging for others to go without adequate shelter, or enough food, so they themselves can have extra luxuries that they could get along quite well without.

I can still hear the venom in the voice of a big rancher in the San Joaquin Valley as he cursed the Chicano farmworkers who wanted an additional twenty cents an hour. He owned three cars, a hundred-thousand-dollar house, and a ranch of several thousand acres. The farmworkers lived in tin shacks and hitchhiked. And he cursed them because they wanted more. The irony is that Pepe and Rosalia and Alfredo and others I knew were warm, alive people who found moments of joy and beauty even amid their hard lives, while the rancher's eyes were cold and dead.

"Right livelihood" was one of the central principles of Buddha's philosophy. It means at the least not working at any job that brings harm to you or others, and if possible, finding work that can help you learn and grow.

Wrong livelihood is when I'm making my living, but feel dissatisfied with my life and the time I spend on my job. My dissatisfaction may be due to the effects of what I do either on me or on other people.

Some of us do things we don't like doing in our work because we have no options. Many others among us do things we don't like doing because we haven't considered that we do have options.

If I'm following what I feel at some level of my awareness to be a wrong livelihood, I can try to change the way I do my work, or I can change jobs. I can look for a way to earn my daily bread that benefits rather than harms other people—work I can feel good doing. In a job like that, I'm likely to get rid of my share of the nightmares, the headaches, and the chronic tension that cripple so many of the people who keep the effects of what they do out of their awareness.

What can you do starting right now? In whatever you do, wherever you are, whatever your job, you can *refuse to do anything that deceives or misleads or cheats or defrauds or in any other way injures other people.*

Many of us are required to exploit one another by the very structure of our jobs. Refusing to do that is the real revolution. When enough people refuse to act in the old ways that are oppressive or deceptive or otherwise toxic, those jobs will have to be radically changed. For example, advertising could become an important educational enterprise, rather than an industry committed to deception.

As each of us learns to identify our own welfare with the welfare of the people as a whole, the incentive for one person to exploit other people drops away.

In my own work, I've found that with some ways of working, I'm renewing myself all along. In others, I become exhausted and drained.

Some days I work ten hours almost nonstop and end the day feeling tired but good. Other days, I have but to go to one meaningless committee meeting, and I'm exhausted.

As I find ways to feel turned on and alive as I work, my work itself becomes a valuable part of my life, instead of something I struggle through so I can be alive in the other hours of the day. I'm not willing to let eight hours a day, year after year, go down the rathole.

Many jobs, such as assembly lines, are far from satisfying. We need to deal with this problem at an organizational level. In certain factories in China and Sweden, they've learned to work on a mass production basis without using assembly lines. There are work centers in which people carry out a number of tasks, creating an entire component that then moves on to another work center. The workers pace themselves, and actually see something taking shape, so that the whole process is more meaningful and satisfying.

We can all demand and work toward changes like that, changes that will make it possible to be more *alive* in our working lives. For example, labor contracts could put more focus on work conditions that help people feel good in their jobs. As we make these kinds of changes, it will be easier for all of us to work with love instead of with resignation and frustration. We will each become able to, as Gibran says, "weave the cloth with threads drawn from [our] heart, even as if [our] beloved were to wear that cloth" (P, 27).

POSSESSING

I feel good when I own a nice pair of pants and a shirt I like. And I look good because I feel good.

At some point, however, when I have fourteen pairs of pants, eighteen shirts, and thirteen pairs of shoes, I'm not sure that adding another item to my wardrobe contributes anything to how I look to anybody out there. I suddenly find myself trapped in the idea of owning as an end in itself.

That is, of course, my choice: I can ignore the valuable time I'll have to put into paying for my endlessly expanding collection of possessions; I can ignore the fact that I may have to build an addition to my home to house all the things I own; and I can ignore any qualms I might have about how much of the world's precious resources I'm using up by having all those things.

On the other hand, I can be concerned about all three of these side effects without feeling obliged to limit myself to the bare minimum I need for survival: I don't really like to wear the same pair of pants every day. Unless I have to. Then, if that's the way conditions are, I want to be able to say, "Yeah, that has to be enough."

In our complex social order, the possessions I depend on for transportation, shelter, and warmth are an essential part of my life. However, instead of owning our possessions, often they own us. The more my self-image depends on having a fancy car and home and clothes and jewelry, the more afraid I am of losing them. Through my fear, I restrict my freedom.

I also restrict my freedom through my need to look after my possessions. Economist John Kenneth Galbraith has pointed out that many American housewives have become full-time managers of their families' possessions. Their families own so many things that paying for them, keeping track of them, and maintaining them is a full-time job. They literally become possessed by their possessions (EPP).

When Jeb was divorced, his wife said, "You can keep the house and everything in it," and breathed a deep sigh of relief as she left her job as household manager behind. Within two months, Jeb was going crazy trying to take care of everything he owned. Half a year later, he'd sold it all and breathed his own sigh of relief as he piled what he had left into a U-Haul trailer and moved into an apartment.

There are few material things I really need: food, shelter, clothing, a source of warmth, and sometimes medicine. Beyond that point, I start to complicate my cave.

The complications in my cave that are worth most to me are *those that enlarge my world of experiences in ways that feel good to me or that contribute to my growth.*

I own other things because I think they will impress other people and make them love me more or make them think I'm a "big man," or because I feel special and important as the owner of something.

I own still other things because I've allowed myself to be a victim of consumer marketing and advertising. I walk into a store and my nerve endings start to tingle. A place starts to flash inside my head that says, "Buy, buy!" even though I don't need what I'm looking at.

The cost of any item to me is the amount of *life* I exchange for it, immediately or in the long run. As social psychologist Harold H. Kelley points out, a certain amount of my life goes into the work I do to make the money to pay for anything I buy, and I balance that against the returns it offers me.

The cost to us all of providing me with some item is the value of the raw materials used in making it, and the time and effort other human beings have put into creating it. In the United States, which is the most wasteful society in recorded history, we often forget these things. In poorer countries, people can't afford to forget. In China, for example, each person has a keen appreciation of the cost in labor and materials of each item he or she possesses, and most of the people are careful to take little more than they need. We are using up our own irreplaceable resources —and those of many other countries too—so rapidly that if we don't quickly learn that same lesson, it will soon slam us in the face.

SIMPLICITY.   The more keys I carry in my pocket, the more I'm likely to be complicating my life. My keys mean I have things I must protect, things I must be responsible to and for.

When I go on vacation, I leave my key ring behind. I have fewer things that I need to attend to, and more space in my life to be in touch with myself and the people around me. Taking time for that kind of simplicity, and finding ways to include more of it in my daily life, is important to me.

Certain aspects of our lives can make it harder to live simply. For example, credit cards can take us away from the fact that when we buy something, we're exchanging our time, our energy, our "life's blood" for what we buy. If we're not careful, the credit card can trap us into the illusion that things are free.

When I go into hock to buy things I want, I lose some of my ability to choose where and how I want to spend my work time. The fear that I might lose my job and be unable to pay my bills leaves me little space to say what I want to on the job, or do what I think I should do.

For many years I didn't buy anything on credit except my house. The less I'm in debt, the more freedom I have to change my job, or to take a risk on the job that might mean losing my income. And so, Mr. and Mrs. America, now you know why the powers-that-be want you to buy, buy, buy, and be in hock.

The more I complicate my life, the harder it is for me to pay attention to what's going on around me and to be with this moment now.

When I remember the value of the simple things in life, I more easily keep my perspective. Then I don't let my life get so complicated that every event, with its many implications, becomes burdensome and deadening to me.

MONEY.   "My generation was always trying to make enough money to do what we wanted to do, and we never quite got there," comments Thomas.

Remember that statement "He's always got dollar signs in his eyes"? If my eyes are filled with dollar signs, I'm likely to be blind to a lot of other things that could add richness and beauty to my life.

We can all remember Emerson's line, "Only that good profits which we can taste with all doors open, and which serves all men."

Lao-tzu adds, "He who knows when he has got enough is rich. . . . Truly, one may gain by losing; and one may lose by gaining" (49, 63).

As I give up my feeling that something outside me will give me what I need, I begin to find myself.

LAND.   In contrast to our system of land as private property that we can "possess" is the system of *usufruct* practiced by many peoples: all land is held in common, and is allotted to any given person for only as long as that person cares for it and maintains it.

Some of my own ancestors were Paiute and Shoshone Indians who went one step further: the land was the Earth Mother, and belonged to no one but the Great Spirit. To me this is a truer attitude toward the land than the one most of us hold today.

When I walk through the land I "own," according to White People's laws, I look at the record, carved into a canyon wall, of the millions of years it took to create that canyon. "My" land was there a million million years before I came, I who am a blink on the eyelash of time, and will be there even longer after I have gone. I put my hand on a redwood tree that has stood for hundreds of years, and I know that I am only passing through.

As we think of our Mother Earth, our material possessions, our money, and our ways of complicating rather than simplifying our lives, each of us can ask, as Jesus did, "What shall it profit a man, if he shall gain the whole world, and lose his own soul?" (Mark 8:36).

Possessing each other

"I've made demands of lovers that I'd never dare make of anyone I didn't feel I totally possessed," Monica told me.

Actually, I *can't* totally possess another person without losing something precious, for then that person becomes an object. I can try to possess his or her body or mind, but to the degree that I succeed, I lose the magic of the relationship that exists only when each of us is free and feels neither coerced nor possessed.

As the people we are, we often *want* to possess each other. It's important for the honesty of our relationship that we recognize those possessive feelings when we have them.

Since a lot of our man-woman anxiety around possessiveness centers on not feeling loved and cared for enough, I may be uptight about you going out with friends of either sex, for fear that the time you spend with them will cause you to love me less. That kind of restriction can be deadening to you and to our relationship, because it limits your access to people and experiences that could nourish you. So *at the same time that we accept our possessive feelings about each other now, and respect all of each other's feelings, we can also work to find ways to give each other the space we need.*

JEALOUSY AND ENVY.   Sometimes I feel envious or jealous. When I'm jealous, I'm afraid I'm losing something because you're involved with someone or something else. When I'm envious, I want something you've got that I don't have.

The central element in jealousy is *exclusion*—a feeling that I'm excluded and cut off from something I'd like to have. I feel left out, deprived, lonely.

When you're the one who's jealous, I can fix things up by *including you in whatever I'm doing*, or by helping to find something else that you'd enjoy doing. If I'm willing to do whatever it takes for you to not feel hurt or uptight, and you know that, you're much more likely to feel okay when I do what I want to do.

When I'm the one who's jealous, I can share my feelings with you openly, and also look for ways to feel better about what you want for yourself.

EGO

Ego often gets in the way of sharing. In our attempt to make sense out of the differing conceptions of ego we've found in Eastern and Western psychology, we've arrived at the following classification.

Infantile ego is my process of saying, "Am I getting enough? Do I have enough? Me! Me! Me!" In the beginning, infantile ego is necessary for survival. When I feel that needy now, as an adult, I still say, "Me, me, me!" Infantile ego corresponds to part of Berne's "natural child" ego-state.

Image-based ego is my process of asking, "Am I good enough?" It isn't present at first, but grows out of other people's evaluations. One side of image-based ego is *self-congratulation:* telling myself, and wanting others to tell me, how great I am. (This is different from a realistic *appreciation* of what I do.) The other side is *self-depreciation:* telling myself how crappy and worthless I am, and imagining that others see me that way too. Self-congratulation and self-depreciation both grow out of my need for validation from others. I need this validation to the degree that, at some previous point, my worth as a person has been questioned. Image-based ego includes parts of Berne's "adapted child" and "parent" ego-states.

We get into trouble when infantile ego and image-based ego get intertwined. Together they make up what most Asian psychologists and spiritual teachers have called "ego." This kind of ego usually involves acting as though I'm *more important than* everybody and everything around me. At some level, I feel *less* important, but in my actions, I act as though I'm the only one who counts. I look up at a tree and imagine myself to be bigger than the tree, and in consequence, assume I can do anything to it I want, including cutting it down.

In reality, I am I, and the tree is the tree. Neither of us is more important.

Adult ego is what Freud called "ego," and it also corresponds to Berne's "adult" ego-state. My adult ego is my capacity to take responsibility for directing my life. It is my realistic and confident sense that I can do what I need to do to take care of myself and that I am a worthwhile human being.

To the degree that my adult ego is weak and underdeveloped, I rely on infantile ego and image-based ego. By contrast, to the degree that I have a strong sense of myself, and feel good about who I am, I feel neither inferior nor superior. I don't need constantly to convince myself of how good I am. I have more attention available to discover the world around me and the other people in it. Since I feel more confident that I can take care of myself and get what I need, I can give more easily.

Feeling separate and isolated is an important part of infantile and image-based ego. I see how you and I are different and how you may want to hurt me, but I have a hard time seeing how we are the same and how you care.

Even if I am following a religious path, I may still be running my same old trip, in a disguised form: "*I* must be the one who is saved; *I* must get off the wheel; *I* must achieve immortality; *I* must get to heaven." The paradox is that I can't really alleviate my own suffering until I become equally concerned with alleviating yours.

In the Talmud, a "mitzvah" is an act of goodness that assures me my place in heaven. But there's a catch: If I do the mitzvah out of concern for you, I score; if I do the mitzvah thinking, "More gold stars to get me into heaven," it doesn't count. Good works for the sake of those they'll benefit makes it; good works for the sake of my own salvation misses the mark.

In politics, much ego takes the form, *my* kind of government, *my* country, *my* political system or party is good, and other ones are bad. And if you don't agree, you are my enemy, and I'll impose my way on you in any way I can.

By setting these ego boundaries, we make it extremely difficult for us to agree even in areas where it's to our mutual benefit to do so.

Most political entities today still function from a place of infantile ego.

I can move toward becoming more aware of my ways of acting in the service of my infantile and image-based ego.

When I agreed a few years ago to be director of a new program at my college, one of the reasons I took the job was to boost my feeling of importance. I'd never been director of anything before. And there it was, my image-based ego, sitting smack in the middle of the road grinning at me. Be able to see it? I couldn't *miss* it!

When I see that I have a choice of doing or not doing something that serves and strengthens my image-based ego, I can choose not to do it. For instance, when I find myself trying hard to think of something clever to say, a good thing to do is to say nothing. A person who follows Lao-tzu's philosophy of the Tao is always saying, "Not so fast," to one who is becoming too clever, too witty, too skillful. In Lao-tzu's words,

> Hesitant like one wading a stream in winter; . . .
> Simple like an uncarved block;
> Hollow like a cave;
> Confused like a muddy pool;
> And yet who else could slowly but steadily move from
>   the inert to the living?
> He who keeps the Tao does not want to be full,
> But precisely because he is never full,
> He can always remain like a hidden sprout,
> And does not rush to early ripening.(31)

And again:

> The high must be built upon the foundation of the
>   low, . . .
> Therefore, the Sage reigns over the people by
>   humbling himself in speech;
> And leads the people by putting himself behind.(59, 97)

WINNING AND LOSING

In some situations, everyone comes out a winner. No one has to lose. These are "everyone can win" games. There are also "win-lose" games, where one person loses as much as the other person wins.

With many games, we can choose how we play them. Most of us play win-lose much of the time when we could be playing everyone-can-win. I can watch "my team" and want them to win, but feel okay if they lose in a well-played ball game, and appreciate the skill of the players on both sides. Under these circumstances, to lose does not mean defeat. I can go home feeling good about having seen the game. In every area of our lives, when we can enjoy the interaction and find the fun in whatever we do, then everyone can win.

To the degree that I live my life win-lose, I can only win by the other person losing. So even when I win, I have only losers to relate to. Win-lose is a one-up, one-down relationship. If I'm one down, I'm likely to resent the person who's one up. "You can *have* your damn victory. Go ahead. *Be* the winner. *All by yourself.*"

When we play win-lose, the deck is stacked against both of us. Whatever you do, I can find a way to have you wrong, so I can feel superior, or cover up my painful feelings if you win. When you lose, you're likely to resent me, so that in a real sense, if you're important to me, that's a loss for me too. At the level where it counts—the level of loving, caring, and being good to each other—no one wins in a win-lose game.

When we succeed in making those around us lose so we can feel good by comparison, the only payoff is to the winner's ego. Nobody grows by winning in a win-lose game. Nobody moves toward being a fuller, richer person. Nobody gets any lessons in loving or caring.

For most of us, the habits of living win-lose are old and well-worn. Finding ways for everyone to win takes thought and work. Sometimes it means finding a way for the other person to get what he or she wants. Sometimes it means helping that person appreciate what he or she has.

Comparison and competition

When comparison takes place in a competitive situation, my competitors can be useful models for me to learn from. This is true, however, *only when I enjoy and welcome the competition,* and not when it's an anxious and fearful ordeal for me, as much of the competition in our culture is for many of the participants. Many of us often feel forced to compete against our will when, on our own, we would consistently choose other ways of interacting.

Recent research has shown that competition does not "build character" as once supposed. I've known that ever since I was a kid. All the way through school I used to dread P.E. I got a slow start in sports and never caught up. The P.E. teachers knew nothing of my world. They had always done well in sports.

They called it physical "education," but everyone cared a lot about winning and very little about learning. "Choosing up sides" was especially wretched. I was always one of the last ones chosen.

"Don't choose him, he's no good." "Oh, come on, you're the only guy left." "He's on *our* side? We get all the lousy breaks." It was like Charlie Brown and Lucy. You know how Lucy is always cutting Charlie Brown down when he drops the ball or strikes out or gives up the winning run? I was Charlie Brown, except that I always played right field.

Year in, year out, that's how it went. At first it was only ball games. I was afraid the ball would hit me in the face, and was so anxious that I usually fumbled it.

"Hey, don't throw it to Butterfingers—he'll just drop it." "Ha ha ha—Butterfingers dropped it again. Boy, is he awful!"

Pretty soon I got an image of myself as "no good in sports," and started to do lousy in almost all of them. Every P.E. period was like marching off to jail.

At least I almost always won the spelling bees. If I couldn't compete at one thing, I could at another.

Every now and then, I thought about the kids who were not so good at either sports or schoolwork. Kind of tough to come out last in everything.

For some people in some circumstances, competition *can* be helpful in learning to do things well. At least equally often, however, and for many people almost always, it does just the opposite. Competing takes attention and energy. Learning how to do a thing takes attention and energy. It's hard to do both these things well at once, especially when a lot of energy is also going into feeling anxious about the competition.

It makes more sense to me for each person to develop in his or her own way than for us all to try to be "best" in the same few ways. When we compete, each of us tries to be "best" in the same way. If our skills improve, they improve at doing the same things everyone else does. Pretty soon we're like peas in a pod—almost no uniqueness left.

"Best" is a confusing word. Often it's a sloppy way of saying "most extreme." Fastest, biggest, most skillful—concrete words like these tell what we mean.

"Most" doesn't mean "best." The most intelligent person or the fastest runner or whatever is no "better" than you or me—just the most intelligent or fastest. When we say "best," it means *we value* extremeness in a given thing. "Best" is a qualitative value judgment, while "most" is a quantitative assessment.

People who depend on their feeling that they're "best" because they're biggest or most in something are ALWAYS using that feeling to cover ways they feel inferior.

With many things there isn't even any "most." But we're so used to thinking that way that we make ourselves believe there is, and call it "best" to boot.

Beauty contests, for example. Twenty beautiful women come walking out. Every one is a different, unique, lovely human being. Then a panel of "judges" decides that this one or that one is "most beautiful of all." Incredible but true.

Is an oak tree more pleasing than a maple? Blond hair "better" than brown?

Even when there is a most, only one person can be most in any given thing. So if I think in comparisons a lot, I'll probably be pretty discontented. In any way I compare myself with others, I'll find someone "better" as well as someone "worse."

Even the things that do have mosts often have another side to them, like the well-liked person who doesn't have enough time to himself or herself. As we gain one thing, we often lose a bit of something else.

There are not too many things a person can do better than anyone else—except be himself or herself.

The habit of competing isn't easy to root out. It crops up in subtle and devious ways.

For instance, someone tells me about a thing he or she did. Instead of sharing that person's excitement about that event, I might jump in with something I did. Some place inside me wants the limelight, wants to feel superior. Naturally that blows it. The other person feels ignored. I seem selfish.

Watch to see if you sometimes do the same.

If two firms are competing to put in the lowest bid on a contract, I can certainly feel good with that.

I object strongly, however, when the big supermarket chain uses the word "competition" to justify driving the Mom and Pop grocery store out of business, just as I'd object to the Heavyweight Champion stepping into the ring with a Golden Gloves bantamweight. Those events are not competition.

In a contest between unequals, like the supermarket chain against Mom and Pop, or the neighborhood bully against the shy child who wants only to be left alone, the more powerful party usually sets the rules, as actions by the large oil companies in driving a number of small independent chains out of business show. That's not competition—it's the law of the jungle.

As we move from a competitive, win-lose attitude toward life into a cooperative, everyone-can-win attitude, we will all find it easier to be with one another in caring ways. Through sharing and caring, we can all feel better with our lives.

28 *Love and Caring*

Love

> Let him kiss me with the kisses of his mouth: for thy love is better than wine. . . .
> A bundle of myrrh is my well-beloved unto me; he shall lie all night betwixt my breasts.

Thus begins the *Song of Solomon*, one of the most beautiful books in the Old Testament.

Amid these lives we lead, we all know those special moments when somehow, magically, we touch each other deeply. Those times of loving become part of who we are, and through them we can grow.

Love in its many forms is a way of bringing joy into our lives, and we all treasure the moments of love that we know and have known. Loving is a way of giving, both to you and to myself. Through loving, I come closer to myself, I share myself with you, and open the way for you to share yourself with me.

My reward in loving is the way I feel when I love. Sometimes you love me in return, and in your love, give me what you can. But that's not necessary for me to have the good feelings that come from being with my world in a loving way.

When I love, I'm more likely to find love around me. For when I feel loving toward you, you're more likely to touch your own ability to love, and meet me from that place. And when you can feel that I really care for you, that I'm not trying to exploit you, you're more likely to be willing to work out our difficulties, instead of making little conflicts into big ones.

Travellers sometimes came to the tent of Abraham, who talked to God.

338

Whatever the reason that the stranger was there, Abraham stopped talking to God to give the person food and water. It was more important that he took time for this act of loving-kindness than that he talk to God.

Four ways of loving

Drawing on the ideas of Fromm and of Miller and Siegel and our own observations and experiences, we distinguish four kinds of love: object-centered love, projective love, conscious love, and agape (ah-gah-*pay*). Each of these often partakes in some way of the others. Like any concept, the categories lie within arbitrary lines we've drawn.

1. *Object-centered love.* Love that is based on the concrete satisfactions that come with loving and being loved is object-centered.

We all know object-centered love from the moment of our birth. This is the love an infant has for his or her mother and her breast. The infant *wants* her, and misses her when she's gone.

Think of a child's love for a teddy bear. The child has a real emotional involvement, wants to be close to the teddy bear as much as possible, and likes the physical joy of its touch and smell.

Most of our object-centered love relationships involve not just teddy bears, but other people. If our physical satisfactions remain the only source of our feelings for each other, we're apt to be less than satisfied in our love relationship. But hopefully, as we grow, object-centered love can begin to involve other ways of loving.

The trouble with object-centered love is that I can get so caught up in my craving for emotional or physical satisfaction that I don't care for the other person as another conscious being with his or her own needs and feelings.

The classic "male chauvinist pig" or "macho" attitude is an example of object-centered love. The priority in our relationship is sexual, and I want you to do what I want you to do. If we're making love, I'm likely to forget to stay in touch with where you are, and there's no real relationship, no interchange of consciousness, and little interplay of loving and caressing.

If I want a caring relationship, I don't have to stay in that "me first" place with you. I may want the fullness of our joy and laughter, and also of the quiet, gentle touching that we have for each other. I have to be aware that you have needs and directions of your own, and make space for what you want in our relationship as well as what I want.

2. *Projective love.* This kind of love plays a large part in what we call "romantic love." In the Middle East, Europe, and the Americas, romantic

love is a strong tradition. In certain other parts of the world, it's less common.

I've "fallen in love" so many times! When I "fall in love," I feel the longing and wanting-to-be-with of object-centered love, and I also see you in a highly idealized way. To some degree, I transfer my image of what I want in another person onto you, and then love the image, thinking that I'm loving you. Probably, without realizing it, I see in you some of the things I loved in my parent or other adult who cared for me when I was small.

I may behave toward you in ways I behaved toward others whose qualities I see in you, instead of behaving toward you in ways that fit the unique person you are. To the degree that I do this, you and I miss making contact in ways that could be important to us.

In projective love, I often see qualities in you that are missing in me. You may really possess these qualities, or I may build some way you are into an elaborate fantasy that fits what I want to see.

Todd had a lot of hostility toward his mother that he was never willing to express directly to her. The woman he married was strong and assertive. Todd expected that she would give his mother hell for him and stop her from pushing him around.

When, out of her strong and knowing place, Todd's wife refused to take care of Todd's problems with his mother, the relationship came close to falling apart. Ultimately Todd began to realize that he had to find that kind of power in himself.

When I project onto you, wanting you to have characteristics that I need for me, I'm apt to be most disappointed in you when I find out that you don't have some characteristic I thought I saw in you, or that you do have it but don't use it the way I wanted you to. This can be confusing to you and frustrating to me.

When I'm aware of my projected needs, I no longer need to ask you to be a certain way to fill my empty places.

Through our sharing and being with each other, I can learn from you about the qualities that are well developed in you but less developed in myself, and you can learn from me in a similar way.

Projective love is a way I keep myself dependent. It lets me avoid dealing with my fears about being inadequate in certain ways. It also stops me from moving ahead in my growth.

Rosie uses love relationships with people as an escape from herself, the way some people use drugs or alcohol. She becomes completely merged in the other person's identity and forgets who she is.

Throughout her childhood, Rosie had been told she was no good as a person, and had finally begun to believe it. Whenever she lost herself in romantic love, she forgot her feelings of worthlessness for a few weeks or months. The man she loved was good in every way she was no good, but she was *still no good, still unworthy.*

In a healthy love relationship with you, I keep my sense of myself. I give you myself as I am, and am with you as you are. In projective love, I may feel I can't make it without you. That feeling is a tipoff that I'm giving away my strength, projecting what I need to do for myself onto you and asking you to fulfill those needs for me. In such a relationship, psychologist John Alan Lee points out, I'm likely to be often yearning and unhappy, anxious about the slightest lack of enthusiasm from my lover, and easily crushed by disappointment. All-consuming thoughts of my beloved, furious jealousy, and tragic endings are the stuff of this kind of loving.

Eventually a relationship based solely on projective love begins to come apart. The burdens on us become too heavy, as I carry your image of me on my shoulders, and you carry my image of you on yours. The images start to crumble as we see each other as we are. This is where many marriages get into trouble. We begin to resent each other for being different from "what was promised," usually more by our projections than by our persons. I want desperately to have you accept me as I am, but you're too disappointed by your unfulfilled illusions, and dor't even know them as such.

At this point, any of several things can happen.

One or both of us might be ready to end our relationship. Out of guilt (which may be induced by the other person's manipulations) or for whatever other reason, we feel afraid to say so out front. Instead, we poison each other more and more, making things so bad that eventually there's no way we'd be willing to stay together any longer. A good poison package involves destructive projections that portray the other as no good in many ways.

Alternately, we might recognize what's happening, share our feelings about that as fully as possible, and decide that we've come to a parting place. Under these circumstances, we can separate but still appreciate each other and share a lot of love and caring.

Another alternative is that we may both find that we're willing to do what we have to do to work things out. As we explore and change, we find nourishing ways of relating to each other out of who we really are, and no longer need our distorted images of each other. As this happens, projective love becomes transformed into "conscious love."

3. *Conscious love.* When I love consciously, I remember who I am, and

I love you as you are. I see and hear myself clearly and I see and hear you clearly. Conscious love is loving you not only for how special you can be, but also for how plain. There comes an ease between us then, as we realize that neither of us has to pretend to be different than we are.

Awareness, caring, and trust are important elements of conscious love. I want to feel your caring in concrete ways that nourish me, and to show my caring in concrete ways that nourish you.

Habit can kill conscious love. Through habit I learn to react to you without being aware of you. At those times when I only go through the motions of loving, love is absent.

The more I can love myself, the more I can love you. The more I take care of my own hang-ups and conflicts, the more energy I have available for loving others.

Walter Rinder, in *Love Is an Attitude*, provides a sensitive description of conscious love:

> If you build an archway for your heart, with neither lock nor door, life will pass freely in harmony with your senses.
>
> Touch . . . your friends, your lover; a stranger, then they are a stranger no more. Hold them, feel the beauty of their skin, their face, their hair. . . .
>
> Listen . . . to their words, their breathing, their heartbeat, their footsteps. . . .
>
> See . . . the expressions on their faces of their different moods. . . . See their hands create their being. . . .
>
> When you have experienced these things you will know your heart . . . follow it.

In our loving, we need closeness and we need space. If I impose more closeness on you than you want or need, you're apt to feel crowded, resentful, dependent. If you pull me too close too long, I likewise have mixed feelings: How good it is that you want me so much; how stifling it is to be held so tightly.

When I experience your holding me as clutching me, I may be afraid to ask for the space I need, for fear that you'll feel rejected. Yet, when you ask me to be your whole world, you're asking me to be more than I can be.

When I ask you to be my whole world, at some point my dependence on you turns into fear of losing you. That's the point where I stop holding you and start clutching you. Then I may insist on being your whole world, and stifle you.

In his chapter on marriage in *The Prophet*, Gibran writes,

. . . Let there be spaces in your togetherness,

And let the winds of the heavens dance between you.
Love one another, but make not a bond of love. . . .
Sing and dance together and be joyous, but let each one of you
be alone,
Even as the strings of a lute are alone though they quiver with
the same music.(15–16)

STYLES OF LOVING.   In our love relationships, misunderstandings often
occur when we forget that others' *styles* of loving may be different than
our own.

One person may easily *act* in loving ways toward others, but have a
hard time putting his or her feelings into words. Another person may
have no trouble saying, "I feel very loving toward you right now," but
feel ill at ease reaching out to hold or hug.

We can ask each other for the kinds of expression of love we want.
We can initiate actions that are hard for the other to initiate, like holding
out our arms to someone who has a hard time reaching out to us. Yet,
we can also be sensitive to others' ways of showing love, and appreciate
the expressions of caring that come easily to them.

J. A. Lee describes some of the different styles of loving that are common
in man-woman relationships. Some people plunge immediately and intensely into love relationships, while others share time and space together
until love "just comes naturally," preferring a reasonable, predictable
relationship that lacks the complications of intense passion.

Some are given to candlelight and roses and laying the world at the
feet of the beloved, making every new relationship a Great Romance,
while others more often love in the style of "a peaceful and enchanting
affection . . . without fever, tumult, or folly."

Some people typically have only one lover at a time, while others tend
to be involved in several relationships at once, and avoid becoming too
tied to any of them. "When you're not with the one you love, love the
one you're with" is their theme song.

Some people typically make love soon after meeting, while others
view sex as a deeply intimate self-revelation, and often postpone it until
they know each other well in other ways.

And while some people consciously balance the payoffs from various
relationships, and pay careful attention to signs of compatibility or incom-
patibility, others would never conceive of such a calculating approach,
and operate much more intuitively (43–51).

You can imagine the trouble that two lovers with very different styles
might have in trying to work out a relationship that suits them both.
We can use our knowledge of different styles of loving to find people
whose styles fit with our own, and to get along better when our styles

differ. And of course, as we grow and change, our styles of loving too can and often do change.

4. *Agape.* There's a stage in loving beyond conscious love. It has different names in different parts of the world. In the West, it's called agape, or *loving-kindness.*

Probably you know it. Probably you have had flashes of it that lasted for an instant, an hour, a day, or even longer.

When I am in this "mystical" state of consciousness, I experience my life on this earth as very good and very beautiful. I express a deep caring in my acts and attitudes.

I would like to know that egoless place, *where I am loving rather than lover,* more often. Coming to know who I am, and appreciating the places where I and others are beautiful, helps me find that place. Meditative practices, such as those described in Chapter 24, can create states of consciousness from which I'm more apt to move into that very special kind of consciousness.

On the other hand, if that state becomes a "goal to achieve," I'm keeping my ego involved, and I'm less likely to find it.

VIOLENCE

I have within me both the Great Mother who is love and the Great Warrior who is fire and lightning; and the Great Mother who is fire and lightning and the Great Warrior who is love. Without denying that these are parts of me, I can choose to what extent, and in what ways, I want to let each of them be part of my life.

I have within me the capacity to murder and destroy. Once when my own survival was at stake, and I was both afraid and enraged, I murdered a man. (The War Department later tried to give me a medal for it.) Anyone who says, "I could never do a thing like that," deceives himself or herself.

On the other hand, I also have the capacity to act with great love and gentleness. I can care for a wounded animal, soothe you in your sorrow, love you in your anger, and rock a child to sleep.

Violence has long been part of our human tradition. An innate tendency toward acting violently exists in every one of us. When I hit my head on a door, and in my pain and anger, belt the door in return, that's natural.

Where we get into trouble is through the many ways our culture approves of the *vicious* expression of violence. By vicious I mean destructive, non-problem-solving reactions that ultimately lead to further violence in a self-perpetuating way. We have too often tried to solve complex, frustrating problems with the oversimplified response of axe or A-bomb.

I enjoy a well-staged boxing or wrestling match. I enjoy a little friendly wrestling or mock fighting with a friend or lover, with such handicaps as seem appropriate. We get our anger and tension out, and no one gets hurt.

The essence of much of our violence, as I understand it, is this: *We project the cause of our own unhappiness and dissatisfaction outward onto others, and try to attack it and eradicate it there.* Our violence is a symptom of a deeper psychological disturbance within us. It goes back to fear and pain and punishment. In my psycho-logic, I equate my "enemies" with those who punished and injured me when I was a child, with those who had little love for me, and with those (whoever they are) who create conditions that make it easy for my life to be empty and loveless and unsatisfying now. Out of my deep-lying rage that is so suppressed that I never let myself express it outwardly, I want to smash the bastards into total and complete oblivion.

Genuine concern for the welfare of the people in my life-space never takes the form of violence toward them. Rather, I become violent when I feel frustrated and impotent, and know that I have power I can use (or abuse). Then, while using violence to gain my own ends, I convince myself that it's "good for them," as when a parent becomes oppressive toward a child, a teacher toward a student, or a boss toward a worker.

It's hard for me to acknowledge my acts of violence and oppression for what they are—statements of my own feeling of incompetence. Isaac Asimov's character Hardin in *Foundation* says, "The temptation was great to muster what force we could and put up a fight. It's the easiest way out, and the most satisfactory to self-respect, but nearly invariably, the stupidest. . . . Violence is the last refuge of the incompetent" (84–85).

The reason violence is usually the stupidest way of handling a problem is that, as Ouspensky has pointed out, *violence ultimately leads, in most cases, to results just the opposite of those it was intended to produce* (ISM, 266). This is due in large part to the anger, resentment, and hatred it usually incites, and the reactions that grow out of those feelings.

Besides the distinctions made by the law itself, economic, ethnic, and racial factors also typically influence how a matter is treated by law-enforcement authorities and by the courts. An act of self-defense by a Black or Chicano or poor person is viewed with more suspicion than such an act by a middle-class white person.

When carried out by the State, violence is usually expected and accepted by the law, which is itself often another instrument of the State rather than a real servant of the people. When the State is being violent toward me, I lose many of my rights. Rarely is an instance of unnecessary violence by an agent of the State dealt with effectively.

When I was living in the ghetto, I encountered many policemen who were on various occasions unjustifiably and unnecessarily violent with people who were my close friends. One of the big problems in our culture is that this kind of abuse of legitimate authority provides models for imitation that ultimately many of us follow.

In some areas, police officers face death, injury, and abuse from the public every day. Being a policeman is a damned hard job. But there are ways of making it easier. In the town where I work, a few years ago members of one of the two classes of people in the town were often harassed and intimidated by the police. After an election in which the old city council was thrown out, many of the police resigned, a new chief was brought in, and the town wound up with a whole new police force. Now when I drive down the street I see the police car drive by and I think, "Hey, this guy is there to protect me. He's taking care of me and all of the people in the town," and I no longer feel the resentment and anger that I felt every time I saw a police car drive by in the old days.

I had that same kind of good feeling in San Francisco recently as I watched a dozen or so Black children clustered around a friendly Black policeman who was obviously their hero and idol.

Our society encourages violence in many ways. It starts when children are given their first toys. Christmas morning, looking out my window, I see a street full of kids shooting each other and launching model nuclear missiles against imaginary cities. That's a hell of a way to celebrate the birthday of the Prince of Peace.

The case against television for its commitment to violence has been documented so thoroughly, in so many places, that it would be redundant here.

But there are so many other subtle places where that same kind of encouragement of violence occurs. Go to the penny arcade in any amusement center. Ingenious ways are provided to stimulate the imagination toward violence. You can drop a nuclear bomb or wipe out a fleet of ships. The more you kill and destroy, the higher your score.

So many of our "cheers," from junior high to college, have to do with smashing, killing, hitting, and the like. They're blunt statements of violence. Steve's son Walter was a husky six-footer. When he entered high school, the football coaches drooled with joy and expectation. Walter refused to go out for the team because of its violence, saying, "I don't like to bang into other people's bodies, and I don't like other people crashing into me." As a result, he was criticized, hounded, and made fun of to a point where his parents finally took him out of school. He was able to return to school only by joining and doing well on the swimming team.

The speeches of many of our Presidents and lesser politicians, when dealing with matters that have no inherent connection with anything violent at all, are repeatedly cast in violent terms. "The *weapons* we will use in the coming *battles* to *combat* inflation," "The *war* we will wage to *destroy the forces* that . . . ," and so on. We insert the imprint of violence into our consciousness at many levels. We could speak instead of a problem-solving approach. We could speak of "the tools we will use to explore and solve these problems," or of "the hard work to find solutions."

This kind of thing happens even in nonverbal ways. I recall watching one recent President make a speech about achieving peace. As he talked about peace, he shook his clenched fists and pounded them together. Events of the months that followed showed that his violent gestures spoke more truly than his words.

We are a people of contradictions. We laud peace, yet the God we most revere is presented to us in the most violent form, nailed to a piece of wood. Actually, the cross did not come into use as a symbol of Christianity until the Dark Ages. Before that, the symbol was a fish. That in our religious yearning for peace, a man nailed to a cross is the image we keep before us, is a statement of ultimate violence. Lenny Bruce commented that we're lucky Jesus was executed two thousand years ago instead of recently, or all the Christians would be wearing necklaces with miniature electric chairs hanging from them.

War is a socially sanctioned and approved form of violence. The military services of many nations, including ours, drill young men over and over until they perform the act of killing automatically and choicelessly when a certain signal comes. When the war is over, nothing is done to extinguish this conditioned readiness to kill, so that, under stress, the ex-soldier may turn it even toward his own countrymen. He also often lives with a lifetime of prejudice toward the people he learned were "the enemy."

America's habit of making war is no accident. The message in what our children read and see as they grow up is clear: caring and kindness are embarrassing and unmanly. Honesty is the exception. Making love is dirty and taboo. Killing and cruelty, deceit and hypocrisy are the Regular Thing, from the Morning Paper to the Late Late Show.

Even so, fewer and fewer people in our culture are willing to accept war as a "solution" to anything. Instead, young men are saying, "This man could laugh and cry with me. How can I lay an 'ambush' in which I lie in wait until he walks past me along the path, and then shoot him in the back? This woman could lie gently in my arms and stroke my hair with loving tenderness. How can I burn her house and kill her animals and drive her into the barbed-wire compound of a 'fortified hamlet,' or into the city where she has no way to live but to sell her body to my fellow soldiers? I will not do these things."

In its oppressive frustration, our government has jailed and exiled these young men. Here again we encourage violence and punish nonviolence.

But though the path of someone who refuses to have anything to do with war is not an easy one, it is a path of courage. If enough of us choose it, we will come to the end of war, for the generals aren't going to pick up M-16s, and the executives aren't going to work on the assembly line to make bombs and missiles.

I saw a sign on a restroom wall: "Fighting for peace is like fucking for chastity."

Recognizing our potentiality for violence, the great religious leaders have consistently pointed to nonviolence as a source of our salvation.

Rather than feeling guilty about our potential for violence, if we can recognize that potential and the conditions under which we are apt to be violent, we may begin to seek solutions that grow out of our love, caring, gentleness, and compassion, instead of those that grow out of our fear, frustration, hardheartedness, and oppression.

There have been cultures in the world's history where violence was practically unknown, cultures that did not make war (a few of these still exist). We can develop our potentiality for living in those same nonviolent ways in our industrial cultures of today.

We can learn to live at peace with ourselves, with one another, and with our earth. I hope one day we will all join in the vow of Chief Joseph of the Nez Perce, one of America's great generals, who after watching the futility of many years of war, proclaimed: "I will fight no more forever."

DEATH

The more squarely I face the inevitability of my death, the more fully I can be alive now.

"A human life is like that moment when a raindrop skates and bounces on the surface of the ocean before merging with the sea," says biologist Don Isaac. My life is brief, and when I die, the great stream of life itself goes on, reborn in new bodies and new forms, evolving onward from its ancient origin. "Our human life but dies down to its root," says Thoreau, "and still puts forth its green blade to eternity."

When I met Calvin, he was putting so much energy into not accepting his mother's recent death and not wanting to accept the inevitability of his own that he began to lie awake nights, afraid that Death would sneak up on him while he slept. When he did sleep, he tortured himself with fearful nightmares.

In a counseling session, he got into a dialogue with his own death. He found his death saying, "I do not regret your mother dying or that you will die. I have compassion for the way you feel, but I am absolute, and I do what I do. So know me in your life, that you may live more fully."

As Calvin accepted his own death as inescapable, his symptoms disappeared.

In our culture, we shy away from looking death in the eye. Funerals and everything associated with them are often mechanical and antiseptic. Death itself is an event that seldom comes up in our speech. It is the unspeakable. And since many of us shy away from facing the prospect of our death, we avoid considering what our death means in terms of the way we live our lives. It seldom enters our humor.

Jeannie's father died slowly, and they spent several weeks together before he died. As he reviewed his life, he talked most about the opportunities he had missed—the things he would have done but didn't. "I said no to life too many times, Jeannie," he said. "I left too much of it unlived. I hope you don't do the same."

That really hit Jeannie. Within the next several months, she began to make some major changes in her life. She found a new job working with people she liked, got involved in doing things for her community that meant something to her, and took a vacation she'd been talking about for years. (She made off with the company funds, got knocked up in Acapulco, and was last seen running through the Yucatan with a banana in her ear.)

Elisabeth Kuebler-Ross, a Chicago psychiatrist, interviewed several hundred people who were revived after they'd been declared medically dead. "We came to fantastic findings, terribly intriguing," she says. These people describe how they "float out of their body . . . they have a feeling of peace and wholeness, a tremendous feeling of 'stop all this attempt [to revive me], I'm all right'. . . . Not one of them has ever been afraid to die again" (UPI, 5/8/75).

We can all take some comfort from this fascinating study.

Some of us let our individual identity die by identifying ourselves completely with some mass organism—i.e., "the company," "the corporation," or "the agency." The pseudo-immortality we can gain through that identification can lead to neglecting the sources of nourishment we need to keep ourselves alive as individuals.

Likewise, old age is often seen as a prelude to dying, rather than as a place to do another kind of living.

"Take kindly the counsel of the years, gracefully surrendering the things of youth," says the *Desiderata*. As we surrender the things of youth, we can gradually enter into the things of maturity and age.

In proportion as we let each day go by without tasting it, we will curse our lives and fear our death. In proportion as we live fully in the now of each day and each time in our lives, we can love and laugh and play in all the seasons of our years.

LIVING WITH NATURE

All living beings live by the grace of other living beings. If we are to survive, we must learn to respect and honor every form of life.

A Navajo who was enrolled in the university decided to drop out and go back to living with his people.

"Why?" asked my biologist friend Don Isaac. "You're doing so well here!"

The Navajo drew two circles. In each one, he drew a collection of symbols around the inside of the rim: corn, clouds, rain, animal figures, etc. In the left-hand circle, he put a human figure in the middle. In the right-hand circle, he placed the human figure among the other figures around the inside of the rim, the same size as all the other figures.

He pointed to the circle on the left and said: "This is the white man's world." He pointed to the circle on the right and said, "This is the Indian's world. I cannot live in the white man's world any longer."

We need to regain our sense of proportion, our awareness that we are just one strand of the interwoven fabric of life on our earth. This is the great lesson that the American Indian peoples offer us.

I like to feel the earth in my hands each day. I like to let it crumble through my fingers, and remember that I am made from that same stuff, that I share this earth with all my fellow beings that in this way are the same as I. Then I remember who I am.

Even in the midst of the concrete and asphalt of a city, I can find a park here and there where I can touch the earth. Or at least I can put my hand against a wall and feel the texture of a brick that has been fashioned from red clay.

Yesterday afternoon I stood on a high cliff above the sea. A group of seagulls caught the currents of the wind nearby and rode them back and forth, calling out to each other and answering in obvious delight as they soared and turned.

That reminded me of a winter day several years ago when I came on a group of twenty or thirty ducks in a field. As I watched them, the clouds parted, and for about two minutes the sky broke into beautiful colors of crimson and gold. One duck looked up, saw it, and started quacking. Then all the rest stopped what they were doing and looked up too, directly at the spot where the light came through the clouds, and started quacking joyfully. When the clouds closed the opening and the sky turned gray again, they watched for ten or fifteen seconds more, and then turned back to their other activities.

Those ducks appreciated the beauty of that moment as much as I did, and the seagulls appreciated the joy of their play as much as I appreciate the joy of mine.

I see myself mirrored in many creatures in the forest. The lizard's little arms and hands are startlingly human. A deer looks at me from several feet away with as much curiosity in its soft eyes as I have as I look back at it. My neighborhood raccoon takes the tightly screwed-on lid off my peanut butter jar, eats all the peanut butter—three jars in one week!—and even samples my vitamin pills. A rabbit caught immobile in my flashlight beam reminds me of my own panic and confusion when I'm faced with danger and don't know what to do. It is almost as if, as naturalist Loren Eiseley says, "I find many versions of myself, with fur and grimaces, surveying my activities from behind leaves and thickets" (UU, 161).

Eiseley likens us humans to the latest bloom on a great tree that stretches backward into the dim recesses of pre-recorded time. The tree is the great stream of life itself, and each creature is a leaf or a branch on that tree.

In areas of North America where Native American culture is still alive, an Indian does not kill for "sport." He kills for food only when he must, and offers a prayer and an apology to the creature he will kill before he kills it. For he knows the look in the eyes of a dying animal, and that animal's pain is his own pain.

We have no choice, now, but to understand the interdependence of all living beings. Our Earth Mother holds us in her trembling hands, and cares for us even now as best she can, but she cannot endure our brutality and arrogance forever. Even the timeless seas, which have become our cesspools of last resort, are gravely ill. Captain Jacques Cousteau, who has spent a lifetime studying the world beneath the seas, speaks with alarm of the pollution—including globules of oil—he has seen deep in the remotest oceans, in waters that were clean and pure when he first dived in them.

The ethics of ecology demand to be recognized. If we are to survive and prosper, we must evaluate our individual actions, our politics, and our economics according to their effects on the entire network of life of which we are one element. And these effects must become the most important factor affecting our actions and decisions.

This will cost us something. Cousteau estimates that saving our environment will take an investment of about 6 percent per year of our gross national product—somewhat less than the price of the credit it takes to keep our economy going. We can afford that. It's not such a radical idea. China is a very poor nation compared to the United States, but its people spend whatever they must to protect their environment, for they have realized that *that is more important than anything else we do.* As a result, that relatively poor but highly industrial nation, with its teeming population, has clean air, clean water, quiet and pleasant towns and cities, total recycling of all reclaimable materials, and near-total use of all the raw materials it uses in production. It's sad to note that despite this ecologically enlightened attitude, China too has exploded nuclear bombs in our already-polluted atmosphere.

Irreplaceable resources are becoming scarce now, and the more of us there are, the less for each of us there is. This is already obvious: the prices of raw materials and increasingly scarce foodstuffs are going up sharply as they become harder to get, and that means that we all will have to learn to live with less. Similarly, the more of us there are, the harder it is for us to live in a balanced relationship with other living beings.

I suspect that our descendants *will honor and respect us to the degree that we pass the earth along to them in a condition no worse than we received it.* That may be the most important gift that we can give them.

The time has come to listen to the wisdom of our Indian ancestors, and live with our Earth Mother rather than against her.

The Indians know that sharing the earth with our fellow beings is a privilege, not an irritation. As we live with this message that they offer us, we will experience within us a rebirth of our sense of the sacredness of nature, and of all living things.

RESPECT

The world is a sacred vessel, which must not be tampered with or grabbed after.

To tamper with it is to spoil it, and to grasp it is to lose it (Lao-tzu, 41).

Not caring is telling a child to stop laughing and dancing. Not caring is needlessly paving a piece of ground where a patch of grass could grow.

An attitude of respect for the world I live in means remembering my sense of wonder at everything around me.

When I create, respect means creating something that is beautiful, and that will fit into its surroundings. *Really look* at what you intend to build or create. Is it pretty? Will it look good with what's around it? Will it fit in with the character of the land?

Respecting other people means asking, "How can we nurture one another? How can we act toward one another in ways that will help us live and love and laugh and grow?" It means finding ways to make sure each of us has enough to eat, a warm place to sleep, decent health care, and a worthwhile job to do. It means using our community agencies, our government, and our business community to preserve and extend our liberties rather than to take them away, so long as we don't interpret our "freedom" as including the opportunity to act in ways that harm others.

Folksinger Ric Masten wrote these lines: "Haven't we all stood helplessly in hospital halls? Haven't we all been to the grave together? I been down in the kitchen, looking through the empty cupboard same as you. There are streets of people who seem to have it made, but we've all been down in the kitchen, lonely and afraid."

As we begin to recognize this oneness we all share, and I see my own heart reflected in your eyes, we don't lose the individuality of you and me. We have the unity we share, and the wonder of the uniqueness of each one of us.

Bibliography

Note: Titles listed here, when cited in the text of this book, are abbreviated in the form of the initial letters of key words. Page references follow the title abbreviations. In the case of a single listing for an author, only the page reference is given.

Adler, Alfred. *The Individual Psychology of Alfred Adler: A Systematic Presentation in Selections from His Writings.* Edited by Heinz L. Ansbacher and Rowena R. Ansbacher. New York: Harper and Row, 1964.
——. *Superiority and Social Interest: A Collection of Later Writings by Alfred Adler.* Edited by Heinz L. Ansbacher and Rowena R. Ansbacher. New York: Viking, 1973.
Alberti, Robert E., and Emmons, Michael L. *Your Perfect Right: A Guide to Assertive Behavior.* Rev. ed. San Luis Obispo, Calif.: Impact, 1974.
Alexander, Hartley Burr. *The World's Rim: Great Mysteries of the North American Indians.* Lincoln: University of Nebraska Press, 1953.
Allport, Gordon W. *The Nature of Prejudice.* Garden City, N.Y.: Doubleday (Anchor), 1958.
Arms, Suzanne. *Immaculate Deception: A New Look at Women and Childbirth in America.* San Francisco and Boston: San Francisco Book Co./Houghton Mifflin, 1975.
Aronson, Elliot, with Nancy Blaney and others. "Busing and Racial Tension: The Jigsaw Route to Learning and Liking." *Psychology Today,* February 1975, pp. 43–50.
Asimov, Isaac. *Foundation.* New York: Avon, 1970.
Assagioli, Roberto. *Psychosynthesis: A Manual of Principles and Techniques.* New York: Viking, 1971.
Azrin, Nathan. "Pain and Aggression." *Psychology Today,* May 1967, pp. 26–33.
Bach, George, and Wyden, Peter. *The Intimate Enemy: How to Fight Fair in Love and Marriage.* New York: Avon, 1970.
Baez, Joan. *Daybreak.* New York: Avon, 1969.
Bahm, Archie J. *Philosophy of the Buddha.* New York: Capricorn, 1969.
Bandura, Albert. *Principles of Behavior Modification.* New York: Holt, Rinehart and Winston, 1969.

355

___, and Walters, Richard H. *Adolescent Aggression: A Study of the Influence of Child-Training Pracitces and Family Interrelationships.* New York: Ronald, 1959.

___, and _____. *Social Learning and Personality Development.* New York: Holt, Rinehart and Winston, 1963.

Bates, Marston. *The Forest and the Sea: A Look at the Economy of Nature and the Ecology of Man.* New York: New American Library (Mentor), 1960.

Becker, Ernest. *The Birth and Death of Meaning: An Interdisciplinary Perspective on the Problem of Man.* 2d ed. New York: Free Press, 1971.

Behaviordelia. *An Introduction to Behavior Modification.* Kalamazoo, Mich.: Behaviordelia, Inc., 1973.

Benjamin, Harry. *Basic Self-Knowledge: An Introduction to Esoteric Psychology.* London: Health-for-All, n.d.

Benton, Alan A.; Kelly, Harold H.; and Liebling, Barry. "Effects of Extremity of Offers and Concession Rate on the Outcome of Bargaining." *Journal of Personality and Social Psychology,* October 1973, pp. 73–83.

Bergson, Henri. *Creative Evolution.* New York: Modern Library, 1944.

Berne, Eric. *Games People Play.* New York: Ballantine, 1974.

___. *Transactional Analysis in Psychotherapy: A Systematic Individual and Social Psychiatry.* New York: Grove, 1961.

Bhagavad-Gita, The. Translated by Swami Prabhavananda and Christopher Isherwood. New York: New American Library (Mentor), 1944.

Bible, Jerusalem. Edited by Alexander Jones. Garden City, N.Y.: Doubleday, 1971.

Bible, King James. Nashville: Gideon Bible Society.

Bible, New English. London: Oxford University Press, 1970.

Boyd, Doug. *Rolling Thunder: A Personal Exploration into the Secret Healing Power of an American Indian Medicine Man.* New York: Random House, 1975.

Brehm, Jack W., and Cohen, Arthur R. *Explorations in Cognitive Dissonance.* New York: Wiley, 1962.

Brice, Norman B. "Blame Is the Name of a No-Win Game." Unpublished paper, Chico State College, Calif.

___. "A New Look at Old-fashioned Honesty." Talk given at the Unitarian Church, Chico, Calif., 1967.

Brown, George I. *Human Teaching for Human Learning: An Introduction to Confluent Education.* New York: Viking, 1971.

Bruce, Lenny. *How to Talk Dirty and Influence People: An Autobiography.* Chicago: Playboy Press, 1965.

Buber, Martin. *I and Thou.* 2nd ed. New York: Scribner, 1958.

___. *Ten Rungs: Hasidic Sayings.* Translated by Olga Marx. New York: Schocken, 1947.

Bugental, J. F. T. *The Search for Authenticity: An Existential-analytic Approach to Psychotherapy.* New York: Holt, Rinehart and Winston, 1965.

Castaneda, Carlos. *Journey to Ixtlan: The Lessons of Don Juan.* New York: Simon and Schuster (Touchstone), 1972.

___. *The Teachings of Don Juan: A Yaqui Way of Knowledge.* New York: Ballantine, 1974.

Chabon, Irwin. *Awake and Aware: Participating in Childbirth through Psychoprophylaxis.* New York: Delacorte, 1966.

Chaudhuri, Haridas, and Frank, Leonard Roy. *Mahatma Gandhi.* San Francisco: Cultural Integration Fellowship, 1969.

Chögyam Trungpa. *Cutting through Spiritual Materialism.* Edited by John Baker. Berkeley: Shambala, 1973.

___. *Meditation in Action.* London: Stuart and Watkins, 1969; Berkeley: Shambala, 1970.

Collins, Barry E., and Raven, Bertram H. "Group Structure: Attraction, Coalitions, Communication, and Power." In *The Handbook of Social Psychology,* edited by Gardner Lindzey and Elliot Aronson, vol. 3, pp. 1–101. 2d ed. Reading, Mass.: Addison-Wesley, 1968.

Comfort, Alex. *The Joy of Sex.* New York: Simon and Schuster, 1972.

Cousteau, Jacques. Brochure soliciting membership in the Cousteau Society, to save the seas.

Craig, James H., and Craig, Marge. *Synergic Power: Beyond Domination and Permissiveness.* Berkeley: Proactive Press, 1974.

De Bono, Edward. *New Think: The Use of Laterial Thinking in the Generation of New Ideas.* New York: Basic Books, 1968.

Deibert, Alvin N., and Harmon, Alice J. *New Tools for Changing Behavior.* Champaign, Ill.: Research Press, 1970.

Dennis, Wayne. *The Hopi Child.* (Reprint of 1940 ed.) New York: Wiley, 1965; Arno, 1972.

Dewey, John. *Human Nature and Conduct.* New York: Modern Library, 1930.

Dogen. *A Primer of Soto Zen: A Translation of Dogen's Shobogenzo Zuimonki.* Translated by Reiho Masunaga. Honolulu: East-West Center Press, 1971.

Downing, George. *The Massage Book.* New York and Berkeley: Random House/ Bookworks, 1972.

Eiseley, Loren. *The Firmament of Time.* New York: Atheneum, 1960.

___. *The Immense Journey.* New York: Vintage, 1957.

___. *The Unexpected Universe.* New York: Harcourt Brace Jovanovich, 1972.

Emerson, Ralph Waldo. *Emerson: A Modern Anthology.* Edited by Alfred Kazin and Daniel Aaron. Boston: Houghton Mifflin, 1959.

___. *The Living Thoughts of Emerson.* Edited by Edgar Lee Masters. New York: Fawcett (Premier), 1958.

Erikson, Eric H. *Childhood and Society.* 2d ed., rev. and enl. New York: Norton, 1963.

Estes, W. K. "An Experimental Study of Punishment." *Psychological Monographs* 57, no. 263 (1944), entire issue.

Eysenck, H. J., ed. *Behaviour Therapy and the Neuroses: Readings in Modern Methods of Treatment Derived from Learning Theory.* Oxford: Pergamon, 1960.

___. *Experiments in Behaviour Therapy: Readings in Modern Methods of Treatment of Mental Disorders Derived from Learning Theory.* Oxford: Pergamon; New York: Macmillan, 1964.

Fagan, Joen, and Shepherd, Irma Lee. *Life Techniques in Gestalt Therapy.* New York: Harper and Row (Perennial), 1973.

___, and ___. *What Is Gestalt Therapy?* New York: Harper and Row (Perennial), 1973.

Faraday, Ann. *The Dream Game.* New York: Harper and Row, 1974.

___. *Dream Power.* New York: Berkeley (Medallion), 1973.

Fast, Julius. *Body Language.* New York: Pocket Books, 1971.

Feldenkrais, Moshé. *Awareness through Movement: Health Exercises for Personal Growth.* New York: Harper and Row, 1972.

Festinger, Leon. *A Theory of Cognitive Dissonance.* Stanford: Stanford University Press, 1957.

Fischer, Louis. *Gandhi: His Life and Message to the World.* New York: New American Library (Signet), 1954.

Freud, Sigmund. *The Basic Writings of Sigmund Freud.* Translated and edited by

A. A. Brill. New York: Modern Library, 1938.

——. *Collected Papers.* 5 vols. New York: Basic Books, 1959.

——. *Interpretation of Dreams.* Translated by James Strachey. New York: Avon, 1967.

——. *Psychopathology of Everyday Life.* New York: New American Library (Mentor), 1972.

Fromm, Erich. *The Art of Loving.* New York: Harper, 1956; Bantam, 1970.

——. *Escape from Freedom.* New York: Avon, 1971.

——. *Man for Himself: An Inquiry into the Psychology of Ethics.* New York: Rinehart, 1947; Fawcett, 1973.

Fujimoto, Rindo. *The Way of Zazen.* Cambridge, Mass.: Cambridge Buddhist Association, 1961.

Galbraith, John Kenneth. *Economics and the Public Purpose.* Boston: Houghton Mifflin, 1973; New York: New American Library (Signet), 1975.

Gandhi, Mohandas. *The Essential Gandhi: An Anthology.* Edited by Louis Fischer. New York: Random House, 1962.

——. *Gandhi on Non-Violence.* Edited by Thomas Merton. New York: New Directions, 1965.

Geba, Bruno H. *Breathe Away Your Tension.* New York and Berkeley: Random House/Bookworks, 1973.

Gerrard, Don. *One Bowl: A Simple Concept for Controlling Weight.* New York and Berkeley: Random House/Bookworks, 1974.

Gibran, Kahlil. *The Garden of the Prophet.* New York: Knopf, 1968.

——. *The Prophet.* New York: Knopf, 1966.

——. *Sand and Foam.* New York: Knopf, 1964.

——. *The Voice of the Master.* Translated by Anthony R. Ferris. New York: Citadel, 1958.

Giorgi, Amedeo. *Psychology as a Human Science: A Phenomenally Based Approach.* New York: Harper and Row, 1970.

Glasser, William. *Reality Therapy: A New Approach to Psychiatry.* New York: Harper and Row, 1965.

Goleman, Daniel. "The Buddha on Meditation and States of Consciousness, Part I: The Teachings." *Journal of Transpersonal Psychology* 4, no. 1 (1972): 1–44.

——. "The Buddha on Meditation and States of Consciousness, Part II: A Typology of Meditation Techniques." *Journal of Transpersonal Psychology* 4, no. 2 (1972): 151–210.

——. "Meditation as Meta-Therapy." *Journal of Transpersonal Psychology* 3, no. 1 (1971): 1–26.

Gordon, Thomas. *Parent Effectiveness Training: The No-Lose Program for Raising Responsible Children.* New York: P. Wyden, 1970.

Govinda, Lama Anagarika. *The Way of the White Clouds: A Buddhist Pilgrim in Tibet.* Berkeley: Shambala, 1971.

Greenberg, Herbert M. *Teaching with Feeling: Compassion and Self-Awareness in the Classroom Today.* New York: Macmillan, 1969.

Greenwald, Jerry A. *Be the Person You Were Meant to Be: Antidotes to Toxic Living.* New York: Dell, 1974.

Gunther, Bernard. *Sense Relaxation below Your Mind.* New York: Collier, 1968.

——. *What to Do Till the Messiah Comes.* New York: Macmillan, 1971.

Gurdjieff, G. I. *Meetings with Remarkable Men.* New York: Dutton, 1963.

Gustaitis, Rasa. *Turning On.* New York: Macmillan; New American Library (Signet), 1969.

Haley, Jay. *Strategies of Psychotherapy.* New York: Grune and Stratton, 1963.

Hall, Calvin. *The Meaning of Dreams.* New York: McGraw-Hill, 1966.

Hall, Robert K. Unpublished lectures given at the Lomi Foundation, Mill Valley, Calif., 1971–72.

Harlow, Harry F. "Motivation as a Factor in New Responses." In *Current Theory and Research in Motivation: A Symposium,* pp. 24–48. Lincoln: University of Nebraska Press, 1953.

Harris, Thomas A. *I'm OK—You're OK.* New York: Harper and Row, 1967; Avon, 1973.

Hayakawa, S. I. *Language in Thought and Action.* 2d ed. New York: Harcourt, Brace and World, 1964.

___, ed. *The Use and Misuse of Language; Selections from Etc.: A Review of General Semantics.* New York: Fawcett (Premier), 1964.

Heider, Fritz. *The Psychology of Interpersonal Relations.* New York: Wiley, 1958.

Hesse, Hermann. *Siddhartha.* New York: New Directions, 1951.

_____. *Steppenwolf.* New York: Holt, Rinehart and Winston, 1963.

Homans, George Caspar. *Social Behavior: Its Elementary Forms.* New York: Harcourt, Brace and World, 1961.

Horney Karen. *Our Inner Conflicts.* New York: Norton, 1945.

Howard, Jane. *Please Touch: A Guided Tour of the Human Potential Movement.* New York: McGraw-Hill, 1970.

Hubbard, L. Ron. *Dianetics: The Modern Science of Mental Health; A Handbook of Dianetic Theory.* New York: Paperback Library, 1968.

Huxley, Aldous. *Island.* New York: Harper, 1962.

Huxley, Julian. *Knowledge, Morality, and Destiny.* New York: New American Library (Mentor), 1960.

I Ching; or, Book of Changes. Translated by Richard Wilhelm and Carl F. Baynes. 3d ed. Princeton: Princeton University Press, 1967.

Inkeles, Gordon, and Todris, Murray. *The Art of Sensual Massage.* San Francisco: Straight Arrow Books, 1972.

Isaac, Donald. Unpublished lecture given at California State College, Sonoma, 1974.

Jager, Bernd. Unpublished lectures given at California State College, Sonoma, 1972.

James, Muriel, and Jongeward, Dorothy. *Born to Win: Transactional Analysis with Gestalt Experiments.* Reading, Mass.: Addison-Wesley, 1971.

Janov, Arthur. *The Primal Scream; Primal Therapy: The Cure for Neurosis.* New York: Putnam, 1970; Dell, 1971.

Johnson, Wendell. *People in Quandaries: The Semantics of Personal Adjustment.* New York: Harper, 1946.

___, and Moeller, Dorothy. *Living with Change: The Semantics of Coping.* New York: Harper and Row, 1972.

Jourard, Sidney M. *Disclosing Man to Himself.* Princeton: Van Nostrand, 1968.

Jung, Carl G. *The Collected Works of Carl G. Jung.* 2d ed. Bollingen Series, 20. Princeton: Princeton University Press, 1960–72.

___. *Dreams.* Translated by R. F. C. Hull. Princeton: Princeton University Press, 1974.

___. *The Portable Jung.* Edited by Joseph Campbell. New York: Viking, 1971.

___. *Psyche and Symbol: A Selection from the Writings of C. G. Jung.* Edited by Violet S. de Laszlo. Garden City, N.Y.: Doubleday, 1958.

___, and others. *Man and His Symbols.* New York: Dell, 1968.

Kabir. *The Fish in the Sea Is Not Thirsty.* Translated by Robert Bly. Northwood

Narrows, N.H.: Lillabulero Press, 1971.

Kafka, Franz. *The Trial*. New York: Vintage, 1969.

Kapleau, Philip, comp. and ed. *The Three Pillars of Zen: Teaching, Practice, and Enlightenment*. Boston: Beacon, 1967.

Kaufmann, Walter, ed. *Existentialism from Dostoevsky to Sartre*. New York: Meridian, 1956.

Kazantzakis, Nikos. *Zorba the Greek*. New York: Ballantine, 1964.

Keleman, Stanley. *Living Your Dying*. New York and Berkeley: Random House/ Bookworks, 1974.

___. *Sexuality, Self, and Survival*. San Francisco: Lodestar Press, 1971.

Kelen, Betty. *Gautama Buddha*. New York: Avon, 1969.

Kelley, Harold H. "Interaction Process and the Attainment of Maximum Joint Profit." In *Decision and Choice*, edited by Samuel Messick and Arthur H. Brayfield, pp. 240–50. New York: McGraw-Hill, 1964.

___, and Stahelski, Anthony J. "Social Interaction Basis of Cooperators' and Competitors' Beliefs about Others." *Journal of Personality and Social Psychology*, September 1970, pp. 66–91.

___, and Thibaut, John W. "Group Problem Solving." In *The Handbook of Social Psychology*, edited by Gardner Lindzey and Elliot Aronson, vol. 3, pp. 1–101. 2d ed. Reading, Mass.: Addison-Wesley, 1968.

Kelly, George A. "Man's Construction of His Alternatives." In *Personality: Readings in Theory and Research*, edited by Eugene A. Southwell and Michael Merbaum, pp. 344–61. Belmont, Calif.: Wadsworth, 1964.

Keyes, Ken, Jr. *Handbook to Higher Consciousness*. 3d ed. Berkeley: Living Love Center, 1973.

Khantipalo, Phra. *Tolerance: A Study from Buddhist Sources*. London: Rider, 1964.

Koestenbaum, Peter. *Managing Anxiety: The Power of Knowing Who You Are*. Englewood Cliffs, N. J.: Prentice-Hall, 1974.

Köhler, Wolfgang. *Gestalt Psychology: An Introduction to New Concepts in Modern Psychology*. New York: New American Library (Mentor), 1964.

Koran Interpreted, The. Translated by Arthur J. Arberry. New York: Macmillan, 1964.

Korzybski, Alfred. *Science and Sanity: An Introduction to Non-Aristotelian Systems and General Semantics*. 4th ed. Lakeville, Conn.: International Non-Aristotelian Library Publishing Co., 1958.

Krippner, Stanley, and Rubin, Daniel, eds. *Galaxies of Life: Human Aura in Acupuncture and Kirlian Photography*. New York: Gordon and Breach (Interface), 1973.

Krishnamurti, J. *The First and Last Freedom*. Wheaton, Ill.: Quest, 1968.

___. *The Flight of the Eagle*. New York: Harper and Row, 1971.

___. *Freedom from the Known*. Edited by Mary Luytens. New York: Harper and Row, 1969.

Krumboltz, John D., ed. *Revolution in Counseling: Implications of Behavioral Science*. Boston: Houghton Mifflin, 1966.

Krutch, Joseph Wood. *The Great Chain of Life*. New York: Pyramid, 1966.

Kuebler-Ross, Elisabeth. "How It Feels to Die." UPI release, in *The Sacramento Union*, March 8, 1975.

Kwong Sensei, Jakusho. Unpublished lectures given at California State College, Sonoma, 1971–72.

Laing, Ronald D. *The Divided Self*. New York: Pantheon, 1969.

___. *Knots*. New York: Vintage, 1972.

___. *The Politics of Experience*. New York: Pantheon, 1967.

___. *The Politics of the Family, and Other Essays.* New York: Pantheon, 1971.

Lao-tzu. *Tao Teh Ching.* Translated by John C. H. Wu; edited by Paul K. T. Sih. New York: St. John's University Press, 1961.

Latner, Joel. *The Gestalt Therapy Book.* New York: Bantam, 1974.

Leary, Timothy. *Interpersonal Diagnosis of Personality: A Functional Theory and Methodology for Personality Evaluation.* New York: Ronald, 1957.

Lecky, Prescott. *Self-Consistency: A Theory of Personality.* New York: Island Press, 1945; 2d ed., Hamden, Conn.: Shoe String Press, 1973.

Lederman, Janet. *Anger and the Rocking Chair: Gestalt Awareness with Children.* New York: McGraw-Hill, 1969.

Lee, Dorothy. *Freedom and Culture.* Englewood Cliffs, N.J.: Prentice-Hall (Spectrum), 1959.

Lee, John Alan. "The Styles of Loving." *Psychology Today,* October 1974, pp. 43–51.

LeShan, Eda J. *What Makes Me Feel This Way? Growing Up with Human Emotions.* New York: Macmillan, 1972.

Lewin, Kurt. *A Dynamic Theory of Personality.* New York: McGraw-Hill, 1935.

___. *Resolving Social Conflicts: Selected Papers on Group Dynamics.* Edited by Gertrud Weiss Lewin. New York: Harper, 1948.

Lewis, Howard R., and Streitfeld, Harold S. *Growth Games: How to Tune In Yourself, Your Family, Your Friends.* New York: Harcourt Brace Jovanovich, 1970.

Lindner, Robert. *Prescription for Rebellion.* New York: Grove, 1962.

Lowen, Alexander, and Levin, Robert J. "The Case against Cheating in Marriage." *Redbook,* June 1969, pp. 70–71, 112–116.

Luce, Gay Gaer. *Body Time: Physiological Rhythms and Social Stress.* New York: Pantheon, 1971.

McIntire, Roger W. *For Love of Children: Behavioral Psychology for Parents.* Del Mar, Calif.: CRM Books, 1970.

Maharishi, Mahesh Yogi. *Transcendental Meditation.* New York: New American Library (Signet), 1968.

Maharshi, Ramana. *The Collected Works of Maharshi.* Edited by Arthur Osborne. New York: S. Weiser, 1969.

Mao Tse-tung. *On Contradiction.* Peking: Foreign Languages Press, 1967.

Maslow, Abraham. *The Farther Reaches of Human Nature.* New York: Viking, 1971.

___. *Toward a Psychology of Being.* 2d ed. Princeton: Van Nostrand, 1968.

May, Rollo. *Love and Will.* New York: Dell, 1969.

___. *Man's Search for Himself.* New York: New American Library (Signet), 1967.

Meher Baba. *Discourses.* 3 vols. 6th ed. San Francisco: Sufism Reoriented, 1967.

Merleau-Ponty, Maurice. *The Primacy of Perception.* Edited by James M. Edie. Evanston: Northwestern University Press, 1964.

Miller, Howard L., and Siegel, Paul. *Loving: A Psychological Analysis.* New York: Wiley, 1972.

Miller, Neal E. "Studies of Fear as an Acquirable Drive, I: Fear as Motivation and Fear Reduction as Reinforcement in the Learning of New Responses." *Journal of Experimental Psychology* 38 (1948): 89–101.

___, and Dollard, John. *Social Learning and Imitation.* New Haven: Yale University Press, 1941.

Mishra, Rammurti S. *Fundamentals of Yoga: A Handbook of Theory, Practice, and Application.* New York: Lancer, 1959; Garden City, N.Y.: Doubleday (Anchor), 1974.

Miura, Isshu, and Sasaki, Ruth Fuller. *The Zen Koan: Its History and Use in Rinzai Zen.* New York: Harcourt, Brace and World, 1965.

Moustakas, Clark. *Creativity and Conformity.* Princeton: Van Nostrand, 1967.

——. *Loneliness.* Englewood Cliffs, N.J.: Prentice-Hall, 1961.

Mowrer, O. J. *Learning Theory and the Symbolic Process.* New York: Wiley, 1960.

Naimy, Mikhail. *The Book of Mirdad.* Baltimore: Penguin, 1971.

Naranjo, Claudio. *The One Quest.* New York: Ballantine, 1972.

Neihardt, John G. *Black Elk Speaks.* Lincoln: University of Nebraska Press, 1961; New York: Pocket Books, 1972.

Newcomb, Theodore. *The Acquaintance Process.* New York: Holt, Rinehart and Winston, 1961.

Nietzsche, Friedrich. *The Portable Nietzsche.* Edited and Translated by Walter Kaufmann. New York: Viking, 1954.

"Older Father, The: Late Is Great" (results of studies by Corinne Nydegger). *Psychology Today,* April 1974, pp. 26, 28.

Orage, A. R. *Essays and Aphorisms.* London: Janus, 1954.

——, ed. *Psychological Exercises.* New York: Farrar and Rinehart, 1930.

Ornstein, Robert E. *The Psychology of Consciousness.* New York: Viking, 1972.

Osgood, Charles E., and Tannenbaum, P. H. "The Principle of Congruity in the Prediction of Attitude Change." *Psychological Review* 62 (1955): 42–55.

Ouspensky, P. D. *The Fourth Way.* New York: Vintage, 1971.

——. *In Search of the Miraculous: Fragments from an Unknown Teaching.* New York: Harcourt, Brace, 1949.

——. *A New Model of the Universe.* (Reprint of 1943 ed.) New York: Knopf, 1967.

——. *The Psychology of Man's Evolution.* New York: Bantam, 1968.

Pearson, Leonard, and Pearson, Lillian R.; with Karola Saekel. *The Psychologist's Eat-Anything Diet.* New York: P. Wyden, 1973.

Peri, David. Unpublished lecture given at California State College, Sonoma, 1974.

Perls, Frederick S. *Ego, Hunger, and Aggression: The Beginning of Gestalt Therapy.* New York: Random House, 1947.

——. *The Gestalt Approach and Eye Witness to Therapy.* Ben Lomond, Calif.: Science and Behavior Books, 1973.

——. *Gestalt Therapy Verbatim.* Compiled and edited by John O. Stevens. Moab, Utah: Real People Press, 1969.

——. *In and out the Garbage Pail.* Lafayette, Calif.: Real People Press, 1969.

——; Hefferline, Ralph F.; and Goodman, Paul. *Gestalt Therapy: Excitement and Growth in the Human Personality.* New York: Julian Press, 1951; Dell, 1965.

——, and others. *Gestalt Is.* Moab, Utah: Real People Press, 1975.

Peter Pauper Press. *Zen Buddhism: An Introduction to Zen.* Mt. Vernon, N.Y.: Peter Pauper Press.

Phelps, Stanlee, and Austin, Nancy. *The Assertive Woman.* New ed. San Luis Obispo, Calif.: Impact, 1975.

Poiret, Maude. *Body Talk: The Science of Kinesics.* New York: Award, 1970.

Polanyi, Michael. *Personal Knowledge: Towards a Post-critical Philosophy.* New York: Harper and Row (Torchbook), 1964.

Poncé, Charles. *Kabbalah: An Introduction and Illumination for the World Today.* San Francisco: Straight Arrow Books, 1973.

Prabhavananda, Swami, and Isherwood, Christopher. *How to Know God: The Yoga Aphorisms of Patanjali.* New York: New American Library (Signet), 1969.

Premack, David. "Reinforcement Theory." In *Nebraska Symposium on Motivation, 1965,* edited by David Levine, pp. 123–80. Lincoln: University of Nebraska Press, 1965.

Prince, George M. *The Practice of Creativity: A Manual for Dyanmic Group Problem Solving.* New York: Harper and Row, 1970.

Progoff, Ira. Unpublished lecture at Esalen Institute, Big Sur Hot Springs, Calif.

Pursglove, Paul D., comp. *Recognitions in Gestalt Therapy.* New York: Harper and Row, 1971.

Rahula, Walpola. *What the Buddha Taught.* New York: Grove, 1962.

Ram Dass, Baba. "Lecture at the Menninger Foundation." *Journal of Transpersonal Psychology* 2, no. 2 (1970): 91–140.

___. "Lecture at the Menninger Foundation, Part II." *Journal of Transpersonal Psychology* 3, no. 1 (1971): 47–84.

___, and the Lama Foundation. *Be Here Now.* New ed. New York: Harmony, 1971.

Rasberry, Salli, and Greenway, Robert. *The Rasberry Exercises: How to Start Your Own School and Make a Book.* Sebastopol, Calif.: Freestone, 1970.

Reich, Wilhelm. *Character-Analysis.* 3d, enl. ed. New York: Noonday Press, 1961.

Reps, Paul, comp. *Zen Flesh, Zen Bones: A Collection of Zen and Pre-Zen Writings.* Garden City, N.Y.: Doubleday (Anchor), n.d.

Rimm, David C., and Masters, John C. *Behavior Therapy.* New York: Academic Press, 1974.

Rinder, Walter. *Follow Your Heart.* Millbrae, Calif.: Celestial Arts, 1973.

___. *Love Is an Attitude.* Millbrae, Calif.: Celestial Arts, 1970.

Rogers, Carl. *Becoming Partners: Marriage and Its Alternatives.* New York: Dell, 1973.

___. *Carl Rogers on Encounter Groups.* New York: Harper and Row, 1970.

___. *Client-centered Therapy: Its Current Practice, Implications and Theory.* Boston: Houghton Mifflin, 1951.

___. *On Becoming a Person: A Therapist's View of Psychotherapy.* Boston: Houghton Mifflin, 1961.

___, and Stevens, Barry. *Person to Person.* Lafayette, Calif.: Real People Press, 1976; New York: Pocket Books, 1971.

Rohe, Fred. *The Zen of Running.* New York and Berkeley: Random House/Bookworks, 1974.

Rokeach, Milton. *Beliefs, Attitudes, and Values: A Theory of Organization and Change.* San Francisco: Jossey-Bass, 1968.

___. *The Open and Closed Mind: Investigations into the Nature of Belief Systems and Personality Systems.* New York: Basic Books, 1960.

Rolling Thunder. Unpublished lecture given at California State College Sonoma, 1973. (See also: Boyd, Doug.)

Rosenberg, Jack. *Total Orgasm.* New York and Berkeley: Random House/Bookworks, 1973.

Rosenberg, Milton J. "An Analysis of Affective-cognitive Consistency." In M. J. Rosenberg and others, *Attitude Organization and Change.* New Haven: Yale University Press, 1960.

Rossi, Ernest L. *Dreams and the Growth of Personality: Expanding Awareness in Psychotherapy.* New York: Pergamon, 1972.

Rubin, Theodore Isaac. *The Angry Book.* New York: Collier, 1970.

Russell, Bertrand. *The Conquest of Happiness.* New York: Liveright, 1930.

Saddhatissa, H. *The Buddha's Way.* New York: G. Braziller, 1972.

___. *Buddhist Ethics: Essence of Buddhism.* New York: G. Braziller, 1971.

Sampson, Edward E. *Social Psychology and Contemporary Society.* New York: Wiley, 1971.

Samuels, Mike, and Bennett, Hal Z. *Be Well.* New York and Berkeley: Random

House/Bookworks, 1974.

—, and ———. *The Well Body Book*. New York and Berkeley: Random House/Bookworks, 1973.

Sanford, John A. *Dreams: God's Forgotten Language*. Philadelphia: Lippincott, 1968.

—. *The Kingdom Within: A Study of the Inner Meaning of Jesus' Sayings*. Philadelphia: Lippincott, 1970.

Satchidananda, Yogiraj Sri Swami. *Integral Yoga Hatha*. New York: Holt, Rinehart and Winston, 1970.

Sears, Andrew. "Communication and the Peak Experience." Ph.D. dissertation, California School of Professional Psychology, 1973.

Secret of the Golden Flower, The: A Chinese Book of Life. Translated and explained by Richard Wilhelm; with commentary by C. G. Jung. New York: Harcourt, Brace and World (Harvest), 1962.

Shah, Idries. *Caravan of Dreams*. Baltimore: Penguin, 1972.

—. *The Sufis*. Garden City, N.Y.: Doubleday, 1964.

—. *Tales of the Dervishes*. New York: Dutton, 1970.

—. *The Way of the Sufi*. New York: Dutton, 1970.

Simkin, James. Unpublished lecture given at Esalen Institute, Big Sur Hot Springs, Calif.

Singer, June. *Boundaries of the Soul: The Practice of Jung's Psychology*. Garden City, N.Y.: Doubleday (Anchor), 1973.

Skinner, B. F. *About Behaviorism*. New York: Knopf, 1974.

—. *Beyond Freedom and Dignity*. New York: Knopf, 1971.

—. *Science and Human Behavior*. New York: Macmillan, 1953.

—. *Walden Two*. New York: Macmillan, 1948.

Solomon, David, ed. *LSD: The Consciousness-expanding Drug*. New York: Putnam (Berkeley Medallion), 1966.

Stanislavski, Konstantin. *An Actor Prepares*. Translated by Elizabeth Reynolds Hapgood. New York: Theatre Arts Books, 1956.

Steiger, Brad. *Medicine Power: The American Indian's Revival of His Spiritual Heritage and Its Relevance for Modern Man*. Garden City, N.Y.: Doubleday, 1974.

Stephen. *Monday Night Class*. Santa Rosa, Calif.: Book Farm, 1970.

Stevens, Barry. *Don't Push the River (It Flows by Itself)*. Lafayette, Calif.: Real People Press, 1970.

Stevens, John O. *Awareness: Exploring, Experimenting, Experiencing*. Lafayette, Calif.: Real People Press, 1971.

Stewart, Kilton. *Pygmies and Dream Giants*. New York: Norton, 1954.

Storm, Hyemeyohsts. *Seven Arrows*. New York: Ballantine, 1972.

Sullivan, Harry Stack. *Clinical Studies in Psychiatry*. New York: Norton, 1956.

Suzuki, Daisetz Teitaro. *Manual of Zen Buddhism*. New York: Grove, 1960.

—; Fromm, Erich; and De Martino, Richard. Edited by Erich Fromm. *Zen Buddhism and Psychoanalysis*. New York: Harper, 1960.

Suzuki, Shunryu. *Zen Mind, Beginner's Mind*. Edited by Trudy Dixon. New York and Tokyo: Weatherhill, 1970.

Tappan, Gordon. Unpublished lectures given at California State College, Sonoma, 1972–74.

Teilhard de Chardin, Pierre. *The Phenomenon of Man*. Translated by Bernard Wall. New York: Harper, 1959.

Tharp, Roland G., and Wetzel, Ralph J. *Behavior Modification in the Natural Environment*. New York and London: Academic Press, 1969.

Thera, Nyanaponika. *The Heart of Buddhist Meditation*. New York: S. Weiser, 1970.

Thibaut, John W., and Kelley, Harold H. *The Social Psychology of Groups.* New York: Wiley, 1959.

Thomas, Hobart F. (Red). "An Existential Attitude in Working with Individuals and Groups." In J. F. T. Bugental, *Challenges of Humanistic Psychology.* New York: McGraw-Hill, 1967.

___. Unpublished lectures given at California State College, Sonoma, 1972.

Thommen, George. *Is This Your Day? How Biorhythm Helps You Determine Your Life Cycles.* Rev. ed. New York: Crown, 1973.

Thoreau, Henry David. *Thoreau on Man and Nature.* Mt. Vernon, N.Y.: Peter Pauper Press.

___. *Walden, and Other Writings.* Edited by Joseph Wood Krutch. New York: Bantam, 1971.

Tolman, Edward Chace. *Behavior and Psychological Man: Essays in Motivation and Learning.* Berkeley: University of California Press, 1958.

Unterman, Isaac. *The Talmud: Origins and Development, Methods and Systems, Causes and Results, Contents and Significance.* 2d ed. New York: Bloch, 1965.

Upanishads, The: Breath of the Eternal. Translated by Swami Prabhavananda and Frederick Manchester. New York: New American Library (Mentor), 1957.

Van Dusen, Wilson. *The Natural Depth in Man.* New York: Harper and Row, 1972.

Van Nuys, David. "A Novel Technique for Studying Attention During Meditation." *Journal of Transpersonal Psychology* 3, no. 2 (1971): 125–34.

Walker, James L. *Body and Soul.* Nashville: Abingdon, 1971.

Walters, John. *The Essence of Buddhism: A Practical Introduction.* . . . New York: Apollo, 1964.

Watts, Alan W. *The Joyous Cosmology: Adventures in the Chemistry of Consciousness.* New York: Pantheon, 1962; Vintage, 1965.

___. *Psychotherapy East and West.* New York: Ballantine, 1969.

___. *This Is It, and Other Essays on Zen and Spiritual Experience.* New York: Macmillan, 1958; Collier, 1967.

_____. *The Wisdom of Insecurity.* New York: Pantheon, 1951; Vintage, 1968.

Whyte, Lancelot Law. *The Next Development in Man.* New York: New American Library (Mentor), 1950.

Wiesel, Elie. *Souls on Fire.* New York: Vintage, 1973.

Willoya, William, and Brown, Vinson. *Warriors of the Rainbow: Strange and Prophetic Indian Dreams.* Healdsburg, Calif.: Naturegraph, 1962.

Wolpe, Joseph. *The Practice of Behavior Therapy.* 2d ed, New York: Pergamon, 1974.

Wood, Ernest. *Concentration: An Approach to Meditation.* Wheaton, Ill.: Quest, 1968.

Wood, John. *How Do You Feel? A Guide to Your Emotions.* Englewood Cliffs, N.J.: Prentice-Hall, 1974.

Yates, A. J. "The Application of Learning Theory to the Treatment of Tics." *Journal of Abnormal and Social Psychology* 56 (1958): 175–82.

Yogananda, Paramahansa. *Autobiography of a Yogi.* 11th ed. Los Angeles: Self-Realization Fellowship, 1971.

Index

2. GENERAL INDEX

VICTOR DANIELS was born in Tooele, Utah, in 1941, and received his Ph.D. in psychology from the University of California at Los Angeles in 1966. He has worked as a Public Health Service Research Fellow in Southern California and as a Peace Corps Volunteer in Chile. Today he is a professor of psychology at California State College at Sonoma. A bachelor, he lives in Bodega, California.

Virginia Horowitz

LAURENCE J. HOROWITZ has been a professor of psychology at California State College at Sonoma since 1970. Born in Brooklyn in 1925, he served as a paratrooper with the U.S. Army during World War II. He was educated at Long Island University, the University of California, and San Francisco State University, and earned his Ph.D. in counseling psychology at Stanford University in 1958. He is currently director of the Ananda Institute in Santa Rosa, California, where he lives with his wife Virginia and their two children.

SAN FRANCISCO BOOK CO., INC.
2311 Fillmore St., San Francisco, CA 94115
(Distribution by Simon and Schuster)